Damage Limitation or Crisis?

CSIA Studies in International Security

Brassey's, Inc., in conjunction with the Center for Science and International Affairs (CSIA) of Harvard's John F. Kennedy School of Government, publishes CSIA Studies in International Security. Issues addressed in the series run the full spectrum of international security affairs, with particular emphasis on the post–Cold War security agenda and the new challenges facing American foreign policy–making. The series editors are Steven E. Miller and Teresa Johnson Lawson, the editor-in-chief and deputy editor of the quarterly journal *International Security*. The first two studies are available from CSIA — phone (617) 495-1464, or fax (617) 495-8963. Subsequent volumes are available from Brassey's, Inc.

No. 1, *Soviet Nuclear Fission: Control of the Nuclear Arsenal in a Disintegrating Soviet Union*, by Kurt M. Campbell, Ashton B. Carter, Steven E. Miller, and Charles A. Zraket. 1991, 144 pp., $10.00.

No. 2, *Cooperative Denuclearization: From Pledges to Deeds*, Graham Allison, Ashton B. Carter, Steven E. Miller, and Philip Zelikow, eds. 1993, 308 pp., $15.50.

No. 3, *Russian Security After the Cold War: Seven Views from Moscow*, Teresa Pelton Johnson and Steven E. Miller, eds. 1994, 206 pp., $15.50.

No. 4, *Arms Unbound: The Globalization of Defense Production*, by David Mussington. 1994, 150 pp., approx., $14.00 approx.

Damage Limitation or Crisis?
Russia and the Outside World

Edited by Robert D. Blackwill
and Sergei A. Karaganov

CSIA Studies in International Security No. 5

BRASSEY'S, INC.
Washington • London

Copyright © 1994 by the Center for Science and International Affairs
John F. Kennedy School of Government
Harvard University
Cambridge, Massachusetts 02138
(617) 495-1400

All rights reserved. No part of this book may be reproduced, stored in a retrieval system, or transmitted in any form or by any means — electronic, electrostatic, magnetic tape, mechanical, photocopying, recording, or otherwise — without permission in writing from the Center for Science and International Affairs, 79 John F. Kennedy Street, Cambridge, MA 02138.

The Carnegie Corporation is not responsible for any of the statements or views expressed in this volume.

Brassey's, Inc.

Editorial Offices
Brassey's, Inc.
8000 Westpark Drive
First Floor
McLean, Virginia 22102

Order Department
Brassey's Book Orders
c/o Macmillan Publishing Co.
100 Front Street, Box 500
Riverside, New Jersey 08075

Brassey's books are available at special discounts for bulk purchases for sales promotions, premiums, fund-raising, or educational use.

Library of Congress   Cataloging-in-Publication   Data

Damage limitation or crisis? : Russia and the outside world / edited
  by Robert D. Blackwill and Sergei A. Karaganov.
     p.   cm. -- (CSIA studies in international security : no. 5)
  ISBN 0-02-881119-4 : $17.00
  1. Russia (Federation)--Foreign relations.   I. Blackwill, Robert
D. II. Karaganov, S. A. (Sergei Aleksandrovich) III. Series.
DK510.764.D36   1994
327.47--dc20   94-18520

Designed by Miriam Avins
Maps drawn by Jeffry Pike

10   9   8   7   6   5   4   3   2   1

Printed in the United States of America

Contents

	Preface	ix
	Contributors	xi
1	Introduction and Conclusions *Robert D. Blackwill* *Sergei A. Karaganov*	1
2	The Outlook for Democracy in Russia *Igor Kliamkin*	25
3	Russia's Elites *Sergei A. Karaganov*	41
4	Russian National Interests *Alexei G. Arbatov*	55
5	Russian National Interests *Steven E. Miller*	77
6	Russia and the Western Post-Soviet Republics *Dmitri A. Fadeyev* *Vladimir V. Razuvayev*	107
7	Ukraine and Russia *Dmitri Vydrin*	123
8	Russia and Eastern Europe *Oleg T. Bogomolov*	139
9	Eastern Europe and Russia *Peter Hardi*	153

| 10 | Russia and Western Europe
Igor F. Maksimichev | 169 |
| 11 | Western Europe and Russia
Karl Kaiser | 183 |

| 12 | Russia and the States of Central Asia and the Transcaucasus
Vitaly V. Naumkin | 199 |
| 13 | The States of Central Asia and the Transcaucasus and Russia
Tonya L. Putnam | 217 |

| 14 | Russia and China
Vladimir S. Miasnikov | 227 |
| 15 | China and Russia
Li Jingjie | 241 |

| 16 | Russia and Japan
Konstantin Sarkisov | 259 |
| 17 | Japan and Russia
Tsuyoshi Hasegawa | 273 |

| 18 | Russia and the United States
Andrei Kortunov | 289 |
| 19 | The United States and Russia
Philip D. Zelikow | 307 |

| 20 | Afterword
Robert D. Blackwill and Sergei A. Karaganov | 329 |

Maps

The Russian Federation	57
Europe	138
Transcaucasia and Central Asia	201
The Russian Far East and Japan	261

Preface

We have worked in our small ways to promote the closest possible cooperation between Russia and the outside world. However, as these relations have become more complicated, we have become increasingly concerned that insufficient analysis, differing national interests, and diplomatic mismanagement would produce a downward spiral in Russia's interaction with its primary external interlocutors.

The contributors to this volume do not come to uniform conclusions regarding Russia's likely domestic trends and foreign policies. But they do all worry about the danger of a marked deterioration in Russia's foreign relations. So do we, and thus the impetus for this book and the policy prescriptions therein.

In producing this effort, we wish to thank our editor, Miriam Avins. We also appreciate the help of Kirsten Hildebrand, Maura Lambert, Arkady Moshes, Erin Powers, and Tonya Putnam. Steven E. Miller and Teresa Johnson Lawson welcomed our project into the CSIA Studies in International Security series.

The Carnegie Corporation of New York made this book possible through its generous support. In particular, we wish to thank David Hamburg, David Speedie, and Jane Wales for their encouragement.

Robert D. Blackwill
Cambridge, Massachusetts

Sergei A. Karaganov
Moscow, Russia

Contributors

Robert D. Blackwill is a Lecturer in Public Policy at the Kennedy School of Government at Harvard University, and the faculty chairman of a Kennedy School program for Russian general officers. Previously, he was special assistant to President Bush for European and Soviet Affairs on the staff of the National Security Council. He served as U.S. Ambassador and Chief Negotiator at the negotiations with the Warsaw Pact on conventional forces in Europe, 1985–1987. Ambassador Blackwill is the author of many articles on European security and East-West relations, and is co-editor of *Conventional Arms Control and East-West Security* (1989); *A Primer for the Nuclear Age* (1990); and *New Nuclear Nations* (1993).

Sergei A. Karaganov is the Deputy Director of the Institute of Europe at the Russian Academy of Sciences. He holds a degree in Economics from Moscow State University and a Ph.D. from the Institute of USA and Canada Studies at the USSR Academy of Sciences. Since 1993 he has been a member of the Presidential Council. Dr. Karaganov also serves on several other advisory bodies of the Russian government. He has written and edited many scholarly articles and twelve monographs including, most recently, *Why Western Aid Failed* (1994).

Alexei G. Arbatov is a departmental chair at the Institute of World Economics and International Relations at the Russian Academy of Sciences, and Director of the Center for Geopolitical and Military Forecasts in Moscow. In 1993, he was a visiting scholar at the Center for Science and International Affairs at the Kennedy School of Government. His most recent publications include *Nuclear Weapons Reductions and Limitations — Strategic Views from the Second Tier: The Nuclear Weapons Policies of France, Britain and China* (1994); and the article "What Will Be Russia's Choice?" (1993).

Oleg T. Bogomolov is the Director of the Institute of International Economic and Political Studies at the Russian Academy of Sciences. In 1989 Professor Bogomolov was elected to the Congress of People's Deputies of the USSR, and served on the Committee for Economic Reform of the Supreme Soviet of the USSR. From 1990–1993 he was a member of the Presidential Consultative Council. Since 1993 he has served as the Deputy Chairman of the International Relations Committee in the State Duma of the Russian Federation. Professor Bogomolov has written and edited about 400 published works.

Dmitri A. Fadeyev is a Senior Research Fellow at the Institute of Europe at the Russian Academy of Sciences. During 1993–1994 he was a Muskie Fellow at the Institute for Policy Studies at Johns Hopkins University in Baltimore. He received his Ph.D. in history in 1988 from the Institute for Social Sciences in Moscow. His most recent publications include *Russian-Ukrainian Relations: Tendencies and Perspectives* (1993); and *Democratization and Political Culture* (1993).

Peter Hardi is a Professor of Political Science at the Budapest University of Economic Sciences. From 1988–1990 he was the Director of the Hungarian Institute of International Affairs and, from 1990–1993, the founding Director of the Regional Environmental Center for Central and Eastern Europe. Presently he is a Senior Fellow at the International Institute for Sustainable Development (Canada). His most recent publications include *Impediments to Environmental Policy Making in Eastern Europe* (1992); and *Security Issues and Nation Building in East-Central Europe* (1993).

Tsuyoshi Hasegawa is currently a Professor of History at the University of California at Santa Barbara. He received his BA from Tokyo University, and his MA and Ph.D. from the University of Washington. He co-edited *Perestroika: Soviet Domestic and Foreign Policies* (1990); and *Russia and Japan: An Unresolved Dilemma between Distant Neighbors* (1993).

Karl Kaiser is a Professor of Political Science at the University of Bonn and is the Otto Wolff Director of the Research Institute of the German Society for Foreign Affairs in Bonn. He was a member of the Council of Environmental Advisors of the Federal Republic of Germany and of the Government Commission for the Reform of the Armed Services. He received his Ph.D. from the University of Cologne and an honorary doctorate from the Russian Academy of Sciences. He has recently written *Germany and the Iraq Conflict* (1992), and co-edited *The Future of German Foreign Policy* (1993); and *The Future of European Integration* (1993).

Igor Kliamkin is a specialist in Russian history and public opinion. He has done research at the Institute of International Economics and Politics at the Russian Academy of Sciences and is Chair of the Public Opinion Foundation. He has spent the past year studying the problems facing governments making the transformation from a totalitarian regime to democracy. His writings include *People and Politics: Russia and Ukraine, Today and Tomorrow* (1992); *Post Communist Democracy and its History,*

Particularly Russia (1993); and *The Political Sociology of Transitional Society* (1993).

Andrei Kortunov heads the Department of Foreign Policy at Moscow's Institute of USA and Canada Studies. He is a columnist for various Russian newspapers and has written for the *Washington Post* and *Newsweek*, as well as approximately 120 publications analyzing Soviet foreign policy and international security issues. His present research focuses on the emergence of security systems and the development of foreign policies in the states of the former Soviet Union.

Li Jingjie is Deputy Director of the Institute of East European, Russian and Central Asian Studies at the Chinese Academy of Social Sciences where he is also a professor. He has written over ninety articles about Russia and its foreign and domestic politics. His most recent publications include *The Collapse of the Soviet Union and its Historical Lessons* (1992); and *The New Pattern of Sino-Soviet Relations* (1989).

Igor F. Maksimichev holds a doctorate in political science and is the Head of the Political Problems of European Security Section of the Institute of Europe at the Russian Academy of Sciences in Moscow. From 1956 to 1992 he was in the Diplomatic Service of the former Soviet Union and Russia. His last function in the Diplomatic Service was Minister of the Embassy of the Soviet Union in Berlin, Germany.

Vladimir S. Miasnikov graduated from the Moscow Institute of Oriental Studies in 1954 and the Institute of International Relations at Moscow State University in 1955. He is Deputy Director of the Institute of the Far East and is a Corresponding Member of the Russian Academy of Sciences. His most recent publications include *The Prospects for Korea in the Asia Pacific Era* (1992); and *The History of Russian Foreign Policy: New Approaches* (1993).

Steven E. Miller is currently Director of the International Security Program at the Center for Science and International Affairs at the Kennedy School of Government at Harvard University and Editor-in-Chief of the quarterly journal *International Security*. Previously he taught Defense and Arms Control Studies at the Massachusetts Institute of Technology. He is editor and co-author of numerous books, including *Cooperative Denuclearization:*

From Pledges to Deeds (1993); *America's Strategy in a Changing World* (1992); and *Europe and Naval Arms Control in the Gorbachev Era* (1992).

Vitaly V. Naumkin is Deputy Director of the Institute of Oriental Studies at the Russian Academy of Sciences. He is a member of the Council for Foreign Policy at the Ministry of Foreign Affairs of the Russian Federation, and Head of the Russian Center for Strategic and International Research. He has edited and contributed to the collective monographs *Central Asia: State Religion and Society;* and *Central Asia and Transcaucasia: Ethnicity and Conflict.*

Tonya L. Putnam holds a Bachelor of Arts in Russian Literature, a Bachelor of University Studies in Soviet Area Studies from the University of Utah, and an MA from Harvard University in Regional Studies: Russia, Eastern Europe and Central Asia. She is at the Kennedy School of Government at Harvard University.

Vladimir V. Razuvayev is the Director of the Center for International Relations at the Institute of Europe at the Russian Academy of Sciences. He was an advisor to the Ministry of Foreign Affairs of the USSR. He received his Master's Degree from the People's Friendship University in 1979. In 1993, he received his doctorate of Political Science at the Institute of Europe. He served as columnist for the *New Times Magazine* from 1989 to 1991.

Konstantin Sarkisov graduated from Leningrad State University in 1966. Currently, he heads the Center for Japanese Studies at the Institute of Oriental Studies at the Russian Academy of Sciences and is Deputy Director of the Institute. He has written many articles on Japanese foreign policy, Russian and Japanese relations and Russian policy in the Asia-Pacific Region. His publications include *Japan at the United Nations* and *Japanese Policy in Southeast Asia.*

Dmitri Vydrin is the Director of the Ukrainian International Institute on Global and Regional Security. From 1989 to 1991, he was Chairman of the Political Science Department at the Kiev Institute of Politics. From 1992 to 1993 he headed the International Security Department at the Institute of World Economics and International Relations. He has a Ph.D. from the USSR Academy of Sciences and is author of *Ukraine on the Nuclear See-Saw.*

Philip D. Zelikow is Assistant Professor of Public Policy at Harvard University. Formerly a career diplomat with the United States Department of State, he served as Director for European Security Affairs on the staff of the National Security Council from 1989 to 1991. His work has appeared, most recently, in the journals *International Security, Foreign Affairs,* and *Survival.* He is co-author of the book *Cooperative Denuclearization* (1993), which outlined a program to reduce nuclear danger; this program was adopted by the United States' government.

Chapter 1
Introduction and Conclusions

Robert D. Blackwill
Sergei A. Karaganov

The future of Russia is international security's most important long-term question. This book seeks to analytically untangle the variables that will affect Russia's internal and external policies, and to delineate and prescribe actions that will reduce the strains between Russia and the outside world.

Robert D. Blackwill

This volume identifies four powerful and negative domestic trends in Russia that promise little good news regarding Russia's internal reform and external policies.[1] First, the development of Russia's economy will be a critical factor in determining the future configuration of Russia's national security interests and the range of policy instruments that will be available to secure them. Although privatization has been occurring on a major scale,[2] most other Russian economic indicators are foreboding. The real

---

1. The incapacitation or death of President Boris Yeltsin would, of course, seriously worsen all these negative trends. Dimitri Simes believes the Yeltsin era is already almost over. "The Twilight of Boris Yeltsin: Facing Russia Without Romance," *Washington Post*, March 27, 1994, p. C1.

2. "Not the Real Thing Yet," *Economist* (March 12, 1994), p. 58; and Lee Hockstader, "Russia's Big Winners and Big Losers," *Washington Post*, December 1, 1993, p. A1.

Robert D. Blackwill is a Lecturer in Public Policy at the Kennedy School of Government at Harvard University and is faculty chairman of a Kennedy School program for Russian general officers. Previously, he was special assistant to President Bush for European and Soviet Affairs on the staff of the National Security Council. From 1985 to 1987 he served as U.S. Ambassador and Chief Negotiator at the negotiations with the Warsaw Pact on conventional forces in Europe.

Sergei A. Karaganov is the Deputy Director of the Institute of Europe at the Russian Academy of Sciences. He has been a member of the Presidential Council since 1993, and is also a member of several other advisory bodies of the Russian government.

standard of living for most Russians will continue to be dreadful.[3] The Russian government's economic policies will probably not entail a return to the kind of fiscal austerity and free market policies that are favored by the West. As Igor Kliamkin in his chapter on the prospects for democracy in Russia notes, this is because Gaidarism, which most Russians equate with shock therapy, is too discredited to make an early comeback. It has virtually no political base in the country. Russian citizens will no longer respond to a political message that they should bear more pain on behalf of Western-style reform. In short, what is thought by the West to be economically necessary in Russia turns out to be politically impossible.[4]

Second, developments in Russia's political sphere are also discouraging. A primary conclusion of this book shared by virtually all its contributors is that the period of democratic breakthroughs (and the accompanying comprehensive cooperative stance in foreign policy with the West), that began midway through Mikhail Gorbachev's presidency and continued until early 1993 is over. In this respect and despite the rosy pronouncements of some Western governments at the time, the December 1993 parliamentary election was a severe setback for the proponents of reform in Russia. The election, and the Russian national sentiment it exposed,[5] undermined and significantly slowed for years to come Russian reform and the following worthy objectives of Western policy:
- steady and brisk movement toward a market economy;
- strict control over the money supply, which would mean fewer subsidies for military industry;

---

3. John Lloyd offers a thorough account of Russia's economic problems in "A Push and They'll All Fall Down," *Financial Times*, March 22, 1993, p. 17. The Russian government is reporting unemployment as high as 8 million people, or 7 percent of the work force, with independent sources estimating a total of 10 million unemployed. Michael Specter, "Soaring Unemployment is Spreading Fear in Russia," *New York Times*, May 8, 1994, p. 3.

4. The following economic forecast for 1994 has been approved by the Russian government: a fall in GNP of 8 percent; a drop of 12 percent in industrial production; an unemployment rate of 5-6 percent, or about three million unemployed; annual inflation of 500 percent, with a monthly rate of 7-9 percent by the end of the year. *ITAR TASS*, March 25, 1994. Most experts believe this dismal economic projection by the Chernomyrdin government is decidedly optimistic.

5. Jacob W. Kipp cautions against the tendency to downplay Vladimir Zhirinovsky's electoral success, writing that "post-election surveys indicate voters support [Zhirinovsky's] ideas, and not just as a protest against economic conditions." See "The Zhirinovsky Threat," *Foreign Affairs* (May/June 1994), pp. 72–86.

- the creation of a civil society united in democratic values and supported by democratic institutions and practices; and
- the pursuit of a benign and cooperative Russian foreign policy toward its neighbors and the West.

Third, crime and corruption are additional corrosive characteristics of today's Russia. This growing lawlessness will continue to poison Russian society and, crucially, government actors and state structures, and will influence the activities of the Russian armed forces. In the absence of a civil society and with no balancing tradition of protection of individual rights, the need to respond to profound concerns about law and order expressed by ordinary Russians will often produce government policies that do not meet the standards of the industrial democracies. In this context, as Kliamkin notes, there is an increasing Russian tendency to support "iron hand" solutions to social and economic problems within the country.

Fourth, anti-Western feeling is strong among ordinary Russians and a significant part of the Russian political elite. This feeling draws on Russian cultural roots and is fed by the widespread perception that at summit after summit the West promised Russia massive aid and simply did not deliver. Indeed, polls show that many Russians think that Western advice regarding Russian reform was designed from the outset to weaken, even fragment, the Russian state.[6] This was a primary factor in bringing about the new activism among the Russian foreign policy and military elites, and partly explains Russia's growing unwillingness to follow the Western lead on international security matters that have a direct impact on its national interests.[7]

These four dominant domestic trends will feed nationalist and chauvinistic forces already gaining ground in the country, and will manifest themselves, as they have since early 1993, in Russian policies toward the outside world that the United States and its partners will often

---

6. Harvard Professor Timothy J. Colton, presentation at a Council on Foreign Relations Study Group at Harvard University's John F. Kennedy School of Government, "Russia and the West: Policy Dilemmas and Future Directions" (January 11, 1994). Russians, like others in the world including our oldest allies, often see malevolent strategic design in U.S. policies when instead there is only innocence or incompetence.

7. The United States is nervous about this Russian activism in Bosnia, the Middle East and regarding the North Korea nuclear problem. Fred Hiatt, "Moscow Proposes Conference to Deal with North Korea," *Washington Post*, March 25, 1994, p. A25.

not like.[8] As a consequence, Russia will increasingly present the West with painful policy choices and tradeoffs. Alexei Arbatov argues that as Russia drives to regain its great power status, it cannot distance itself from the conflicts and crises on the territory of the former Soviet Union. Russia will intervene in the affairs of these states because Russians worry that they must seek to influence decisively the outcome of disputes in these states or the rights of Russians living outside the Federation in the former Soviet Union (FSU) will be threatened; because Moscow believes that these instabilities and wars could spread to Russia itself; and, although no Russian author says so explicitly, because Moscow believes that these countries, including Ukraine, naturally belong under the great Russian umbrella rather than as independent states.[9] Nonetheless, Steven Miller properly questions the soundness of Russian policies toward the FSU states that would edge out Moscow's relations with Western Europe, the United States, and China from top priority in Russia's foreign policy.

THE CHANGED RELATIONSHIP
There was a time of Russian acquiescence to Western wishes, what has been termed the "romantic period" in Russia's relations with the West. Russia voted for Gulf War United Nations resolutions, agreed to UN resolutions on former Yugoslavia, signed the START II (Strategic Arms Reductions Treaty) and Conventional Forces in Europe (CFE) Treaties, largely completed its troop withdrawals from Eastern Europe and the Baltic states, and co-sponsored the Madrid peace process. But that time is now over and has been since at least early 1993. As President Yeltsin has stressed, "As regards relations with the United States, we want to be equal in everything, as two great powers. Concessions on any matter humiliate our patriotic feelings, and this indeed has been so."[10]

---

8. Jack Snyder argues that Russia is now "poised between a tarnished hope in liberal reform and the growing fear that habitual patterns are reemerging, both in domestic and foreign affairs." See "Russian Backwardness and the Future of Europe," *Daedalus*, Vol. 123, No. 2 (Spring 1994), pp. 179–203.

9. Alexander Rutskoi has dramatically affirmed this idea: "We are destined by Lord God himself to live as one family, one nation, one state — a great power...today people have fully understood the price of the irresponsible and ill-thought-out decision to liquidate the USSR." *ITAR TASS*, March 16, 1994.

10. Serge Schmemann, "Yeltsin Calls Vote a Rebuke but Vows to Pursue Reforms," *New York Times*, December 23, 1993, p. A1.

The communiqué at the January 1994 Clinton-Yeltsin summit meeting in Moscow heralded the achievement between Russia and the United States of a "mature strategic partnership based on equality, mutual advantage, and recognition of each other's national interests." Moscow and Washington indicated their eagerness to "move forward on the path of openness and mutual trust." This statement and the concept it represents is a misleading caricature of Russia's relations with the United States and the West. What type of strategic partnership is possible between Russia and the industrial democracies? Partnership with regard to the future of the other nations of the former Soviet Union including Ukraine and the Baltic states, or concerning Eastern Europe? Not likely.

Philip Zelikow's warning about the dangers of over-simplifying images of Russia and Russian reform in order to sell policies to Western parliaments and public opinion is apt. This sort of inflated rhetoric raises public and congressional expectations as to what kind of Russia the West can expect to deal with, and increases the likelihood of public and congressional overreaction when Russia disappoints.[11] In short, by ignoring the plain truth about Russia — that it is not a democracy, that it is far from a market economy, and that it is now pursuing a foreign policy that in some cases means trouble for the West — the industrial democracies foolishly ignore reality.[12]

THE RUSSIAN NATIONAL SECURITY ELITE'S VIEWS OF THE WEST

The Russian national security elite has very little good to say about Western security policy. It often discerns Western intent to exclude or isolate Russia internationally, even to render it weak and defenseless. In this context, Andrei Kortunov stresses that Russian hopes for a new era of U.S.-Russian cooperation have been disappointed.

---

11. An example of such overreaction is the demand by various senators, in the aftermath of revelations about the Ames spy scandal, to review or suspend all economic assistance to Russia. See such calls by Senator Mitch McConnell (R-Ky.) and Dennis DeConcini (D-Ariz.) in "Russian Foreign Minister Wants $1 Billion from U.S. Despite Charges of Espionage," *Washington Post*, February 28, 1994, p. A13.

12. See the Clinton administration's retreat from the concept of strategic partnership in U.S. Secretary of Defense William Perry's Address at Georgetown University, "United States Relationship with Russia" (March 14, 1994).

Russian policy makers regard current conventional arms control limitations on Russia as unfair.[13] They resent Western opposition to Russian conventional arms transfers and the U.S. blocking of Russian sales of missile technology to India. They conclude that by Russian defense conversion, many Westerners mean unilateral Russian disarmament. They think that the West, and especially the United States, has been too soft regarding Ukraine's unwillingness to follow through on its commitments to allow the removal of nuclear weapons from its soil. (Although this irritant has been somewhat relieved by the praiseworthy Trilateral Nuclear Statement signed in January 1994 in Moscow, it remains unclear whether Ukraine will actually give up its nuclear option.) They believe that the West does not understand that Moscow is fighting Islamic extremism in Central Asia, and argue that the West does not appreciate the real security problems Russia faces on its borders. They find the Japanese position on the Kurile Islands unreasonable and arrogant.

These Russians question whether the latest U.S. defense plans to maintain a capability to fight two regional wars simultaneously will be implemented anywhere near the territory of the Russian Federation. They criticize the West's unwillingness to consult with Moscow before making decisions that affect Russia's interests. They reject the Western judgment that the Serbs are the villains in the Bosnian tragedy. They protest that the United States is too pro-Israel in its approach to the Middle East peace process. They fault the U.S. opposition to arms sales to Iran. They ask who appointed the United States as threatening global policeman in the former Yugoslavia, Haiti, Somalia, Iraq, and North Korea.[14] They complain of Western hypocrisy regarding human rights, particularly what they assert is Western indifference to human rights violations against Russians living in the other former Soviet states. They blame the West for many of the domestic ills that Russia has suffered since 1991 and are convinced that Western advice regarding democracy and the free market has brought near catastrophe to Russia. In short, many in the Russian elite think that

---

13. This has been dramatized by the amassment of Russian troops returning from Central Europe along Russia's northern and southern borders. Michael R. Gordon, "Russian Troop Movements Rouse NATO Concern on Treaty Limits," *New York Times*, April 3, 1994, p. 1.

14. In this regard, note Andrei Kozyrev's recent op-ed piece, "Don't Threaten Us," in which he stated that "Some views suggest an almost maniacal desire to see only one leading power in the modern world — the United States of America — and to obsessively proclaim American leadership everywhere and in all respects." *New York Times*, March 18, 1994, p. A29.

important forces in the West do not wish Russia well, and do not accept that Russia has important security interests that are different than those of the West. These Russian views are hardly the stuff of strategic partnership with the West.

THE SHAPE OF RUSSIA'S RELATIONS WITH THE "FAR ABROAD"
In assessing Russia's relations with the Western European states, Karl Kaiser argues that West Europe is all to easily overwhelmed by the difficulties of a Russia in turmoil, stymied by the radical noises emanating from certain Russian politicians. In contrast, Igor Maksimichev asserts that Russian integration into European political, economic, and security institutions is imperative, and he cautions that Western policies and actions that increase Russia's sense of isolation from the rest of Europe intensify the very features of the Russian political and social context from which the countries of Eastern and Western Europe seek protection and security guarantees.

Maksimichev's perspective reflects the view of many Russians that the West has developed a conception of the new Europe that excludes Russia. They oppose the extension of NATO membership to the states of Eastern Europe, regarding it, as Oleg Bogomolov believes, as an effort to cut Russia off from its traditional intermediaries with Western Europe, and to deprive Russia of important potential partners in its economic and political transition.[15] Russians have no sympathy for Peter Hardi's conviction that the interests of at least the Visegrad group of Eastern European states would be best served by avoiding the attentions of Moscow altogether.

With regard to general trends in Russia's relations with the outside world, a point of near consensus is that East Asia will play an increasingly important role in Russia's economic and political development. The outlook for Russia's interaction with Japan, according to both Konstantin Sarkisov and Tsuyoshi Hasegawa, is bleak. China has been much more willing to engage Russia both economically and politically, and may represent a sizeable counterweight to Western influence in Russia. While Li Jingjie argues that prospects for long-term economic and political cooperation between China and Russia are good due to the compatibility of their long-term interests, Vladimir Miasnikov emphasizes the potential

---

15. See "Press Conference by Yevgeny Primakov, Head of RF External Intelligence Service on the Interests of NATO and Russia," *Official Kremlin International News Broadcast*, November 26, 1993.

for antagonisms to arise if the balance of economic strength tips in favor of the Chinese, leaving Russia playing a game of catch-up, or even becoming dependent upon China.

RUSSIA'S PERIPHERY

In trying to anticipate the likely character of Russia's relations closer to home with the other states of the former Soviet Union, it is important to dispel the notion that the Russian military has been dragging a reluctant political elite into a more aggressive national security policy. Rather, a broad consensus has now been formed within the Russian government about the future direction of Russian policy toward its periphery.[16]

Nearly all Russians believe unselfconsciously and unapologetically in the geographic boundaries of the former Soviet Union. This means that few Russians genuinely accept the independence of Ukraine, Georgia, Tajikistan and so forth. This does not suggest that there is a neo-imperial blueprint for reconquest in the Kremlin; Russia is far too chaotic for that and faces some constraints on its activity with its neighbors (detailed below). But it does promise that all things being equal, Russia's instinct will be to seek to firmly return in one configuration or another all the former republics of the Soviet Union except the Baltic states to Moscow's security orbit.[17] This Russian pressure has already produced results in Belarus, in the Caucasus, and in parts of Central Asia. It will increasingly be directed against Ukraine.

This expansive instinct is compounded by the security problems Russia faces in the south. Vitaly Naumkin argues that regardless of the political impulse both in Russia and in the countries of Central Asia and Transcaucasia to sever ties between them, these new nations are inextricably bound to Russia economically and militarily. Conflicts in these states, many of which are internally generated and some of which Moscow exploits for its own purposes, draw Russia into the affairs of its neighbors in a dynamic interaction that can only lead to greater Russian influence in these new, weak and unstable nations.

The fear of Islamic extremism that permeates the Russian political elite plays an important role in pushing Russia toward an increased presence

---

16. For further details, see Suzanne Crow, "Russia Asserts its Strategic Agenda," *Radio Free Europe/Radio Liberty Research Report*, December 17, 1993, pp. 1–8.

17. For example, note the assertion by Colonel General Andrei Nikolayev, the commander of Russia's border guards, that Russian forces will stay in Tajikistan forever. "Border Guards To Stay Forever," *Moscow Times*, April 1, 1994, p. 5.

in Central Asia. And even the most ardent Russian reformers worry that events to the south will eventually infect Russia itself and bring about the mass return of ethnic Russians, further radicalizing the domestic political situation.[18] While emphasizing the considerable variation in Russia's relations with the individual states of these regions, numerous contributors to this volume conclude that Russia will increasingly intervene in the conflicts along its southern border. While Moscow is not inventing all the problems in neighboring former republics, it will certainly use these conflicts to advance its interests as it perceives them.[19]

This should come as no shock to the West. Tonya Putnam opines that Russian intervention in these regions should not be of serious Western concern, given the much greater priority the West has in maintaining good relations with Russia, especially in the nuclear sphere. In any event, no responsible Russian government could ignore the civil wars along or near its periphery. Furthermore, the West has not shown great interest in involving itself in these ethnic wars in the FSU. It is not surprising that Russia has decided to go to the sources of these conflicts and to intervene directly with military force, rather than allow the instability to spread and gradually undermine Russia itself.

The 25 million ethnic Russians living outside the Russian Federation in the former Soviet Union also pull Moscow into the affairs of these countries. Again, it is instructive to note that even Russian westernizers worry seriously about the treatment of ethnic Russians in the Baltics, Ukraine, Kazakhstan and other Central Asian states. Any Russian government, no matter how reformist, will be preoccupied with this problem both because of a real sense of responsibility and Russian public opinion on the subject. Over time, looking after these Russians living outside the Russian Federation will inevitably involve Moscow more and more in the internal affairs of its neighbors. The developing crisis in the Crimea is a case in point.

At the same time, there are some constraints upon any swift and comprehensive Russian attempt to recreate the Soviet Union, even if it is assumed this is the working objective of the Yeltsin government, which it

---

18. Shari Duren, "Millions May be Returning to Russia," *Moscow Tribune*, March 31, 1994, p. 5; and Carey Scott, "End of Empire: Look Homeward, Russians," *Moscow Times*, April 1, 1994, p. 1.

19. For military implications, see Paul Quinn-Judge, "Moscow Places Military Focus on Creating Elite, Mobile Force," *Boston Globe*, March 18, 1994, p. 17.

is not.[20] Several of the countries that emerged from the former Soviet Union are killing fields where most Russians do not want their sons to die. The political and economic weaknesses of the Russian central government and of Russia itself also limit Russian activities regarding its neighbors. Finally, the Russian government does continue to wish for good relations with the West, and should recognize that those relations would become soured if aggressive interference in its neighbors' affairs became a persistent pattern of Russian behavior.

These constraints will not decide Russia's future external behavior. In terms of Russian military involvement on the territory of the former republics, Russian public opinion — which is fractured and mostly uninterested — can be managed as long as large numbers of casualties are avoided, which should be possible given the self-restraint that will likely characterize the actions of the Russian general staff. Nor will Russian economic weakness prohibit Russian ventures in neighboring states, as relatively small expenditures of men and resources can decisively affect the internal dynamics of many of these small and vulnerable countries, as in Georgia.

And while the Russian government continues to value good relations with the West, the likely downturn in levels of Western economic assistance (because of looser Russian macro-economic policy and increasing Western-Russian friction) is not likely to provide sufficient Western leverage to produce a significant impact on Russian policies regarding its neighbors. This is particularly the case because Moscow believes that increasing its influence in the former republics of the Soviet Union is its first external priority.

RUSSIA, UKRAINE AND THE WEST

In contemplating the conflicting interests of Russia and the West, the issue of Ukraine is of cardinal importance.[21] The relationship between Russia and Ukraine is the most serious security threat now confronting Europe. What are the odds that Ukraine will be an independent nation within its present borders in 1997? The chances may be no better than one in two. Most Russians believe that most of Ukraine — the historic epicenter of the

---

20. Dorinda Elliott expounds a different view in "The Long Arms of the Bear: Russian Aims in the 'Near Abroad,'" *Newsweek* (January 31, 1994), p. 13.

21. A thoughtful discussion of Russian-Ukrainian relations is found in William H. Kincade and Natalie Melnyczuk, "Eurasia Letter: Unneighborly Neighbors," *Foreign Policy*, No. 94 (Spring 1994), pp. 84–104.

Russian nation — should return to mother Russia. Moscow's political, economic and security policies will increasingly be devoted to forcing Ukraine back into the Russian fold.

These Russian objectives do not posit a military invasion. Rather, many Russians, Vladimir Razuvayev and Dmitri Fadeyev included, believe that Ukraine cannot long endure economic and strategic isolation, and that Ukraine's disastrous economic circumstances will push it into Russia's orbit. The economic situation in Ukraine is indeed dire. Hyperinflation is raging, industry remains largely unprivatized, and industrial production has dropped precipitously.[22] The deficit has spun wildly out of control, public services are stopping, and pensions are worthless. The health care system is in ruin, and the current fuel crisis may be the most severe in half a century.[23] Ukraine's 11 million ethnic Russians in the south and east are restive. Along these lines, Dmitri Vydrin identifies the fragmentation of national politics in Ukraine and the regionalization of political power, and stresses that the disintegration of Ukraine — if it occurs — is likely to be bloody.

This fragmentation would be especially dangerous because of the 1600-plus nuclear weapons remaining on Ukrainian soil. The Trilateral Statement, signed by Russia, Ukraine and the United States on January 14, 1994, provides for the removal of warheads from Ukrainian territory in return for energy compensation from Russia and economic assistance from the United States. If implemented, it will facilitate the denuclearization of Ukraine, pave the way for the implementation of START I, and ease Ukraine's enormous $2.5 billion debt to Russia. While Ukraine has made and broken denuclearization commitments on several occasions, this document is significant in that 1) Ukraine pledged that it would join the Nuclear Non-Proliferation Treaty (NPT) as a non-nuclear state and remove *all* nuclear weapons on its soil; 2) it apparently was associated with a side agreement setting a timetable for denuclearization; and 3) it provided specific written security assurances from the United States and Russia, though limited to standard CSCE (Conference on Security and Coopera-

---

22. Steven Greenhouse, "Clinton Vows to Improve Relations with Ukraine," *New York Times* March 5, 1994, p. 5; and Fred Kaplan, "Ukraine's Morass: A Rich Potential Lost," *Boston Globe*, March 3, 1994, p. 18.

23. Russia began charging Ukraine world energy prices on January 1, 1994, and threatens to cut off energy shipments to Ukraine for its failure to pay its fuel debt, which exceeds one billion dollars. Robert Seely, "Ukraine Casts Doubt on Disarmament: Removal of Warheads Linked to Energy Supplies from Russia," *Washington Post*, March 7, 1994, p. A12.

tion in Europe) and NPT formulations. Crucially, however, the Rada did not vote on the Trilateral Statement itself, and did not consider Kravchuk's proposal to accede to the NPT.[24] The fate of nuclear weapons in Ukraine remains quite uncertain.

The situation in Ukraine is a building crisis that could be the most serious in Europe in more than thirty years. For a variety of reasons, the West should strongly prefer that Ukraine remain an independent nation. A sovereign Ukraine within in its present borders would:
- increase the likelihood that Ukraine would allow the removal of all nuclear weapons from its soil;
- reduce the risk that Ukrainian fragmentation and attendant instability and violence would endanger the command, control and safety of the nuclear weapons on its territory, and endanger the civil nuclear installations in Ukraine;
- lessen the chance of conflict between Ukraine and Russia;
- give evidence to East and Central Europe that Russia intends to be a good neighbor; and
- minimize the possibility that Ukraine could become a destructive element in Russia's relations with the West.

Unfortunately, most Russians see this problem quite differently and seem to believe that Ukraine can be somehow peacefully drawn back into the Russian orbit without seriously damaging Moscow's relations with East and Central Europe and with the West. Indeed, this issue has significant potential to rupture Russia's relations with the West, or at least the United States.

IMPLICATIONS FOR WESTERN POLICY
1. The West can expect Russia to pursue a policy of bringing its neighbors back within its orbit. This will not entail the recreation of the Soviet Union but it will mean that most of the nations of the former USSR will lose much freedom of action in their domestic and foreign policies as Russia reestablishes a strong sphere of influence and intervention regarding these nations. This will be primarily done by non-military means, which is certainly the Russian preference.

2. With the Baltic states less threatened by Russian direct action of the kind indicated above, policies to support the independence and territorial

---

24. Steven E. Miller, "Ukraine, the Trilateral Agreement, and the Future of Denuclearization," prepared for IISS *Strategic Comments* (February 23, 1994), pp. 1–13.

integrity of Ukraine are the dominating priority for the West. As indicated above, this is because of nuclear weapons on Ukrainian soil that would be at risk if Ukraine comes apart, and because a fragmenting Ukraine would send destabilizing shocks well into East and Central Europe. To put it conceptually, Western energies should be focused upon the region first, then Russia, then Yeltsin and the reformers[25] — not, as in the past, Yeltsin first, then Russia, then the region.[26] This requires a major Western effort to save Ukraine, if that is still possible. If the Ukrainian government is willing to cooperate (including by adopting sensible economic policies — a big if), then the G-7 (group of seven major industrialized nations) should put together a multi-billion dollar financial assistance package to try to help stabilize the Ukrainian economic situation which is feeding Russian separatism in the Crimea and eastern Ukraine. In addition, the West should offer major and continuous high-level political support for Ukrainian independence. Finally, the West should tell Moscow that Russia's relations with the industrial democracies will suffer significantly if Russia seeks to undermine Ukrainian statehood, and should mean it.

Ideally, the West and Russia should be working together in managing the Ukrainian crisis, but their objectives are not compatible. The West wants a genuinely independent Ukraine; Russia does not. And the industrial democracies unfortunately are showing no sign of mounting such an ambitious program of assistance to Ukraine. One must also doubt whether Ukraine's leadership will have the political will to carry out the necessary painful economic reforms on which any Western aid would be contingent. Thus, the West had better get ready for a crisis generated by Ukrainian fragmentation,[27] and also prepare to react to a less dramatic but creeping de facto annexation of Ukrainian territory by Russia.

---

25. The Clinton administration began moving in this direction by March, 1994, evidenced by the visits of the Ukrainian, Kazakh, and Georgian leaders to the United States, by increased economic assistance to Russia's neighbors, and by U.S. Defense Secretary William J. Perry's proposal of a non-aggression pact among Russia, the U.S., Kazakhstan and perhaps Britain. For details, see Steven Greenhouse, "U.S. to Focus More on Ex-Soviet Republics," *International Herald Tribune*, March 22, 1994, p. 2; and Steve LeVine, "Perry Seeks Security Pact for Ex-Soviet Republics," *Washington Post*, March 20, 1994, p. A32.

26. Philip Zelikow is particularly critical of the Clinton administration's preoccupation with Yeltsin in "Beyond Boris Yeltsin," *Foreign Affairs*, Vol. 73, No. 1 (January/February 1994), pp. 44–55.

27. Ukrainian President Leonid Kravchuk has said that if Moscow attempts to reconstruct the Soviet Union, "there will be blood." Quoted in "Ukraine Leader Sees Strife in Any Bid to Recreate USSR," *Boston Globe*, April 3, 1994, p. 8.

3. Unless it is ready to commit major resources to the area, which it should not, the West should lower its voice regarding Russian actions in the Caucasus and Central Asia.[28] With the partial exception of Kazakhstan, important Western national interests are not engaged in these two regions.[29] The United States and its allies are unwilling both to send peacemakers there to dilute the Russian presence and influence, and to expend the necessary Western resources to try to blunt the Russian advance. Moreover, the West is unlikely to punish Russia in practical ways for its activities in these distant regions. Such empty threats regarding these areas to the south reduce the credibility of Western expressions of concern to the Russian leadership about Ukraine and the Baltic states. And feckless warnings by the United States here as elsewhere do not contribute to international stability.

4. The G-7 countries should redouble their efforts to provide much more technical assistance to the Russian reform effort: to help Russians build democratic institutions over the long term is the critical task.

5. Despite seriously negative trends in Russia, the West should engage more, not less, with the Russian leadership and elites. This is a point Sergei Karaganov has been making eloquently for some time. The West should attempt to pursue narrow but important issues on which it can cooperate with the Russians: strategic nuclear reductions, implementation of other existing arms control agreements, counter-proliferation, counter-terrorism, counter-narcotics, and, if there is agreement on what the term means, opposing the spread of Islamic extremism. These matters will be the core of possible Western collaboration with the new Russia. Even here the record will be at best mixed and progress will be ever more difficult to sustain given internal developments in Russia, and the probable directions of Russia's foreign policy. But to now abandon the Western effort to find a broadly profitable relationship with the new Russia, difficult as that will be, would be deeply misguided and would contribute

---

28. The Clinton administration has stressed that Russia must only engage in the affairs of its neighbors after having received their explicit invitation, and such engagement must be fully consistent with international norms. "Presidential Address Before Joint Session of Congress on the State of the Union," January 25, 1994. These ambitious criteria are not being fulfilled in Russia's activities on the territory of the FSU, so why set forth Western standards that Russia has not met and will not meet in most situations on its periphery? With so much at stake in the U.S.-Russian nuclear relationship, will Washington really damage bilateral ties because Russia does not meet international norms in Tajikistan?

29. Kazakhstan has nuclear weapons on its soil and abundant natural resources of interest to the West.

to a self-fulfilling prophecy whose ruinous effects would be felt in Europe and beyond for decades.

6. If Western governments cannot improve the situation with respect to Russia anytime soon, they should at least take care not to make it unnecessarily worse. This means systematically consulting with Russia before important Western initiatives — not shutting Russia out from the new Europe, its deliberations, its institutions, and its future. The European Union has been especially at fault for giving Russians this feeling of exclusion, including in the trade sphere. And while we should move methodically to bring Poland, the Czech Republic and Hungary into full NATO membership by the end of the century (this time frame could be accelerated if events to the east made that necessary), Russia should also be given every opportunity to deepen its relationship with NATO.

NATO authorities have thus far been hampered in this critical goal of engaging Russia by insufficient resources, other priorities, and a tendency to indulge in what the Russians now call "military tourism." If the entrance into the Alliance of the three East European countries causes a crisis between Russia and the West, which is likely if present trends continue, let that be Russia's choice. NATO should try to open up the Alliance in creative ways to Russian involvement, including in defense planning and crisis decision making, if Russian external behavior permits such cooperation. In sum, NATO should give Russia a clearly unique place within the Partnership for Peace framework.[30] If Russia chooses self-isolation from a NATO that is the only plausible core of an effective future European security system, so be it.[31] But the West should itself certainly avoid exciting the historic Russian sense of isolation and vulnerability. Indeed, it would be foolish at this point to rule out eventual Russian membership in NATO or to speak of a deterministic long-term Russian threat to European security.

7. Finally, the West, led by the United States, should develop a coherent set of policies to deal with the Russia of the rest of this decade and beyond, not the Russia of recent dreams. Western governments need to work much harder to forge Western strategic purpose and hold their own geopolitical cohesion together in the absence of the Soviet threat. That

---

30. The Clinton administration thinks differently; see U.S. Ambassador to NATO Robert Hunter's comments in John Palmer, "NATO Denies Russia Big-Power Status," *The Guardian*, March 7, 1994, p. 8.

31. For the internal Russian debate on Partnership for Peace, see Jon Auerbach, "Russians Appear at Odds on NATO Plan," *Boston Globe*, April 2, 1994, p. 4.

cannot happen without the intense personal involvement of the American president.

CONCLUSION

The above analysis and policy prescriptions presume that the Russian Federation will not disintegrate, which would make the world a much more dangerous place.[32] On the other hand, the prognosis would be overly pessimistic if any of the following transformations were to occur:
- macro-economic stabilization in Russia, significantly reducing inflation and improving the economic condition of ordinary Russian citizens;
- political revival of the Russian democratic reform movement that arouses widespread popular support in the country;
- the creation of institutions of political pluralism throughout Russia that compete well with older and less congenial Russian expressions of national identity;
- a national revolt against crime reverses the current profoundly corrupting trends;
- Russian nationalism becomes the engine of Russian renewal based on democratic values, rather than being channeled into foreign involvements, and the national security elite's consensus on the reassertion of Russian influence in the FSU is reversed;
- Russia's neighbors to the south become quiet and stable;
- Russians abroad are safe, prosperous and loyal to their new nations, and the Russian government is satisfied by this; or
- the Ukrainian economic situation decisively improves, reducing the possibility of Ukraine's disintegration, and Russia stands by passively.

Unfortunately, these developments are not likely.[33]

This sobering picture does not portend a return to the Cold War or anything approaching it. There are no great power rivalries that threaten the peace of Europe or the world. The Soviet nuclear sword no longer hangs over the countries and peoples of the West. The Soviet Union is in

---

32. Jessica Eve Stern raises the possibility of the Russian Federation's fragmentation in "Moscow Meltdown: Can Russia Survive?" *International Security*, Vol. 18, No. 4 (Spring 1994), pp. 40–65.

33. Stephen S. Rosenfeld and Stephen Sestanovich offer less pessimistic prognoses in (respectively) "Russia Scare," *Washington Post*, March 18, 1994; and "Russia Turns the Corner," *Foreign Affairs*, Vol. 73, No. 1 (January/February 1994), pp. 83-98. Yuri N. Afanasyev offers an even bleaker view in "Russian Reform is Dead," *Foreign Affairs*, Vol. 73, No. 2 (March/April 1994), pp. 21–27.

the dustbin of history; its global reach is only a memory. Russian military power has gone from East and Central Europe. Russia poses no military threat to Western Europe or to North America, and could not do so for many years. Thus, for the first time in six decades, there is no hegemonic danger to Europe. Russia's power projection capabilities have vastly shrunk. Communism and the police state are discredited among a large majority of the Russian population. Basic human rights and a considerable degree of freedom of the press have become a central part of Russian life. Privatization is occurring at a rapid and transforming pace. And millions in the new Russia still aspire to reforms that will eventually bring the nation securely toward democracy and away from brutal, corrupt, and inefficient statism. The West must, of course, do everything it can to build on these profoundly positive developments.

But as has been true for centuries, Russia is a great European power, with a particular history and perspective. As the following chapters make clear, it will have national security policies that will often be at odds with Western preferences. So with "partnership" an empty slogan, Russia and the West should instead energetically pursue policies of damage limitation designed for narrow cooperation when possible, and seek to forestall crisis in Russia's relations with the outside world. This will not be easy. Ukraine is the key. The outlook is bleak.

Sergei A. Karaganov

Robert Blackwill's largely realistic and gloomy conclusions are less pessimistic than those from the Russian perspective. There are even more problems that will cloud Russian-Western relations — problems on both sides.

Western Europe is experiencing a deep psychological crisis. Politically, the European Union is still too fragile to withstand real crises in the outside world, and post-Maastricht difficulties exacerbate the intra-Western orientation of core West European countries. Germany is still preoccupied with the assimilation of its eastern lands.

The West has proven itself incapable of devising and implementing a cohesive long-term strategy to integrate Russia, other independent states of the former Soviet Union, and even the East Central European states into the Western world. Worse, the current quality of Western policy making suggests that the West is losing its ability to develop any coherent long-term strategy, whether friendly engagement or hostile containment. The Russian government is weak and still too poorly organized to develop a long-term strategy, or even an effective reaction to a major crisis. The gradual degradation of Western security structures created during the Cold War has increased the longing of some Western security elites for an organizing principle — an outside threat. Russia is also confronted by such sentiments from its elites.

The world is experiencing a gradual yet steady erosion of the structure of international relations created after the Second World War. This structure provided for dominance by the West and North, and an uneasy but robust stability within the North. It is relatively clear that the emerging system will be far less stable. Traditional dominating actors — the United States, the West in general, the Soviet Union or its main heir, Russia — will have far fewer possibilities to influence this system than they did in the past, unless they organize themselves in a different mode.

Not only is Russia experiencing a backlash against "only yes" foreign policies and a revival of nationalist feelings; it is also witnessing a gradual slide toward economic collapse, disintegration of state structures, and the political fragmentation of most of the countries on its periphery (except for the Baltic countries, gas-rich Turkmenistan, the currently roughly authoritarian Uzbekistan, and Belarus, which is effectively joining Russia's economy). Most of the causes of this degradation are systemic — the changing of the pricing system, which transformed Russia from an economic colony, as it was in the USSR, into an economically dominating power; the absence of reforms; the significant damage incurred by smaller republics from the cutting of traditional economic ties to Russia; and a desperate lack of managerially and technically capable elites. Russia is blamed for this general deterioration, but, for example, the transformation of Georgia from one of the richest republics of the USSR into one of the poorest happened before Abkhazian secession and possible Russian involvement. Furthermore, Russia continued to subsidize most of its neighbors, officially independent states, long after the dissolution of the Soviet Union.

Multiple vacuums are being created in the former Soviet Union due to crises, mismanagement, unbearable living conditions, and the weakening of governments. Ukraine is a prime example of this. As a result, there are powerful impulses for Russia to become involved in the affairs of neighboring states, and the positions of Russians who are anxious to intervene are strengthened as well.

Russia's choice is not between a policy of 1) democratic benign neglect, full respect for sovereignty, and support for reforms; or 2) full-scale imperial revanche and forceful Russian takeover of most of the republics of the former USSR. In most of these states there is very little democracy, virtually no reform, and declining sovereignty due to the weakening of government. Russia's assets are inadequate to pursue the second policy, and a growing majority of the Russian elite and the population are beginning to appreciate the prohibitive cost of taking over turbulent societies and ruined economies.

Instead, Russia must choose between 1) partial reintegration of parts of the former Soviet Union in a confederative-like structure, along with management of instability in the rest of the former Soviet Union; and 2) the creation of a system of dependent and dominated states with only formal independence, very much along the model of U.S. relations with Central American states. The second choice is bad, but preferable to the first. This decision will face Moscow no matter who is in power — even a government comprised of a late-day Mikhail Gorbachev as Russian President, with early Yegor Gaidar as prime minister, early Boris Yeltsin as head of Parliament, Eduard Shevardnadze as foreign minister, and Andrei Kozyrev as minister of defense.

The West is unpleasantly surprised and irritated by Russia's less compliant tone, disillusioned by the sluggishness of Russian reforms (which were previously pushed forward by only a tiny minority of

Russian economists, but are now rejected by an overwhelming majority of politicians, even reformists), and worried by Russia's new posturing and signs of a revived capacity to compete. These factors — in addition to increased concern about signs of Russian dominance, if not neo-imperialism, in the space of the former USSR — could prompt the West to try to start a new Cold War, a policy of neo-containment.

The majority of Russian elites would rather avoid such an outcome. They understand that Russia has nothing to gain and much to lose in such a confrontation. Russia has a deep strategic interest in rapprochement with the West. The ultra-imperialists and the iron-handers would secretly applaud such a Western reaction; their ascension to power is facilitated by a belligerent external environment.

But even formerly liberal Russians are contributing to the anti-Russian drift of Western policies. They cannot formulate coherent policies adequate to the new challenges. In part they fear those who criticize a compliant foreign policy. Partly innocent of the possible consequences, these formally liberal Russians are creating and adhering to concepts such as the "Monrovsky Doctrine" and "zone of special responsibilities," and are calling for the integration of the former Soviet Union. Such statements are superfluous and dangerous. They are superfluous because no nation or international effort could replace Russia; Russia's "special responsibility" in this region is gradually (if only by default) being acknowledged by the nations on Russia's periphery. Such aggressive comments are dangerous because they provoke fear and anti-Russian sentiment in the "near" and "far" abroad. Above all, they pave the way conceptually for indiscriminate Russian involvement in innumerable crises that would bleed Russia white and create a strong reaction from the outside world.

A new Cold War would strengthen the conservative elements in Russian society, not achieve Western goals. Russia is too weak to become a real enemy. The new Cold War would not prevent Russian dominance over most of the former Soviet countries; they are weak and the West cannot help them in a meaningful way. The West has proved incapable of providing serious aid even to Russia, where the investment could have made a difference.[34] A new Cold War would be shallow: the differences that would fuel the conflict would be unrelated to the two sides' core interests. The ideological confrontation is over. Russia is not competing for

---

34. For an evaluation of the Western policy of aid to Russia see Sergei Karaganov, et al., "Why the Western Aid Failed" (Moscow: Bertelsmann Press; and Germany: Gutersloh, 1994).

influence as a global power. It could not in the foreseeable future pose a meaningful military threat to the West.

An active Russian peacemaking role in Central Asia is actually in Western interests because it would curtail the spread of instability and Muslim extremism. The situation is far more complex in the Caucasus: there is no chance that the West could manage this vortex of wars and conflicts without Russia. Despite Caspian oil deposits and sympathy for Eduard Shevardnadze, Western disengagement will continue.

The Baltics are a special case, but are not really challenged by Russia. Belarus is gradually merging with Russia (but retaining its political independence). The real issue over which a new Cold War could start is the fate of Ukraine. Here again I agree with Blackwill: The West's inability to help Ukraine and its unwillingness to form a common strategy with Russia toward Ukraine (except on nuclear matters) will produce a gradual deterioration of the state and social order on Ukrainian territory. (This is not to say that reunification of a collapsing Ukraine or its parts with Russia is in Russia's interests. In fact, such a unification could deal a *coup de grace* to Russia proper.)

One could argue that the first Cold War was a tragedy, the second, at the beginning of the 1980s, was dangerous, but contained elements of a tragic comedy, and the third, if it happens, would be a farce. Many people would suffer, and Russia and the countries around it would be delayed in their development and would have to look for allies in the South. If in the meantime NATO expands eastward, Russia under any government will become a revisionist power striving to undermine the already fragile European order. Europe and the Euro-Atlantic area will lose a historic possibility to create a robust and stable post–Cold War order.

What is the alternative? To lower inflated expectations, to understand that a country with the size, history and complexity of Russia, along with its intellectual, military, and potential economic power, will not act like a scaled-up version of Monaco. To judge the social transformation of Russia, one must weigh not only the obvious shortcomings but also the unbelievable achievements. Russia has done away with communism within three years, and privatized or at least de-étatized half its industry and more than half its trade. Reforms will most probably continue, though at a slower pace, and may go deeper than the first gallant but relatively shallow attempts of the young monetarists. Now comes structural policy, demonopolization, and the creation of the institutional base for a capitalist economy. That was not achieved or, indeed, attempted by the first wave of reformers.

Russia is not a full democracy, nor will it be for many years. One could regret or condemn that; one could also understand that politically Russia is living in an earlier historical stage. The state of democratic freedoms in Britain in the mid-nineteenth century or in the United States even half a century later would outrage most contemporary democratic purists. Nor does Russia fully belong to Western civilization. Through centuries of defending itself from Asian invasions, it has become partly an Asian country as well.

RECOMMENDATIONS FOR THE WEST

So what should the West do to avoid a third Cold War?

1. The West should understand that Russia is undergoing a long evolution with ups and downs, breakthroughs and reversals.

2. If the West is unable to help, let it adopt a policy of not hindering this evolution. It must stop its inflated talk about aid that never came and will not come.

3. The West should act upon its interests and expect Russia to do the same. These interests largely converge, or at least do not conflict with each other. When they do, both sides should try to resolve them or accept some level of disagreement as normal.

4. The West should accept the possibility that Moscow's influence on the territory of most of the former USSR will be reinstated, probably in the form of domination over a periphery of weak states rather than the recreation of an empire.

5. The only viable strategy toward Ukraine is massive and coordinated Western-Russian aid to Ukraine, given on condition of reform. If the West will not participate, let it be prepared for the consequences, including Ukraine's possible disintegration. Nor should the West pretend that Russia is to be blamed; many Russians want to show Ukraine the price of independence by letting it boil in its own juices. But Russia will inevitably be drawn into the emerging crisis in Ukraine with an inexorable increase in its political influence there.

6. The West must decide whether in historic, geostrategic, and, later, economic terms, it wants Russia as its ally, or whether Russia will be left to wander alone or join with other countries in the South or East Asia.

7. Finally, both Russia and the West should compare their interests — they converge much more often than they conflict, especially in the strategic sphere:
- management of the superpower nuclear legacy;
- non-proliferation;

- containment of regional conflicts and of Islamic extremism in Asia;
- prevention of Russian neo-imperialism or the creation of a geostrategic "black hole" in the center of Eurasia, if Russia cannot provide for some stability in this area (with outside help), or if Russia itself falls apart;
- management of the emerging Chinese leviathan;
- creation of a new stable core of the international system, which cannot be built only around Western institutions; and
- the linking of Russian resources (and later its human and economic capital) to the West.

A strategic association between Russia and the West, as well as Japan and South Korea, is not only advisable but also possible. In the near term, such an association could only function in a relatively narrow military-political and geostrategic sphere. The crucial role in such an association would be played by an evolving Russian-U.S. military-political partnership.

But after saying as a strategic analyst that such an association is possible and advisable, as a political scientist I cannot assert with assurance that such an association is probable. Equally likely is mismanagement by all concerned and a decline in Russia's relations with most of the outside world.

Chapter 2
The Outlook for Democracy in Russia

Igor Kliamkin

The more than reserved attitude of Russian public opinion toward the word "democracy" is one reason why the future of Russian democracy can hardly be viewed in optimistic terms.[1] The concepts of democracy and democratization entered into Russia's perestroikan new-speak overburdened with ideological connotations and symbols that are alien to it; democracy has come to mean not so much a system of specific political institutions and procedures as an abstract alternative to communism and an easy and quick way to solve the problems that could not be solved under communism. But for many people life under democratic rule has proven more difficult than life under the communist regime. According to data gathered by the Public Opinion Foundation, for millions of Russians the concept of democracy has no inherent political value and is perceived as propaganda peddled by the semi-official Russian media. This is also true of concepts such as "the market," "reform," and "perestroika."

This disappointment in democracy and democrats is cause for concern. Russia's history is full of cases when democratic development was sacrificed to stability and security; for contemporary Russia, the primary national security challenge is internal. The core security problems facing Russia stem from the situation within Russia itself and between Russia and the Soviet successor states — that is, the danger of internal political and economic collapse.

---

1. The success of Vladimir Zhirinovsky's Liberal Democratic Party in the December 12, 1993 elections is by no means related to the name of the party.

Igor Kliamkin is a specialist in Russian history and public opinion. He has done research at the Institute of International Economics and Politics at the Russian Academy of Sciences and is Chair of the Public Opinion Foundation. He has spent the past year studying the problems facing governments making the transformation from a totalitarian regime to democracy.

Guiding Ideologies in Russia

Russia's security challenge is rooted in the catastrophic situation of its economy and an unstable political system, which is incapable of guiding economic reform. This internal security challenge is one reason why the new Russian military doctrine contains a dangerous clause allowing the Russian armed forces to participate in the suppression of internal conflicts. In fact, Russia has not yet chosen whether it will gravitate toward democratic or undemocratic means for guaranteeing its security.

But while the choice has not yet been made, democracy in Russia is not doomed to be rejected. Rather, popular conceptions of the democratic system must be cleansed of the view that democracy is merely another version of a "bright future." In this sense, the current general disappointment with democracy may be an important transformative step from democratic rhetoric to democratic reality.

More important, Russia has, in a historic sense, outgrown totalitarianism. Its revival is only possible if large sectors of the Russian population drop out of the developing social and political structures and the current way of life, and the state proves unable to protect them. Only in that case could Russian society again be swayed by universalistic ideologies, a prerequisite for totalitarianism. So far, none of the ideologies claiming to be totalitarian could attract sufficient popular support. As a leading ideology, communism, it would seem, is a thing of the past for Russia. While the Communist Party will be active on the parliamentary and governmental scene, it will never reacquire its former rank and functions. Instead, a variety of other ideologies are attracting the Russian people.

Political interest in the ethnic "Russian idea"[2] — which may lay claim to a certain totality in its outlook — is growing rapidly; the success of Vladimir Zhirinovsky's nationalist party is part of a larger trend and cannot be attributed to mere luck. Many other Russians are very suspicious of the Russian idea because of its revolutionary nature. Despite the appeals of its champions to Russian origins, roots, and traditions, the Russian idea is, in fact, at odds with tradition; it is radical, not conservative.

---

2. The "Russian idea" can be summarized as the messianistic predestination of the Russian nation and its selection to fill an extraordinary role in world history. In contemporary Russian journalism and intellectual circles, the Russian idea means the cultivation of the special interests and a special role for Russians, both within the Russian Federation and across the territory of the former Soviet Union.

Two years of cooperation by communists and Russian nationalist-patriots, from August 1991 to October 1993, failed to add to the popularity and prestige of either movement. This is evidence that the idea of social revolution has exhausted its mobilizing power in Russian society, while that of ethnic revolution has not so far revealed its full potential. The success in the December 1993 elections of nationalist groups is attributable not to the ethnic, but to the social and national-étatist sympathies of the Russian population. The nationalists distinguished themselves by their use of legalistic rather than revolutionary rhetoric. An ethnically-based revolution might be demanded by the Russian masses, but only if the country's economic and political development takes a catastrophic turn.

To be sure, a number of people are skeptical about or ill-disposed toward democracy and want to revive the good old days of state control. But this does not mean that Russia is once again prepared to sacrifice democracy for the sake of social stability. In fact, what people want is not so much stability *instead* of democracy, but democracy *coupled with* stability. Ideally, they would like to bring back the social and economic stability of the Brezhnev era while preserving the political gains of the post-Brezhnev years.

The current economic and political disarray plaguing Russia is increasing social and political demands for "law and order" and, by extension, for a political regime that can secure this order. According to data gathered by the Public Opinion Foundation, half of Russia's inhabitants favor the establishment of an "iron hand" political regime. The proportion of such people is even higher among certain population groups — managers of state-owned enterprises, collective and state farm leaders, Russian army officers, urban laborers, and others disadvantaged by recent changes. This preference might seem incompatible with the claim that Russians are unwilling to give up their newly acquired political freedoms. In the Russian mass consciousness, however, such apparently contradictory ideas easily combine and coexist.

The iron hand notion is extremely vague. Generally speaking, people do not bother to think much about who should establish order, by what means it will be accomplished, and what it will mean in practice. In the Russian mass consciousness, such a regime is associated with abstract notions of order — above all in the economic sphere — rather than with dictatorship. According to Public Opinion Foundation data, very few supporters of the iron hand notion assume it would include a reintroduction of state censorship or a ban on the activities of political parties and other social organizations; rather, Russians believe it implies first and foremost the adoption of strict laws against corruption and economic crimes, and tough enforcement.

The Russian understanding of the word "law" is key to comprehending the present state of post-communist democracy in Russia and to evaluating the prospects for its transformation into a developed modern democracy. The craving for law and order is a basic demand of Russian people — part of their reaction to the collapse of the old economic and social system, and the resulting instability. However, most people continue to understand the idea of law in the old collectivist way, which is different from the idea of individual-based law, a fundamental element of Western liberal democracies.

For the majority of people, the law is a weapon in the hands of the state, which is bound to use it to maintain order even if this infringes upon the legal rights of individuals or groups.[3] Two assumptions underlying this mentality are first, that the law should effectively protect the individual from criminals; and second, that the purpose of law is not to guarantee people the opportunity to achieve success, but rather to guarantee the satisfaction of basic requirements for living. In an economic sense, therefore, Russians do not value economic freedom, but protection against it.[4]

---

3. In the course of a representative opinion poll conducted in 1993 among 1,060 Russian citizens, the respondents were asked to answer the following question: "What would you do with those individuals whose activities are harmful to Russia, but which are not in violation of existing legislation?" Only one in four respondents answered against the infringement of the legal rights of such individuals. At the same time, 29 percent of the respondents replied that the activities of such individuals should be blocked, and another 29 percent argued that the access of such groups to the media and other means of publicly arguing their cause should be blocked.

4. According to an opinion poll conducted among 10,547 Russian citizens in March-April 1993, 52 percent of the respondents believed that the state must guarantee that their basic requirements are satisfied, and only 34 percent preferred the guaranteed opportunity to achieve success by their own efforts. The distribution of these attitudes in all basic population groups (workers, collective farmers, etc.) was roughly the same, except for pensioners, who generally advocated a large role for the state. As for the elite groups, only among the military was the share of advocates of state patronage higher than that of champions of liberal freedoms. There was a sharp division between representatives of the private and the public sectors: advocates of liberal freedoms made up roughly 75 percent of the former, and only about 50 percent of the latter.

Russia's Parliamentary Democracy

The desire by Russians to be guaranteed the satisfaction of their basic needs gives rise to some of the features that distinguish Russia's version of democracy from that of modern developed democracies.

To begin with, parliamentary democracy in the former Soviet Union began to take shape even before market-economic agents appeared in the country and private ownership emerged. As during much of the Soviet era, the owners of private property do not call the shots in the parliamentary arena and are not the economic mainstays of the Russian parliamentary system. On the contrary, Russian post-communist democracy, coupled with a strong presidency, contributes to a political environment where the new economic agents have little visible success in playing a more assertive role in the political process.

Second, Russia's post-communist parliamentary democracy has been so far unable to wed the ideas of political legality and law to become a law-based democracy. Individual and group rights, including the right to own property, were legally formalized, but before the state quit its economic role and the property owner began to be an active force in economics. Thus, these rights were formalized before the broader Russian population became aware of the role played by the property owner in raising general social welfare.

The third unique attribute of the Russian parliamentary system is that until September 21, 1993, it preserved its Soviet-era form, which was adapted specifically to a society with no private economic agents. Post-communist Soviet-style parliamentarianism has been attempting to merge a state-run economy with the ideological and legal acceptance of private ownership. Hence the peculiar phenomenon in which two branches of federal power have become the two largest (albeit formally unorganized) party-like entities in the political system. The status of the Supreme Soviet and the Congress of Peoples' Deputies was in line with their continued domination of the public sector, while the president relied upon the support of a small group of property owners and industrialists prepared to work under market-economic conditions. Problems of internal and international security resulting from this instability of power will be present for a long time.

The economic and political principles of the new parliament will not differ substantially from those of its predecessor. This is because in Russian society, *producer* interests are virtually absent; the society is influenced by almost purely *consumer* interests. (Producers do exist, but they are not interested in the social value of their products. They are concerned about profit, but this concern is not reflected in the quality of their products.) Russians view each other as rivals in consumption rather than production. A totalitarian communist regime is the perfect complement to this structure of interests. Such a regime ensures that everyone is employed, and to a significant degree rids people of the need to ponder the essence of their work, while assuming all responsibility for the distribution of the fruits of their labor.

If representative democracy is established, the parliament is bound to turn into a club of angry consumers. Representatives will demand a redistribution of income in favor of their own electorate at the expense of other population groups, and will compete among themselves in an attempt to expose whichever authorities do not want to comply with their demands. However, the historic mission of post-communist democracy is not to upgrade distribution, but to reform production. This invariably involves a temporary infringement upon the interests of a substantial section of the population. Hence, post-communist democracy is doomed to be torn apart by internal conflicts. The infringement upon the majority's interests is, in itself, undemocratic.

The New Urban Burgher

It would be wrong to infer that the immediate future of Russian democracy is completely without promise. Ideology may not play the most important role; the private consumer interests of the post-Soviet man-in-the-street are by nature totally devoid of ideology. A legacy of the USSR's totalitarian regime was the emergence of an urban burgher whose mentality is dominated by private interests. This individual has a definite social niche of his own; he has something to lose. The urban burgher is more suitable for the transition to a modern democracy and a market economy than was the pre-revolutionary communal peasant or the marginal former peasant.

The Soviet burgher came into being contrary to all ideological dogmas of the communist regime. Despite all efforts to contain it, this consumer-oriented class began to emerge in Russia on a large scale in the second half of the 1950s, and came into its own during Leonid Brezhnev's tenure as General Secretary of the Communist Party, when a unique totalitarian-communist type of consumer society took root in the USSR under the slogan "Everything for Man, Everything for the Benefit of Mankind." The attitudes of the Russian urban burgher differ from those of the pre-industrial peasant or the formal communist line.

First, people worked to improve private life, achieve personal gain, and secure the welfare of their families and the future of their children.[5] At the same time, ideological and more socially militant motivations for behavior have been severely weakened or are completely absent. These include a desire to realize the "bright communist future" and guard against the threat of war from outside, as well as moral and psychological dependence upon the collective, and the fear of administrative recrimination. Meanwhile, social interest, if it is at all present, more often than not takes the form of an economic-pragmatic guideline with direct bearing on the individual's welfare, rather than an ideological dogma.[6]

Urbanization has virtually removed the threat that broad population groups will drop out of mass culture, as typically occurs in transitions from an agricultural to an industrial society. This creates the possibility of a peaceful, evolutionary transition from communism to capitalism. However, there are no grounds to believe that such a transition will be sufficiently rapid to ensure the desired outcome before countervailing social and political forces emerge. While the Russian psyche is no longer ideological and militaristic, and is oriented toward private interests, it has not fully accepted the idea of capital. Motivations such as the need and desirability of acquiring land or enterprises, buying stock, accumulating money to invest in business, and securing the economic independence from the state have yet to take root.

Thus, there may not be any appreciable invigoration of the population's labor effort, nor a fundamental change in Russians' attitudes toward production and economic activity. In fact, this could not happen in a society in which legalized private interest is not rooted in private ownership, and is still dominated by a state-run or semi-state-run economy.

---

5. This is unambiguously borne out by the findings of the Foundation's sociological surveys. Such impulses are typical of over two-thirds of the respondents out of a massive sample. For details see *Trudovoye soznaniye naseleniya (Russian population: attitude toward labor)* (Moscow: Public Opinion Foundation, 1993.)

6. For example, this comes through in statements about the need to get the country out of its crisis and to improve the overall economic situation.

The Role of Elites and Industry

Even if private interest gains the upper hand, reforming the Russian economy will inevitably be a very long process: the more democratic Russia's political regime, and the more attentive it is to the mood of the electorate, the more painful and slow this country's transition from communism to capitalism will be. Whether the country will continue to develop along democratic lines or will slide into some kind of autocratic modernization will largely depend upon the balance of strength between various parts of the public sector, and between various groups of workers and managerial elites.

Judging by all indications, the emergence of new elites — essentially a new ruling class — will take years to complete. It is an open secret that Russia's new elite structures are taking shape on the basis of the old ones. So-called *"nomenklatura* privatization" — the division of property belonging to the former Soviet state among the old-time communist and state bigwigs — is a fact of Russian political and economic life; despite the outrage of many people, it is an organic element in the current stage of the system's evolution. The former *nomenklatura* were bound to perceive a decisive disadvantage to standing by idly in the transition from communism to capitalism; the communist functionaries are becoming Russia's property owners.

This transformation provides the key to understanding certain distinctive features of Russia's post-communist democracy — its lack of social and political authority, aggravated by an unending struggle for power between various governmental branches, and its lawlessness and corruption. This system constitutes the political and legal environment in which the consolidation of Russia's new ruling class — or rather, the self-renewal of the old one — is occurring.

The struggle for power is waged first for control over the rules and conditions of play within the system, and second for the means to determine the starting conditions for various groups of the old managerial, CPSU (Communist Party of the Soviet Union), and state *nomenklatura* in the struggle to acquire this property. The third coveted prize is the right to appeal to the "interests of the entire people" in order to be less vulnerable to popular discontent.

The present trend of lawlessness will only end when the redivision of property is completed and one of the competing economic and political groups proves strong enough to take full responsibility for production and social stability. The future will belong to the economic and political force that first monopolizes the process by which the further division of property is carried out.

Contrary to the opinions and glosses of many politicians and experts, Russians are not being confronted with a simple choice between democracy and reformist authoritarianism.[7] Until private property is fully institutionalized and civil society emerges in Russia, no strong form of parliamentarianism will be able to take root. Similarly, until there are influential elite groups able to serve as pillars for the development of reforms while simultaneously neutralizing the forces of opposition and preserving stability, there can be no strong authoritarian regime in Russia of the type described. In the meantime, Russia will probably be in a rather unstable state, in which the core of the decision-making power will shift to executive and presidential structures.

Given the industrial nature of Russia's current economic system and the fact that industry employs the bulk of the population, it is safe to say that the future of Russian democracy depends directly upon the economic and political weight of industrialists, many of whom are among the former *nomenklatura*, and thus tend to be conservative. The Soviet system gave rise to a relationship between managers and workers in which managers performed special functions for the social protection of workers. Workers have always valued their bosses not for their efficiency as managers, but rather from the viewpoint of how well they took care of their workforce. That is, a good boss was effective at combining the roles of manager and labor leader.[8]

To try to do away with this legacy overnight by forcing large numbers of enterprises to get by on their own without support from the state, as some radical liberal economists suggest, would subject Russia's social fabric to a stress it will not be able to withstand.[9] A majority of former Soviet enterprises are non-competitive due to objective economic and

---

7. Reformist authoritarianism is defined here as the consensus of influential elite groups controlling the economy and other force structures, accompanied by the suppression or limitation of political liberties.

8. It was in these industrial communes that the above-mentioned breed of consumer with a predominantly private interest and an orientation toward guaranteeing the satisfaction of his basic needs came into being.

9. Advocates of this approach often use the "bureaucratic market" concept, the idea that the market within the USSR's economic space acquired the form of a system of administrative trade deals. This involved the distribution of resources and positions among departmental, regional, and political structures, as well as among individual bureaucrats.

technological reasons, not because their managers are less competent than managers at other enterprises. This initial qualitative heterogeneity is one of the main problems complicating the transition from one economic system to another, and explains why the strength and weight of various groups of industrialists will determine the pace and nature of the transition, the future role of the state in the national economy, and, probably, the type of political system that will emerge.

Russian private capital is too weak to buy out whole enterprises; this is an additional reason why the public sector will continue to play a decisive role in the development of Russia's economic and political system in the foreseeable future. (Attempts to artificially increase private capital by handing out vouchers can do little to solve the problem.) But more important than the differences between the private and public sectors are differences within the public sector — between competitive (at least in the domestic market) enterprises and weak, "sponger" enterprises that can be kept afloat only with the help of state subsidies. It is for the sale of these types of enterprises that authorities are trying to find new owners by means of "voucher privatization."

The weaker part of the public sector is not so helpless as it may seem; its interests are intertwined with the interests of the bureaucrats and financiers whose main function is to wring subsidies out of the government. In addition, the potential for social protest by the millions of people employed by this sector must be considered. These groups are becoming increasingly politicized; in other words, Russian politics is becoming increasingly fixated upon issues of distribution, which is quite natural considering employees' dependence on their managers. Thus, the outcome of any elections will largely be decided on the shop floor; consequently, so will the future of Russian democracy.

Still, even if the modernizer-industrialists emerge victorious in the struggle for political control, this will not guarantee a democratic future for Russia. It is unclear whether Russia will be able to use democratic means to consolidate its battered statehood and ensure concord between the competitive, vanguard groups and outsiders, whose ranks will be swollen with workers from economically weak enterprises. The alternative is to resort to authoritarian methods of management and administration.

Much will depend upon the international community. Outside actors should seek to support those forces in Russia that optimally combine development and stability, and to prevent these forces from sliding into the abyss of authoritarian rule. This would threaten the interests of many of Russia's neighbors and partners; as explained, Russia is not prepared for such a system and has no reliable socio-economic base to support it.

Democratic Reintegration

In the final count, the main issue of contention is who will manage the consolidation of the Russian state and bring it out of its current crisis, and how. This question is directly linked to Russia's national security and, given Russia's status as a nuclear state, global security as well. The most important issue is Russia's relations with other former Soviet republics, above all Ukraine, Belarus, and Kazakhstan. This problem is central to Russia's internal security, international security, and the future of Russian democracy.

Why are ongoing and future conflicts in the former Soviet republics, especially along their borders with Russia, so important to Russia's security? The threat is that territorial disputes could escalate into inter-ethnic conflicts; these conflicts could become militarized, and spill over onto Russia's own territory. This danger would be particularly acute if Ukraine and Kazakhstan were to experience inter-ethnic conflicts.

This challenge is becoming more serious because the newly independent states of the former Soviet Union are largely too weak to manage conflicts without help from the outside, and the international community has not been successful in bringing about concrete results. Thus, the problem in the post-Soviet security space is intimately connected to the issue of the reintegration of Commonwealth of Independent States (CIS) member countries. The continued sovereignty of each state is, of course, not called into question.

The need for such a reintegration, at least economically, is clear. There is a certain integrity to the economic and security space of the former Soviet Union. The broader economic and political stability of Georgia, Ukraine, Kazakhstan and Russia, with their ethnic heterogeneity and regional concentration of ethnic groups, is unthinkable without the establishment of close allied relations between them, bolstered by a handful of coordinating supranational structures. Today, none doubt the need for reintegration, as illustrated by demonstrations in Ukraine, the compelled entry of Georgia and Azerbaijan into the CIS, and the economic difficulties of many of Russia's neighbors. But what kind of reintegration will it be, which states will it involve, and what political forces will it bring about?

If the core of the CIS (Russia, Ukraine, Belarus, and Kazakhstan) falls apart, even this would not indicate a rejection of reintegration, but rather that the worst and most chaotic path toward reintegration has been chosen. Such a path would entail the diminution of the democratic process in Russia (and not only in Russia) and the rise of imperialist-oriented forces brandishing the Russian national idea. This group will advocate a form of ethnic empire in Russia, with a regathering of Russian and Soviet imperial lands. The success in the December 1993 parliamentary elections of the nationalist party led by Zhirinovsky, who champions this type of reintegration, was an obvious indication that political moods have been developing in this direction. It should not be ignored.

For Russia's nationalist patriots, the disintegration of the CIS core would mean a chance to take power, and gain access to the instruments of power in the wider region. It would also inevitably give rise to conflicts in many hotbeds of tension, such as Crimea, where the infringement of the national and state interests of Russia is a factor. It will undermine the rickety pillar of political stability in the post-Soviet security environment, and, by extension, will directly threaten the process of democratization and democratic reintegration. Reintegration will become first and foremost a military issue. The hawks in the Russian army and military-industrial complex have already made it clear that this turn of events is much to their liking.

Under certain circumstances, Russian society may also accommodate itself to such a trend. While Russia does not want to wage war against Ukraine or any other country, moods and sentiments in Russian society can be played to by the nationalistic patriots and those who stand behind them. That is precisely why nationalists rallied around the July 1993 parliamentary resolution proclaiming that Sevastopol was part of Russia. This resolution is one example of how CIS disintegration will pave the way for a forcible reintegration along less liberal lines.[10]

Today, the threat that some form of empire will be restored stems from the possible disintegration of the CIS, rather than from its strengthening. Nowadays, strengthening the CIS does not mean taking a step toward restoring a Russian or Soviet empire. Rather, it is the only opportunity to structure political relations among the states of the former USSR; if it disintegrates, attempts will inevitably be made to consolidate

---

10. An opinion poll conducted among Russia's urban population in July 1993 immediately following the passage of the parliamentary resolution on Sevastopol revealed that 51 percent of the respondents supported that decision, and only one-sixth denounced it.

some form of order based upon ethnic ideologies. In Russia, such an ethnic ideology could easily become coupled with the desire to annex the Russian-populated territories of the other former Soviet republics.

Thus, the strengthening of the CIS is today the most important guarantee of the security, independence, and territorial integrity of its member states. It is also a major safeguard for the democratic process in those CIS countries where it has already begun to assert itself.

None of the CIS member states can count on speedy integration with the West. Hence, they must preserve their own common market, which is unthinkable without some coordinating structures at the supranational level. Any delay in attempting to solve basic logistical problems will have the effect of promoting antidemocratic forces in Russia.

Attitudes in Russia toward the CIS and its members are mixed. Substantial changes have taken place in the political awareness of Russian citizens since the majority of the population of the Russian Federation voted in March 1991 to preserve the USSR. While the blow dealt to the pride and collective consciousness of Russian society by the collapse of the Soviet system is proving very slow to heal, most people do not let themselves get carried away by revenge-seeking sentiments.

Initially, the CIS was seen as the primary means for building a new, more federative form of multinational statehood. The idea of constructing another form of multinational statehood outside this framework was as unpopular in polls as the idea of restoring the USSR. Yet even a few months after the decision to dissolve the Soviet Union, certain distinctive features in the political awareness of Russian citizens testified to their far from uniform attitude toward the Russian state and other CIS nations.

According to Foundation data, in June 1992 many Russian citizens were unable to reconcile themselves to the fact that Ukraine was no longer a part of Russia, but an independent state politically equal to Russia. That was why they welcomed anything to promote the CIS and resolutely rejected Ukraine's quitting the Commonwealth. They could not bring themselves to accept anything that strengthened the Ukrainian state, but at the same time they hailed all measures to promote Russian statehood. When asked about attitudes toward maintaining strong Russian armed forces, 70 percent of the respondents supported the idea. The corresponding attitude toward the establishment of the Ukrainian army was the opposite: slightly over 50 percent denounced it. This may be chalked up to Russia's injured imperial pride. The categorical opposition in Russia to Ukraine's withdrawal from the Commonwealth expressed a growing awareness of Russia's special role and status in the CIS.

Table 1 shows the evolution of state awareness among the population of the Russian Federation according to polls of individuals from various professional groups conducted between February 1992 and September 1993.

Table 1. Aims and Priorities of State Development

	Restoring a Centralized State		Strengthening the CIS		Strengthening the Russian State	
	Feb. '92	Sept. '93	Feb. '92	Sept. '93	Feb. '92	Sept. '93
General Population	18%	16%	50%	38%	20%	28%
Managers of State Enterprises	17%	14%	66%	45%	13%	34%
Collective & State Farm Managers	28%	21%	53%	37%	13%	31%
Businessmen	10%	11%	65%	39%	23%	41%
Workers	18%	16%	48%	37%	22%	32%

The growth of state awareness among Russian citizens may produce opposite results, depending upon how it is channeled. Democratic forces interested in a civilized process of reintegration, with Russia as the economic and political coordinator, could take advantage of this trend in public opinion, as could nationalists seeking to pursue an extremely tough policy toward the Soviet successor states in order to further destabilize them. In other words, the ongoing changes in the perception of Russian political and security interests bring into even bolder relief the essence of the choice facing the peoples of the former Soviet empire — the choice between forced or voluntary reintegration.

It would be no exaggeration to say that relations among the CIS member-states, above all among its four largest members, are the key to both regional and global security as well as to the prospects for the consolidation of democracy in Russia and the other CIS countries. The former Soviet republics remain the most developed and structured political entities on the territory of the former USSR; relations among them may become a pivotal element in the democratization process in the CIS.

The global democratic community is faced with a fairly straightforward mission. It should do all that it can to promote the democratic reintegration of the post-Soviet economic and security space and to prevent the forcible reintegration of CIS member-states into a system of close cooperation with Russia. The international community should recognize the special role of Russia as the only entity that can guarantee the security and stability of this region. This support should, of course, be preconditioned first by Russia's continued adherence to the democratic course, and second by Russia's readiness to fulfill its stabilizing role under the supervision of and in cooperation with international organizations.

Such an effort on the part of the West will not, of course, guarantee that democracy will triumph in Russia and the former Soviet republics. The problems and hardships mentioned in the above analysis, along with many others, are indeed enormous and will require a great deal of time and effort to overcome. But if some form of democratic reintegration fails to materialize in the post-Soviet economic and security space, Russia and the international community will be confronted with quite different problems and hardships. The failure to realize democratic reintegration will usher in an altogether different and infinitely more acute challenge to international stability and security.

Chapter 3
Russia's Elites

Sergei A. Karaganov

The rapid growth of Russia's new social strata, the replacement of the old political elite, and the transformation of the new elite's interests will naturally and inevitably influence the development of Russia's foreign policy. Few systematic studies of the opinions of Russia's new political elites have yet been made,[1] but it is clear that social democratization has sharply increased both the number of elites that have a say in the formulation of Russian foreign policy, and the number of channels for exercising political power outside the government. Foreign policy is most directly influenced by the visible players: parliamentarians, the press, and political parties. In general, these actors directly and indirectly reflect the broader interests of fundamental groups within the Russian policy elite, and to some degree define and articulate those interests. Occasionally these actors become independent agents and campaign for their own specific interests; the previous Russian parliament, which became a largely independent force during 1992 and 1993, is a prime example. Because of the active and varied role of Russia's elites, an understanding of the interests they promote is critical to anticipating developments in Russian foreign policy.

At least two changes in Russian society account for the greater influence of elites. The first is the absence or semi-absence for the foreseeable future of a general ideological framework for the formulation of national security strategy. In the past, a mix of Marxism and pragmatism provided such a framework, which sorted and distorted impulses

---

1. The only systematic overview of the ideologies professed by the foreign policy elite was conducted in summer, 1993 by the national public opinion center (VTsIOM), which polled diplomats, various other civil servants, scholars and researchers, journalists, and parliamentarians. These rough data are referred to in this chapter. In most cases, the author was forced to draw upon his own ample, albeit subjective, experience.

Sergei A. Karaganov is the Deputy Director of the Institute of Europe at the Russian Academy of Sciences. He has been a member of the Presidential Council since 1993, and is also a member of several other advisory bodies of the Russian government.

generated at various levels of the society and state. The absence of such ideological and institutional guidelines has created an environment where elite interests influence policy directly.

The second change is a profound reorientation that is probably taking place in the Russian national psychology, and definitely occurring in the social system. Tired of generations of almost inhuman suffering, the well-educated populace is becoming more pragmatic and survival-oriented. The tradition of Russian messianism is nowhere to be found.

At the same time, the rapid capitalization of Russia is making economic interests much more visible on the national agenda. Economic motivations influence Russian social and political life in a much more direct and evident way than ever before. Of course, the situation is full of contradictions.[2] The greater role of economic interests is paralleled by the increasing "secularization" of Russian politics and policy debates. Threats to the security of the Russian Federation and its citizens are clearer than in the Cold War period.

It will be this mix of economic and security interests (as opposed to the older notion formulated largely in globalistic and ideological terms) and the elites that espouse them that will determine Russia's policies. The interaction among the various elites will not generate a consistent policy, especially considering the relative weakness of Russia's bureaucratic structures which, rather than helping to shape political events, tend to be dragged by them. Elite interests are, therefore, perhaps the most reliable basis for casting and analyzing Russian policies. This chapter discusses the interests of Russia's most important elites.

The Traditional Foreign Policy Elite

The traditional foreign policy elite is composed of diplomats, intelligence officers and top figures in academia traditionally associated with foreign policy, as well as certain journalists. It is mainly concentrated in Moscow. This elite is not large, nor does it enjoy any powerful economic influence. However, this traditional elite does pursue its own interests, and continues to maintain a good measure of authority. To a large degree it

---

2. One should, of course, avoid hasty generalizations about the total predominance of economic interests among factors influencing the future development of Russian foreign policy and security strategy.

has retained access to the decision-making mechanisms, if only due to geographic proximity to the center of power.

For the past few years, the strength and prestige of the traditional foreign policy elite has declined tremendously. The Russian diplomatic corps is in disarray. More than any other group of political elites, this community suffered from and was greatly bereaved by the breakup of the Soviet Union. It seems that many in this community still stubbornly refuse to accept that the USSR has disintegrated. Although generally more liberal and more educated than the rest of the old Soviet political elite, the Soviet foreign policy community was nurtured in the Cold War environment and its members profess a philosophy of political realism with regard to Russian foreign policy.[3]

On the whole, the foreign policy elite will seek to keep the mechanisms of Russian foreign policy within the mainstream; that is, more conservative than the Ministry of Foreign Affairs shortly after the failed coup in 1991, but much more liberal than the communist and nationalist opposition. Despite its traditionalism, the foreign policy establishment will promote Russia's openness, as well as consistency in disarmament and other policies. It will ideologically support the reincorporation of some former Soviet republics into the Russian Federation, but in practice will seek to orient Russia's foreign policy toward the broad international context and away from issues exclusive to the post-Soviet republics. This elite includes numerous experts on the West, particularly the United States, and is largely inclined to keep Russian policy focused on the West.[4]

---

3. Accordingly, the path of Russian foreign policy pursued by Russian Foreign Minister Andrei Kozyrev in the year following the August 1991 coup attempt received only limited support within the traditional foreign policy establishment. Instead, Kozyrev was supported primarily by radical democratic politicians who came to power in the post-putsch political shake-up. In fact, the policy of openly courting the favor of the West was doomed because it was secretly rebuffed by many in the foreign policy elite; it was severely criticized by communists and nationalists; and it ignored and thereby aggravated the psychological pain inflicted by the rapid weakening and demise of the USSR, which greatly disturbed most members of the Russian elite, even the more liberal ones.

4. Only 19 percent of respondents to the VTsIOM poll cited the CIS as the top priority area for Russian foreign policy (approximately 13 percent of respondents cited Belarus and Kazakhstan as top priority, and 24 percent cited Ukraine). At the same time, 50.5 percent mentioned Western Europe, and 35 percent cited the United States. The responses of the foreign policy elite generally corresponded to this pattern.

The Armed Forces

The institutional crisis at the federal level allows the armed forces to exercise greater influence on Russia's foreign and strategic policy than they did under Communist rule, when the role of the military elite in devising even military policies was limited.[5] One obvious example was the role of the armed forces in breaking the stalemate between the legislative and executive branches of political power in autumn 1993.

Numerous factors have contributed to the increase in the influence of the armed forces in Russian foreign and domestic policy. The weakening of the central institutional framework has reduced the level of control over defense, security, and law-enforcement structures. The controls that remain have become even more important to the consolidation and exercise of power, so that executive and legislative authorities have launched a process of competitive bidding for the loyalty of officers of the Russian armed forces, never hesitating to slip in a political perquisite or two. As a result, when any political crisis breaks, the first question asked in the Kremlin or in parliamentary corridors is "Which side does the army support?"

The dissolution of the USSR and the resulting instability have made the Russian armed forces a direct instrument of policy. The climate of general economic, political and social instability has altered the perceptions of the Russian public on this issue. Whereas previously, the armed forces were viewed as a deterrent against a distant and almost mythical threat, they are now perceived as necessary to protect Russia and Russians against very real threats — such as spillover from conflicts along Russia's borders and the possibility of the fragmentation of the Russian Federation due to internal forces. Anti-military sentiment has subsided, and the prestige associated with military service has again been elevated. This trend may have been sustained by the traditional Russian feeling of compassion for the abused and the humiliated. The Russian army was seen as neglected due to, among other things, a severe shortage of housing for officers.

The armed forces do not yet realize the extent to which their influence has grown. The effects of plunging morale, most acute between 1990 and

---

5. For example, procurement policies were largely decided by the all-powerful Soviet military-industrial complex along with related departments of the Central Committee of the Communist Party.

1992, are still felt.⁶ Since August 1991, the armed forces have felt increasingly negative toward any involvement in politics; this trend will undoubtedly persist for some time. The participation of the army in the October 4, 1993 storming of the Russian parliament building was engaged only after repeated pressure from President Boris Yeltsin and Prime Minister Victor Chernomyrdin. For now, this has strengthened the antipathy of the Russian armed forces toward direct involvement in politics. However, the visible growth of the political influence of the armed forces, an inadvertent result of this episode, could in the long run whet the appetite of these elites for such involvement if not checked by stronger political and legal control over the military.

After a long fight, the leadership of the Russian armed forces has yielded on the issue of whether troops can be involved in the regulation of internal disputes. Allegedly under pressure from democratic politicians, the military elite agreed to state in the new military doctrine that regular troops can be used to contain the destabilizing activities of extreme nationalists and secessionists, and to counter violent attempts to overthrow the constitutional order.⁷

Given the slow pace at which stable political and security institutions are being consolidated, the political authority of the Russian armed forces will almost certainly grow. In many respects, Russian military commanders are already playing an independent role in these crisis-stricken regions: the northern Caucasus, Transcaucasus, and Trans-Dniester. The growing influence of the armed forces will not, however, automatically create a sharper military flavor in Russia's relations with the West. Threats from Russia's "near abroad" now look quite detached from the challenges emanating from the West. Only if the West were to intervene against the perceived interests of Russia in conflicts on Russia's immediate periphery might Russian policy toward the West be partly remilitarized.

A conservative posture is popular in the armed forces, and most officers are critical of the dissolution of the USSR. However, servicemen are reluctant to become involved in complicated and politically ambiguous conflicts. In the coming years, the army must undergo a reorganization and reform process that includes measures to alleviate many of the social

---

6. On this matter, see the interview of Defense Minister Pavel Grachev: "Rossiyskaya Armiya: Novoye Vremya" ("The Russian army: new times"), *Nezavisimaya Gazeta*, June 6, 1993 pp. 1, 5.

7. "Osnovniye polozheniya voennoi doktrini Rossiyskoi Federatsii" ("Main clauses of the military doctrine of the Russian Federation"), *Isvestiya*, November 18, 1993, p. 2.

problems of servicemen. The armed forces are unlikely to undertake any programs or initiatives that might damage their new positive image in Russian society. As a result, senior military officials are becoming increasingly favorably disposed to cooperation with the West. It is yet unclear how deep these sentiments run; they likely will become more prevalent as new generations inherit control of Russia's military machinery.

The army will contribute to the bolstering of a neo-conservative patriotic consensus among the Russian political elite, and will assist in the formation of a "pro-defense consciousness." However, on the whole it will discard its old reactionary role and will stop politicians from meddling in major conflicts outside Russia. To date, threats of military adventurism and the militarization of Russia's foreign policy come not from the military elite, but rather from Russian political circles.

Regional Political Elites

The normal and healthy process of delegating authority to local governments leads to a strengthened influence of regional political elites on the national level.[8] If the country evolves in a more or less democratic way, these local and regional elites will be crucial in shaping Russia's strategy, as the process is channeled through parliamentary elections and rotation among executive authorities.

Local elites are sprouting so rapidly that their ranks can scarcely be analyzed systematically. However, it is clear that the new local elites are much more pragmatic and less ideologically bound than their communist or radically democratic predecessors, though many originally identified with one or the other of those camps. These elites advocate a moderately nationalist ideology of self-preservation. Ethnic elites consider foreign policy as a tool for shoring up their status within Russia, along with other applications. So far, regional elites inside Russia seem most interested in promoting economic links with foreign partners. At the current stage of economic development and foreign trade in Russia, these elites will look to close regions: China, Japan, and South Korea for Siberians; South Asia and the Middle East for southern Russians; and Finland and other Nordic countries for the population of Russia's northwest. This pattern is not

---

8. This fact has occasionally assumed a distorted and ugly twist in the post-Soviet political situation.

rigid; for example, Siberian energy producers are looking closely at economic opportunities in European countries.

The diffusion of power from Moscow to the provinces would impede the success of a radical coup attempt by communists or nationalists in Moscow. All groups that would consider staging such a coup know that the regions could simply disobey new orders from the center and cause the coup to flounder by default, especially since there are no longer any organs of central power (such as the Communist Party apparatus and the all-powerful KGB) to force these elites into compliance.

As the influence of regional elites grows, the orientation of Moscow's foreign policy will also shift. For example, in recent years authorities in Moscow have been more politically attentive to potential partners in Asia; this is due in part to an increase in the relative weight carried by Siberia and the Russian Far East in Russia's domestic policy since the dissolution of the Soviet Union.

Russia's local elites are largely nostalgic about the "good old times" in the USSR. In most cases the primary interest of local elites is to ensure the stability of their own regions. They can be counted on to neutralize the effects of any harsh actions that might threaten such stability, including any shift toward dangerous and costly imperial adventures. At the same time, these elites are bound to uphold, and in many cases even to galvanize, the efforts of the federal government toward the economic integration of the post-Soviet republics.

Interested mostly in pork-barrel issues, Russia's local elites will oppose any attempt to remilitarize the country. These elites are interested in keeping military manufacturers located in their districts afloat, but on the whole will fight against any attempts to redistribute national income from civilian to military uses. However, the moderate nationalism and étatism of these elites, their somewhat simplistic view of the outside world, combined with traditional Russian suspicion and the humiliation stemming from the ongoing crisis in Russia, will contribute to a moderate-conservative drift in Russian foreign policy. Much will depend upon the foreign policy experience rapidly being accumulated by local elites, and the ways in which it shapes their still vague outlook on the world.

The New Russian Security Elite

Largely unnoticed by Russia's academic and policy-making communities, a new groups of elites is emerging on the Russian political landscape. This group is mostly composed of officers of the interior and security forces, some military officials, officials of the State Committee (Ministry) of Emergency Situations and Civil Defense, local functionaries, and a handful of diplomats. These officials deal personally with the resolution of crises, handle migration problems, aid in the prevention of and clean-up of accidents, and grapple with natural disasters. The efforts of these officials may seem reminiscent of a proverbial time of yore, but they do, in fact, save human lives, localize conflicts, and even assist in the resolution of those conflicts, if sometimes only temporarily.

This new Russian security elite has not yet been fully integrated into domestic or international political structures. It most probably professes neo-isolationist views and a doctrine of unilateralism vis-à-vis the former Soviet republics. Because of its relatively recent emergence, Russia's new security elite has not yet succeeded in perceiving and articulating its own interests and in developing a common ideological framework. It is not yet evident how the new security elite will influence Russia's foreign policy. As Russia becomes a looser federation with increasingly independent regions, this new elite, in conjunction with other groups of new local elites, will wield a great deal of influence over the foreign and security policies of the Russian Federation.

The Military-Industrial Elite

The military-industrial complex was never a solid, monolithic structure under the communist system, and is even less so today. Some industries within Russia's military-industrial complex are adapting themselves to defense conversion and the new economic environment, including the competitive demands of external markets. These industries, for example aerospace, radio electronics, and new materials production, have at least come to understand that adaptation is an option.

Some Russian defense enterprises still benefit from hefty state orders. These include factories and design offices engaged in the production of highly accurate weapons systems and electronic means of warfare, and specialized munitions factories. Other sectors are clearly doomed, as they cannot possibly reorganize themselves without sizable capital injections, for example factories that produce armored vehicles, artillery pieces, munitions, and parts for strategic armaments.[9]

The Russian military-industrial complex still boasts spectacular intellectual and scientific potential. This explains the powerful position of its elite, which controls one of the few pools of potential for the future development of Russia: advanced technologies and skilled managers well-versed in sophisticated technological systems.

Nonetheless, the difficulties of the economic transition reduce the opportunities for the military-industrial elite to exert pressure on policy makers. Many factories are competing for a limited number of contracts; some managers who already professed traditionalist views have moved toward the most reactionary political forces, such as Vladimir Zhirinovsky and his group. Suspicions about the motivations of Western governments have increased as hopes for an influx of foreign capital into Russia were dashed. Some in the more advanced military sectors now firmly believe that the West, and the United States in particular, is striving to destroy Russia's defense and other advanced industries altogether.

Yet even the most right-wing, who profess a policy of bellicose isolationism for Russia, increasingly realize that a revival of a siege mentality will not raise military spending to Soviet levels, nor restore their former prosperity. This prompts them to look for other, non-socialist ways to ensure their survival. Many in the military-industrial sector favor a quasi-state and pseudo-capitalist path of economic development, which would be upheld by the plan for dividing the Russian economy into thirty to one hundred conglomerates. In this plan, each conglomerate would include both profitable and losing enterprises in the hope that the strong ones would balance and save the weak. Such a path of economic development would most likely lead to protracted economic stagnation and restraints on democratic development, though the economy would probably become more manageable. This type of economy would be perfectly complemented by an authoritarian political system with a cautiously neo-isolationist attitude.

The members of the military-industrial elite have enlisted the support of most of the other Russian policy elites in an issue that will heavily

---

9. According to Russia's First Deputy Minister of Defense, Andrei Kokoshin, state defense orders will shrink by 65-68 percent by 1994, compared to 1991. (Arms production could drop less if exports are maintained at a steady level and defense enterprises take care of their in-house resources.) See *Nezavisimaya Gazeta*, June 4, 1993, pp. 1, 4.

influence Russian foreign policy for years to come: arms sales abroad.[10] This support will be buttressed through the establishment of better relations with potential foreign governmental customers, and the sorting out of relations with competitors in the state sector. The elite consensus on the importance of arms sales for Russia's economic and security development is unlikely to be thwarted in the foreseeable future.

Arms traders can exert effective pressure on Russia's foreign policy makers for two reasons. First, the military-industrial complex accounts for a larger share of Russia's domestic economy than in most Western countries.[11] Second, Russia has a comparatively narrow export base, and therefore has relatively few short-term options for modifying its export portfolio.

So far, the West's policy has included very limited involvement in defense conversion in Russia, accompanied by brisk efforts to fill in the void in the arms market created by the dissolution of the USSR; the West has elbowed Russia out of any Western arms markets it has attempted to penetrate. This short-sighted policy has had the effect of distancing this influential group of Russian elites from a cooperative posture with the West, and will promote more intensive Russian interaction in this critical sphere with China, the Far East, and South Asia, at the expense of Western interests. Discouraged by the thwarted opportunities for collaboration with the West on arms and security issues, many among the Russian military-industrial elite have become xenophobic; this attitude could also be viewed as a newly forged philosophy of Russian self-reliance.

---

10. The poll taken by VTsIOM among political elites in June 1993 to outline their foreign policy views revealed that 72.6 percent of the respondents were in favor of greater arms sales. Only 15 percent were against.

11. On Russia's arms trade policy, see S. Akshintsev, "Vigodno li nam ne prodavat oruzhie stranam blizhnego zarubezhiya?" ("Is it profitable for us not to sell arms to the near-abroad?"), *Krasnaya Zvezda*, June 17, 1993; P. Vassilyev "Kupitye avianosets" ("Buy an aircraft-carrier"), *Novoye Vremya*, No. 17, 1993, pp. 18-21; V. Shepotkin, "Export oruzhiya: zlo ili blago?" ("Arms exports: boon or bane?"), *Isvestiya*, January 29, 1993.

Factory Managers in Civilian Industries

Factory managers in civilian industries have many interests in common with their military-industrial colleagues, especially in enterprises that produce both civilian and military equipment. This group is diverse and changing rapidly, as formerly die-hard communist managers adapt to the capitalist mentality and seek ownership of their enterprises. Formerly a monolithic force of opposition to Gorbachevian reforms, factory managers no longer constitute a cohesive political group. Nevertheless, civilian enterprise managers are in many ways distinct from other Russian elites. These managers are highly interested in cultivating foreign trade and exert pressure for the creation and maintenance of strong foreign economic ties. Because it craves access to foreign markets and Western technologies, this elite comprehends the extent to which a slide back into autarky would threaten its interests.

At the same time, factory managers and the new class of Russian businessmen are likely to become the prime source of pressure for government protectionism and the closing of Russian markets to foreign competitors. Politically, the majority of Russia's enterprise managers hold views associated with the conservative left-of-center but are gradually moving toward more rightist and liberal positions, at least in an economic sense. In fact, the majority hold views that are not much different from the lopsided pro-Western policy espoused by Russia in the year after the August 1991 putsch.[12] The foreign policy course preferred by Russia's enterprise managers as a group is one of cooperation, with greater emphasis placed upon their own interests, and closer attention paid to relations with the countries of Asia, Central and Eastern Europe, and the CIS. Strictly speaking, these preferences constitute less an alternative than a readjustment.

Hallmarks of the foreign policy vision promoted by Russia's factory managers are first, a laundry list of grievances stemming from the collapse of the USSR, and second, a strong preference for the reintegration of the Russian economy with the economies of other ex-Soviet republics. The desire of this group for the political resurrection of the USSR is still relatively strong, but has recently shown signs of weakening as part of the adjustment to new economic conditions and due to the growing realiza-

---

12. Though they collectively deny it when confronted directly, discussions with individual enterprise managers, combined with analysis of the foreign policy sections of the programs hammered out by associations that speak on their behalf, show this to be the case.

tion of the prohibitive cost of this policy. Managers still favor reintegration because, more than other groups, they feel directly the impact of broken supply links, and rising monetary and customs barriers. Their partners in other CIS countries share their view. The dissolution of the USSR is, in short, a fact that completely confounds them.

Organized factory managers pressure Moscow authorities and CIS leaders to meet their demands for economic integration, and have also created organizations and structures to promote strengthened ties independent of the Russian government. Other managers are motivated by distinctly nationalist considerations in formulating their policy demands. Russia, they argue, should sever its economic ties with other post-Soviet republics completely and concentrate upon developing its own considerable wealth. Such voices are still few, but are likely to grow in number.

The New Bourgeoisie

Secessionists are more numerous among the new bourgeoisie, which largely supported the policies of the first Gaidar government. This group includes many radically democratic figures who are anxious to ward off other post-Soviet republics, which are allegedly culturally backward, less democratic, and more economically centralized.[13] Those among Russia's new bourgeoisie who are involved in domestic production are particularly wary of all attempts to create a new political or economic union, both because of the potential cost of such an undertaking, and because expansion is seen as likely to undermine the stability of Russia's national economy and its domestic markets.

Most new capitalists combine political and economic liberalism with a liberal attitude toward foreign trade. Economic liberalism is equally popular among the vast class of middlemen that has recently emerged on the Russian social landscape. As an outgrowth of their professional interests, these self-made and often very self-assured individuals occasionally develop an ideology of economic expansionism along with corresponding foreign policy formulae. This is not surprising, given the emerging ideology of nascent capitalism.

---

13. By mid-1993 these views were rare, but still represented in the press. See, for example, A. Zagorsky, "Kto ureguliruet konflikt?" ("Who will settle the conflict?"), *Moskovskie Novosti*, May 4, 1993, p. 7A.

A decline in the number of foreign market opportunities along with the gradual reorientation of the bourgeoisie toward production rather than trade, and from the foreign to the domestic market, will ensure a slow transformation of the interests of Russia's fledgling capitalists. Both growing projectionist sentiments[14] and moderate nationalism and self-reliance are felt to a heightened degree in this community. Segments of the new bourgeoisie will probably support a moderately nationalist and authoritarian regime for a time, especially since many in this group are, in any case, still being fed from the hand of the state. In contrast, Russia's new bourgeoisie will never support a communist or a rampant nationalist and fascist regime.

How the Interests Combine

This combination of interests will ensure that — unless enormous mistakes are made and enormous disasters occur, and then, on top of everything else, Zhirinovsky comes to power (which is unlikely) — Russian foreign policy will not shift toward an extreme nationalist line. The partial reintegration of some former Soviet republics will openly be put on the political agenda; however, growing appreciation of the economic costs of full reintegration of these states is beginning to seriously curtail remaining impulses toward full reintegration.

It is highly unlikely that Russia will pursue overtly anti-Western policies. This is prevented by the growing concurrence of the Russian political and economic system with those in the West, and the very real interest of most major groups of Russian elites in close cooperation with the West. Russia is deeply interested in achieving a strategic rapprochement with the West for economic, cultural, historical, and, above all, geostrategic reasons. Russia has no natural allies in the South or the East; to become locked out of Europe would spell tragedy for Russia.

The combined impact of the self-assurance of the new economic and political class, the lingering trauma resulting from the disintegration of the USSR, and the loss of illusions about the possibilities for massive Western aid, has brought about a better understanding of Russia's national

---

14. For example, one of the leaders of the Economic Freedom Party, a party of liberal entrepreneurs, has called for protectionism notwithstanding the name of the party. Even more protectionist is the private banking community, fighting penetration of foreign banks onto the Russian market. See the series of articles in *Financial Isvestiya*, July 17–24, 1993.

interests. This new clarity has already produced new trends in Russian foreign policy: Russia is more assertive in voicing specific interests. It does not hesitate to differ with Western views; it is not fixated upon attempts to improve relations with the West in the hope of immediately becoming like the West, or part of the West. Russia's new foreign policy is more even-handed, acknowledging the necessity of active policies not only toward the former Soviet republics, but also toward Asia, Southern Europe, and the Middle East.[15]

At this point, there are no grounds to predict any further large-scale shifts in Russia's foreign policy, except in the unlikely event that a nationalist-socialist regime comes to power. Recent readjustments in Russian foreign policy represent a backlash against previous policies that did not adequately consider Russia's vital national security interests, and a return to a more stable and pragmatic policy line.

After all, it should not be expected that Russia, with its unique geopolitical and geostrategic position, will continue to play the "yes-man" in the international political and security dialogue without eventually experiencing some type of recoil. With black luck and unwise policies in both Russia and the West, combined with a lack of mutual understanding and an unwillingness to engage to find early solutions to problems, even the goodwill of Russia's policy elite — which is itself by no means a given — cannot guarantee the smooth development of relations between Russia and the West.

---

15. Interestingly, this twist of policy was executed without major changes in the leadership of the Russian foreign policy establishment.

Chapter 4
Russian National Interests

Alexei G. Arbatov

However surprising, against the background of bitter controversies surrounding virtually all issues of domestic and foreign policies, there is an overwhelming consensus in Russia on the main goal of strategic and national security: that Russia should remain one of the world's great powers in a real sense — not just by formal United Nations (UN) status — in the tumultuous and unexpectedly violent post–Cold War era.

With very few exceptions, every political faction and party in Russia today counts this objective among Russia's highest national priorities; however, there are wide-ranging differences as to the meaning of this notion for Russia. For some, the preservation of Russia's great power status represents a legitimate goal in its own right, while for others it is a means to achieve other ends. For some it is an unavoidable burden, for others a glorious mission. And of course, there are acute disagreements over how this aim should be achieved, its practical implications for Russian domestic and foreign policy, and its likely impact upon the choice of state and social organization.

Many of these controversies are quite natural and result from post-Soviet Russia's transitional character. Throughout history, Russian and then Soviet power relied on four inseparable pillars: the centralized state-run economy, dedicated primarily to sustaining an enormous military power; the oppressive and strictly hierarchical authoritarian or totalitarian political system and messianic ideology, which were indispensable for governing such an economy and providing for an enormous military force; empire-building, limited only by geography and resistance of indigenous peoples; and finally, as a result of these, permanent confrontation with the outside world.

It was not possible to begin to chip away at any one of the four pillars without undercutting the solidity of the remaining three. Conversely, it

---

Alexei G. Arbatov is a departmental chair at the Institute of World Economics and International Relations at the Russian Academy of Sciences, and is the Director of the Center for Geopolitical and Military Forecasts in Moscow.

would be impossible to preserve the stability of any one of them without the support of the others. Russian domestic and international politics have reflected the difficulties and conflicting needs involved in dismantling the four pillars. The evolving national debates on security and foreign policy, and their impact on Russia's practical course (or drift) will determine not only its relations with the outside world, but its domestic evolution as well. Moreover, these debates will greatly affect Russia's prospects for national survival and resurrection, and with that the future of the international strategic landscape.

The Shift in Russia's Foreign Policy Debate

During most of 1992–1993, the first year of President Boris Yeltsin's administration, issues regarding relations with the near abroad (with the exception of the conflict in Moldova and controversies with the Ukraine about the Crimea) and Russian foreign policy were to some extent on the back burner. But by the fall of 1992, Russian foreign policy had become one of the major issues of domestic politics. This was primarily the consequence of the government's domestic economic and political failures, but its international conduct has also proved a liability rather than an asset to the Yeltsin administration inside Russia.

First, in 1992 Yeltsin and his team failed to formulate or even to specify in general terms a hierarchy of Russia's national interests and priorities abroad that moved beyond utopian slogans (such as "strategic democratic initiative") and could serve as a guide for decision makers. Also, the administration failed to recognize in time that the most critical priority of Russian policy after the disintegration of the USSR was not relations with the United States or the World Bank, but relations with Ukraine, Kazakhstan, Georgia and other republics of the former Soviet Union.

Another deficiency was that in dealing with the West, the Yeltsin administration established a clear precedent in its unilateral concessions with respect to UN sanctions on Yugoslavia, Iraq, Libya, the provisions of START II, the issue of exporting missile technology to India, the Western position on the rights of Russian minorities in the Baltics, the readiness to give away the South Kuriles to Japan, and other issues. Finally, the policies of the Yeltsin government did not have the support of any substantial domestic constituency or the cooperation of Parliament. Foreign Ministry operations were characterized by disorder and numerous

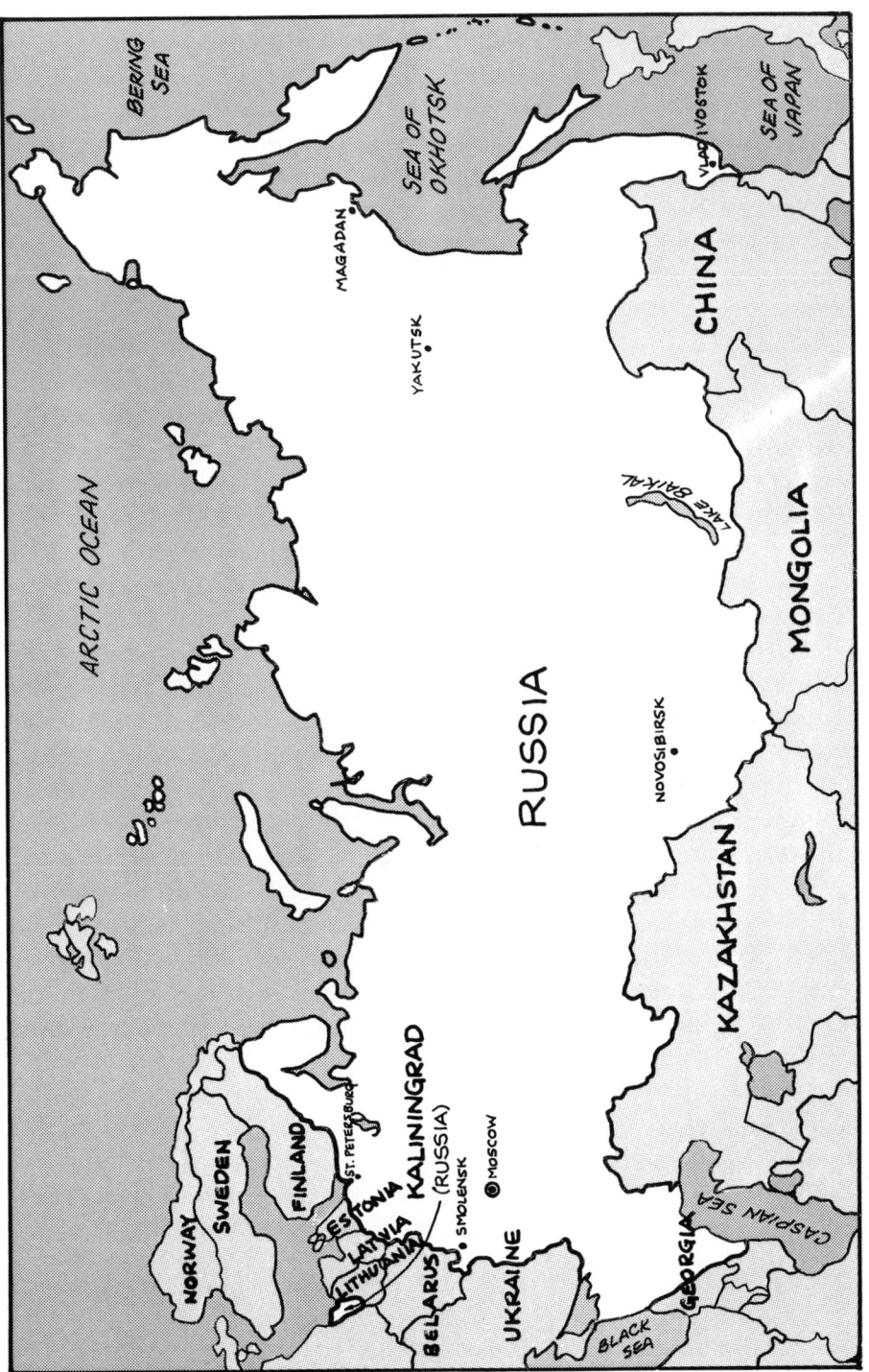

The Russian Federation

mishaps. There was a complete lack of interest in independent analysis of major policy issues.[1]

The turning point in the domestic controversy over Russian foreign policy was probably the aborted presidential visit to Japan in September 1992.[2] The last-minute cancellation of this summit was the first time that Boris Yeltsin so obviously yielded to the nationalist campaign. After that, the conservative offensive against the government's foreign policy gained momentum.

Until the end of 1993, Russian foreign policy, with the exception of Russia's relations with the near abroad, was largely neglected, with all the attention concentrated on the escalation of the domestic political, economic, and constitutional crises. Foreign policy again captured the public eye only after the tragic events in October 1993, and in quite an odd way: through the parliamentary election campaign of radical nationalist leader Vladimir Zhirinovsky.

In November 1993, Yeltsin approved a new military doctrine, which legalized the deployment of the Russian armed forces for the purposes of settling domestic conflicts, and postulated a much more aggressive conventional and nuclear posture toward the other former Soviet republics and tacitly toward NATO. In many ways this new doctrine signifies the end of military reform and the reduction and withdrawal of Russian armed forces from many regions of the former USSR.[3]

But even before the October-December 1993 crisis, during most of 1993 a major underground shift in the foreign policy debate had been taking place. This shift had several aspects. First, there was a growing mood in favor of Russian self-assertiveness, of finding a clear-cut formulation of Russian national interests and the mission to defend those interests with all available means. There was also an increasing aversion to so-called "universal values" and norms, and to the requirements of international law and other "idealistic" propositions as guidelines to policy. Anti-

---

1. V. Nadein, "The West's delay in supporting economic reforms could be a tragic mistake," *Isvestiya*, February 7, 1992, p. 4; A. Shalniev, "The new state secretary of the USA promises to increase support of the reforms in Russia," *Isvestiya*, January 15, 1993, p. 2; and A. Kozyrev, "The party of war is attacking in Moldova, Georgia, and Russia," *Isvestiya*, June 30, 1992, p. 3.

2. A. Arbatov and B. Makeev, "The Kurile barrier of Russian diplomacy," *Novoye Vremya*, No. 40–41 (November, 1992).

3. See "Main guidelines of the military doctrine of the Russian Federation," *Isvestiya*, Nov. 18, 1993, pp. 1–5.

Western sentiment started to surface more prominently in the public mood and in political debates. Finally, Russian relations with the near abroad came to the foreground of both theoretical debates and practical policy making, leaving all other international issues far behind. Most important, all these currents cumulated in expanding support for what came to be termed the Russian "Monrovsky Doctrine."[4]

There were a number of reasons for this profound shift. The fundamental explanation was the deteriorating economic and social situation and growing dissatisfaction among the population with the results of reforms. This made Russia's political leadership more vulnerable to mounting pressure from nationalist and other aggressive moods stemming not only from the public and the Supreme Soviet, but also from within the bureaucracy, from military and security institutions, and much more importantly, from the rival factions of the new ruling elite who were trying to attract support through neo-imperialist appeals. A final factor in Russian security debates and policies is the emergence in the Russian Federation of a new foreign policy elite. (See Chapter 3.)

While Russia has made significant changes in its foreign policy, their effect on Russia's relations with the West has been delayed by a number of factors, especially economic considerations and the personal rapport between Russian and Western leaders. Still, the consequences will be unavoidable. The first serious example of how this new stance is likely to affect Russia's relations with the West was Moscow's reluctance to join the NATO "Partnership for Peace" initiative in early 1994. An official from Russia's Ministry of Foreign Affairs claimed that the West's goal in proposing the plan was "to sanctify the disintegration of the Soviet Union, weaken the military-political positions of Moscow, and put its foreign and military policies under Western control."[5] Coterminous with this policy shift has been a realignment of the principal groups in foreign policy debates in Russia.

---

4. V. Portnikov, "Andrei Kozyrev defines priorities," *Nezavisimaya Gazeta*, No. 11 (January 20, 1994), pp. 1–3.

5. V. Chernov, "Moscow must think well," *Nezavisimaya Gazeta*, No. 35, February 23, 1994, p. 4.

Russian Foreign Policy in the Near Abroad

By early 1994, the predominant position on Russia's affairs in the near abroad among the political elite became something akin to the "Monrovsky Doctrine."[6] Supporters of this doctrine are to be found among former pro-Western liberals, centrists and moderate-conservatives.[7] According to them, Russia is entitled to a "special role" due to its size, historic preponderance in the region and other advantages over smaller states that give Russia a range of out-of-area strategic and political interests. Preserving and, wherever necessary, reinstating its dominant role throughout the former USSR is the principal goal of this version of Russian foreign policy.[8]

In his 1994 foreign policy agenda, President Yeltsin states that "unconditional emphasis...will be placed upon the defense of Russia's national interests, of the rights of Russian and Russian-speaking populations within the guidelines of international law and proceeding from the idea of all-national solidarity."[9] Foreign Minister Andrei Kozyrev, in his speech of January 1994 at the conference of Commonwealth of Independent States (CIS) and Baltic ambassadors, claimed that "the states of CIS and the Baltics constitute the area of concentration of Russia's vital interests. This is also the area from which the main threats to these interests emanate.... I think that raising the question about complete withdrawal and removal of any Russian military presence in the countries of the near abroad is just an extreme, if not extremist suggestion, comparable to the idea of sending [Russian] tanks to all of the former republics to establish there some imperial order..."[10]

---

6. The analogy is quite erroneous. The Monroe Doctrine was proclaimed by a young and vulnerable United States against attempts of the European colonial superpowers of the time to regain their colonies in the Western Hemisphere, and in particular against military interventions there.

7. See A. Zubov, "CIS: Civilized divorce or a new marriage?" *Novoye Vremya*, No. 36 (September 1992), pp. 8–9.

8. V. Chernov, "National interests of Russia and threats to its security," *Nezavisimaya Gazeta*, April 29, 1993, pp. 1–3.

9. In A. Dubnov, "This great word: Solidarity," *Novoye Vremya*, No. 2 (January 1994), p. 10.

10. In A. Pushkov, "Kozyrev has started the game at the alien field," *Moskovskie Novosti*, No. 4, January 23–30, 1994, p. A13.

This new dominant Russian thinking apparently underestimates the power of nationalism and historic grievances in smaller republics, just as it overestimates Russian resources, and the ability of Moscow authorities to keep extreme Russian nationalists at bay. Ironically, the present "democratic" ruling elite, which came to power as a result of the collapse of the Soviet empire, has completely forgotten the lessons of the USSR's eclipse, or else wrongly assumes that the collapse was caused by actions of Mikhail Gorbachev and Eduard Shevardnadze.

Moscow mistakenly believes that the full independence of the former republics would mean great economic, political, humanitarian and strategic losses to Russia; it also misjudges the outside world's tolerance of Russian neo-imperialistic policy and the regular use of force, a probable outcome if this course were adopted. Another deficiency is that this doctrine deprives its partisans of a rational and pragmatic choice of national interests and priorities. They lose the ability to distinguish between events that really matter to Russian economic, political, humanitarian or defense interests in the new regional and global environment, and those that are irrelevant. According to the "Monrovsky Doctrine," Russian involvement and intervention would be automatically provoked by local troubles and opportunities, depending on the location of Russian ethnic minorities and military presence inherited from the perished Soviet and czarist empires.

Neither the timing and scope of Russian involvement, nor its forms, would be fully under Moscow's control. Local players who may have other motives for prompting Russian involvement, independently acting institutions (such as the military, security forces, volunteers or the Cossacks[11]), and the counter-reaction of the opposition would have a large hand in determining the dynamics of Russia's involvement. Finally, the tolerance of the Russian people for the material and human losses that such actions would entail, as well as their readiness to make further sacrifices in the name of reviving an empire for the glory of their leaders, is greatly overestimated.

In view of all the deficiencies of this policy, it may achieve results opposite from the goals stated above. Russia could become bogged down in local civil or ethnic wars with growing Russian casualties, rising numbers of refugees and expenditures, and unconventional burdens such as retaliatory terrorist strikes in Russian cities. Some smaller states will be

---

11. See L. Minasian. "Kazaki want to guard Russia's borders and do not recognize borders of the Commonwealth." *Nezavisimaya Gazeta*, No. 32 (February 18, 1994), p. 3.

motivated to join efforts for economic, political, and military opposition to Russia, and eventually might receive support from the West, South, or East. This would likely be accompanied by political and economic sanctions against Russia and the revival of a Cold War-like security situation, placing Russia in a situation much worse than it faced at the end of the 1940s. Of course, these developments would be incompatible with the continuation of Russian democratic reforms; they would lead to the revival of an authoritarian, besieged, militarized state, with a large degree of central economic planning and the reintroduction of rationing.

The real national interests of Russia require a policy very different from the "Monrovsky Doctrine." Recognizing Russia's "vital interests" in some areas of the former USSR is justified; claiming its "special role" and "responsibilities" is quite a different story. Obviously, it should not be expected that Moscow sit quietly on the sidelines when its vital interests are at stake: the issue is largely how these interests are defined, and what policy instruments are available to provide for these interests. Preventing domination by outside powers hostile to Russia in the near abroad is one thing; striving for such domination itself is another matter. Using diplomacy and economic levers to enhance its influence in a particular state, and actively mediating in conflict resolution is fine; fueling internal tensions in a neighboring state, providing volunteers and arms to separatists across the border, or intervening directly with military force (except for rescue operations to save civilians) is something else.

There are indeed strong common economic, humanitarian, cultural and security interests among the former Soviet republics, and fair and equal cooperation in various fields would be the best way to halt their centrifugal tendencies. The first priority of Russia's foreign policy is to support the emergence of independent, stable, peaceful and neutral new states in place of the former Soviet colonial republics.

Many of the new states are inherently unstable and in conflict with Russia and each other. Hence, the primary Russian goal should be to help these states achieve at least a minimum of stability and to resolve conflicts without overcommitting its own diminishing resources. It is in Russia's interest to actively involve the advanced industrial West in creating economic and political networks of stability in these regions. At a minimum, Russia should not exacerbate instability and conflicts through its own policies.

Russia should be extremely cautious about intervening in the affairs of other states, even when invited by the local government (as in Tajikistan), so as not to incur direct responsibility for the development of these conflicts, or waste resources and lives in support of one faction in a messy civil war. Peace-enforcement or peacekeeping interventions should be based on multilateral (UN, CSCE, or CIS) decisions and actions. The principal Russian role should be that of an active, impartial and creative broker and mediator in settling conflicts — and only when sought by others.

Much of the tension and conflict in Russia's relations with other former Soviet republics stems from Moscow's ambivalence on one basic issue: the territorial integrity of these states. The Helsinki principle of the inviolability of frontiers to change by force should form the basis of the relationship between the republics. Under this provision, the revision of borders could only be brought about as a result of peaceful negotiations. Ethnic separatism within individual republics should be discouraged, and military support by one state of ethnic separatists in another state should be prohibited. Exceptions to this rule may be necessary, if an individual state itself initiates a revision of its frontiers, for instance by deciding to unite with another state (for example, Moldova with Romania), or if a state carries on outright genocide against a national minority, as occurred against Armenians in Azerbaijan. In these cases a demand for secession or unification with another republic by the ethnic minority would be legitimate. To protect the rights of minorities various sanctions are permissible, including the use of military force as a last resort. To exclude any abuse of these norms, as with provoking ethnic conflicts to justify military intervention, all necessary rules and mechanisms should be established in advance at CIS forums. Those guidelines should be submitted for international approval and recognition to the UN and the CSCE.[12]

This applies in full measure to the approximately 25 million Russian-speaking individuals living outside the Russian Federation; their fate is an inseparable aspect of Russia's vital foreign interests.[13] The situation is complicated by the presence of armed forces under the jurisdiction of the

---

12. See A. Arbatov, "Empire or great power?" *Novoye Vremya*, No. 19 (November, 1992), pp. 20–21.

13. Defense of the rights of this population is undoubtedly a sacred duty of all Russians, particularly Russian political authorities, since the sovereignty of the Russian Federation was achieved in 1991 at the cost of leaving millions of Russians abroad, often discriminated against and deprived of their rights and property, and sometimes even physically threatened. Unfortunately, Russia has not been able to effectively protect them or mobilize the support of world public opinion.

Russian Federation in a number of republics. Their presence exacerbates anti-Russian sentiments, aggravating the situation of the Russian-speaking population. This, in turn, leads to demands to indefinitely retain troops abroad in order to ensure the protection of that same Russian-speaking population;[14] this has recently become a part of Russia's official policy.[15]

Without denying the guilt of the political elites and populations of some former Soviet Union (FSU) republics, one important observation is in order: the experiences of many countries in the world, especially during the process of decolonization, have shown that a military presence — while capable of preventing a massacre of civilians, or of evacuating endangered individuals — can never achieve a permanent guarantee of minorities' civil rights. Often the armed forces placed in such a situation become involved in internal ethnic and civil conflicts, and morale and discipline suffer. They end up supplying mercenaries to both warring sides, selling weapons, taking a position in local affairs. At various times in Moldova, Crimea, Abkhazia, Tajikistan, and Nagorno Karabakh, Russian forces have acted independently of Moscow.

In the current situation, the immediate withdrawal of Russia's troops may provoke new destabilization and violence. But in the long run, protection of the rights of minorities will be achieved by different means. In general, as soon as the FSU republics are treated by Moscow as truly sovereign states, when the integrity of their territories is fully recognized and guaranteed by Russia, and when all claims to the opposite, wherever they come from, are rigorously rebuked by Russia's authorities (including the Ministry of Defense), then states that violate the rights of minorities will be held accountable on the basis of legal and moral norms, and will be held responsible for their misdeeds. Russia may then apply political and economic sanctions as legitimate instruments, and even military intervention, as a last resort in the case of pogroms or genocide. It would also be much easier to mobilize world public opinion to support such sanctions and to apply pressure in support of human rights.

RUSSIAN INTERESTS IN THE NEAR ABROAD

Within the general framework outlined above, Russia's relations with individual states in the near abroad should be adapted to particular circumstances. Indeed, the framework that attempts to formulate policy

---

14. Cit. by A. Dubnov, "This great word: Solidarity," p. A-13.
15. A. Pushkov, "Kozyrev has started the game at the alien field," p. A-13.

toward the near abroad as a whole is inspired by an imperial bias, which treats the states of the former Soviet Union as Russia's former colonies. In contrast, recognizing them as independent states would imply specific relations in each case, analogous to Moscow's policy in Europe, the Middle East or the Asia-Pacific region. Without addressing all the republics individually, it is possible to define five principal groups, which would imply five principal differentiated courses of Russian policy.

The first group consists of the Baltics and Moldova, which are not likely to reintegrate with Russia in any sense. In a best-case scenario, the basis of security relations with Russia would be the neutrality of these states. There will be no security threat to Russia from these republics, if only Russia can refrain from pushing them into military alliances with other states by its position-of-strength policies.

The second group includes Georgia, Armenia and, to a lesser degree, Kirgizstan; Russian security interests largely overlap with those of these states. The economic and political integration of these states with Russia (as distinct from the establishment of trade relations) is hardly possible or necessary. But these states need Russian security guarantees and military presence to protect their outer borders against perceived foreign threats.

Belarus is a special case and represents a class of its own. It never really strove for the independence that was imposed upon it by Russia and Ukraine in their efforts to disband the USSR. Minsk has preserved its old communist elite and has not pursued a program of economic or political reform since 1991; however, should Russian democratic reforms be resumed in some revised version and democracy take hold, the growth of internal tensions in Belarus would be unavoidable and would create great problems for its relations with Russia. Coordinated democratic reforms in both countries would be the best, most mutually beneficial option, and a precondition to their rapid reintegration within a federal state.

The fourth group consists of Azerbaijan and the Central Asian states of Tajikistan, Uzbekistan and Turkmenistan. Azerbaijan joined CIS and its collective security organization because of its lack of success in the war with Armenia over Nagorno Karabakh, which prompted domestic revolts against Baku. But the alliance with Russia is essentially empty, and Azerbaijan will never become a Russian security ally and will not voluntarily consider reintegration with Russia. This does not, however, mean that Azerbaijan will be an enemy of Russia, or that normal political and economic relations are impossible after peaceful settlement.

Central Asia is the least important sub-region for Russian interests in all the former Soviet geopolitical space. Uzbekistan, Turkmenistan, and Tajikistan are willing to be closer to Russia, but their reasons for desiring integration are hardly compatible with Russian interests. The former communist regimes in these states are trying to secure Russian military support in order to fight local opposition movements by labeling them as Muslim fundamentalists. This threatens to involve Russia in a hopeless series of neo-colonial wars that are not compatible either with its foreign interests or its domestic political preferences. Russia should avoid direct military intervention in this region under the slogan of opposing the spread of Muslim extremism, which was adopted even by Andrei Kozyrev, the liberal Foreign Minister of Russia.

Finally, the fifth group includes Ukraine and Kazakhstan. Ukraine is by far the most important of the former republics to Moscow, and Russia's vital interests dictate a consistent policy of recognition of Ukraine's independence and territorial integrity, which will strengthen the position of the moderate group in Kiev. Russian security commitments and proposals for military alliance and integration are hardly feasible in view of Kiev's prevalent fear of a revival of Russian domination.

At the same time, cooperation on foreign policy in the UN, the CSCE and the NACC (North Atlantic Cooperation Council), as well as united peacekeeping operations and some joint defense programs are quite possible. Over the long term, falling short of a formal military alliance, close relations between Russia and neutral Ukraine are possible. It is up to Moscow to consistently maintain the initiative in promoting equal bilateral relations, based on the unequivocal recognition of Ukrainian sovereignty and statehood.

This policy, coupled with U.S.-Russian security guarantees and Western financial help to Ukraine, would also be the best way to achieve the elimination of nuclear weapons in Ukraine.[16] Crimea must be clearly recognized by Russia as part of Ukraine, regardless of how Kiev and Simferopol rearrange their relations. As for the Black Sea Fleet, neither Russia nor Ukraine can support it. Russia must start radical reductions of the Fleet unilaterally, which would remove most of the problems of sharing it with Ukraine.

In contrast, Moscow's policy of permanent pressure on Ukraine will be self-defeating for Russia's long-term vital security interests. The best

---

16. A. Arbatov, "Nuclear-missile prestige or real security?" *Moskovskie Novosti*, No. 49, December 5, 1994, p. A-4.

possible result of such a policy would be the growing estrangement of Ukraine from Russia, the severance of natural ties, and a search for support from Germany, Poland or Turkey.[17] Attempts to get closer to NATO through its Partnership for Peace to gain protection against Russia would likely follow. In a worst-case scenario, there may be serious social and political destabilization in Ukraine, the secession of Crimea and some or all of Ukraine's eastern territories, armed clashes with the central authorities, and finally Russia's military intervention. This would initiate a Bosnian-type scenario in a country with nuclear weapons and nuclear power stations that could have horrible consequences for Ukraine, Russia, and Europe. At present, this scenario is the single greatest external threat to Russia's national security. It could bring Russia to national catastrophe.

To a degree, such a description also applies to relations with Kazakhstan. Kazakhstan is genuinely an area of vital Russian interests for ethnic, economic and security reasons. The spread of nationalism and Muslim extremism would be fatal for the economic and strategic security of Kazakhstan and tragic for the Russians living there. Ethnic violence and the forced partitioning of Kazakhstan would certainly involve Russia. On the other hand, there are profound mutual interests in economic integration between Russia and Kazakhstan, and Kazakhstan may be interested in Russian security guarantees against potential threats from China or Muslim radicalism pressing from the South.

Russia's Regional Priorities and Global Responsibilities

Russia's relations with the near abroad, its geographic proximity to and historic involvement in many of the region's conflicts, and its international role as a great power, make it impossible for Moscow to stand aside from the politics playing themselves out in the vast expanses of Eurasia.

COOPERATION WITH THE WEST

A crucial precondition for Russian political cooperation with the West and its military participation in multilateral peacekeeping or peace-enforcement operations should be much greater Western sensitivity and willingness to accommodate Russian foreign interests than has been the case. Following the Western lead on policy toward the former Yugoslavia

---

17. See V. Razuvayev, "The crisis in Ukraine and Russia," *Nezavisimaya Gazeta*, December 17, 1993, p. 5.

has done an enormous disservice to Russian interests and the Yeltsin administration's foreign policy record. Moscow has undercut its position in its relations with the United States and Western Europe, and was largely marginalized in international policy-making on this issue, in spite of its much greater stake in developments than any other major power. Russia has missed an opportunity to gain the initiative in stopping the war, using its special relationship with the Serbs, by simultaneously pressuring them to make concessions and protecting them from discriminatory UN sanctions.

The February 1994 decision to search for an alternative to the NATO bombing ultimatum was the right step for the wrong reason. Moscow's more independent stance, which was instrumental in reaching a temporary compromise, was assumed because of pressure from Russian conservatives and nationalists, in particular those in the new Parliament (State Duma). Such a position should have been Russia's from the very beginning. Moscow should neither yield to domestic hard-liners nor passively follow NATO; instead, it should play a more active and creative role in mediating between the Serbs and the West, and in shaping an unbiased UN posture on the resolution of the Balkan conflict.

RUSSIA AND EUROPEAN AFFAIRS

The profound transformation of Europe's political and strategic environment in recent years requires a major revision of Moscow's security course. Of first priority is the implementation of the CFE (Conventional Forces in Europe) Treaty; its shortcomings are more than compensated for by its political and strategic advantages. For economic and many other reasons, Russia would hardly be able to attain greater military power in the foreseeable future without the limits and stipulations of the treaty. On the contrary, if other states had sufficient political motivation, they would be capable of rapid build-up and the achievement of military superiority over Russia. The advantages they share are economic, military-technical and demographic potential, an advantageous geostrategic position, and the ability to join forces in collective defense.

It would be extremely shortsighted of Moscow to issue ultimatums and to threaten to reject the treaty, even if the quickly changing situation leads to reopened discussion over some of its provisions.[18] However, it is

---

18. For example, there were controversies around the CFE quotas for the flank regions, which created obstacles to Russia's build-up of forces in the North-Caucasus military district.

not clear whether these problems are really so formidable and cannot be solved in other ways.

Russia remains, from a military point of view, a leading power in Europe and the world. On the other hand, as a state confronting NATO, or NATO together with the countries of Eastern Europe (to say nothing of adding the Western republics of the former USSR), Russia doesn't stand a chance. As recently as 1989 the Warsaw Pact enjoyed an almost 2.7:1 superiority over NATO in Europe in the main classes of weapons of ground and air forces (subsequently limited by CFE). After the mid-1990s the ratio will shift to 4.5:1 to Russia's disadvantage in terms of the potential cumulative power of states in the West (NATO, Eastern Europe, and the republics of the former USSR).[19]

Hence, the second priority is to avoid the rebirth of an anti-Moscow coalition of states on an expanded scale. The good news is that the achievement of this goal mostly depends on Russia's own policy. Apart from implementing CFE and further force reductions, its democratic reforms at home, its good-neighborly relations with adjoining states, the suppression of Russian neo-imperialist ambitions, and the consistent defense of reasonably formulated national interests are the principal means by which to promote Russia's security interests in Europe.

The retreat of Russian military power by 1,500 kilometers from the center of Europe — from Magdeburg to Smolensk — brought an unaccustomed strategic vulnerability: for the first time in hundreds of years, the Moscow district was not in the deep rear, but in the forward defense line. On the other hand, force disengagement in Europe conferred an unprecedented advantage: a wide separation between the forces of the great Western military powers and Russia. Even technically, the administrative and industrial heartland of Russia is now beyond the operational combat range of the most advanced tactical aircraft and conventional missiles of the strongest military powers in the West. A corridor of many hundreds of kilometers works both ways. Fortifying and formalizing such a separation is one of the most important tasks of Russian national security strategy, making it the third priority. This means ensuring the neutral and non-nuclear status, and the independence and sovereignty of the Eastern European states and Western republics of the former USSR. For many centuries these countries have served as a bridgehead for Western aggression against Russia or Russian aggression against the West. In the

---

19. Calculated by D. Crawford, Conventional Armed Forces in Europe (CFE), U.S. Arms Control and Disarmament Agency, Washington, D.C.

future, Western Europe, the United States and Russia should become the guarantors of the neutrality and security of these countries, and should make them a bridge for economic and political cooperation between Russia and the West.

The armed forces of the neutral countries should be cut and restructured on the principles of non-offensive defense. This would be in keeping with their modest economic capabilities and would reassure those in Russia who think of "worst-case scenarios." In return, to reassure these states, Russia's forces should be further reduced and restructured. Setting aside the quotas of the CFE Treaty, there is no good reason to maintain 18,000 armored vehicles and more than 4,000 aircraft in the European part of Russia — more than on the eve of the Second World War. Similarly, there is no valid reason for Ukraine to retain 9,000 tanks and armored vehicles, along with 1,400 aircraft and helicopters. The territories of Ukraine, Belarus and the Baltic states, as well as the military districts of Moscow, Leningrad and the Western part of the North Caucasus, should become a zone of reduced concentrations of ground and air forces. In its European part 5,000-7,000 armored vehicles and 1,000-2,000 combat aircraft (including air defense) would be sufficient for Russia's training purposes and as a reinforcement reserve for the Southern and Eastern theaters. Still less is needed by other republics.

It is clear that the withdrawal of Russian troops from foreign territories requires the preparation of rear infrastructure. This makes their temporary deployment in the European part of Russia admissible. But as a long-term perspective, when the reduction of the armed forces and their reform have made sufficient progress, the rear infrastructure should be made to correspond to the necessary deployment of troops to respond to potential military threats, which emanate mainly from the south and east.

The agreements with Russia and the neutral countries should be linked to obligations by NATO. For instance, NATO might undertake not to extend eastward, and members of the alliance should not deploy their forces and military facilities there. The number and level of NATO troops and forces should be further lowered and restructured for the purpose of peacekeeping missions. Joint exercises, the development and deployment of compatible weapons systems and equipment, and other kinds of interdependence between the rapid deployment forces of Russia and NATO should be encouraged to the utmost. This is not only a way to save resources, but also a guarantee that enhanced power projection capabilities will never present a threat to each other, will not create a danger of inadvertent escalation, and will always be employed in a joint and coordinated manner with the sanction of multilateral security institutions.

From this standpoint the extension of NATO to the east (by accepting Poland, Hungary, the Czech Republic, Slovakia, and the Baltic states) would cause a negative Russian reaction and would greatly strengthen Moscow's hard-liners. Instead of further reduction in forces, the hawks would argue for their build-up and the extension of deployments and facilities to the west, which would bring more tensions with former Soviet republics and new fears in the larger Eastern European region.

This is, of course, not to suggest that the time has already come to dissolve NATO. It represents a factor of stability and without it there would be a vacuum on the European continent, which would be dangerous in every respect, first and foremost due to uncertainty about the role and policy of united Germany. Over the long run, however, NATO — an alliance conceived and structured for collective defense against a common enemy — should be superseded by a different organization for multilateral security: one directed not against an outside enemy, but designed to ensure compliance with the norms of civilized relations between states and the peaceful settlement of conflicts between its members. Of course, the consolidation of democratic principles in Russia's domestic and foreign policies would be the primary precondition for that.

RUSSIA'S SOFT UNDERBELLY

Russian policy in the volatile regions to its south, including Turkey, the Middle East, and South Asia, should be determined by its interests in the Transcaucasus and Central Asia. Potentially, Turkey, Iran, Iraq, Pakistan, and Afghanistan may be its opponents. In the nearest future Russia may gain from conducting a policy of balancing powers in these regions, since it is too early to contemplate realistically any lasting collective security arrangement.

Iran may be Russia's preferred partner to counterbalance possible Turkish expansion in the Transcaucasus and Central Asia. Of special geopolitical importance is preserving the so-called Megrin corridor of Armenian territory, separating Turkey and the Azerbaijani enclave of Nakhichevan from the rest of Azerbaijan, which has direct communication with Central Asia across the Caspian Sea.[20] In addition, the restoration of

---

20. This is why the suggested territorial exchange between Armenia and Azerbaijan, including Nagorno Karabakh, would not be in Russian interests.

Russia's traditional partnership with India (without encouraging its nuclear, offensive conventional, and naval ambitions) will be instrumental in containing potential Pakistani and Afghani expansion to the north.

To the greatest extent possible, Russia's policy toward Turkey, Iran, Pakistan, and India should be coordinated with those of the United States, NATO and China, so as not to spoil Russia's relations with these more important partners. On the other hand, Russia's clumsy policy on the missile technology deal with India and the tough U.S. policy toward China and India have already prompted these two great Asian powers to seek more cooperative relations with each other.[21] Understanding the mechanisms of multi-polar relations and maintaining a well-balanced policy is a great challenge for Russia in its involvement with its powerful neighbors in Asia.

THE FAR EASTERN REGION

In the Far East, the interests of Russia (in contrast to those of the USSR) may be best served by the maintenance of the American political role and limited military presence. If the United States were to withdraw, the Japanese reaction could be none other than remilitarization in view of the rapid growth of economic and military power in China. A clash between these two giants over Korea, Taiwan, Hong Kong or Southeast Asia could draw Russia into the conflict as well. But the U.S. presence is not enough.

Since Russia will remain weak and vulnerable in the Far East for many years to come, its interests are tied to a more stable regional alignment of powers, and would be served by a new system of multilateral security there. The greatest problem is that Moscow's present slant in favor of China could put Russia in a position of one-sided dependence on Beijing. This would be highly detrimental in view of China's rapidly increasing power and its long history of territorial claims on Russian territory in the Far East.

After the crucial short-term problems with Ukraine and Kazakhstan and the medium-term challenge of adapting to the new political and military environment in Europe, China may represent the greatest external security threat to Russia and Russian interests over the long run.

The resolution of the Kurile Islands dispute with Japan is the key to Russia's security in the Far East. It would provide Moscow with a much more advantageous political and strategic position and greater freedom to

---

21. See N. Roslova, "India and China are trying to resolve conflict in Tibet," *Segodnia*, September 11, 1993, p. 8.

maneuver in the Western Pacific. This subject should not be addressed from a legal or historic angle, and certainly not in the "islands-for-credits" mode attempted by the Russian government in summer 1992.

The islands might be eventually transferred (not necessarily "returned") to Japan in a phased way over 10 to 15 years, in the context of agreements on a zone of deep reductions in armed forces, limits on antisubmarine warfare operations in the Sea of Okhotsk Sea, confidence-building measures in the Far East. This zone might include the entire Kurile chain, Sakhalin and the Hokkaido Islands, and the Sea of Okhotsk as an application area. In this way, both parties' security interests would be accommodated, and the territorial agreement will be a part of a fundamental revision of political and security relations between Russia and Japan. Economic cooperation could follow, provided that Russia creates attractive conditions for foreign investments in Siberia and the Far East.[22]

Unfortunately, large-scale solutions of this type will have to wait for some better future. Moscow's policy of concessions to the West in 1992–1993, including the scandalous handling of the territorial issue with Japan in 1992, was so greatly discredited in Russia that the present turn toward a tougher stance excludes any rational compromise on this subject. Moreover, conservatives are pushing for a further expansion of one-sided political and military reliance on China, including massive exports of arms and military technologies.[23] Avoiding this should be the minimal goal in the short run.

There are two other issues of immense importance to Russia in this region. One is the goal of stability on the Korean peninsula, with subsequent peaceful reunification of the two states. A strong unified Korea would be an important stabilizer in the Far East, conducive to Russia's security as a buffer between China and Japan. A second issue is Mongolia, with its huge territory and small population; were it to become a hotbed of instability, Russia's defense requirements in its eastern zones would triple.

Despite the present domestic crisis Russia has important global responsibilities. These flow from its position as a permanent member of the UN Security Council, its role in other international organizations, and

---

22. See A. Arbatov and B. Makeev, "The Kurile barrier," *Novoye Vremya*, No. 42 (November 1992), pp. 24–26.

23. V. Chernov, "National interests of Russia and threats to its security," *Nezavisimaya Gazeta*, April 29, 1993, pp. 1–3.

its participation in peacekeeping operations in line with UN resolutions. Russian cooperation is essential to ensure the non-proliferation of nuclear and other weapons of mass destruction, better control over the export of missiles and missile technology, and the introduction of quotas and restrictions on the arms trade.

In relations with the United States, much depends on the implementation of the START II Treaty of January 1993. Nationalist hard-liners, advocating the adoption of a first-strike strategy[24] (which has affected the new military doctrine of November 1993), are adamantly against this agreement with the United States.

Under the dominance of conservatives in the State Duma, and with seemingly never-ending problems with Ukraine (and potentially Kazakhstan) on nuclear weapons, the chances of START II ratification and implementation are quite uncertain. The two sides may be obliged for several years to undertake unilateral reductions, as they are now in view of the obsolescence of their strategic forces and the curtailment of modernization programs. The evolution of general political and security relations between Russia and the West will determine the prospects for further bilateral and multilateral arms control and reductions agreements.

The longer this interval of time, the greater will be the need for new negotiations to ensure the implementation of START I and START II, or even more radical cuts and limitations.[25] Some new options may include implementing more rapid reductions by removing warheads in advance (and storing them separately) from the missiles slated for dismantling. Apart from radically lowering alert rates, this would defuse the problem of nuclear proliferation through nationalization of strategic weapons by Ukraine and Kazakhstan.[26]

---

24. V. Repin, "Once more about strategic dilemmas," *Nezavisimaya Gazeta*, September 24, 1992, p. 2.

25. See "START II and Russia's national interests," Report of the Foreign Policy Association, *Nezavisimaya Gazeta*, March 23, 1993, p. 5; and V. Litovkin, interview with G. Berdennikov, V. Dvorkin, and A. Arbatov, "START II strengthens Russia's security," *Isvestiya*, April 10, 1993, p. 15.

26. A. Arbatov, "Yeltsin, Kravchuk and ballistic missiles," *Nezavisimaya Gazeta*, August 6, 1992, p. 4.

Recommendations for the West

There is no doubt that for the foreseeable future Russian foreign policy will shift from its early pro-Western paradigm to a much more assertive stance regarding Russian national interests and its foreign policy in many international problems, most of all on Russian "special responsibilities" in the post-Soviet geopolitical space. In many areas the evolving policy should be a matter of concern: in some of them it exactly opposes Russia's genuine security interests. Nevertheless, Western overreaction and hasty recourse to a new containment strategy would be as bad as complacency and indecisiveness, and might easily turn into a self-fulfilling prophecy.

It is certain that there is no "grand design" of imperialistic expansionism behind Russia's foreign policy. The so-called "Monrovsky Doctrine" is a policy by default, not an elaborate long-term strategy. Its meaning is vague and subject to various interpretations, from quite benign to very aggressive, and its implementation proceeds by tugging and pulling many actors.

The new Russia's foreign policy, or more correctly its foreign policy moods, are the consequence of three factors. First, the failure of domestic economic and political reforms in 1992–1993 made a revival of nationalism the outlet for frustration, and increased the desire for self-reassertion among broad sections of the public and political elite.

The second factor is the initial lack of interest and clear position on the relations with the near abroad by Russia's leadership. Problems grew out of control; the Gordian knot tempted the inexperienced political elite to cut it with one stroke: the imposition of Russia's dominance on the smaller unstable and violent states.

Third, the disappointment and shame over the subservient policy of 1992–1993 produced a great deal of humiliation for the Russians, with very few tangible benefits, and did not help to resolve many international problems. The arrogance and shortsightedness of the United States' policy were just as counterproductive, as was its too great (and personal) involvement in Russia's internal economic and political developments, assuming responsibilities it never could or should fulfill.

These considerations should help to define the proper U.S. and Western reaction to the shift of Russia's foreign policy. Obviously, the West can only marginally affect the conduct of domestic reforms in Russia, which will be the principal determinant of its foreign policy. The main task for the United States is to learn from past mistakes and not to repeat them in the future.

As for Russia's foreign conduct, the West should not be irritated or offended by Moscow's more independent stance on such problems as Bosnia. On the contrary, Russia is to be encouraged into more active policy on all international issues, as long as this is not an anti-Western confrontational strategy, but the expression of a great power's national interests, which it is. Moscow's policy in some regions may be wrong, but not necessarily expansionist or subversive. It will be severely constrained by economic and political problems at home, and by the reactions of public opinion, mass media and the Parliament. It will also be limited by dependence on Western economic aid, credits and investments. It will be restricted by a multi-faceted arms control regime, behind which lies potential Western strategic preponderance, as well as by the weakness of Russian armed forces and degradation of defense industries.[27]

On the other hand, Russia's relations with other former republics of the Soviet Union may create real and dangerous problems, draw Russia into an expanding number of conflicts, undercut its democratic reforms, and precipitate a new confrontation with the West. In Russia's political elite, apart from a few individuals, there is no serious liberal opposition to this policy in early 1994. It may emerge after big failures, but the cost could be too high, if not irreparable.

Preventing Russia from being drawn into expanding conflicts in the states of the former USSR will require an active, creative and sophisticated policy on the part of the United States, Western Europe and Japan, acting through major international organizations, with much greater investments of time, energy and resources than in 1992–1993. What is needed may be called a strategy of "engagement" with various partners, as opposed to what may be defined as a strategy of "confinement,"[28] which has been recently emerging. An active Russia's engagement in world affairs, and its gaining respect in the West, are crucial preconditions for Western involvement in conflict-resolution and the protection of the rights of minorities in Russia's near abroad. Otherwise, Western activism might revive Moscow's traditional paranoia about hostile encirclement and lead to confrontation just as surely as the strategy of "confinement."

---

27. See Report of the Council on Foreign and Defense Policy, "Strategy for Russia," *Nezavisimaya Gazeta*, August 19, 1992, p. 4.

28. Basically, this means the West leaving the CIS to Russia, and Moscow following the Western lead in other areas. See Alexei G. Arbatov, "Russia's Foreign Policy Alternatives," *International Security*, Vol. 18, No. 2 (Fall 1993), pp. 42–43.

Chapter 5
Russian National Interests

Steven E. Miller

For several reasons, defining and assessing the new Russia's national security interests will be particularly difficult. First, this process necessarily takes place in the domestic context, and reflects the character of the internal political system and the relative fortunes of political leaders, parties, factions, and schools of thought. The severe political instability that prevails in Russia produces substantial uncertainty about how it will come to define and defend its national security interests.

Second, by virtue of its size and location, and the number and identity of its neighbors, Russia inevitably occupies a complex geostrategic position — as do all centrally located continental powers. It must confront an unusually large number of potential security threats, inescapable diplomatic relationships, worrying scenarios, and neighboring trouble-spots. Russia will have security interests from one end of Eurasia to the other; establishing priorities among them will be difficult and often painful.

Third, Russia, like the fourteen other states that emerged from the former Soviet Union, gained its independence suddenly and unexpectedly. Moreover, it is, in many significant respects, a new state; politically, economically, ethnically, and geographically, it is different from earlier Moscow-centered states. Naturally, this new state could not immediately have in place a coherent and widely accepted conception of its national security interests and requirements, nor even a well developed national security debate. As one analyst put it, "The new Russia has yet to

---

Steven E. Miller is the Director of the International Security Program at the Center for Science and International Affairs at the Kennedy School of Government at Harvard University. He is also Editor-in-Chief of the quarterly journal International Security.

determine its identity, its character, its national interests, its place in the world."[1]

Finally, calculating Russia's national security interests will be complicated by the fact that Moscow inherits the imperial legacy of the Soviet Union and czarist Russia. As one Russian politician expressed it, Russia "retains the psychological detritus of a superpower."[2] This means that some in the Russian national security debate will perceive rights and responsibilities, opportunities and temptations, and threats and challenges in states formerly controlled or dominated by Moscow; imperial mentalities will surely not be absent from the Russian debate.[3]

In view of these considerations, it is not surprising that Russia is in the midst of a contentious debate over its security interests and policies.[4] There are, of course, some common elements across these various schools of thought.[5] But more striking is the range of disagreement about Russia's identity, interests, and place in the world. The menu of choice is broad.

---

1. Sergei Rogov, ed., *Russian Defense Policy: Challenges and Developments* (Washington D.C.: Center for Naval Analyses, February 1993), p. 1. See also Iain Elliot, "Russia in Search of an Identity," *RFE/RL Research Report*, Vol. 2, No. 20 (May 14, 1993), pp. 1–4.

2. Oleg Rumyantsev, chairman of Russia's Parliamentary Constitutional Committee, quoted in William C. Bodie, "The Threat to America from the Former USSR," *Orbis*, Vol. 37, No. 4 (Fall 1993), pp. 510–511.

3. See Vera Tolz, "The Burden of the Imperial Legacy," *RFE/RL Research Report*, Vol. 2, No. 20 (May 14, 1993), pp. 41–46.

4. Useful overviews and categorizations of the Russian debate include Alexei G. Arbatov, "Russia's Foreign Policy Alternatives," *International Security*, Vol. 18, No. 1 (Fall 1993); S. Neil MacFarlane, "Russia, the West, and European Security," *Survival*, Vol. 35, No. 3 (Autumn 1993), pp. 8–12; Andrei Kortunov, "Strategic Relations Between the Former Soviet Republics," Backgrounder No. 892, The Heritage Foundation, April 17, 1992, especially pp. 9–11; Alexei K. Pushkov, "Russia and America: The Honeymoon's Over," *Foreign Policy*, No. 93 (Winter 1993–1994), pp. 77–90; Olga Alexandrova, "Divergent Russian Foreign Policy Concepts," *Aussenpolitik*, Vol. 44, No. 4 (1993), pp. 363–372; Neil Malcolm, "The New Russian Foreign Policy," *The World Today*, February 1994, pp. 28–32; Vladimir P. Lukin, "Our Security Predicament," *Foreign Policy*, No. 88 (Fall 1992), p.65; and Konstantin E. Sorokin, *Russia's Security in a Rapidly Changing World*, Center for International Security and Arms Control, Stanford University, January 1994. A representative sampling of views on the subject can be found in Teresa Pelton Johnson and Steven E. Miller, eds., *Russian Security after the Cold War: Seven Views from Moscow*, CSIA Studies in International Security No. 3 (McLean, Va: Brassey's [US], 1994). Slightly dated but relevant is Alexei G. Arbatov, ed., *The Security Watershed: Russians Debating Defense and Security Policy after the Cold War* (Yverdon, Switzerland: Gordon and Breach Science Publishers, 1993).

5. See, for example, Paul A. Goble, "Russia's Extreme Right," *The National Interest* (Fall 1993), pp. 95–96.

The aim of this essay is to examine the choices that confront Russia as it seeks to define its national interests, and to identify the tendencies evident in Russia's external behavior so far.

Russia's national security interests can be viewed through three lenses. The first is Russia's acute internal crisis, which potentially threatens the survival of the current Russian state. Second, Russia must sort out its relations with the other newly independent states of the former Soviet Union (FSU). These states are not only Russia's new neighbors, they are linked by various political, economic, and military legacies of the USSR. Last, Russia's national security interests need to be analyzed in the context of traditional geostrategic considerations. The sections that follow examine each of these contexts.

Russia's Crisis and Russian Interests

Russia's most urgent near-term interest is to survive as a state within its presently constituted borders. Unlike most states most of the time, Russia faces a significant (if debatable) immediate threat to its survival. This threat is largely internal in character; it involves the risk that Russia, like the Soviet Union before it, will disintegrate. Some of the same centrifugal forces that undermined the Soviet Union — ethnic and economic nationalism, for example — are evident in Russia. Further, its central authority is greatly weakened. Its economic and political problems are acute. The durability of the current Russian state cannot be taken for granted.[6]

While the solutions to this crisis are unlikely to be found primarily in Russia's external relations, it is impossible to avoid consideration of its implications for Russia's national security interests. What external interests derive from the desire to maximize Russia's chances to survive the present internal crisis? Several very different sets of answers are possible. One approach simply discounts the threat to the Russian state. Further disintegration, in this logic, is inconceivable: Moscow simply will not

---

6. See, for example, Jessica Stern, "Moscow Meltdown: Can Russia Survive?" *International Security*, Vol. 18, No. 4 (Spring 1994); and Bogdan Szajkowski, "Will Russia Disintegrate into Bantustans?" *The World Today*, Vol. 49, Nos. 8–9 (August–September 1993), pp. 172–176; John Lloyd and Leyla Boulton, "Iron Fist and Iron Glove," *Financial Times*, September 25, 1993; and "Russia: Things Fall Apart," *The Economist*, January 30, 1993, p. 47.

permit it to happen; potential breakaway states are not viable; Russia's military power guarantees that it will not happen. In this logic, Russia's current crisis deserves no special weight in determining Russia's near-term security interests.

A second approach, which takes the threat to the Russian state seriously, emphasizes the importance to Russia of integrating with the Western industrial world and of keeping Russia at peace. It aims to minimize the costs of Russia's external relations while seeking help from the West as part of Russia's struggle with its internal difficulties. The logic of this approach has several components. First, it is generally presumed that the severe economic crisis in Russia is the primary taproot of its troubles. Hence, Moscow has an urgent need to find ways of averting economic catastrophe and improving economic performance. In its external relations it should pursue paths that seem likely to produce the maximum economic benefit in the short run.

In practice, this suggests that Russia has a strong near-term national security interest in pursuing a strategy oriented toward the industrial powers. This is true for several reasons. First, despite the limitations on the West's ability and willingness to provide aid, it is the only significant source of emergency assistance that might be necessary to stave off disaster if Russia suffers further steep economic deterioration. Second, Western capital investment on a large scale is probably necessary, and certainly desirable, if the Russian economy is going to be turned around over the coming few years. Third, the industrial world offers the biggest and wealthiest markets, access to which could also increase Russia's economic prospects. To be sure, Russia will need to find internal solutions to its economic problems, and looking westward is no doubt at best an incomplete answer; moreover, Moscow has ample reason to be disappointed with the behavior of the West so far. But, in this logic, it is hard to see what alternative approach to Russia's external policy offers better prospects of helping Moscow surmount the present internal crisis.

Second, Russia needs international political support, both for the continued integrity of its present borders and for its integration into the Western international system. Again, a Western-oriented strategy would seem to serve this interest, since this would involve building good — or at least better — relations with most of the most powerful states in the international system. Moreover, a policy that aligns Russia with and attempts to integrate Russia into the West may also help to foreclose the potential danger that some among the most powerful states in the international system might come to see the disintegration of Russia as in their interest. A Russia that looks unfriendly, aloof, aggressive, or chronically troublesome could well produce this outcome.

Third, Russia would appear to have a strong interest in avoiding entanglement in conflicts along its lengthy borders, for at least two reasons: this would siphon resources from the Russian economy, a drain it can ill afford; and such conflicts could damage Russia's relations with the West, undermining or eliminating the benefits desired from a Western-oriented strategy.

A third approach sees jeopardy to the Russian state but rejects the notion that cultivating the West is necessary or desirable, and instead emphasizes the restoration of Russia's strength and status. This approach comes in several variants. One attributes the Soviet Union's collapse and Russia's problems to the malign intentions and schemes of outside powers.[7] The interest of the West, according to this logic, is in a weak and troubled Russia. The more extreme adherents of this view, according to one analysis, "depict the United States as the center of a Western anti-Russian, anti-Slavonic, and anti-Orthodox conspiracy that aims to destroy Russia as a state and reduce it to a Western colony."[8]

A less virulent variant emphasizes Moscow's need to recover from the humiliation associated with the disintegration of its empire, to rebuild Russia's power and influence (especially in the FSU), to preserve Russia's great power status, and to stand up for Russia's interests. A Russia that appears weak and supine, in this argument, is more vulnerable to disintegration than one that is influential and independent — Russia needs a strong state to survive. This approach does not lead necessarily to poor or confrontational relations with the West, but does mandate that Russian interests not be sacrificed for the sake of relations with the West — a view that implies some friction since not all of Russia's perceived interests will be congenial to the West.[9]

A complementary argument suggests that any help from the West will be too little, too late. Again, this leads to the conclusion that there is little point in being deferential to the West at the expense of other Russian interests.

---

7. See, for example, Wendy Slater, "The Center Right in Russia," *RFE/RL Research Report*, Vol. 2, No. 34 (August 27, 1993), p. 11.

8. Pushkov, "Russia and America," p. 81.

9. See, for example, Pushkov, "Russia and America," p. 79.

A final variant focuses on the important role of the Russian military in the new Russia. The military's support of Yeltsin's government is thought crucial if that government is to have any chance of success. Military force may be the glue that holds Russia together. And Russia's military is a key factor in the restoration of Russia's power and influence in the FSU and more broadly. In this logic, it is far more important to remain on good terms with the military than to remain on intimate terms with the West but face a divisive, disgruntled, unsupportive Russian army. Indeed, if support of the Russian military is thought necessary to the survival of any regime in Moscow, favoring ties with the West over the preferences of the army may be impossible.[10]

Of these three approaches, the Western-oriented approach, which focuses on the potential support and help that may derive from close and good relations with the industrial West and on the potential costs of Russian activism in the former Soviet Union, is most attractive to the West (although it brings with it the onus of having to deliver assistance). In the early months after Russia became an independent state, this was the clear policy of the Russian government. But the pronounced trend over the past year has been in the direction of the third approach.[11]

Russian Interests and Options in the Near Abroad

Moscow's proximity to and special connections with the other states of the former Soviet Union — the "near abroad" — guarantee that they will figure prominently in calculations of Russian national security interests. At least seven factors come into play.

RUSSIAN INTERESTS IN THE FORMER SOVIET UNION

First, and perhaps most important in terms of politics within Russia, are the 25 million ethnic Russians who live outside the borders of Russia. All

---

10. See "Russia's Armed Forces: The Threat that Was," *The Economist*, August 28, 1993, pp. 17–19; David Remnick, "Letter from Moscow: The Hangover," *The New Yorker*, November 22, 1993, p. 51; "Russian Foreign Policy: Your Policy or Mine?" *The Economist*, October 30, 1993, pp. 57–58; and Serge Schmemann, "Russia's Military: A Shriveled and Volatile Legacy," *New York Times*, November 28, 1993. A more extensive discussion is Stephen Foye, "Updating Russian Civil-Military Relations," *RFE/RL Research Report*, Vol. 2, No. 46 (November 19, 1993), pp. 44–50.

11. See, for example, "Russia Resurgent," *The Economist*, December 4, 1993, pp. 14–16.

of the other fourteen newly independent states of the former Soviet Union include ethnic Russian minorities, and in every one save Armenia, the minority is more than a token percentage of the population.[12] It is extremely unlikely that any Russian government can remain indifferent to the fate of the ethnic Russian diaspora. Real or perceived mistreatment of these populations will cause problems between Russia and the offending state, and could provoke Russian intervention.[13]

Second, a substantial level of economic interdependence exists between Russia and the other FSU states.[14] Until January 1992, these fifteen states were part of a highly centralized, tightly integrated, and substantially autarkic economic system. However keen some of these states may be to reduce their dependence on the residual Soviet economic system, political independence cannot disinvent these economic connections — at least for some time to come. Being larger and more blessed with natural resources, Russia is probably less dependent than the others, but cannot be wholly immune from the effects of interdependence within the former Soviet economy. Moreover, other of the newly independent states are, in some respects, economically dependent on Russia, particularly in the energy sector; Russia is by far the primary supplier of oil, nuclear fuel, and even electricity.[15] To some extent Russia is entangled in the affairs of other FSU states regardless of its preferences or theirs. And Russia itself cannot afford to ignore profitable economic ties with other FSU states.

Third, some FSU states may be important to Russia because of their natural resources. For example, indications that the Caspian Sea basin may be a major source of oil could give Moscow incentive to influence, dominate, or even reintegrate FSU states that turn out to be oil-rich — particularly given Russia's own oil production problems and the importance of oil exports as a source of hard currency.

---

12. See the table in Zbigniew Brzezinski, "Post-Communist Nationalism," *Foreign Affairs*, Vol. 68, No. 5 (Winter 1989/1990), p. 7.

13. See Anthony Hyman, "Russians Outside Russia," *The World Today*, November 1993, pp. 205–208.

14. See, for example, Susan L. Clark, "Security Issues and the Eastern Slavic States," *The World Today*, October 1993, pp. 189–190.

15. See, for example, "Ex-Soviet States Meet amid Disputes," *Boston Globe*, October 19, 1992; "Russia to Halve its Oil Exports to Other Former Republics," *Boston Globe*, September 27, 1992; and Erik Whitlock, "Ukrainian-Russian Trade: The Economics of Dependency," *RFE/RL Research Report*, Vol. 2, No. 43 (October 29, 1993), pp. 38–42.

Fourth, the risk of instability or conflict along its borders (particularly to the south) is a concern for Moscow. This could jeopardize or harm Russian populations outside of Russia, which would likely cause Moscow to consider or undertake military intervention. Turmoil in the near abroad could also produce large-scale migration of Russians back into Russia; this would only exacerbate Russia's own severe socio-economic problems. And conflict in the near abroad could impinge on Russian territory and populations in border areas. Accordingly, conflict along the periphery has loomed large in Russian thinking about security. As Minister of Defense Pavel Grachev said, "Local wars are the main threat to peace, and the possibility of their eruption in certain regions is growing."[16]

Fifth, a substantial non-Russian population of some 25 to 30 million lives within Russia's borders, almost all of it with ethnic links to other newly independent states of the former Soviet Union. Thus, a considerable constituency within Russia will be interested in and influenced by developments in the near abroad. Particularly notable are Russia's 20 million Muslims; Moscow fears that if Islamic fundamentalism takes root in Central Asia or the Caucasus, the contagion might spread to Muslims within Russia and cause problems at home.[17]

Sixth, the near abroad will be regarded by Russia as an arena in which it may have to compete for influence with outside powers. The worst case would be a situation in which states hostile to Russia establish dominant positions of influence in newly independent states of the former Soviet Union. This explains the wary eye that Moscow casts on the interests of states such as Turkey, Iran, Pakistan, and Saudi Arabia in the Caucasus and Central Asia.[18] On the other hand, it is desirable from the Russian point of view that states of the former Soviet Union serve as buffers between Russia and significant rivals.

---

16. Quoted in Daniel Sneider, "New Russian Doctrine Raises Western Suspicions," *Defense News*, November 8–14, 1993, p. 34. Also see Lukin, "Our Security Predicament," especially p. 62.

17. See, for example, "Where Does Russia End?" *The Economist*, November 13, 1993, p. 58; Maxim Shashenkov, *Security Issues of the Ex-Soviet Central Asian Republics*, London Defence Studies No. 14 (The Centre for Defence Studies, King's College London, 1992), pp. 51–53; and Sergei Stankevich, "Russia in Search of Itself," *The National Interest*, Summer 1992, p. 49.

18. See, for example, Stankevich, "Russia in Search of Itself," p. 49; and J. Mohan Malik, "Central Asia Astir," *Pacific Research*, May 1992, pp. 3–4.

Finally, there are a variety of geostrategic considerations that can influence Russia's perceptions of its national security interests in the near abroad. For example, Russian forces are still deployed outside Russia in the near abroad.[19] There may be military bases and facilities to which Russia might like to retain access: the large phased array radar in Latvia, for example, is an important component of the strategic early warning system that had been created by the Soviet Union; similarly, Russia clearly wishes to complete an early warning radar that had been under construction in Belarus.[20] Desire to have more or better access to the sea could affect Russia's relations with some FSU states, a factor in its relations with the Baltic states, Ukraine, and Georgia.[21] And a desire to push Russia's air and land defense perimeter out as far as possible, and to exploit the defensive perimeter created by the USSR, provides yet another military rationale for regarding the near abroad as strategically significant; in this logic, Russia is better defended in Tajikistan than along its own frontier.[22]

In short, ethnic, economic, political, and security considerations cause the near abroad to figure prominently on the Russian policy agenda. From an outsider's point of view, some of these Russian concerns seem sensible and legitimate, such as economic and resource interests. Others seem exaggerated: the threat of Islamic fundamentalism in Russia is unlikely to be great; and the threat to Russia from remote conflicts in Tajikistan or other small FSU states does not seem large. And some seem questionable: if all states claimed a right of intervention on behalf of ethnic brethren, this would be a recipe for disaster — particularly in an ethnically diverse area like the FSU; and the desire to preserve and exploit the USSR's defense perimeter seems to reflect mentalities left over from the Soviet period rather than a careful assessment of Russia's security interests.

---

19. Steven Erlanger, "Troops in Ex-Soviet Lands: Occupiers or Needed Allies?" *New York Times*, November 30, 1993, reports that an estimated 200,000 Russian troops are still deployed outside Russia, mostly in the near abroad.

20. See "Nuclear Warning Station Discussed with Belarus," *Moscow ITAR-TASS*, November 18, 1993 (in FBIS-SOV-93-221, November 18, 1993, p. 5).

21. See the comments made by Colonel-General I. Rodionov, head of the Russian General Staff Academy, excerpted in Mary C. Fitzgerald, "Chief of Russia's General Staff Academy Speaks Out on Moscow's New Military Doctrine," *Orbis*, Vol. 37, No. 2 (Spring 1993), pp. 282–283.

22. See, for example, John Lloyd, "Russian Military Seeks Permanent Baltic Presence," *Financial Times*, June 15, 1992; and Steven Erlanger, "Troops in Ex-Soviet Lands."

Nevertheless, as Alexei Arbatov suggests, many Russians believe that "The first and highest foreign policy priority for Russia is its relations with other former republics of the USSR."[23] It is debatable whether the near abroad deserves highest priority, when one considers the importance to Russia of relations with China, Western Europe, and the United States. But there can be no doubt that developments in the near abroad will be seen to have significant implications for Moscow.

There remains the question of how Russia ought to pursue its interests with respect to the fourteen states of the FSU. It has a wide range of options, and need not embrace one single strategy. Indeed, the states vary considerably in size, power, location, importance, hostility or friendliness toward Moscow, and domestic character and stability. Russia's strategy ought to reflect this variety.

Russia can choose among three broad postures toward the other states of the FSU: it can seek a circumscribed role that aims at limiting Russia's involvement in the near abroad; it can attempt a policy of benign engagement that allows Russia to play the role of security guarantor and peacekeeper in the region; or it can adopt a more domineering strategy that seeks to preserve and expand Russia's influence and control in the region.

LIMITED ENGAGEMENT

A strategy of limited engagement might seem unlikely in view of the interests outlined above. Nevertheless, a case can made for such a strategy. First, most of the states (with the notable exceptions of Ukraine and Kazakhstan), are not major power assets. Russia appears, for example, to have engaged in considerable maneuvering to reassert its influence in Georgia, but it is hard to see that this represents a significant improvement in Moscow's international position. Indeed, Moscow's complete control of all of these states during the Soviet period did not prevent the Soviet Union's relative decline and eventual collapse. In addition, there is a risk that an activist Russian policy in the near abroad will cause it to get bogged down in costly peripheral conflicts and interventions, consuming money, resources, and political capital already in short supply.[24] Further, a more activist policy could easily damage Russia's relations with the

---

23. Arbatov, "Russia's Foreign Policy Alternatives," p. 26. This is a common refrain in Russian writings on foreign policy. See also Pushkov, "Russia and America," p. 90.

24. A point recognized by some Russian commentators.

West by suggesting heavy-handed Russian imperialism. Thus, it is arguable that with respect to a number of FSU states, Russia has little to gain and much to lose by an activist policy. A strategy of limited engagement would minimize the possibility of such an outcome.

Moreover, this strategy does not imply abandonment of Russia's interests in the near abroad. Rather, it defines those interests narrowly and seeks to advance them as cheaply as possible. A strategy of limited engagement could be pursued in several not mutually exclusive ways.

NEO-ISOLATIONISM: A policy of neo-isolationism would seek to minimize Russian involvement in the FSU. Russian isolationism would be compatible with continuing economic links where these proved mutually desirable, but would imply indifference to the internal affairs of the other states of the FSU and a policy of detachment from conflicts between them. In this framework, Russia would see internal or regional conflicts not as opportunities for expansion of its influence, nor as responsibilities it must accept as the leading power in the former USSR, but as problems to be avoided. Russian relations with Kirgizstan appear to approximate this model (although there has yet to be trouble there that might tempt Russia to intervene).[25]

FINLANDIZATION: A second variant would emulate the model of Soviet relations with Finland during the Cold War. This would involve wide tolerance in Moscow of the internal and foreign policy orientations of its FSU neighbors, provided that they refrain from joining hostile alignments and from serving as agents of influence for Russia's rivals. Finlandization would amount to a sort of conditional isolationism in which Russia, in effect, promises to leave its FSU neighbors alone so long as they avoid anti-Russian external policies. Russia's policy toward its former allies in the Warsaw Pact resembles this approach, in that it has combined recognition of their independence and their sovereign rights as international actors with strong opposition to the idea that they might become members of NATO.[26]

---

25. See "Russia's Southern Flank: Who's Winning and Who's Losing," *The Economist*, November 13, 1993, p. 61.

26. See, for example, "Russian Foreign Policy: Your Policy or Mine?" *The Economist*, October 30, 1993, pp. 57–58; "East Europe Waves Off NATO Stand by Yeltsin," *International Herald Tribune*, October 2–3, 1993; and Suzanne Crowe, "Russian Views on an Eastward Expansion of NATO," *RFE/RL Research Report*, Vol. 2, No. 41 (October 15, 1993), pp. 21–24.

MULTILATERALIZATION: Russia might also attempt to limit its own role in, and to minimize the trouble that might arise from the FSU by trying to multilateralize its security concerns in that area. Such an approach could have two dimensions. One would focus on issues of peace and stability within and between the other states of the FSU. Russia could, for example, promote a large CSCE role in FSU troublespots. Or it could encourage NATO to assume responsibility for keeping or restoring peace in the near abroad. If Russian relations with the West are good, and integration with the West is a prime Russian goal, this approach should be compatible with Moscow's interests.[27] Nor is this inconceivable from the CSCE or NATO perspective. On the contrary, such an arrangement is compatible with visions of what role CSCE and NATO ought to play in post–Cold War Europe.[28] The involvement of the CSCE in trying to resolve the Trans-Dniester dispute in Moldova contains a hint of this approach.[29]

A policy of multilateralization must also focus on the protection of minority rights of Russians in the FSU; Russia could attempt to devolve this burden, to international institutions, such as the CSCE or the NACC (North Atlantic Cooperation Council).[30] Any realistic policy along these lines must take cognizance of the possibility that international action on behalf of ethnic Russians will not be forthcoming or will be ineffective; but Russia could at least try to be the protector of last, rather than first, resort.

In short, a combination of neo-isolationism, finlandization, and multilateralization might permit Russia to safeguard its interests in the FSU while minimizing its own role and costs. This could appeal to an inward-looking Russia absorbed in its own problems, or to a Russia

---

27. However, Russia has generally responded coolly to offers of outside mediation or involvement in the near abroad, dismissing them as efforts to create spheres of influence. See, for example, "Danger in the Near Abroad," *International Herald Tribune*, October 2–3, 1993.

28. See, for example, Craig Whitney, "NATO Sees a Role with Peacekeepers for Eastern Europe," *New York Times*, June 5, 1992; "NATO Weighs New Role in Peacekeeping," *Basic Reports*, No. 22 (June 3, 1992), pp. 1–3; Adam Daniel Rotfeld, "The CSCE: Towards a Security Organization," in *SIPRI Yearbook 1993: World Armaments and Disarmament* (Oxford: Oxford University Press, 1993), especially pp. 179–182; and Konrad J. Huber, "The CSCE and Ethnic Conflict in the East," *RFE/RL Research Report*, Vol. 2, No. 31 (July 30, 1993), pp. 30–36.

29. See David Shorr, "CSCE Action on Moldova Awaits Envoy's Meeting With Yeltsin," *Basic Reports*, No. 27 (December 23, 1992), p. 1.

30. See "Russia and its Neighbors," *Financial Times*, November 22, 1993.

preoccupied with forging close links with the West and eager to avoid trouble along its periphery.

BENIGN ACTIVISM

A strategy of benign activism, in contrast, would cast Russia in the role of leader, protector, and peacekeeper within the FSU. In this logic, Russia's interests in the FSU are too substantial, and its ties to the other states of the FSU are too many and too deep, to allow a strategy of limited engagement. Rather, Russia should take the lead in constructing a new international order in the FSU, and should be prepared to defend and promote that order through collaboration and cooperation.

Accordingly, this strategy requires that other FSU states are prepared to confer a leading role upon Russia and to accept that Russian power is unthreatening and that Russian activism and intervention in the FSU is genuinely benign. As the troubled relations between Russia and several of its FSU neighbors attest, this is a problematic assumption; hence the limits of this strategy will be defined by the reactions of others. But some states of the FSU do desire close and friendly relations with Russia; over time others might if Russia's internal character and external policies evolve in ways that inspire greater trust than now exists. This strategy would require Russia to bear greater costs, but arguably would provide a more direct and certain way to protect Russian interests in the FSU.

An obvious instrument of such a strategy is the Commonwealth of Independent States, formed in December 1991 as the USSR was disintegrating. Its membership includes twelve of the fifteen states of the FSU; only the three Baltic states remain outside. It provides a framework for collaboration among these twelve states, but its ultimate form, content, and importance remain to be worked out. Some CIS members (most importantly, Ukraine) harbor doubts about its utility and desirability; not all join in every CIS agreement or arrangement; and many CIS agreements appear to be observed largely in the breach. Many have doubts about its importance and durability; nevertheless, so far the CIS has played a key role in Russia's relations with about half of the other FSU states, and at least some role in its relations with all the other CIS members. Moreover, the various conceptions associated with the CIS suggest the range of options available to Russia in the context of a strategy of benign activism; many of these options can be applied bilaterally as well as multilaterally.

The strategy of benign activism can manifest itself in several different ways, depending on the level of collaboration thought to be desirable and feasible:

"COMMONWEALTH" MODELS: At one end of the spectrum are approaches involving relatively modest forms of international collaboration among FSU states; these will be the most attractive options to those states that see advantage in cooperation but remain suspicious of Russian power and intentions. Various forms of loose association among independent states have served as models for Russia's bilateral or multilateral relations with the other states of the FSU. Other examples include the British Commonwealth, which reflects the special historical, political, military and economic ties among the states that once comprised the British Empire but does not bind them extensively into common institutions or compromise their sovereignty, and the European Free Trade Association (EFTA), the free trade arrangement among West European states not members of the European Community.[31] Similarly, there are a variety of military assistance, military cooperation, and status of forces agreements that do not entail formal alliance, joint obligations, or integrated command structures.[32]

INTEGRATIONIST MODELS: At the other end of the spectrum are approaches that envision very substantial levels of political, economic, or military integration. In its initial Russian conception, the CIS fell very much into this category;[33] however, this approach was unacceptable to at least several members of the CIS, including Ukraine, Azerbaijan, and Moldova, which wished to form their own national militaries and, at least in Ukraine's case, were unwilling to accept any disproportionate Russian role in the CIS.[34]

---

31. See, for example, Ruslan Khasbulatov, "The Commonwealth of Independent States: Conflicts, Problems, Perspectives," in Johnson and Miller, eds., *Russian Security after the Cold War*, pp. 179–180.

32. See, for example, Sergei Rogov, et al., *Commonwealth Defense Arrangements and International Security* (Washington D.C.: Center for Naval Analyses, June 1992), pp. 80–81.

33. Rogov et al., *Commonwealth Defense Arrangements and International Security*, pp. 1–17, provide a good account of the formation and early evolution of the CIS. See also David Mendeloff, "The Potemkin Army? The Joint Armed Forces of the Commonwealth of Independent States," *Soviet Defense Notes*, Vol. 5., No. 1 (May 1993), and Richard Woff, "The Joint Command Commonwealth of Independent States: December 1991–March 1992," *Defense Analysis*, Vol. 8, No. 2 (1992), pp. 179–197.

34. See Christopher Donnelly, "Evolutionary Problems in the Former Soviet Armed Forces," *Survival*, Vol. 34, No. 3 (Autumn 1992), especially pp. 35–38.

The failure of this conception of a tightly integrated CIS did not end the interest in achieving substantial integration among FSU states. In the security realm, an alternative model is NATO, a coalition of independent sovereign states, each with its own military, but committed to defending one another and joined in common planning and command arrangements. It combines the autonomy prized by various of the FSU states with a high degree of military collaboration. For a Russian strategy of benign activism, this is an attractive outcome.[35]

For those FSU states that regard Russia as a potential threat to their security, even this level of integration remains unacceptable. But Russia has succeeded in achieving a Treaty on Collective Security, signed by six states (Armenia, Kazakhstan, Kirgizstan, Russia, Tajikistan, and Uzbekistan) in Tashkent on May 15, 1992. The signatories agree not to join military alliances directed against one another, commit to consultation and coordination on "all important questions of international security affecting their interests," and embrace NATO's famous formulation that an attack on one is an attack on all.[36] Subsequent efforts to form joint command arrangements under this treaty have been unsuccessful. Nevertheless, clearly such an arrangement, if feasible, goes far toward advancing Russia's interests and influence in the near abroad. Similarly, in the economic realm, the European Community represents a model that has influenced Russian views of the CIS. Ongoing discussions among some CIS states over uniting their economies are a reflection of this impulse.

RUSSIA AS PEACEKEEPER: If conflict and instability in the FSU threaten Russia's interests, then Russia has an incentive to help keep or restore peace where conflict threatens or erupts. Other FSU states that fear conflict in the region may also perceive an interest in having Moscow play this role, since it is the only state in the FSU capable of doing so.[37] In a strategy of benign activism, Russia can attempt to assume the role of impartial peacekeeper within the CIS, presumably with the support, and conceivably the participation, of other CIS members.

---

35. See Rogov et al., *Commonwealth Defense Arrangements and International Security*, p. 79.

36. For the text of the treaty, see "Treaty on CIS Collective Security," *RFE/RL Research Report*, Vol. 2, No. 25 (June 18, 1993), pp. 4–5.

37. See, for example, Boris Z. Rumer, "The Gathering Storm in Central Asia," *Orbis*, Vol. 37, No. 1 (Winter 1993), p. 95.

Efforts along these lines have been visible in Russian policy toward the CIS. The Treaty on Collective Security, for example, envisions a peacekeeping role for member states. Further, at a CIS summit in July 1992, the ten member states agreed to form peacekeeping forces, and soon thereafter a Russian-Georgian peacekeeping force, operating under the blue colors of the United Nations, intervened in South Ossetia.[38] Russian involvement in Moldova, Tajikistan, and Georgia has also been justified in terms of peacekeeping. Moreover, Russia has, without notable success, also sought international blessing for this role, suggesting that it be granted "special powers" in the territory of the FSU in order to ensure peace and stability.[39]

The limits of benign activism will be determined by the perceptions and reactions of the other FSU states, which fall into three categories: those that wish to have no part of collaborative arrangements with Russia, notably the three Baltic states; those prepared to consider very substantial levels of integration, a category defined by the five signatories of the Collective Security Treaty plus Belarus; and those FSU states that prefer the CIS to remain limited, and refrain from participating in greater institutionalization and integration, a category that includes Ukraine, Moldova, Georgia, Azerbaijan, and Turkmenistan. Accordingly, Russia has no choice but to pursue a multi-tiered policy if it wishes to opt for a strategy of benign activism.

DOMINATION

A third option for Russia is to pursue a strategy of domination, treating the FSU as Russia's sphere of influence and emphasizing Russia's unilateral interests and prerogatives; at the extreme, this strategy amounts to revanchism, seeking to reincorporate other FSU states, or parts thereof, into a Moscow-centered state. The motivation could be national pride, after what is regarded in Russia as a humiliating loss of international status.[40] This approach could also reflect Russia's difficulty in accepting the sovereignty of "a host of nominally independent states, many of

---

38. "CIS Plans Peacekeeping," *Arms Control Today*, July/August 1992, p. 33. On the intervention in South Ossetia, see "Peacekeepers Occupy Former Soviet Region," *New York Times*, July 15, 1992.

39. See, for example, "Russia and its Neighbors," *Financial Times*, November 22, 1993; and "Peacekeeping Forces May Fly CSCE Flag," *Moscow Mayak Radio*, November 17, 1993 (FBIS-SOV-93-221, November 18, 1993, p. 3).

40. See Tolz, "The Burden of the Imperial Legacy," p. 43. See also Goble, "Russia's Extreme Right," p. 96.

which, from the Russian perspective, have little or no historical legitimacy, are economically dependent on Russia, and are home to sizable Russian minorities."[41]

A strategy of domination could also appeal because of the belief that the disintegration of the USSR has been a disaster for Russia and that the FSU is inherently a vital interest for Moscow.[42] According to the logic of the strategy of domination, Russia is the rightful guarantor of peace and stability in the FSU, and its interests in the FSU are best served by maximizing its influence and control.

In short, Moscow can seek to promote its interests in the FSU by creating a sphere of influence in which it is the dominant player. Moscow's aim would be to create or to exploit instruments of influence and domination. The tactics of such Russian neo-imperialism could take several forms.

DIVIDE AND DOMINATE: Russia can prevent wide collusion against itself among FSU states, weaken the capacity of other FSU states to engage in undesirable behavior, punish those that pursue an independent line, and create opportunities for influence and intervention, by causing or contributing to trouble within and between FSU states. This could involve arming and supporting protagonists in internal or regional conflicts, encouraging separatist movements in other FSU states, contributing "volunteers" to participate in ongoing conflicts, or intervening directly to influence the outcome of conflicts.

There is wide suspicion, both within the FSU and in the West, that Russia has undertaken just such a policy with respect to certain FSU neighbors, particularly in the Caucasus.[43] In the cases of Moldova, Georgia, and Azerbaijan, for example, states that appeared to be eager to

---

41. John Lough, "Defining Russia's Relations with Neighboring States," *RFE/RL Research Report*, Vol. 20, No. 2 (May 14, 1993), p. 53.

42. See, for example, Fitzgerald, "Chief of Russia's General Staff Academy Speaks Out on Moscow's New Military Doctrine," p. 283.

43. See "Still on the Prowl," *The Economist*, August 28, 1993, p. 11; "Danger in the Near Abroad," *International Herald Tribune*, October 2–3, 1993; Goltz, "The Hidden Russian Hand"; Elizabeth Fuller, "Russia's Diplomatic Offensive in the Transcaucasus," *RFE/RL Research Report*, Vol. 2, No. 39 (October 1, 1993), pp. 30–34; and Fiona Hill and Pamela Jewett, "Back in the USSR: Russia's Intervention in the Internal Affairs of the Former Soviet Republics and the Implications for United States Policy Toward Russia," Strengthening Democratic Institutions Project, Kennedy School of Government, Harvard University, January 1994.

strike out on their own autonomous paths have been rendered less independent and more compliant. Indeed, some believe that Russia's response to the independent policies of these states was to foment strife and conflict, partly with the intention of bringing them to heel but partly to send a message to other FSU states about the limits of Russia's tolerance; in this argument, by punishing some for their "wayward" behavior, Russia deters others.[44]

PEACEKEEPING OR INTERVENTION? In a strategy of domination, Russian peacekeeping amounts to Russian intervention — even if some international mandate, whether UN, CSCE, or CIS, provides a fig leaf of legitimacy. But even Russia's efforts to obtain international sanction for present and future peacekeeping missions have seemed rather transparently to be aimed at gaining license for a special unilateral role in FSU peacekeeping — a role justified largely in terms of the need to guarantee Russian security.[45] Russia has asserted both a responsibility and a right to intervene in conflicts in the FSU, and the unilateralist tendencies in Russia's approach to peacekeeping are reflected in Russian military doctrine: local conflicts along Russia's borders are identified as one of the primary threats to the new Russian state, and military intervention is seen as justified and necessary if Russian interests are thought to be jeopardized in any way.[46]

Indeed, the doctrine announced by Minister of Defense Pavel Grachev in November 1993 claimed a right of intervention and emphasized mobile intervention forces.[47] Russia's embrace of the peacekeeping role within the FSU coexists with a rationale for unilateral intervention. It is hardly

---

44. See, for example, Goltz, "The Hidden Russian Hand," p. 97.

45. See Theresa Hitchens, "Russians Rile NATO Over Peacekeeping," *Defense News*, July 19–25, 1993, p. 1.

46. See, for example, John W.R. Lepingwell, "Restructuring the Russian Military," *RFE/RL Research Report*, Vol. 2, No. 25 (June 18, 1993), p. 18; and Vladimir Petrovskiy, "What Form Will Russia's Military Doctrine Take?" *Rossiyskiye Vesti*, October 26, 1993 (In FBIS-SOV-93-208, October 29, 1993, pp. 42–43).

47. See Sneider, "New Russian Doctrine Raises Western Suspicions," pp. 1, 34; and Michael Gordon, "As its World View Narrows, Russia Seeks a New Mission," *New York Times*, November 29, 1993. Defense Minister Grachev's press conference announcing the new doctrine, and additional commentary, is available in "Grachev, Other Officials Comment on New Military Doctrine," FBIS-SOV-93-212, November 4, 1993, pp. 34–43.

surprising that at least some of Russia's FSU neighbors view this with distress.

INTERNATIONAL INSTITUTIONS OR INSTRUMENTS OF INFLUENCE? In a strategy of domination, Russia can seek to tie other FSU states into institutional relationships that reflect Russia's preponderant weight. Initially, for example, the CIS was regarded by some Russians as a looser version of the USSR, thereby providing a mechanism for continued control by Moscow. This vision of the CIS has proven infeasible given the desire for autonomy of other FSU states. But incarnations of the CIS far short of the "loose USSR" model can serve as an instrument of Russian influence. Indeed, the fear of this result makes a number of CIS members reluctant about any moves toward tighter integration. For Ukraine, for example, the CIS is "nothing more than a way station in Russia's attempt to reestablish a Russian-dominated empire."[48]

Such fears are fueled by indications that Russia aims for predominance rather than equal collaboration. In CIS discussions about giving institutional expression to the Collective Security Treaty, for example, many CIS members advocated emulation of the NATO model, including the subordination of any joint command to a collective CIS security council in which all would have an equal voice. Russia, however, "backed a proposal based on the old Warsaw Pact command structure that would have subordinated the CIS commander in chief directly to the Russian Defense Ministry and made him a Russian deputy defense minister."[49] In the end Russia rejected all alternative proposals for CIS command arrangements and by June 1993 preferred dissolution of the CIS Joint Command to compromise. This suggests that Russia is primarily interested in institutional arrangements that would enshrine its primacy, and that it has little enthusiasm for arrangements that fail to do so. Similarly, in the economic realm, Russia's approach to the creation of CIS institutions has often appeared to allocate all discretion to itself and derogate the others to the position of mere followers.

---

48. Roman Solchanyk, "The Ukrainian-Russian Summit: Problems and Prospects," *RFE/RL Research Report*, Vol 2, No. 27 (July 2, 1993), p. 27. See also Roman Solchanyk, "Ukraine and the CIS: A Troubled Relationship," *RFE/RL Research Report*, Vol. 2, No. 7 (February 12, 1993), pp. 23–27.

49. Stephen Foye, "End of CIS Command Heralds New Russian Defense Policy?" *RFE/RL Research Report* (Vol. 2, No. 27), July 2, 1993, p. 46.

INTERDEPENDENCE OR DEPENDENCE? Another potent lever in a strategy of domination is Russia's indispensable role in the economy of the FSU. What is characterized as interdependence is actually dependence for many FSU states. The economic vulnerability of most of the FSU provides ample opportunity for Russia to exercise its dominance: Russia's "banks provide credits that run at least six economies, its resources fuel the system of intertwined and interdependent factories throughout the fifteen former republics, and its policy makers set the tone for virtually everything else."[50] Many of the newly independent republics have little choice but to accept Moscow's economic help and policies, no matter what the implications for their independence.

There are indications that Moscow has manipulated its economic advantages in order to pressure other FSU states. For example, Ukraine is enormously dependent on Russia for supplies of oil, gas, and nuclear fuel, and is financially deeply indebted to Russia as a result of previous deliveries of energy. These facts make Kiev very vulnerable to Russian pressure, since a decision by Moscow to withhold energy deliveries would devastate the Ukrainian economy. Russia has recurrently reduced energy exports to Ukraine well below agreed levels,[51] and appears to have explicitly linked the energy and debt issues to Ukrainian concessions on other issues.

ETHNIC RUSSIANS: HOSTAGES OR ASSETS? In a strategy of domination, Russians abroad represent not only an interest to be protected, but an asset to be exploited: they provide an ever-present rationale for Russian involvement in the affairs of the FSU and an all-purpose legitimization for an assertive policy.[52] Their mistreatment, real or alleged, can justify Russian criticism and threats. The presence of ethnic Russians in the FSU can provide grounds for putting or keeping Russian forces there, or slowing their withdrawal. It can limit the freedom of action in other FSU states; for example, "Kiev has been forced to slow down its 'return to Europe' and has been unable to adopt radical economic reforms because

---

50. Jon Auerbach, "Russia Tightening its Grip on Former Republics," *Boston Globe*, December 6, 1993.

51. See, for example, Vadym Frunze, "Oil and Gas in Ukraine May Disappear," *Lvov Post-Postup*, October 7, 1993 (FBIS-SOV-93-202, October 21, 1993, p. 52).

52. See, for example, Lough, "Defining Russia's Relations with Neighboring States," p. 59.

of fear of what the reaction would be in eastern Ukraine."[53] FSU states with geographic concentrations of Russians are vulnerable to separatist threats or challenges — as is true in both Ukraine and Estonia. And Russia has reserved the right to intervene militarily on behalf of the ethnic Russians in the FSU. Thus, ethnic Russians in the near abroad could be another potent lever in the hands of Moscow — and are so regarded by other FSU states.[54]

In sum, Russia is well positioned to pursue a strategy of domination should it choose to do so; there is evidence that this tendency is not absent from Russia's behavior.

Russia's Geostrategic Problem

Some states are blessed with relatively unchallenging geostrategic positions: states with few or weak neighbors, easily defended borders, distance or water insulating them from major threats, or geostrategic insignificance. Russia's geography provides it with the basis for great power, but confers none of the security blessings enjoyed by some other states. Rather, its vast size, lengthy borders, and strategically important location present Moscow with a chronic and always potentially daunting security predicament.

RUSSIA'S SECURITY PREDICAMENT
At least three factors account for Russia's security predicament.

RELATIVE POWER IN EURASIA. Russia is ringed by relatively powerful states, from Japan in the far east to Germany and Ukraine in Europe. Seven of Russia's neighbors or near-neighbors — China, Germany, Iran, Japan, Korea, Turkey, and Ukraine — are large enough to be substantial players on the international scene, even if only in a regional context in

---

53. Andrew Wilson, "The Growing Challenge to Kiev from the Donbas," *RFE/RL Research Report*, Vol. 2, No. 33 (August 20, 1993), p. 8. See also Susan Stewart, "Ukraine's Policy Toward its Minorities," *RFE/RL Research Report*, Vol. 2, No. 36 (September 10, 1993), pp. 57–58.

54. See, for example, Douglas Jehl, "Ukraine: A Nuclear Power, but Untested Loyalties," *New York Times*, December 2, 1993.

some cases, and to be potent rivals or adversaries in the event of troubled relations with Russia.[55]

None of these states, save China, possess the vast natural resources and the long-term economic potential of Russia. But in the near term, Russia's acute economic problems mean that for some time it will operate with an economic power base that is estimated to be little more than one-third larger than South Korea's. The Japanese and German economies are substantially larger than Russia's.

Especially significant for Russia has been the extraordinary takeoff of the Chinese economy in recent years. China may already have the second or third largest economy in the world after the United States, and even the lower estimates of Chinese economic performance suggest that it has surpassed Russia in gross economic output; it has also proven far more effective than Russia at penetrating the international marketplace, appears to have been successful at implementing economic reform, and has achieved extremely high rates of economic growth. Unless China too experiences some large-scale internal crisis that disrupts its political order and economic performance, it seems likely that Russia will never again exceed China as an economic power, and it will have to grow accustomed to sharing several thousand kilometers of border with the emerging Eurasian powerhouse.[56] This may well come to be the single most important factor shaping Russian national security interests.

These considerations are significant for several reasons. First, economic strength is one of the foundations of national power. Indeed, it is frequently suggested that in the post–Cold War era, economics has become the decisive arena of international competition, that this is an age of "geo-economics." Russia clearly starts out with a weak competitive position compared to most of its larger neighbors.

---

55. See Central Intelligence Agency, *The World Factbook, 1993–1994* (Washington, D.C.: Brassey's [US], 1993); and Institute for Strategic Studies, *The Military Balance, 1993–1994* (Washington, D.C.: Brassey's [US], 1993).

56. On China's rapidly growing power, see Kenneth N. Waltz, "The Emerging Structure of International Politics," *International Security*, Vol. 18, No. 2 (Fall 1993), p. 68. See also Gerald Segal, "The Coming Confrontation of China and Japan?" *World Policy Journal*, Vol. 10, No. 2 (Summer 1993), p. 27; and Nicholas D. Kristof, "The Rise of China," *Foreign Affairs*, Volume 72, No. 5 (November/December 1993), pp. 59–74.

Second, even small differentials in economic performance can accumulate to fundamentally alter the international distribution of power.[57] Relatively poor performance over a long period can cause a state to slide from the first rank of powers in the international system. Russia must not only halt its present economic decline, but grow at rates that equal or exceed those of its Eurasian economic "competitors" if it is not to lag ever further behind.

Third, there is a direct connection between the economic performance of states and their ability to generate military power.[58] Hence, Russia's economic problems and constraints are significant factors in its security situation.

For these reasons, correcting Russia's present economic problems and maximizing its economic performance over the long term is crucially important to its national security. This is of course a matter of domestic politics and internal organization. But according priority to economic development to avoid a severe deterioration in Russia's international power position can also have significant implications for its external policies; clearly Russia should pursue those external policies that are most likely to facilitate economic progress and success, and avoid policies that may impede economic development.

Still, even a vigorous Russian economy could not hope to keep pace with all the powers arrayed beyond its frontiers. While some level of economic success is necessary to prevent Russia's decline and to strengthen its comparative position, this will not be sufficient to offset all the potential challenges to Russian security. The extent of Russia's security problems will depend heavily not only on the strength of its neighbors, but also on the extent to which they are hostile to Russia. Apart from the Cold War, Russia historically has been able to find major allies and to avoid isolation and encirclement. Except when dealing with implacable foes, this is a factor that Russia can influence by its choice of policies and strategies.

SUSPICIOUS NEIGHBORS, HOSTILE COALITIONS AND THE PROBLEM OF ENCIRCLEMENT. The risk is that Russia's neighbors will form coalitions

---

57. Differential economic growth rates are identified in the Western literature as one of the basic sources of change in the international balance of power. See, for example, Robert Gilpin, *War and Change in World Politics* (Cambridge: Cambridge University Press, 1981).

58. See Paul Kennedy, *The Rise and Fall of the Great Powers: Economic Change and Military Conflict from 1500–2000* (New York: Random House, 1987), p. xxii.

against it. In the worst case, encirclement, Moscow will find itself ringed by powerful states, all formally or implicitly aligned against it. During the Cold War, the Soviet Union confronted a massive coalition that included all the other industrial powers of Eurasia, plus the United States and Canada. By strenuous (and self-destructive) exertions, the USSR held its own in terms of mobilized military power, but by most other criteria of power, it was heavily overmatched by the opposing coalition.[59] Russia has an obvious strong interest in avoiding a similar fate.

However, it will be difficult for Russia to completely escape this problem. First, most, if not all, of the neighboring or nearby states that lived under the czarist or Soviet yoke are suspicious of Moscow's intentions; they will not soon lose their uneasiness about living next to the imperial power that once dominated them. Second, the large power disparity between Russia and its smaller neighbors may cause even the more powerful of Russia's neighbors to worry about taking on Moscow alone. If they fear Moscow, such states will be strongly motivated to find allies who can help to negate Russian power. Third, within Russia, there are advocates of imperial policies whose views fuel the fears of neighboring states; Russia's neighbors will be acutely sensitive to the existence of such opinions, even if they are shared only by a small minority. Fourth, Russian involvement (especially military involvement) on its periphery, however benignly intended, is sure to provoke concern on the part of many neighboring states. Evidence of malign Russian intentions, however ambiguous, will produce incentives for neighboring nations to balance Russian power.

Finally, the size and character of Russia's military will be disturbing to its neighbors. Because of the number and capabilities of its potential adversaries, Russia will be driven to possess a large military. Its enormous perimeter will mandate that its forces be highly mobile, which will cause them to look offensive to worried neighbors even if Moscow's intentions are defensive. Thus, for Russia, what Western scholars have termed the "security dilemma" (the propensity for the defensive preparations of one state to look threatening to its neighbors or rivals) will be acute.

In short, many of Russia's neighbors will have, or will perceive, reason to coalesce against it. What will matter most is the orientation of the largest and most powerful states, especially Japan, China, Germany, and the United States; many of Russia's FSU neighbors are relatively weak and

---

59. See, for example, Stephen M. Walt, "Alliance Formation and the Balance of World Power," *International Security*, Vol. 9, No. 4 (Spring 1985), p. 35.

much more vulnerable to Moscow than Russia is to them, even if they do attempt to ally against it. Moreover, some of its neighbors may fear others more than they fear Russia, in which case Moscow may be the ally of choice. Similarly, some of the FSU states may be so at odds with one another, or so torn internally, that Russia is regarded as a desirable ally or necessary protector.

Still, a number of Russia's neighbors to the west, for example, including former Warsaw Pact members in East-Central Europe as well as Ukraine and the Baltic states, are eager to join NATO or to otherwise gain security guarantees from the West, provoking worries in Moscow of isolation.[60] There have been proposals for a Black Sea–Baltic Confederation along Russia's western border, proposals clearly motivated by a desire to build coalitions against Russian power.[61] Similarly, Russia's activist policy in Central Asia is provoked in part by fear that an Islamic group, with links possibly to Iran or Turkey, might emerge on its southern border.[62] If Russia is unwise or unlucky, it may have to deal with a series of anti-Russian alignments around its periphery.

It is therefore a very strong national security interest of Russia to avoid isolation and to minimize the likelihood and extent of hostile coalitions. This will require Russia's leaders to recognize the danger that Russia's own behavior may provoke the hostile coalitions that are so inimical to its security. It is widely believed in the West that the security policies of the USSR had this effect, and that its enormous security burden was at least somewhat of its own making.[63]

MULTIPLE THEATERS, SIMULTANEOUS CONTINGENCIES. Moscow is inevitably a player in four different regional security alignments: Europe, the Caucasus, Central Asia, and the Far East.[64] Russia must not only play simultaneously in four different balance of power games, but it must

---

60. See "Russian Foreign Policy: Your Policy or Mine?" *Economist*, October 30, 1993, pp. 57–58.

61. See Andrei Kortunov, "Strategic Relations Between the Former Soviet Republics," Backgrounder No. 892, The Heritage Foundation, April 17, 1992.

62. See, for example, Shashenkov, *Security Issues of the Ex-Soviet Central Asian Republics*, pp. 53–54.

63. See Stephen Sestanovich, "US Policy Toward the Soviet Union, 1970–1990: The Impact of China," in Robert S. Ross, ed., *China, The United States, and the Soviet Union: Tripolarity and Policy Making in the Cold War* (Armonk, NY: M.E. Sharpe, 1993), p. 144.

64. See Kortunov, "Strategic Relations Between the Former Soviet Republics," p. 6.

contend with the fact that conflict is a possibility in all four. However, even a troubled Russia is so much more powerful than almost all of its immediate neighbors (save China) that bilateral conflicts with them do not pose a serious challenge for Moscow; apart from war with China or other major powers, it is probably only simultaneous contingencies that can cause serious problems for Russia.

The reality of multiple theaters imposes a need to establish priorities among contingencies. Thus, Russia faces major tradeoffs in assessing its security requirements: Should its forces give priority to west, south or east? Should they be geared toward less likely but more demanding scenarios involving major regional war (with Ukraine or China, for example) or should they give priority to less demanding but more likely scenarios involving the FSU? Clearly, such questions do not require "either-or" answers, but the balance struck will determine Russia's capabilities and options if Russia's security policy is tested by war.

Whatever choices are made, Russian defense planners will need to take into account the possibility that Russia will need to fight in more than one theater at the same time. Inevitably, the threat of simultaneous contingencies increases military requirements; Russia will find large forces and a substantial defense effort to be necessary.

Russia can try to minimize the risk of simultaneous contingencies through diplomacy, but its defense planners will almost certainly be unwilling to rely on such reassurances. A major reason is the fear that having forces sufficient for only one large contingency invites others to attack should Russia be involved in a conflict. This logic should operate powerfully in the case of Russia.

For Moscow, the problem is compounded by geography: its border is extremely long, much of it is not protected by easily defensible terrain, and long stretches of it are remote and not easily reachable due to poor infrastructure. Russia cannot solve its simultaneous contingency problem simply by fortifying and manning the entirety of its border. Thus, Russia's vast size implies large and highly mobile forces — a fact reflected in Russian military thinking.[65] The dilemma for Russia will be to develop offensive mobile forces sufficient for its defense needs without provoking fear and balancing behavior on the part of its neighbors.

On the other hand, Russia is still a powerful state, few of its immediate neighbors possess the capacity to credibly threaten its sovereignty,

---

65. See John W.R. Lepingwell, "Restructuring the Russian Military," pp. 20–22.

many of its neighbors have difficulty getting along with one another, and, as noted below, it possesses a nuclear deterrent. Thus, while Russia faces a challenging security predicament, it is hardly without assets and options in dealing with its security challenges, particularly if it can avoid counterproductive policies that provoke hostile coalitions or isolate Russia among the great powers.

RUSSIA'S STRATEGIC OPTIONS
How well Russia copes with its security predicament will depend heavily on how it situates itself with respect to the other major states in the international system. It has three broad options.

ADOPT A "GO-IT-ALONE" STRATEGY. In view of Russia's eagerness to forge ties with the Western industrial democracies, it may seem unlikely that it would revert to an autarkic or isolationist strategy. But should it become deeply disillusioned by the West, or convinced that the West seeks a weak and submissive Russia, or should ardent nationalists come to rule in Moscow, such a policy might become attractive.

A "go-it-alone" strategy would focus on reestablishing Moscow's dominance in the former Soviet Union and on restoring Russia's military strength. It would revert to internal solutions to its economic difficulties — an approach arguably facilitated by binding the FSU together again. This strategy does not imply complete isolation from international trade and investment, although economic relations with the West would undoubtedly be significantly inhibited.

The obvious advantage of this approach is that it allows Russia to pursue, unfettered by any external constraints, its maximum interests in the former Soviet Union. Insofar as this region constitutes a vital interest for Russia, this is a major plus. But the cost is potentially very high: it may be difficult and costly to restore and maintain the empire; and Russia will be much more isolated, raising risks of hostile coalitions and encirclement and denying Russia the benefits of integration with the industrial world.

PLAY GREAT POWER "BALANCE OF POWER" GAMES. Because Moscow is no longer the isolated pole in a bipolar security confrontation, it has, for the first time since the interwar period, the opportunity to engage in great power games. Because Moscow has a strong interest in avoiding or minimizing its isolation, it may be powerfully motivated to play such games. Several factors give Russia room to maneuver.

First, the United States and Russia are no longer automatically deep rivals and bitter enemies. Indeed, with the retreat of Russian power from Central Europe, Moscow's retrenchment from the Third World, and the bilateral moves to dampen the nuclear danger, their vital interests are no longer inevitably in direct collision. To be sure, their interests will not always be identical, particularly in places like Central Asia and the Caucasus, but in these places the United States is not a major player, does not want to be a major player, and does not have much at stake even if it does find aspects of Russian policy to be uncongenial. Nor are their relations necessarily always going to be close, hopes for "strategic partnership" notwithstanding. But the United States has ceased to be Russia's central security problem, friendly relations are possible, and collaboration with Washington has become an option for Moscow.

Second, China may be emerging as the new primary geostrategic threat in Eurasia. Its breathtaking economic growth, rapid accumulation of military power, and apparently revisionist foreign policy are provoking wide concern. While this is troubling for Russia in view of its long border and historical enmity with China, Beijing's emergence as a potential geostrategic threat has two beneficial consequences for Russia: other states will have an interest in balancing against and containing Chinese power;[66] and Russia may position itself as a significant asset in efforts to contain China. This could give it common cause with states such as Japan and the United States (much as the Soviet Union and India found common interest in their mutual concern about China). Indeed, it could make Russia a critical player in a new geopolitical configuration oriented around containing Chinese power.[67] Alternatively, Moscow could position itself as the flexible party in a triangle including Washington and Beijing. However Russia orients itself, the rise of China, combined with Russia's ability to engage with the United States, gives Russia some diplomatic elbow room in the new era.

Third, a similar dynamic may operate, if less powerfully, in relation to Germany. In historical terms, Russia has been the traditional counterweight to a powerful Germany in Europe. The unease caused in Western

---

66. See, for example, Richard K. Betts, "Wealth, Power, and Instability: East Asia and the United States after the Cold War," *International Security*, Vol. 18, No. 3 (Winter 1993–1994), pp. 34–77.

67. See, for example, Boris Zanegin, "Beyond the Geopolitical Crash of the 1990s: Towards a New Equilibrium," *Security Dialogue*, Vol. 23, No. 4 (1992), pp. 16–19; and Lukin, "Our Security Predicament," p. 70.

Europe by German unification and by Germany's disproportionate weight may cause Russia to be an attractive partner to other West European states.[68] French President François Mitterand's sudden trip to the USSR in the aftermath of German unification is a pointed reminder of this possibility. Conversely, Germany and Russia have periodically found it mutually beneficial to befriend one another.

In short, engaging in fluid great power diplomacy provides Russia with the possibility of avoiding isolation, preventing encirclement, promoting integration with industrial powers, and gaining formal or implicit help in dealing with some of Russia's geostrategic problems.

OMNIDIRECTIONAL FRIENDLINESS. Balance-of-power diplomacy involves choosing friends and gaining allies, but also aligning against states and making enemies. An alternative strategy would seek to avoid creating enemies and to maximize Russia's engagement with the outside world by attempting to forge good relations with as many of the other major powers as possible. In this logic, for example, rather than position itself as an anti-Chinese asset, Russia would seek good relations with China. In fact, this is what Russia has so far sought to do, via such devices as arms sales, military cooperation agreements, summit meetings, and so on.[69] Similarly, far from exploiting potential divisions in the West, Russia could pursue a "G-8" approach, seeking inclusion in the exclusive club of major industrial powers.

However, the viability of this strategy depends on the reaction of and the relations among the other powers. It may not be available or durable.

NUCLEAR DETERRENCE. Alone among all the Soviet successor states, Russia inherited a coherent nuclear deterrent capability. This means it can seek to address some of its security problems by means of deterrent threats. Obviously, this is how it would try to negate nuclear threats from any source. Russia also has an incentive to try to rely upon nuclear deterrence to neutralize conventional threats to its security, particularly in view of its economic constraints and the transitional disorder in its conventional military forces. This emphasis can be seen clearly in Russia's new military

---

68. See Lukin, "Our Security Predicament," p. 71.

69. See, for example, Patrick Tyler, "Russia and China Sign a Military Agreement," *New York Times*, November 10, 1993. On China's receptivity to these initiatives, see Xuewu Gu, "China's Policy Towards Russia," *Aussenpolitik*, Vol. 44, No. 3 (March 1993), pp. 288–297.

doctrine, which abandons Moscow's pledge of no first use, and pointedly implies that it will use nuclear weapons in the defense of Russia.

Chapter 6
Russia and the Western Post-Soviet Republics

Dmitri A. Fadeyev
Vladimir Razuvayev

Russia's relations with the Western former Soviet republics — Belarus, Estonia, Latvia, Lithuania, Moldova and Ukraine — occupy a special place in Russian foreign policy. These countries are well aware of each other's strong and weak points, their economies are largely interdependent, their political leaders usually know each other fairly well, and their summit meetings are free of such petty but annoying trifles as language barriers that can be overcome only with the help of interpreters. Yet, in no other region has Russia encountered such difficulties.

The heavy burden of the past along with manifestations of Russian nationalism often outweigh rational political considerations. The lack of diplomatic experience in the non-Russian former Soviet republics gives rise to numerous misunderstandings and exacerbates conflicts. The drive for immediate and complete political independence from Moscow goes hand in hand with categorical demands for special economic privileges. Most of these factors are transitional and will disappear; but for now, they seriously complicate Russia's relations with its neighbors.

This paper concentrates on Russia's relations with Ukraine, Belarus, and the Baltic states.[1] Ukraine and the Baltics are the most important for Western policy, while Belarus, of all the former Soviet republics, shows the greatest indications of reverting to Soviet-era patterns of dependency.

---

1. Moldova is discussed briefly in several other chapters.

Dmitri A. Fadeyev is a Senior Research Fellow at the Institute of Europe at the Russian Academy of Sciences. In 1993–1994 he was a Muskie Fellow at the Institute for Policy Studies at Johns Hopkins University.

Vladimir V. Razuvayev is the Director of the Center for International Relations at the Institute of Europe at the Russian Academy of Sciences. Previously, he has served as advisor to the Soviet Ministry of Foreign Affairs.

Russia and Ukraine

Of all the nations of the former USSR, the Russian and Ukrainian peoples are most closely linked with one another by common origin, history, culture, religion, and language. Ukraine became part of a unified Russian state in 1654, and was, in fact, the cradle of Russian statehood. The split with Ukraine resulted in the loss of territory that had been in Russia's domain for several centuries and is still home to 11.4 million Russians, comprising 22 percent of Ukraine's population. Thus, Ukraine's secession from its union with Russia has dealt a serious psychological blow to Russia that will continue to influence the nature of Russo-Ukrainian relationships for years to come.

The disintegration of the USSR and the establishment of an independent Ukrainian state have created new threats to Russia's national security.[2] Russia may become geopolitically isolated from Western Europe if Ukraine enters some form of buffer union with Eastern European countries or with the Western republics of the former USSR. With the possible exception of potential threats to communication lines that link Russia with Western Europe, Russia's economic and military interests have been most damaged by the loss of all its strategic Black Sea ports, except Novorossisk.

Russia is also threatened by the nuclear weapons stationed in Ukraine, especially after Ukraine declared itself the owner of these arms in July 1993, in violation of earlier international commitments. Policy makers are not so much concerned that Ukraine will use these nuclear weapons against Russia, but that these weapons could be launched without proper authorization, or cause an environmental disaster near Russia's borders.

Joint Russian and American pressure on Ukraine should force Kiev to agree to the provisions of the trilateral agreement, which entails the full nuclear disarmament of Ukraine over the coming decade. But political turmoil in Ukraine could render the Ukrainian government incapable of implementing all aspects of the agreement. In addition, the fragmentation of Ukraine and the emergence of new independent successor states would further complicate the issue.

The common Russo-Ukrainian economic environment is a thing of the past. Cross-national ties between many enterprises have been broken,

---

2. For details on new threats to Russia's national security stemming from geopolitical factors, see Vladimir Razuvayev, *The Geopolitics of the Post-Soviet Space* (Moscow: Institute of Europe, Russian Academy of Sciences, 1993).

damaging the economic wellbeing of entire industries in both countries. Russia's defense industry, which had the highest degree of integration, has felt the brunt of this rupture. The disintegration of the common Russian-Ukrainian economic system has also severely destabilized the Ukrainian economy, introducing the possibility of its collapse. Kiev has no economic policy, and cannot manage or direct ongoing economic processes. This creates the danger of an economic slump too severe for the fragile Ukrainian state to endure, and could trigger major social eruptions. Massive emigration of Ukrainian citizens to Russia would pose a serious threat to Russia's own economic and social balance. At the beginning of 1994, some 300,000 to 400,000 Ukrainian citizens already held part-time jobs in Russia.[3]

Russo-Ukrainian relations began to deteriorate immediately following the adoption of the December 1991 decision on the USSR's dissolution. In the first two years of Ukraine's independent existence, the greatest problems were the status of the nuclear weapons stationed on Ukrainian territory, the territorial dispute over Crimea, and questions relating to the division of the ex-USSR's debts and property. These problems still give rise to heated debates, but the core issue is that both Russia and Ukraine have so far failed to clearly define their foreign policies toward one another. Legislative and executive bodies in both Russia and Ukraine make uncoordinated, often contradictory, foreign policy decisions. In addition, specific policy moves are subject to a great deal of political jockeying, and are frequently motivated by foreign and domestic policy considerations beyond the issue at hand. As a result, policy decisions often do not reflect a rational consideration of the interests involved.

STRATEGIES FOR RUSSIA

While Russia's foreign policy toward Ukraine is not clearly defined, it is possible to delineate five strategies that reflect Russian interests.

First, Russia could follow a policy that would lead toward Russia's reunification with Ukraine under a single state. This option is peddled by various neo-Communist and so-called patriotic organizations that refuse to acknowledge the legality of the December 1991 accords disbanding the USSR, as well as by the bureaucratic structures hit hardest by the USSR's disintegration. This model is also supported by radical populist move-

---

3. See *Rossiskaya Gazeta*, January 12, 1994.

ments such as Vladimir Zhirinovsky's Liberal Democratic Party, and some segments of the Russian population that are nostalgic for the Soviet Union.

This option is the most dangerous: it can be implemented only by methods such as placing harsh economic pressure on Ukraine to sap its economy, and by force of arms. The violent and destructive essence of this scenario makes it the least probable, yet it cannot be ruled out, especially given the recent increase in number and virulence of the extremist platforms in Russia's domestic politics. It may even become likely if the democratization process is curbed, allowing a nationalist dictatorship to come to power in Russia.

A second and equally extreme option would be for Russia to effect a neo-isolationist policy toward Ukraine. This could occur if Russia were to focus exclusively on its domestic problems, and refuse to strengthen the multilateral institutions shared by the post-Soviet states. It would involve establishing a non-transparent or almost non-transparent border between Russia and Ukraine with tough customs and visa regimes. Such a strategy would fence off Russia's economy from the more rapidly collapsing Ukrainian economy, and enable Russia to more easily carry out its economic and political reforms. This option is supported by some of Russia's radical democrats, many nationalists, and some étatist-minded economists.

If Russia embarks on that course, it will face serious difficulties. First, it will require a great deal of time and effort to make Russia's economy self-sufficient — some thirty years and huge amounts of so-far unavailable capital investments, according to expert estimates.[4] Second, Russia would lose the opportunity to influence Ukrainian policies, and would be compelled to recognize Ukraine's nuclear status. Third, it would shatter friendship and kinship ties between millions of Russians and Ukrainians, likely boosting nationalist and revenge-seeking sentiments in Russia, and undermining stability in the region.[5]

A third option would be for Russia to establish economic and strategic blocs with other post-Soviet republics, without Ukrainian participation. In terms of its likely negative consequences, this strategy is similar to the previous one. In addition, it could prod Ukraine to launch a more vigorous search for ways to set up blocs with the countries of Eastern and

---

4. *Nezavisimaya Gazeta*, April 1, 1993.

5. There are around 13 million mixed families living in Russia and Ukraine. For example, some 82 percent of the population in Russia's Belgorod Region bordering on Ukraine have close relatives in Ukraine. *Isvestiya*, July 1, 1993.

Central Europe. But this strategy is not likely to be adopted, if only because Russia's probable allies in a military-political and economic union (Armenia, Belarus, Kazakhstan, Tajikistan, and perhaps Kirgizstan and Uzbekistan) would hardly wish to make that union overtly anti-Ukrainian.

Under a fourth option, Russia would maintain "special relations" with Ukraine, helping Ukraine stabilize its domestic situation and bolstering the position of its leadership, in exchange for concessions on economic, Black Sea Fleet, and Crimean issues. Ukrainian leaders are trying to prod their Russian counterparts into effecting precisely this strategy, but for several reasons, it is hardly practicable. First, it is too costly for Russia. It calls for subsidizing the Ukrainian economy via the establishment of preferential prices for Russian products, above all oil and gas, and granting direct loans to Ukraine. Russian International Monetary Fund (IMF) Director K. Kagalovsky has estimated that in 1992, Russia's "special relations" with various former Soviet republics cost it $17 billion, which is equal to 21.7 percent of its GDP.[6] If such an outflow of resources continues, it will hamper Russia's ability to restructure its own economy. Second, without successful concrete measures to move Ukraine toward a transition to a market economy, direct subsidies will only prolong, rather than prevent, the death throes of Ukraine's economic system. Finally, the implementation of this policy could probably only be sporadic and unstable, given Ukraine's sensitivity toward perceived violations of its sovereignty by Russia.

A fifth option would entail the reintegration of the post-Soviet economic and security space based upon fundamentally new principles.[7] With regard to Ukraine, this strategy would mean Russian recognition of the inviolability of the existing borders, agreement to assist in the restructuring of the Ukrainian economy along market lines, and the restoration and promotion of cooperative ties between Russian and Ukrainian enterprises and geographic regions. Such a situation would be untenable without the simultaneous observance of the principle of equivalent exchange, that is, commercial payments according to world

---

6. *Isvestiya*, June 2, 1993. The lion's share of these subsidies went to Ukraine, which is the chief importer of Russian oil and gas among the former Soviet republics. In 1992 alone, shipments to Ukraine accounted for over 44 percent of the oil and more than 72 percent of the natural gas exported by Russia to the former republics. *Finansovye Izvestiya*, May 15-21, 1993.

7. This policy was suggested in 1992 by the authors of "Strategy for Russia: A foreign policy concept," *Nezavisimaya Gazeta*, August 19, 1992.

market prices. As part of this strategy, Russia would seek to set up a common economic, cultural, and humanitarian environment and conclude a military alliance with Ukraine. The chief obstacle to effecting this strategy would be the unwillingness of large segments of the Russian political elite to support it. Likewise, some influential nationalist movements in Ukraine feel that close ties with Russia may jeopardize prospects for building an independent Ukrainian state.

THE FUTURE OF RUSSIAN-UKRAINIAN RELATIONS

The combination of strategic options chosen by Russia and Ukraine might give rise to differing outcomes for the countries' bilateral relations. The quality and nature of Russo-Ukrainian relations will have a considerable if not decisive impact on the entire structure of international relations in the post-Soviet space and in East-Central Europe. Which strategy is ultimately implemented will largely hinge on the degree to which other former Soviet republics, primarily Belarus and Kazakhstan, are prepared to develop closer relations with Russia, and whether or not the Eastern and Central European states agree to form close economic, political and military ties with Ukraine. The rapprochement of these countries with Ukraine may be limited, first and foremost, by differences in their economic potential. Eastern and Central European countries have made far greater headway toward establishing functioning market economies. In addition, they fear Ukraine's military might and prefer to distance themselves from it strategically.

The isolation of Ukraine is unlikely as a long-term outcome; Ukraine would be economically, politically, and militarily unable to bear the brunt of antagonistic relations with a Russia-dominated bloc of states. Nonetheless, far fewer obstacles impede Russia from setting up blocs with the post-Soviet states than stand in the way of Ukraine forming alliances with the Central European states. Even if no serious strategic conflicts were to arise, the likely consequences of a Russian policy to isolate Ukraine would be the collapse of the Ukrainian economy, the growth of separatism, and the intensification of political and social tensions in the country, all of which could lead to Ukraine's disintegration.

There are influential champions of the reintegration of Ukraine into the Russian economic and security sphere in both Russia and Ukraine, and their ranks have considerably swelled as the weakening of bilateral ties has sent the living standards in both countries plummeting. Reintegration could be effected in various forms; the two extremes are the restoration of a single state, and the establishment of confederative-type relations, whereby both countries are politically independent, have their own armed forces and national currencies, but cooperate in tackling strategic problems and maintain open and mutually interacting economies.

Neither of these models would work in the current economic, political, and strategic context. The idea of restoring a single state in any form — centralized, federative or confederative — has few active followers in Ukraine today. In the medium term, it is also unlikely that Russia and Ukraine will establish confederative relations because this requires developed market economies and stable political regimes in both countries, as well as a high level of mutual trust. Ukraine especially cannot yet meet any of these preconditions.

Political and leadership developments in Crimea may, under certain conditions, become a decisive factor in the future of Russian-Ukrainian relations. Yurii Meshkov, the president of Crimea, has demonstrated a tendency to play off opposing forces in Russia and Ukraine in order to further Crimean interests. Extremist forces in both Russia and Ukraine could use this situation as a pretext for the worsening of bilateral relations between them. At the same time, new developments in Crimea could force Moscow and Kiev to find joint solutions to the Crimea's problems.

The prospects for reintegration via multilateral CIS mechanisms are dimmed by the stand taken by Ukraine's nationalist movements and political elites. In their view, reintegration should be limited to the economic field and embodied in continued Russian subsidies to Ukraine, along with the preservation of ties between the state-owned enterprises of both countries. They see the restoration of the level of economic ties that existed in the former Soviet Union as a way to solve the current crisis and subsequently re-orient Ukraine's economy toward the Western market.

Thus, the growing role played by spontaneous local and regional contacts and interactions in the political life of Russia and Ukraine offers the most probable path to reintegration. Managers of large enterprises have taken the initiative in restoring bilateral economic ties. The gradual entrenchment of rudimentary forms of market relations in the economies of both Russia and Ukraine has promoted the transformation of state-owned enterprises into joint-stock companies.[8] Businessmen and managers of state-owned enterprises are exerting the strongest pressure on the governments of both countries, through their demand for the removal of

---

8. To preserve ties with their partners in the former Soviet republics, these companies buy up, often on a reciprocal basis, the stock issued by the enterprises of their partners in order to set up international companies together.

political and legislative obstacles to economic cooperation. As there is no viable alternative to the development of a market economy in either Russia or Ukraine, it is highly probable that in the medium term, grassroots reintegration will continue, despite the resistance of heavyweight political forces.

How Russo-Ukrainian relations evolve depends upon the progress or regression of economic reforms, the changing balance of strength between Russia and Ukraine, which political currents are strongest in each country, and what stand the post-Soviet states and the Central European and Western nations take with regard to the Russo-Ukrainian rivalry. The consolidation of a climate of cooperation in the economic, cultural and military environment of Russia and Ukraine would be most favorable for the long-term national security interests of both countries, and also for global security. This scenario would help to end Russia's divided nation complex, which could be a source of tension for decades to come. And without reintegration with Russia, Ukraine will hardly be able to overcome in the foreseeable future the economic, political and social problems that have threatened its existence as a sovereign state.

The West has perhaps lost its chance to act as a mediator in Russian-Ukrainian relations. First, Western governments have demonstrated their unwillingness to be involved seriously in the international affairs in the post-Soviet space. Second, the influence of the Atlanticist factions in Russian and Ukrainian policy circles has declined dramatically since 1992.

The Baltic Challenge

From a global perspective, Russia's relations with the Baltic states would seem to be of little interest.[9] Geographically, Estonia, Latvia and Lithuania are only tiny islands in the enormous Slavonic sea of Belarus, Poland and Russia. The Baltic states have little impact on the world economy and pose no military threat to their neighbors. However, Russia's relations with the three small Baltic states are important to its foreign policy because Russo-Baltic relations are becoming a symbol and a barometer of the struggle of the former Soviet republics to gain full independence from Russia.[10] If

---

9. Here and elsewhere the term "Baltic states" refers to Estonia, Latvia and Lithuania.
10. See *New York Times*, "Latvia's Worry: What to Do with All its Russians," March 1, 1994, p. 3.

Russia takes a strong hand against the Baltic states using any number of pretexts, this might send shock waves throughout the entire former Soviet security space, Eastern Europe, and the West. The key issue for the international community is whether or not Russia is capable of applying the methods typical of liberal democracies in the post-Soviet security space.

Following the August 1991 events and the recognition by the world community of Estonia, Latvia and Lithuania as independent states, the latter had every opportunity not only to establish good-neighborly relations with the Russian Federation, but also to make use of Moscow's benevolent support to step up their policy of integration into the European community. Following the USSR's final disintegration in December 1991, Moscow could reasonably believe that the Baltic dimension of its foreign policy would be free of conflict; Russia did not think that any grave contradictions could arise in its relations with the Baltic states.[11]

Moscow was prepared to reckon with the interests of the Baltic states, having agreed, for instance, to an accelerated pullout of its troops from Estonia, Latvia and Lithuania. It is no wonder then that Russia's leadership was taken aback by the strategy pursued by the Baltic states in 1991–1993 of constantly building up tensions between them. The Baltic countries' efforts to distance themselves from Russia, and to use the "Russian threat" as a gimmick to enlist the aid of Western democracies, gave the Russian opposition a trump card in its struggle with the Yeltsin regime. It provided a fine pretext for accusing the Russian government of betraying the interests of Baltic-based Russians and for simultaneously fanning anti-Baltic sentiments in Russia. Russia's democrats also started to reconsider their attitude toward Estonia, Latvia and Lithuania. In their view, the realities of the post-Soviet period made it necessary to give up attempts to build Russia's relations with the ethno-nationalistic post-Soviet republics based on models typical of Western liberal democracies. As a result, any possibility of preserving a pro-Baltic lobby in Moscow in the near future was lost.

Estonia's and Latvia's territorial claims to the Russian Federation became a serious headache for Moscow. On January 22, 1992, Latvia's Supreme Soviet declared unlawful the "annexation of the Abrene District" (now the Pytalovo District of Russia's Pskov Region) by the USSR in 1944.

---

11. See, for example, Vladimir Razuvayev, *The Russian Federation and the Near Abroad: Geopolitical Problems* (Moscow, Institute of Information on Social Sciences, 1993), pp. 9, 16–24.

On recent Latvian maps, the Pytalovo District is shown as part of the Latvian Republic. Under Article 122 of Estonia's Constitution, the republic's eastern border runs along the line established by the February 1920 Tartu Treaty — that is, Estonia claims the lands on the right bank of the Narva River in the Leningrad Region as well as part of the territory of the Pechora District of Russia's Pskov Region, which in the past was part of Estonia's Petseri District.

Moscow's position is that the Russian Federation's borders are the administrative borders of the ex-RSFSR (Russian Soviet Federated Socialist Republic), which predated the collapse of the USSR. Russia's experts stress that the 1944 territorial additions to Russia were made to bring its borders into line with the administrative borders of the former Russian Empire and with the settlement patterns of ethnic groups. They also say that for the Bolshevik Government, the 1920 border change was largely a *force majeure* measure, similar in many respects to the subsequent return of these territories to Russia by Latvia and Estonia in 1944.

The status of the Russian and Russian-speaking population in Estonia and Latvia will apparently remain a conflict-laden issue for some time.[12] In Estonia and Latvia, non-indigenous ethnic groups make up some 48 percent of the total population (Russians account for 34 percent) and are concentrated in big cities.[13] The Riga and Tallinn authorities have steered toward a gradual reduction of their number of Russian and Russian-speaking residents, seeing them as a threat to their national interests. The chief of Latvia's National Minorities Department said, for instance, that optimally the number of such people in his country should not exceed 25 percent of the total population, and that the authorities should do their best to achieve that proportion. The ethnic Russians residing in Estonia and Latvia regard the infringements on their rights as a means of squeezing them out of these republics.

---

12. *Izvestiya*, March 3, 1992. Significantly, in Lithuania, where Russians make up a small percentage of the total population, the law has extremely liberal provisions for granting Lithuanian citizenship. Russia's relations with Lithuania have not been as tense as Russo-Estonian or Russo-Latvian relations. As many as 37 percent of the Russians living in Lithuania speak the local language, the highest share for all the post-Soviet republics (cf. 22 percent in Latvia and 15 percent in Estonia).

13. In Latvia, for instance, there are no mono-ethnic districts where the indigenous population comprises over 90 percent of the population. In Estonia, non-Estonians account for some 40 percent of the total population and live compactly in the country's northeast.

The Russian leadership explicitly condemns the tendency adopted in the Baltic countries to term their Russian-speaking residents, many of whom have lived there for generations, as "occupants." For example, Boris Yeltsin has warned Latvia's leaders that under international law and practice, Russia has the right to take economic, political and other measures to protect the legitimate rights of the downtrodden citizens of Russian stock.[14] On July 23, 1993, Russian Foreign Minister Andrei Kozyrev branded Estonia's government policy as "apartheid" aimed at future ethnic purges. The next day, the Russian Federation stressed that "given the natural desire of the Russian-speaking population to defend itself against brazen discrimination, Russia will not be able to remain an indifferent onlooker."[15] The human rights policy pursued by the Baltic leaders has led even non-nationalist-minded Russian experts to believe that a moratorium on the withdrawal of Russian troops from Estonia and Latvia would be a stronger statement than all the homilies to the effect that apartheid is immoral.

RUSSIAN STRATEGIES IN THE BALTICS

Russia has three basic foreign policy options with regard to the national minorities issue in Estonia and Latvia. First, Russia can continue its present policy, which is to appeal to the world community. Unfortunately, this policy is not proving terribly effective, largely, in Moscow's view, because the West has backed down on the principle it proclaimed during the Cold War of upholding human rights, and has started to support states that pursue a policy of apartheid and ethnic purges.

Second, Russia can bring strong pressure to bear on Estonia and Latvia, relying on its own resources, and without appealing to world public opinion. However, this policy would be ineffective if the international community protects Estonia and Latvia from economic and security threats from their giant neighbor.

Third, Russia could combine the first two policies by continuing to rely primarily upon the efforts of the international community, while quietly tightening the screws on Estonia and Latvia through subtle unilateral policy instruments and incentives. The success of this approach would hinge first upon the timing of Russia's effort, and second upon a combination of political and geostrategic factors, including the willingness

---

14. *Nezavisimaya Gazeta*, January 23, 1993.
15. *Rossiskaya Gazeta*, June 25, 1993.

of the international community to become actively involved in the Baltic issue, the relative strength of the Russian and Baltic economies, and the level of volatility in Russia's policy-making process. Since these factors cannot be forecast with an adequate measure of confidence, it is not possible to assess reliably the potential effectiveness of the third option.

In any event, while Moscow will choose a policy, the assessment of its effectiveness will be made largely by the West. For instance, active support by Western governments of the Baltic states against Russia might be seen as a sign of the ineffectiveness of Russia's diplomacy toward the Baltics. On the other hand, if the West signals its dissatisfaction with the Baltic states' handling of their national minorities problems, it will be regarded in Moscow as a minor coup for Russian foreign policy.

Over the longer term, Russian security interests in the Baltic region will play a primary role in Russo-Baltic relations. After Russia's military pullout from the area is complete, its principal security interest will be to prevent the consolidation of any military-political bloc to which Russia is not a party from extending its sphere of operations to the territory of the Baltic states. This includes, but is not limited to, the expansion of NATO to the Baltics if Russia is not also included.

THE FUTURE OF RUSSIAN-BALTIC RELATIONS
Two extreme scenarios illustrate the range of possible outcomes for Russia's relations with the Baltic states. Under the first scenario, new politico-military tensions will arise between Russia and the West. This will result in the establishment of a strategic *cordon sanitaire* around Russia, with the Baltic states as active participants. Under this scenario, the Russian population in the northeastern part of Estonia and in Latvia would rebel against the governments of these states, creating the possibility that Russian troops will intervene in the conflict, which could then escalate into a full-scale war. This scenario may become a reality only if a dictatorial nationalist or communist regime supported by the bulk of the Russian population comes to power in Moscow. Although extremely unlikely in the short or medium term, this prospect should not be excluded altogether.

Under the second scenario, Russia and the West will, for the most part, manage to preserve the cooperative tone of their relations. In Russo-Baltic relations, both sides will proceed in their actions from a rational interpretation of their mutual strategic interests, rather than from ideological or nationalist considerations. This would require that Baltic statesmen drop the frequent evocations of the need to contain "the Russian threat," and that Moscow not object to the Scandinavian orientation of the Baltic states. Such a policy might lead to close cooperation on urgent local problems, such as Baltic Sea ecological issues.

Neither of these extreme scenarios are practicable; Russo-Baltic relationships will probably fluctuate between these two poles, and new factors will likely intervene. For example, while the Baltic states are trying to preserve a common stance toward Russia, differences in the policies of Estonia, Latvia, and Lithuania toward Russia are striking. The once united Baltic front could split into two parts, with Lithuania on one side and Estonia and Latvia on the other. Then Russia would likely play up — as it is already beginning to do — the differences between the Baltic states for its own benefit; a careful policy might secure changes in Estonia's or Latvia's approach to the national minorities issue, ensuring the eventual capitulation of the remaining country. Such a policy can only be successful if the West refrains from supporting the politics of ethnicity in whatever form and context they appear.

Russia and Belarus

Russia's relations with Belarus have been marked by relative stability; the political isolation of Belarussian nationalist forces facilitated the early recognition and acknowledgment of geopolitical realities and interests by both countries.

Several factors are of particular importance to Belarus. The first is the unconditional dependence of Belarussian industry upon Russian deliveries of raw materials, energy resources and spare parts. Under Soviet rule, Belarus's industrial sector acted as an assembly workshop for the entire USSR. Following the collapse of the USSR, this workshop became fully dependent upon economic contracts with Russia.[16]

Second, during 1993 it became clear that the prospects for Belarus to become integrated into Western European institutions such as the European Community, the European Council, and NATO in the foreseeable future are slim. These objectives have, for the most part, been relegated to the realm of political pipe-dreams. In the beginning of 1994, Belarus again began to align a large number of its policies with those of

---

16. According to expert estimates, Belarus can independently produce a mere 4 percent of its total economic output. In 1992, 87 percent of Belarus's finished products used supplies from Russia. *Rossiskaya Gazeta*, July 8, 1993.

Russia, a distinct change from its former desire to be more independent of Moscow. The most dramatic example is the March 1994 agreement that Belarus will merge its monetary structures with those of Russia, and again become dependent on the Russian Central Bank for its monetary policy and currency.

Russia too has a number of interests that will continue to affect its policies toward Minsk. The strategic leanings of Belarus have traditionally been of key importance to Russian strategic security. Both the Napoleonic invasion of 1812 and the 1941 German attack on Russia advanced through the territory of present-day Belarus, making it a particularly sensitive area along Russia's western border.

Russia is highly dependent upon good relations with Belarus for its economic security. The lion's share of the goods shipped between Russia and Western Europe travel on railroads that run through Belarussian territory. These lines of transport are especially significant to Russia because it has lost many of its Baltic port facilities to the north of Belarus, and economic relations with Ukraine to the south are volatile. Additionally, cooperation between Russian and Belarussian commodity producers is important to Russia's economy.

Problems stemming from economic relations feature boldly in Russo-Belarussian relations, and the issue of energy is the most important.[14] Russia's switch to charging world energy prices in 1992 posed a number of very serious problems for Belarus. Belarus cannot afford to pay world prices for Russian oil, while Russia cannot afford to sell oil to Belarus cheaper than to its own consumers. Belarus has been forced to reduce its oil purchases from Russia, buying approximately 8.5 million fewer tons from January–July 1993 than originally contracted.

Another large problem is the stagnation of the Belarussian defense industry, which in 1992 employed around 324,000 people. Minsk is planning to convert its military-industrial complex to civilian production, and reduce its workforce to 20–25 percent of its current level. The future of the situation in the Belarussian military industrial complex depends largely upon Russia, its biggest customer. Of late, however, the volume of Russian defense orders has consistently dwindled. The issue of learning to synchronize its process of industrial restructuring with that of Russia is, therefore, of fundamental importance to Belarus.

---

14. Belarussian refineries could process 42 million tons of oil a year, but their annual oil production is a mere 2 million tons.

Some issues that have been touchy in Russia's relations with other former Soviet republics have not caused difficulties in its relations with Belarus. The nuclear disarmament of Belarus has caused no special problems. At present, only mobile SS-25 missiles remain in Belarus, and these are scheduled to be destroyed before the end of the century. Despite pressure from the nationalist opposition, Minsk maintains that it handles all issues related to the nuclear weapons deployed in the republic bilaterally with Moscow.[15] In addition, the national minorities problem has never been on the agenda of Russo-Belarussian political talks.

If continued over the long term, Belarus's focus on Western Europe could create major problems in Russo-Belarussian relations. The synchronous entry of both nations into European political and strategic institutions and organizations would be the best option for all involved, but is very unlikely in the near future and only somewhat less unlikely in the medium term. In the long term, tensions may arise between the two countries only if Belarus enters a bloc of Central European states acting as a new *cordon sanitaire* around Russia. This is unlikely; Russia will be able to spot any moves in that direction in good time, and will not hesitate to forestall trends in Belarus's foreign policy that may be detrimental to its vital interests.

Conclusion

At first glance, relations between Russia and the Western republics seem chaotic and utterly disorganized. The foreign policy strategies of these countries are either ill-conceived or almost totally absent. Signed treaties are not being observed, and many of these states have yet to develop a coordinated policy with regard to their neighbors. In many cases, the actions of governments and their parliaments are uncoordinated. This fully applies to Russia's relations with its Western post-Soviet neighbors.

Yet the miscalculations of political leaders and the disparity in diplomatic moves are a transient phenomenon. These relations are ultimately governed by the national interests of each of the players.

The notion of the post-Soviet economic and security space will continue to exist in the foreseeable future despite all the differences between the states and the intention of the Baltic states to "escape to

---

15. *Nezavisimaya Gazeta*, October 14, 1992.

Europe." The post-Soviet states are bound to each other by common history, mutual economic interests, and conflicts and disputes that will not be settled overnight. They share a set of common problems, including environmental crises, economic dependence upon one another, and technological backwardness. Finally, Russia is, once again, asserting its role as a conduit between all the former Soviet republics.

Chapter 7 | Dmitri Vydrin
Ukraine and Russia

Russian-Ukrainian relations will have enormous import not only for the future of these two countries, but also for Europe and the future of the international security system. Even ignoring Russia's considerable nuclear might, the Russian Federation has the largest army in the world. Ukraine, in spite of its negligible nuclear status, has the second largest army in Europe. Any armed conflict between these two countries would entail tremendous losses and would send economic and political shock waves throughout Europe.

Thus, any serious decline in relations between Russia and Ukraine is not merely a matter of their own internal affairs, but a serious threat to the stability of Europe and the development of the post–Cold War international security structure. The following pages analyze the most important dynamic elements of these relations, and attempt to sketch likely scenarios for the development of relations between these two countries in both the short- and the long-term future.

Ukrainian Apprehensions

Since gaining its independence, Ukraine's stance toward Russia has fluctuated. Russian-Ukrainian relations plunged in August 1991, when Yeltsin's press secretary declared that the Russian Federation had a right to territorial claims against Ukraine. Since then, apprehensions about Russian designs on Ukrainian territory have been a powerful destabilizing force in relations between these two states. For example, Vladimir Zhirinovsky has become a symbol and the embodiment of all such fears in Ukraine, and has caused considerable unrest in the parliament. This has caused Ukrainian sentiments to lean even more strongly toward seeking security guarantees from outside powers, especially the United States.

Dmitri Vydrin is the Director of the Ukrainian International Institute on Global and Regional Security. From 1992 to 1993 he was the head of the International Security Department at the Institute of World Economics and International Relations.

Any statement or action by a political force or institution that could be regarded as a territorial claim against Ukraine causes an immediate and intense reaction. Specific instances where Russia has attempted to flex its muscle include debates over the status of Crimea and Sevastopol, and the activities of Russian politicians agitating in Eastern Ukraine — where a large number of Russians live — for succession and rejoining Russia.[1] The Ukrainian mass media typically retaliates against such overtures from Russia with a wave of anti-Moscow rhetoric, including vociferations against Russia's "imperialist policies," and "expansionist tendencies." This, in turn, makes the public restless and uneasy, and such moods are promptly exploited by political parties in Ukraine. It will be a very long time before even the most solid and reliable economic and cultural links between the two countries will be immune to the careless handling of political rhetoric. If cooperative relations are established, they could be swiftly destroyed by an off-hand Russian remark on territorial claims.

The stability and integrity of Ukraine is also threatened by secessionist rumblings in various regions that may feel disadvantaged by prevalent economic and political conditions. The fragmentation of the Ukrainian state brought about by the increasing regionalization of Ukraine's political and economic situation represents perhaps the greatest potential threat to Ukraine's vital national interests. There are two general drives behind separatist movements in Ukraine: the first is socio-political, and the second is purely economic. The socio-political drive may be likened to the situation in Quebec, where there is a strong antipathy in one region against domination by the center and other regions. In the east and the south of Ukraine, such a social-political basis for separatism is a force of at least moderate relevance.

The more compelling drive behind separatist movements in Ukraine is economic. If the economic situation in Russia improves significantly,

---

1. The "hand of Moscow" is always painstakingly sought behind any claims of political or economic independence in Crimea or the Donbas; such claims could be dismissed as psychotic if no historical basis for them existed. Ukraine has been repeatedly carved up (the most recent example of this was in the pre–World War II situation when the western section of Ukraine was under the control of Poland, and the Austro-Hungarian Empire before that). This bitter experience has made the country extremely sensitive to even the slightest signs of secessionism being inspired from abroad. The only way for Russia to avoid accusations of fanning the fire of separatism is for Moscow to exercise the utmost caution in publicly assessing developments in Ukraine, and for it to scrupulously refrain from any statements that could be interpreted as attempts to interfere in internal Ukrainian affairs. Unfortunately, it would seem that Russian caution is rarely applied in this sphere.

and the situation in Ukraine fails to improve or becomes worse, this could lead to movements in some regions to break off from Ukraine and to join with the stronger economic force.

Tensions between Russia and Ukraine are visible in foreign policy as well. As an independent state, Ukraine has found itself in competition with Russia for Western credits, investments, and political support. Ukrainian policy makers have not failed to notice Russia's competitive edge in this domain, and Russia's selfish use of its advantages is cause for anxiety in Ukrainian policy circles. Apprehensions only increase when Ukraine is excluded from international summit meetings attended by Russia at which political and economic issues common to all of the former Soviet republics are discussed.

Russia rarely bothers to inform Ukraine of the details and nature of major international agreements in which it participates, and which may directly affect Ukraine's interests. For example, Russia agreed to export uranium to the European Community, which aroused suspicions in Ukraine that Russia was planning to sell the uranium it obtained from battlefield nuclear weapons removed from Ukraine, for which Ukraine received no tangible compensation.

Greater openness in Russian (and Ukrainian) policy within a defined legal framework would help to remove the source of such anxieties. The joint participation of both Russia and Ukraine in major international organizations would also serve this purpose. However, Russian diplomacy is in fact inclined toward greater secrecy, and appears to discard the potential to work together politically and strategically with Ukraine in the diplomatic sphere. Russia has, on occasion, made political and economic decisions that directly affected Ukrainian internal affairs without informing Kiev. For example, the money exchange of 1993, when the Russian government issued new bank notes, declaring the old ones invalid, cost many Ukrainian citizens a great deal. While there are now fewer and fewer opportunities for Russia to wield this kind of influence on internal Ukrainian policy because such ties are almost gone, the attitude which such actions imply is still alive and well.

Another source of conflict between Ukraine and Russia has been the division of the spoils of the defunct Soviet empire. Ukraine is apprehensive that it will find itself severely short-changed. A brawl over the most important and prestigious parts of the Soviet inheritance — nuclear weapons and the Black Sea Fleet — set the tone for Russian-Ukrainian relations during 1992–1993. The not unreasonable suspicion that Russia will attempt to take the choicest scraps from the remains of the Soviet structure is likely to remain a source of contention between the two, at least over the short term.

Unlike in many other former Soviet republics, official discrimination against the Russian minority in Ukraine is unlikely to be a factor in Russian-Ukrainian relations. One of Ukraine's founding provisions was that the relationship of the individual to the state was to be determined by citizenship, not ethnicity as under the Soviet system. However, Kiev no longer has the power to protect the rights of its minorities, due to the regionalization of such matters. The Russian government now purports to speak politically for all Russian-speaking persons residing outside the Russian Federation on the territory formerly encompassed by the Soviet Union. Roman Szporluk has pointed to this phenomenon as a serious destabilizing factor for the consolidation of the concept of statehood and citizenship in Ukraine.[2] Depending upon future developments in Ukraine's internal situation, such claims may fortify separatist and secessionist tendencies.

Finally, Russia's mass media have also contributed to the antagonistic tone of Ukrainian-Russian relations. Immediately following Ukrainian independence, the Russian media assumed a scornful and mocking stance. It was, for example, not uncommon for Ukrainian words to be used derisively and in a ridiculous manner in reports gloating over Ukraine's difficulties in the economic and political spheres. Even the reports of the otherwise politically balanced Mayak Radio occasionally asked needlessly insulting questions during interviews, such as "Do you think Russia may collapse economically, as Ukraine has done?" This attitude of public scorn often does more to distance Ukraine from Russia than more substantive economic and inter-governmental disagreements.

Prospects for a Ukrainian-Russian Partnership

The centrifugal trends that burst the seams of the Soviet Union have not yet fully played themselves out. In this volatile political and economic environment, solid cooperation between Ukraine and Russia is unlikely. Theoretically, though, it is possible to envision some powerful external factors driving Ukraine and Russia closer together. For now the only

---

2. See, for example, "One Year After the Collapse of the USSR: A Panel of Specialists," *Post-Soviet Affairs*, Vol. 8, No. 4 (1992), pp. 324–325.

source of threats to the integrity of Ukraine, other than Russia, is Romania.

Both Russia and Ukraine are confronted with the threat of economic neo-colonialism from the West and of being regarded primarily as sources of raw materials, sites for the production and dumping of toxic materials, and sources of cheap labor using primitive technologies. At the same time both countries are being blocked from penetrating the more sophisticated spheres of the Western market. The West's approach is more likely to stimulate economic competition between Russia and Ukraine than cooperation.

The expansion of Islamic extremism may turn out to be a common threat to the Slavic world which will stimulate the restoration of strong economic, political, and security ties among its members. A popular idea among Ukrainian political elites is that external enemies are needed in order to consolidate national solidarity. If cooperation is going to characterize relations between Russia and Ukraine, the Muslim world is an obvious target, all the more so since anti-Muslim rhetoric is well received in the West, especially in the United States. Similarly, joint actions to combat both terrorism and the trafficking of narcotics, which are already occurring between Ukrainian and Russian intelligence services, might serve as a uniting factor.

A much more likely scenario for the cooperative development of Ukrainian-Russian economic and security relations is gradual integration with a minimum of bombast. This could occur due to the inevitable decentralization and regionalization of political and economic life in both countries during 1994–1995. Increasing cooperation between private trade, financial, and industrial enterprises will help to stimulate the Ukrainian-Russian integration process. In fact, at least two-thirds of the large private capital amassed in Ukraine over the past several years was raised from deals involving Ukrainian metals and Russian oil products.[3] This capital is concentrated mainly in the eastern regions of Ukraine. One result of growing economic collaboration will be the increased politicization of the general business environment and steady pressure from the emerging middle and business classes for smooth Ukrainian-Russian relations. This process has already begun through direct contracts between Russian and Ukrainian regions, and if continued within a framework of official

---

3. Russia is a primary consumer of Ukrainian sugar, meat, and butter, spending over a billion dollars a year on these purchases.

interstate relations could become a powerful factor promoting long-term cooperation between the two countries.

Military-Nuclear Factor

Ukraine has given the policy world a new and unique strategic phenomenon with which to cope: after its ratification of START I and its refusal to ratify the Nuclear Non-Proliferation Treaty, Ukraine became the only nuclear state in the world without any nuclear capability. The more sophisticated among Ukrainian politicians know that strategic weapons without corresponding infrastructures or operational controls are not in the least effective in a purely military-strategic sense: they have a different use for these weapons. Missiles kept by Ukraine will elevate its strategic significance and international prestige, and may, when the time is ripe, be calmly swapped for external security guarantees and aid packages. It would appear that Ukraine prefers a reputation as a famous scandal-maker to that of an obscure citizen of the international community.

The role and status of nuclear arms has become the main focus of Western policy toward the development of Russian-Ukrainian relations. The West, particularly the United States, has been instrumental in keeping this issue at the forefront of Russian-Ukrainian foreign policy and security debates, and has to an extent defined the acceptable terms for the resolution of this issue.

Ukraine currently has no capability to deliver a nuclear strike against Russia. Those missiles still deployed on Ukrainian soil are inter-continental ballistic missiles incapable of striking Moscow, and Ukraine does not possess the codes needed to launch them. Ukraine has approximately twenty planes capable of delivering smaller nuclear weapons, but Russia's western airspace is defended by a number of highly sophisticated systems. The greatest threat to Russia from Ukraine's nuclear weapons lies in the potential for them to be mishandled while still on Ukrainian soil. Ukraine lacks the technology and the facilities to maintain these weapons even over the medium term.

Ukraine's insistence on keeping its nuclear status is indeed difficult to comprehend unless one remembers the political significance that the army, military hardware, and nuclear weapons had in the USSR. Nuclear weapons played a fundamentally different role in Western societies than in the Soviet Union. For the more pragmatic Western world, nuclear weapons were first and foremost weapons, whereas in the Soviet Union they were to be venerated; they were the most direct and immediate image identified with civil pride, courage, and dignity. The Soviet "nuclear priests" insisted that their riches be displayed on the holiday parade grounds so that the public could come to see them, prayerfully and trembling, in a well-orchestrated spectacle of civil ecstasy. Thus for Ukraine, the possession of a large army and especially of nuclear arms is a natural source of pride and national self-esteem.

The United States gave Ukraine a chance to make a nominally honorable exit from an increasingly untenable situation in the form of the January 1994 Trilateral Agreement. American officials conducted a number of meetings with Russian leaders, in which, without the participation of Ukraine, the future of its nuclear status was decided.[4] It is likely that Ukraine was brought in only in the final phases of the process after the framework and many of the details were finalized. Under the provisions of the Trilateral Agreement Ukraine will receive a minimum of $175 million from the United States in order to pay for the procedures of removing and dismantling its weapons, as well as to store the remains and to restore the environment on and around former missile sites. Russia will give Ukraine uranium for its civil nuclear power program, which is already in shortage in Ukraine.[5]

On the one hand Ukraine has reason to be satisfied with the outcome of the Trilateral Agreement: when fully implemented, it will formalize the role of the United States as a guarantor of Ukraine's national security, and provide explicit recognition from the Russian Federation of the territorial integrity of Ukraine.[6] On the other hand, the means by which it was brought about were less than ideal for a country attempting to carve a creditable place in international politics. Russia is unlikely to be terribly disturbed by delays in the official approval of the Trilateral Agreement because these weapons are in any case being removed from Ukraine to Russia on technical grounds.[7] Ukraine does not have the means to dismantle nuclear weapons and weapons systems and to dispose of the

---

4. This, it is strongly suspected, was one of the main reasons for the 1993 Clinton-Yeltsin summit in Vancouver.

5. See John W. R. Lepingwell, "Ukrainian Parliament Removes Start-1 Conditions," *RFE/RL Research Report*, Vol. 3, No. 8 (February 25, 1994), p. 38.

6. Ibid., p. 37.

7. Many of the warheads and weapons systems in Ukraine are nearing the end of their design life and pose serious environmental threats.

remains safely, making it largely dependent upon the continued goodwill of Russia in this respect.

Continuous political turmoil in Russia cannot help but cause concern in Ukraine, where decision makers wonder what will happen if the conservative, pro-imperialist forces suddenly gain control in Russia. Many Ukrainian policy makers and citizens see nuclear weapons as a means of self-preservation in the face of threats from Russian conservatives to restore the empire or to regain control over specific pieces of Ukrainian territory, such as Crimea and the Donbas. In addition, the perseverance and impatience of the United States in its goal of removing all nuclear arms from Ukraine has been interpreted in Ukraine as a rude nudge in a direction that may ultimately go against its real interests, and as interference in internal Ukrainian affairs. This is the source of a great deal of political tension since officially the United States is regarded as the primary guarantor of Ukrainian security and territorial integrity — a status further reinforced by the Trilateral Agreement. Ukraine's sensitivity will leave a scar on both Ukrainian-Russian and Ukrainian-American relations, and will cause Ukraine to be more suspicious and antagonistic in its relations with the great powers.

The Economic Factor

Although the West has succeeded in focusing much attention on the nuclear aspect of Russian-Ukrainian relations, a much more important issue is economic relations. Ukraine's economy and social situation in many ways resembles that of wartime. The inflation rate has reached 100 percent per month. The average wage is around ten dollars a month, compared to around one hundred dollars in Russia, and production is still falling about 20–30 percent per year. Many Ukrainian politicians and journalists refer to Russian "economic pressure and blackmail" when speaking of "the threat from the North."

Both Ukrainian and Russian officials harbor lists of grievances that they consider the causes for their current economic relations. The basic economic claims of Ukraine against Russia are that: 1) Russia sells raw materials to Ukraine (primarily oil, natural gas, lumber, electricity, and light metals) at prices which are too high, thus contributing to the destruction of the Ukrainian economy; 2) Russia grabbed the lion's share of the riches from the former Soviet Union, including gold and diamond reserves and all of the property belonging to the Soviet Union abroad; 3)

Russia is luring away Ukraine's most highly qualified scientists, engineers, and technical experts from key spheres of production, including atomic energy, transportation, and others; 4) Russia is trying to buy property on the territory of Ukraine in order to make parts of Ukraine first economically, and eventually politically dependent upon Russia; and 5) Russia is inaccurate and dishonest in its payment for deliveries and owes a large debt to Ukrainian enterprises.

Russia's basic economic complaints against Ukraine are that: 1) Ukraine engages in the re-export of cheap Russian materials such as oil and light metal to outside markets for a sizable profit; 2) Ukraine has not agreed to cooperate with Russia in its export policy, with the result that the prices which Russia is able to get on the world market for many types of products, including chemicals, metals, and arms, are lower than they would otherwise be; 3) Ukraine is conducting an isolationist economic policy and is interfering with the natural reintegration process, specifically with the formation of joint ventures, inter-state firms, and financial-industrial groups; and 4) Ukraine is inaccurate and dishonest in its payment for Russian deliveries and owes an enormous debt to Russian enterprises.

The emotional tension, mutual recriminations, subjectivity and incompetence of policy makers and experts on both sides make it impossible to decide who is right and who is wrong. Probably both sides are to blame. Ukrainian policy makers have attempted to implement a model of relations in which Ukraine is politically fully independent from Russia, but counts upon receiving materials and resources from Russia at discounted prices. Russian policy makers have taken a long time to begin to take the independence of Ukraine seriously, and have tried to establish an unequal model of relations by relegating Ukraine to the role of a satellite or a diplomatic junior partner.

Experience has shown that there exists a natural limit below which economic relations between Ukraine and Russia will not fall; neither country is currently capable of delivering an economic blow to the other that is strong enough to bring the crisis to the point at which armed conflict is a possibility. It would seem that the policy makers of both countries overestimated their own abilities in this respect. The most effective Ukrainian response to economic pressure from Russia turned out to be a form of partisan economic warfare against Russian lines of transport and communication with Europe. The threat to shut off oil and gas pipelines and systems for the transport of electrical power as well as railroads and highways running through Ukraine was enough to cause Russia to behave somewhat more carefully toward its southern neighbor.

However, Ukraine was unsuccessful in forming an economic *cordon sanitaire* between Russia and Europe from the Black Sea to the Baltic due to the existence of Belarus as an openly pro-Russian link. In the near future, Russia will try to move its lines of transport and communication with Western Europe to Belarus. In addition, Russian experts on foreign trade were extremely quick to restructure Russia's economic affairs and trade deals with European countries to guard against such blockages in the future. By 1994, Ukraine's ability to isolate Russia from Europe had all but disappeared. Consequently, those Ukrainian policy makers who continue to threaten Russia's transport lines cannot provoke Russia into action that would affect global security.

From the other side, Russia likewise overestimated its ability to exert economic pressure on Ukraine. The Russian government does not have exclusive ability to manipulate the supply of resources to Ukraine; the greater quantity of many commodities, such as petroleum products, that go from Russia to Ukraine are sold through private commercial channels only marginally controlled by the government. Nor can the Russian government any longer fully control prices. Some among Russia's political elite predicted that the rupture of economic ties between Russia and Ukraine would result in a sharp decline in the economic situation in Ukraine, and that this would lead to social upheaval and the strengthening of tendencies toward reintegration with Russia. A sharp decline in Ukraine's economic situation did in fact occur, but this did not spark a stormy drive toward reintegration with Russia.

This outcome may be explained by a number of factors. In Western Ukraine, the independence and the sovereignty of the Ukrainian state have a weighty, even religious significance; this region is prepared to tolerate practically any economic difficulties in order to preserve its integrity. Eastern Ukraine still lacks the fully formed institutions of civil society that could adequately transform dissatisfaction with the economic situation into political demands. It is unlikely, therefore, that economic discontent in Ukraine will translate into a general demand for economic reintegration of the two countries.

It is much more likely that further decline in the economic situation in Ukraine will contribute to the stratification of society into confrontational social classes, and the polarization of the Ukrainian state into competing political regions. This is the most likely scenario for the short term, since Ukraine's economic situation will almost certainly continue to worsen. In the course of time, Ukraine's tendency to blame Russia for the deepening of its economic crisis will subside. Even extreme russophobes have begun to understand that Ukraine's own conservative government may be more to blame for the current situation.

As long as the economic situation in both Russia and Ukraine is volatile and unfavorable, relations between the two countries will be characterized by a paucity of cooperative activities and attitudes, and a great deal of competition for markets and resources in which each attempts to undercut the interests of the other. If the economies of Russia and Ukraine continue to do poorly, the antagonistic relationship between these countries is unlikely to improve. Three scenarios illustrate how change in the economic situations of Russia and Ukraine would tell upon their political and security relations.

FIRST VARIATION

The economic crisis in Ukraine assumes catastrophic proportions, and Russia overcomes the majority of its difficulties. Under these conditions, the eastern and southern regions of Ukraine will strengthen their orientation toward Russia, and begin to demand reunification. Such a development would almost inevitably spark civil war. The western regions of Ukraine would never agree to allow unification with Russia, and, as mentioned above, are prepared to pay any price to maintain a unified Ukraine. If the situation in the country were to reach this extreme, it would trigger a massive emigration of Ukrainian citizens into Russia. The need to deal with millions, and possibly even tens of millions, of immigrants from Ukraine would have a chaotic and ruinous effect on Russia's economic situation. The option of pouring large amounts of resources into bolstering the moribund Ukrainian economy will for some time be equally untenable for Russia without some hefty political compensation from the leadership of Ukraine.

SECOND VARIATION

Ukraine is successful in making the transition out of its economic difficulties, and the reform process in Russia ends in failure. This variation would lead to the harshest possible economic, political and strategic isolation of Ukraine from Russia, and possibly provoke aggressive rumblings in Russia for the reintegration of Ukraine by force. Russian citizens would likely seek to settle in Ukraine,[8] threatening Ukrainian economic stability.

THIRD VARIATION

The process of economic reform develops roughly evenly and largely successfully in both Russia and Ukraine. This would quickly lead to the normalization of political and economic relations underpinned by the demands of representatives of private capital in both countries, including corporations and financial groups with a clear interest in the maintenance of good relations between Russia and Ukraine. This process is already underway, but progress is slow.

Thus, in spite of various extremist political opinions, the long-term national interests of neither Ukraine nor Russia would be served by the continuation of destructive economic relations between them. While even in the optimal third scenario, the two countries will compete for resources, labor markets, export markets, and economic and security partners abroad, this rivalry will be primarily economic, and will not attain an overtly political character as it would in periods of severe economic crisis.

Ukraine's Quest for New Allies

The complexity of Ukraine's political and economic relations with Russia and the uncertain prospects for their improvement over the short and medium term have spurred Ukraine to seek economic and security partners in the immediate region and beyond, but with largely disappointing results. Following the disintegration of the Soviet Union a euphoric Ukraine imagined that it would be very easy to find allies. Ukraine first tried to find economic and security partners in the West. Some experts in Ukraine were and remain convinced that Ukraine occupies a unique and crucial position in the geopolitical framework of Europe: it was imagined that once Ukraine gained its independence, Western countries would line up to enter into partnership with it.

The United States was expected to show special interest in such a partnership, as a means of balancing the influence of a united Germany in Europe. Similar considerations were expected to motivate France and Britain, and it was assumed that Germany would also be interested in

---

8. There are some seven million ethnic Ukrainians currently living in the Russian Federation.

forming such a partnership to counter U.S. influence in Europe. However, Ukraine's plan to find Western allies was unsuccessful, due to a simple lack of interest on the part of the West.

The second plan was to find security partners among Ukraine's neighboring countries. It was hoped that by establishing economic, political, and cultural links with other Eastern and Central European states, Ukraine could somehow neutralize the threat of Russian imperial revanchism. That plan too turned out to be largely wishful thinking, at least as an immediate solution, mainly due to the diversity of interests among Ukraine's neighbors, and the overtly westward orientation of political and economic policy in the countries of Eastern Europe, all of which translated into a lack of interest in cooperation with Ukraine.

On the issue of whether NATO should be expanded to include former Communist Bloc countries, Ukraine took the position of Eastern European states, because Ukraine views NATO as much less of a threat to its interests than Russia. However, Ukraine knows well the threat it faces from Russia; it is much less familiar with what it has to expect or fear from European security structures. Given the general disappointment with Western economic assistance and the unwillingness of the West to engage to solve Ukraine's very serious economic and security problems, Ukraine may, after a time, be driven back toward Russia in its need to avoid strategic isolation.

The only former Soviet republic that may be a likely ally for Ukraine is Kazakhstan. These two countries are going through a honeymoon period, and Ukraine seems to have the most in common with Kazakhstan among all of the former Soviet republics. Common problems include the issue of nuclear weapons, large Russian minorities, and difficulties in military-industrial conversion, as well as possible territorial claims by Russia. Ukraine seems to trust Kazakhstan more than it does other former Soviet republics, so Kazakhstan could potentially become an intermediary in Ukraine's relations with Russia.

Despite its efforts, Ukraine is unlikely to develop any large conglomerate of states around itself and grow into a regional superpower to counterbalance Russia. Generally speaking, the time for alliances among the ex-Soviet republics has not yet arrived. All successful economic, political, or security pacts require either a common political will or complementary national interests; in the short term, the former factor is unlikely to materialize, and the latter is a vain hope. But Ukraine has learned from its disappointments in its hopes for close economic and political ties with the

West and with East and Central Europe, and should learn to cooperate with its closer neighbors.

Ukraine is showing signs of drifting toward an authoritarian future, partly because of the country's great disappointment with the pace of immediate returns on the institution of democratic power. In Ukraine, a politically under-developed society, there was a distinct absence of basic institutional and organizational components, such as parties, movements, and political funds. The government was modeled on a division of powers, but more closely resembled a duality of powers: the president interfered freely in the affairs of the parliament, and the parliament attempted to dictate to the president. This rendered the system incapable of acting in an effective or coordinated manner.

The democratic model began to lose popular support, and the "democratic" form of government began to be associated more and more with political, social, and economic chaos. The Ukrainian people began to demand the return of a strong hand, and a political movement emerged that was prepared to channel the popular desire for law and order into authoritarian forms of government. It has become very likely that Ukraine will develop an authoritarian form of government close to dictatorship.

Conclusion

Relations between Ukraine and Russia may still get worse, as there are plenty of destabilizing factors and plenty of illusions to be shattered. Neither country can now find radically new and optimal models of partnership and mutual cooperation; this challenge is likely to be met only by future generations of policy makers less fettered by ideological considerations and more attuned to economic and security realities.

Ukraine's nuclear threat to Russia will continue to diminish as its weapons are removed to Russia for dismantlement on technical grounds. Ukraine's nuclear status will be most useful for ensuring sufficient long-term security guarantees from the West, and especially the United States. These guarantees will be all the more important to Ukraine, as it is unlikely in the short and medium term to find reliable partners among other former Soviet republics or among the countries of Eastern and Central Europe.

In the economic sphere, the most dangerous moments of the economic cold war between Russia and Ukraine have already passed. At one time these countries could have wrought enormous economic damage upon each other, but now the possibility that armed conflict will occur between these two countries due to purely economic factors is unlikely. However, Russia and Ukraine will increasingly compete for markets, in particular for arms, economic resources, labor, and foreign economic partners. Cross-border private enterprise could either promote cooperation between Ukraine and Russia, or could further irritate their relations, depending upon how it is handled.

Politically, the quality of relations between Russia and Ukraine will for the foreseeable future depend more and more upon the relations between individual leaders. If the leaders of Russia and Ukraine operate with similar interests and understanding, then relations will be good. If they do not, they are likely to be tumultuous. This is due to the failure of democratic institutions to take root in either Russia or Ukraine.

Beyond its involvement in the nuclear issue, the West can help to stabilize relations between Ukraine and Russia by aiding in the development of civil institutions in Ukraine through targeted assistance programs in democratic organization and procedures. The West can provide incentives for Russia and Ukraine to work together, rather than setting them up as competitors for aid and attention to their security problems. The Partnership for Peace represents such a possibility, as do international efforts against terrorism and the trafficking of narcotics. The main goal is to create opportunities for both countries to work together to solve common problems and to establish the institutional channels for doing so.

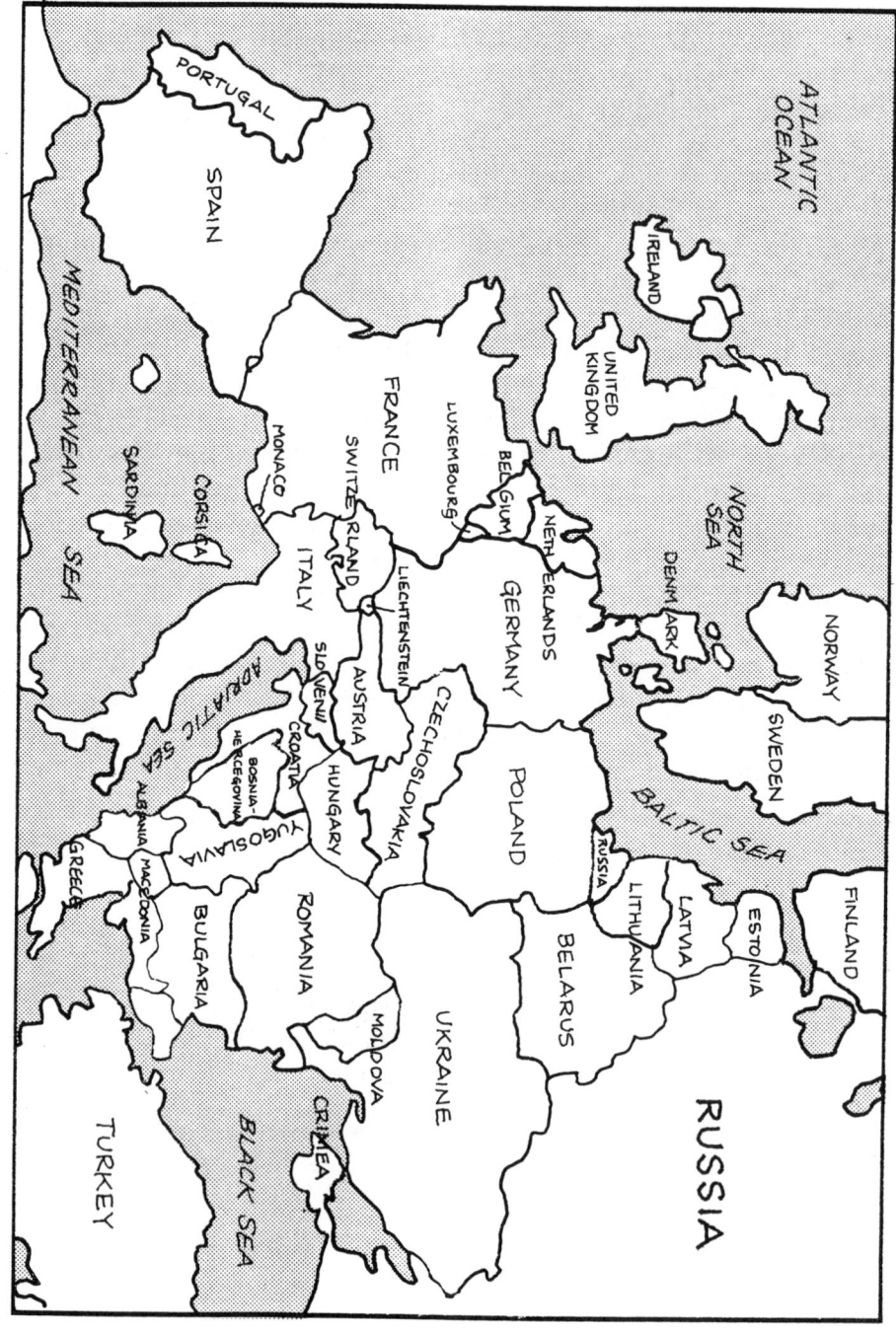

Chapter 8
Russia and Eastern Europe

Oleg T. Bogomolov

One of the greatest challenges facing Russia in its external relations is to develop a foreign policy based upon post–Cold War international political, economic, and security conditions. Russia, as the primary successor to the Soviet state, inherited much from Soviet foreign policy, especially in the sphere of arms control. But Russia now operates in a fundamentally altered geopolitical and geostrategic environment from that of the Soviet era, and its interests do not, in many respects, correspond to those of the former USSR. The new character of Russia's interests in Eastern Europe is a strong example.[1] Under the post–World War II Soviet system, Eastern Europe was regarded as a special zone of Soviet interest and influence. Russia's current approach to relations with Eastern Europe reflects its post-Soviet interests.

This chapter outlines and analyzes Russia's national security interests in Eastern Europe in a policy perspective, the foreign policy interests of East European states, and the West's interests in this region. Factors which will, over the long term, contribute to the strengthening or the weakening of these interests, as well as how Western policy might affect future Russian–East European interaction, are analyzed critically. In the concluding section, several concrete proposals for the invigoration of Russia's foreign policy toward Eastern Europe are discussed.

---

1. One would be hard put to render a strict definition as to what constitutes Eastern Europe. Geopolitically, this region is comprised of the cluster of former socialist East-Bloc countries, with the exception of the German Democratic Republic (Poland, the Czech Republic, Slovakia, Hungary, the former Yugoslavia, Bulgaria, Romania, and Albania). Some analysts, particularly in the West, also tend to regard the three former Baltic Republics of the Soviet Union — Estonia, Latvia, and Lithuania — as belonging to Eastern Europe.

Oleg T. Bogomolov is the Director of the Institute of International Economic and Political Studies at the Russian Academy of Sciences. In 1989, he was elected to the Congress of People's Deputies of the USSR, and served on the Committee for Economic Reform of the Supreme Soviet. He has served as Deputy Chairman of the International Relations Committee in the State Duma of the Russian Federation since 1993.

Russia's Interest in Eastern Europe

Russian foreign policy toward Eastern Europe as a whole and toward individual states is still being formulated, so its long-term objectives remain somewhat vague. Political and social forces in Russia have yet to reach a governing consensus regarding Russia's long-term interests in either the foreign or domestic sphere. But one thing is clear: Russia's actual foreign policy interests and the treatment of these interests by Russian politicians are seldom the same; they may, in fact, differ quite substantially. It can only be hoped that a sound assessment of Russia's long-term vital interests in the political, economic, and military spheres will find its way into current policy discourse.

Russia currently has no enemies that threaten it militarily, but it also has no allies upon which it can depend. The potential for Russia to find itself strategically isolated, unable to enter into partnerships with its neighbors and powerful friends, is perceived as a serious threat to Russia's national security. Thus the acuteness of Russia's problems in consolidating basic components of its national security are the prime motivation for Russia's desire to restore cooperative relations with the countries of Eastern Europe. Russia's unprecedented transition from a totalitarian system to a democratic one, and from a command to a market economy, has given rise to many unexpected internal developments. These now threaten its national security and long-term prospects for democratic development, and could also substantially alter Russia's foreign policy course.

Eastern Europe's current mistrust and enmity toward Russia have deep roots in the history of Russia's relations with these countries. However, this history also includes traditions of friendship, good-neighborliness, and mutually advantageous economic cooperation, but such memories have been obscured during the difficult process of social and economic transformation. In more stable and prosperous circumstances, the brighter pages of this history will again be brought to the forefront. Of course, Russia's relations with individual Eastern European countries have been varied, and thus affect the conduct of current politics differently. (Unfortunately, it is difficult to avoid generalization and to show the specifics of relations between Russia and the individual states of Eastern Europe.)

The dismantlement of communism began along with the collapse of the military-political and economic blocs set up by the Soviet Union. The disintegration of this system significantly upset the existing balance of forces in the international arena, and ushered in a period of sweeping social transformations in the region. These have brought political and social instability, acute conflicts, and new economic problems. However, if reforms take a positive turn, this would open up the prospect for a radical improvement of the political climate prevailing on the European continent.

Democratization in the social, political, and economic spheres has eliminated many ideological and institutional barriers that earlier prevented interaction and cooperation with the West. A more reliable basis for mutual trust and the settling of outstanding political and economic disputes through international law is now being formed.

While perestroika and Mikhail Gorbachev's political thinking gave the countries of Eastern Europe a long-awaited impulse for liberalization from communism, Russia has been affected by the experiences of the transition process in Eastern Europe, most particularly in the social, political, and economic spheres.[2]

The new anti-communist regimes demanded real independence and respect for the sovereignty of their countries and rejected any further encroachments from the East. Russia, itself facing difficult internal problems, lost the ability to ply its influence and force its will on the policies of these countries. Russia has accepted this new reality. The withdrawal of Russian troops from Czechoslovakia, Hungary, and Poland, as well as from Estonia, Latvia, and Lithuania, has helped to consolidate Russia's policy of promoting a genuinely equal partnership with those countries. Characteristically, signs of older stereotyped, paternalistic attitudes toward Eastern Europe on the part of Russia have not been completely eliminated.

Already during the Gorbachev era, Russia began to conduct economic relations with the countries of Eastern Europe on a contract basis, starting with Lithuania's clearing-house system, and ending with payments between these countries using hard currency. Refusals to fulfill the Eastern European demand for the supply of oil, gas, and raw materials from the

---

2. The United States and Western Europe, being aware that the countries of Central and Eastern Europe may act as models for post-communist reform and potential allies for the West, have stepped up their activities in the region. There has been a marked increase in the number of official visits and diplomatic exchanges between Eastern European countries and the West, accompanied by an inflow of aid and credits. Business activities, tourism, and cultural exchanges have also increased dramatically.

USSR occurred simultaneously with a breakdown in the purchase of Soviet finished products in Eastern Europe, partly due to consumers' reorientation toward Western markets. The exchange of official delegations between Russia and the countries of Eastern Europe was curtailed, and the practice of consulting Moscow on matters of foreign policy was terminated altogether. During this period cultivating warm relations with the United States and Western Europe became a primary focus of Soviet foreign policy as well.

After the failure of the August 1991 coup attempt, Russia began again to devote more attention to Eastern Europe, but the drop in trade and cultural exchanges between Russia and Eastern Europe continued, and there was no meaningful improvement in political and economic relations. There are delays in the conclusion and ratification of treaties and agreements between Russia and these countries, including an agreement to settle the issue of Russia's outstanding debts to them.

Russia has displayed great interest in promoting mutual trust in its relations with the Eastern European states, and it has consistently worked to remove the basis for all grievances. Of course, these efforts at the diplomatic level do not always immediately find expression in practice, but over the long term, if underpinned by concrete examples of economic, political, and strategic cooperation, these pronouncements may come to reflect the reality of Russia's relations with Eastern Europe.

It is a vital interest of the Russian Federation to ensure that the countries of Eastern Europe do not feel threatened; a perceived threat from Russia would likely compel many Eastern European countries to join alliances and coalitions that could be directed against Russia. In order to prevent such a scenario, Russia must offer solid guarantees for the security of Eastern European states.

Russia can only benefit from the success of the political and economic reform process in Eastern Europe; Russia has an interest in not disrupting the social stability inside these countries, or the political and economic ties between them.[3] It is here that the interests of Russia and the West largely intersect. Not all the countries of Eastern Europe are stable, and this diminishes Russia's security with regard to the region as a whole. Among Russia's current ruling elite, there is a consensus that stability in Eastern

---

3. Stability is defined here as cohesion within the political system, adherence to normal democratic procedures concerning the rotation of ruling elites, the absence of pressing ethnic and social conflicts, and a healthy, functioning economy.

Europe will be most directly met by supporting democratization and the growth of market reform in these countries.

Russian progressives take a special interest in the consolidation of market-based institutions in Eastern Europe. Although Russia's less than successful experience with Polish-style shock therapy may have dampened enthusiasm for large-scale borrowing among many Russian politicians, other aspects of the Eastern European experience, especially in the microeconomic sphere, still serve as a model for Russia. The desire to learn from the successes and mistakes of Eastern Europe's transition manifests itself in an ever-increasing Russian interest in improving inter-governmental dialogue, and broadening communication in the economic and social spheres.

There will likely be an intensification of the drive to restore vitally important economic ties between Russia and the countries of Eastern Europe if economic conditions in Russia stabilize, and as Eastern Europe overcomes its own difficulties. The end of the Cold War ushered in new geopolitical and geostrategic conditions for both Russia and Eastern Europe. The severance of economic ties between them was greatly damaging for both parties.

It has turned out to be virtually impossible for the Eastern European economies to make up for the loss of trade in the ex-Soviet market. The low relative quality of many Eastern European products and elaborate trade restrictions and agreements have made the Western European and U.S. markets especially difficult to penetrate. As the dismal prospect for rapid integration of most of the Eastern European economies into Western markets becomes ever more apparent, it is reasonable to expect that these countries will show a renewed interest in trade and cooperation with Russia, Ukraine, and Belarus.

It is not difficult to uncover the correlation between restoring and developing close cooperation between Russia and the countries of Eastern Europe in areas such as trade, industry, and science, and improving the economic, environmental, and military security of the entire region. Ties in these and other areas lead to the development of mutual interests. Shared interests across a broad range of spheres will inhibit the deterioration of relations between Russia and the countries of Eastern Europe should political or even military tension emerge in the future.

Eastern European Foreign Policy Interests

Due to their geopolitical position, the countries of Central and Eastern Europe have always been squeezed by the ambitions of the great powers surrounding their region — Germany and Russia in particular — and have at different times been drawn into various political orbits. This trend is likely to continue. Almost all of the Eastern European states currently aspire to complete political, economic, and military independence, to join the ranks of industrialized nations, and ultimately to achieve membership in the European Union. In spite of their common goals, these countries hardly present a united front. They compete with one another for Western favor and access to Western markets. Old arguments and offenses have surfaced. Disagreements resulting from the disintegration of multinational states are particularly acute.

The collapse of the Soviet Union has opened a Pandora's box of nationalism and ethnic strife. Severe economic depression and the breakdown of regional economic ties have also contributed. As a result, Eastern Europe has become stratified, with the East-Central European states, Poland, the Czech Republic, Slovakia, Hungary, the Baltic states, Slovenia, and Croatia enjoying a more advantageous position than the southeastern states of Romania, Bulgaria, the new Yugoslavia,[4] and Albania. These two groups have different levels of economic development, standards of living, and scales of democratic and market reform. The gap between them may widen over the next decade and beyond. With its disparate rates and directions of development, the region will long remain a breeding-ground for nationalism, inter-ethnic conflicts, relapses into authoritarianism, and economic tensions between states.

Over the past several years, the foreign policy of the Eastern European states has become increasingly oriented toward Western Europe and the United States, and has relegated Russia to the background. These states seek support to resolve economic difficulties and advance toward democracy and market-based economies, as well as safeguards for their security and the means to overcome intra-regional differences. For the countries of Eastern Europe, fostering cooperation with Western Europe takes precedence over cultivating relations with the United States — even though the United States is regarded as a stronghold of democracy, an essential factor of European stability and security, a source of economic

---

4. Serbia and Montenegro.

credits and investments, and an important trading partner. This is because Eastern and Western Europe share more geopolitical and geostrategic concerns.

The need to ensure security guarantees has assumed a special urgency for the countries of Eastern Europe, which are relatively small, have limited military potential, and are highly conscious of their vulnerability. The apprehensions of these countries are stimulated by the past, by their awareness of the extremely unstable political and economic situation across the territory of the former Soviet Union, and by the emergence of new neighbors whose goals and policies are as yet unclear. These states are particularly concerned over the fact that the West is preoccupied with Russia as a nuclear power whose destabilization would be dangerous to international security. This attitude has resulted in a degree of neglect for the problems of Eastern European countries. The specter of agreements between Russia and the West at the expense of the interests of Eastern European countries haunts the political leaders of these states.

Poland, the Czech Republic, and Hungary especially want the protection of Western European economic, political, and strategic organizations — including possibly NATO — as soon as possible. The impatience of the Eastern European countries will come up against the restrained position of Western Europe (and on the topic of NATO, of Russia and the United States as well). In short, the situation could become an enormous headache for the West.

Still greater problems would arise if the Southeastern European states are allowed to join the European Union (EU). So far, the EU has preferred to leave these countries to their own resources and to encourage them to restore their regional economic and political ties — with Russia and Ukraine in particular. The West will hardly seek to become too deeply engaged in the prevention and settling of conflicts in Southeastern Europe.

Whether there are real prospects for forming strong regionally based groupings in Central and Eastern Europe and Southeastern Europe to intensify economic and political cooperation and strengthen collective security remains a large question. Viewed broadly, relations among the Eastern European states are marked by a historical legacy of religious and other differences, language barriers, complaints about cross-border environmental pollution, disputes over the status of various ethnic minorities, and fierce competition for scarce economic resources. This leaves little chance for these countries to soon find any common stand in international affairs. Even the Visegrad states — the Czech Republic, Slovakia, Poland, and Hungary — show no inclination to transform their relations into a more substantial union with shared institutions and a coordinated policy.

Russia will be willing to cooperate with any groupings in Eastern Europe that aim to further cooperation in the region, so long as they do not counter the progress of Russia's international efforts along other lines, including the development of the Helsinki process. Russian wariness may be piqued only if the countries of Eastern Europe unite in reaction to an exaggerated fear of the "Eastern threat" or out of mistrust toward Russia. A Russian relapse into great-power politics can be practically ruled out; Russia will be preoccupied with its domestic problems for years if not decades. By the time Russia begins to recover to the point that it may again pose a threat to the countries of Eastern Europe, the region will be fully protected by the emerging legal and diplomatic structure of security guarantees. The countries of Eastern Europe will be shielded by bilateral and multilateral treaties and assurances from Russia that will be reinforced by other guarantees from Western Europe and the United States.

The newly formulated foreign policy objectives of the Eastern European states and the feasibility of these objectives are rather far apart. As the present illusions preoccupying these countries are dispelled, they will come around to a more sober-minded approach to their relations with Russia. The gradual shift to the left now occurring in the political spectrum of some Eastern European countries may help to facilitate this process.

The West's Strategy Toward Eastern Europe

The West's policy with respect to Eastern Europe is still being formed. It is clear, however, that old Cold War–era approaches derived from the "building of bridges" doctrine — a differentiated approach to individual countries depending upon how far they were willing to drift from the Soviet policy line — all require revision. This policy was appropriate at the time, but the international landscape has changed rather drastically, requiring a fundamentally new approach to national and international security problems, both in Russia and in the West. The West's goals in Eastern Europe have been discussed both by specialists and policy makers;[5] when finally decided upon, they are bound to tell upon Russia's foreign policy.

The political, economic, and social crises in Eastern Europe — including Russia — present large policy challenges to the West — and many East European countries do not feel that the West's response has been adequate. The interests of the United States, the European Union, and individual countries of Western Europe diverge more often than not when it comes to making and implementing specific policy choices. Regrettably, there have even been attempts to revive obsolete concepts such as buffer zones and *cordons sanitaires*. Similarly, inertia in foreign policy thinking could stand in the way of establishing a new balance of interests between Russia and the West regarding the role to be assigned to Eastern Europe in the emerging structure of post–Cold War international relations.

To all appearances, Western strategy toward Eastern Europe will be marked by attempts to fill the region's vacuum of influence. The West will strive to assume the role of leader in safeguarding regional security and stability, and to be the model from which the countries of Eastern Europe take their cues in effecting democratic and market transformation, especially for countries that yearn for integration into Western economic and military-political structures.

The West has an active interest in preventing the destabilization of the political and economic situation in Eastern Europe. Among its available policy instruments are credits, subsidies, and the encouragement of private investment. These can help support the progress of democratic and market reforms; however, the West's opportunities in this respect are rather limited since a considerable number of countries are vying for Western aid, both in Europe and worldwide. Nevertheless, Eastern European states have succeeded in obtaining large Western credits. Poland, for example, has been relieved of half its debts to Western creditors, and direct investment in Hungary, the Czech Republic, and Poland has been growing continuously.

---

5. See, for example, the report published by the Center for Strategic and International Studies in Washington, "Objectives and Basic Principles of U.S. Policy in Central and Eastern Europe," 1991; "The Relations of the USA with Central and Eastern Europe," Aspen Institute, 1992; N. Weildenfeld, M. Huterer et al., *Osteuropa: Herausforderungen, Problemen, Stragedien (East Europe: challenges, problems, strategies)* (Gutersloh: Verlag Bertelsmann Shiftung, 1992); and J. Lederer, ed., *Western Approaches to Eastern Europe* (New York: Council on Foreign Relations Press, 1992).

Work is nearing completion in the European Union on a new approach to the countries of Eastern Europe. A report by the Commission of the European Council states that a positive response by the EC to the prospect of those countries joining the Community on acceptable terms could promote trust and stability. A further conclusion of this report is that if the countries of Eastern Europe sign the bulk of existing European accords, this would facilitate their active involvement in the all-European integration process.[6]

The European Union is in no hurry to favor Eastern European states with membership in its structures, making admission contingent upon a number of qualifications, quite apart from the issue of how Russia will react.[7] It is likely to be a while before most countries of Eastern Europe will be able to meet these requirements; this deepens their concerns about their security over the short and long term.

The United States welcomes Eastern Europe's turn to the West and supports the EC's efforts to reach out to those countries. However, Russia will have to reckon with specific U.S. interests in Eastern Europe that will differ from those of Western Europe. These interests are linked to the special role of the United States in Europe's postwar development, the fact that many U.S. citizens are of Eastern European descent, and U.S. economic interests in the region.

A future challenge to U.S. foreign policy could be a new division of Europe, if the economically and politically strong European Union, dominated by a unified Germany, comes to include Poland, the Czech Republic, Hungary, Slovenia, Croatia, and the newly independent Baltic states. This would shut out Romania, Bulgaria, and other remnants from former Yugoslavia — not to mention Russia, Ukraine, and Belarus. Apprehensions about finding themselves on the wrong side of an economic iron curtain may compel these states to unite in opposition to the richer part of Europe. Isolation from the more prosperous and

---

6. "Towards a Closer Association with the Countries of Central and Eastern Europe," Report by the Commission to the European Council, December 1992.

7. Among these qualifications are political and economic systems based upon the rule of law, a record of respect for human rights, including the rights of ethnic minorities, the holding of free elections, commitment to the principles of the market economy, and the possession of stable governmental institutions. A further condition is the readiness of the applicant to undertake and carry out all the obligations of membership in the Community; this means that members must support the cause of establishing a political, economic, and currency union.

democratic core of Europe would likely affect domestic development. Should this scenario come to pass, Russia's relations with the United States and with Western Europe could become quite strained. Thus, it is necessary to find ways to balance the interests of all parties.

Eastern European states depend upon international guarantees for their security, largely because militarily they are in no position to protect themselves from outside threats without the help of others. Without the inclusion of Russia, Ukraine, and Belarus, however, the prospects of finding a formula for lasting peace and stability in Eastern Europe look problematic.

Unfortunately, it is proving to be no easy matter to make the state of affairs in Eastern Europe a priority for the international community. The vacuum of geopolitical influence in Eastern Europe could induce rivalry between those wishing to fill it. Barring the unlikely possibility that some extreme crisis will develop in Eastern Europe that requires immediate action in the short term, Russia will insist that the United States, the EU, Russia, and possibly Ukraine and Belarus seek a joint solution to the problem of ensuring stability and security in the region by ruling out the possibility of domination by any one side. Russia will remain an active protagonist in such a process.

For many, the concept of the Common European Home still evokes skepticism. The value of this idea is that it stimulates European countries to look for new paths to unification and ways to avoid divisions that could threaten the security of Europe. Therefore, the concept should not be discarded, despite the improbability of its implementation in a period characterized by tectonic shifts in the political, economic, and social structures of Eastern Europe. The idea provides a test. In many ways, the proposed integration of Eastern European states into NATO with the exclusion of Russia contradicts the spirit of this idea, and therefore should be avoided.

The West, feeling the pressure from East European states clamoring to join NATO, proposed the "Partnership for Peace" as a compromise. Invited to participate in this initiative were the countries of Eastern Europe, Russia, Ukraine, and others. The Partnership for Peace was proposed, in part, to remove the basis of Russia's concerns about the eastward expansion of NATO's sphere of operations to Russia's western border, which would happen if Poland, the Czech Republic, Hungary, and other states were to be included under the NATO umbrella.

The other goal of the initiative is to satisfy the need of these states to join NATO. The countries of Eastern Europe have been asked to accept that the West is not attempting to block their incorporation into Western military-political and economic structures, but rather requiring a measure of patience in achieving those goals. NATO's member countries may doubt whether the enlargement of NATO will not ultimately weaken the security of all concerned. Therefore, it appears to be in the interest of the West to buy time in the resolution of this problem.

Russian policy makers interpret the Partnership for Peace initiative as a kind of preparation for the eventual enlargement of NATO. This will be achieved through the establishment of close contacts, periodic consultations, facilitating openness in defense planning, and laying the foundation for military integration. Continued Russian support of the Partnership for Peace will require changes in the structure and mission of NATO. If these changes do not begin to appear gradually, then Russian concerns will be heightened and will contribute to Russia's unwillingness to further support efforts in this direction.

On the other hand, if the spirit of the operation does not contradict the letter, Russia's participation in the Partnership for Peace could facilitate the gradual transformation of NATO's structures into a mechanism capable of ensuring peace in Europe, maintaining the balance of interests, and safeguarding the security of all European countries. In addition, Russian involvement will prevent the threats to European security that would arise from its isolation. Russia's participation in the Partnership for Peace could encourage other wide-scale initiatives linked to the creation of new European security structures, along with opportunities for deepening policy coordination between Russia and the West in the military-political sphere. Such initiatives could entail the enlargement of NACC (North Atlantic Cooperation Council) to include the non-aligned states of Europe, as well as the provision of Central and East European states with security guarantees from both Russia and the G-7 partners. It is also too early to conclude that possibilities for further development of CSCE structures have been exhausted.

The impetus behind the above-mentioned initiatives is the conviction that simply enlarging NATO's sphere of operations, either through incorporating new members, or through lesser forms of association, will not make the task of coping with new challenges to European security any easier. These challenges will largely be the result of ethnic conflicts, aggressive forms of nationalism, increased nuclear proliferation, and political instability in individual countries. For this reason, Russia has an interest in ensuring that the military, political, and conceptual transformation of NATO results in its becoming an all-European structure that can guarantee the security of its members, and prevent further armed conflicts on European soil.

Conclusions and Policy Recommendations

An ever-fuller awareness of its national interests will compel Russia to improve and invigorate its relations with Central, Eastern, and Southeastern Europe according to new standards and incentives. There are a number of steps Russia is now taking and could take in the future to help transform its relations with the countries of Eastern Europe.

First, Russia should carry on its efforts to lay a new legal groundwork for bilateral relations with some countries of Eastern and Central Europe. New arrangements for friendly relations and cooperation have already been worked out with Bulgaria, Hungary and Poland, and agreements are signed. In Russia's political relations with Eastern Europe, many unresolved problems, ambiguities, suspicions, and old grudges remain that make negotiations difficult. Nevertheless, the formalization and legalization of Russia's relations with the Eastern European states would constitute a significant step toward building stable contacts with these countries. This means the signing not only of broad treaties of friendship and cooperation, but also more narrow consular conventions, agreements on trade and economic relations, and arrangements for scientific and cultural cooperation.

Second, the building of mutual trust in Russia's relations with Hungary, the Czech Republic, and Poland calls for honesty and candidness in ascertaining the historical truth about the events of 1956, 1968, and 1980, respectively. As the primary legal successor to the former Soviet Union, it is Russia's responsibility to officially condemn the history of Soviet interference in the internal affairs of these countries, and to make due apologies to them. Russian officials have taken steps to ease access to historical archives, and have formed joint investigative commissions of historians and other officials; such steps should be continued.

Third, the restoration of trade and economic relations will require much more than elaborating new forms of legal regulation and organization. It requires bilateral commissions for economic, scientific, and technical cooperation, joint trading companies, banks, and insurance institutions, free-enterprise zones, and other entities to facilitate microeconomic contacts and to increase the incentives for long-term economic cooperation. Russia should take the initiative in overcoming a number of barriers standing in the way of trade with the countries of Eastern and Central Europe, and has shown signs of moving in this direction. A key issue will be Russia's large debt to a number of Eastern European states, especially the Czech Republic, Hungary, and Yugoslavia. Another problem is that Russia and many East European states are short of hard currency, which is necessary for wide-scale economic intercourse.

By virtue of its position between Russia and Western Europe, Eastern Europe has the potential to provide Russian businesses with access to international markets.[8] Russian enterprises will find it easier to establish new business contacts through the mediation of the Czech Republic, Poland, and Hungary and in cooperation with enterprises in those countries. The latter are certain to gain a solid foothold in Western markets well in advance of Russia, and their experience in penetrating these markets will be very useful to Russia. There is vast potential for expanding trade, industrial, and scientific contacts, especially with the Czech Republic, Hungary, Bulgaria, Romania, and the Yugoslav successor states; it is in Russia's interest to use this potential to its advantage.

Finally, Russia is gravely concerned over open and latent conflicts between countries in Eastern and especially Southeastern Europe. Since Russia has a vital interest in settling conflicts in this region through political means and compromise, Russian diplomacy should offer the conflicting sides its good offices more frequently, both bilaterally and under the auspices of international organizations. This could be a key element in the network of East-West security guarantees for the region, including over the long term.

As it seeks to revitalize its relations with the countries of Eastern Europe, Russia will make every effort to establish a new and reasonable balance of interests in the region, and one that will meet with the approval of the participants in the Helsinki process. It is a long-term goal of Russia to make the Eastern European region a zone of stability and peace, and a bridge of cooperation and mutual understanding between Russia and the West.

---

8. Poland will have a special role to play in this context. First, the main communication routes connecting Russia with Western Europe are located on Polish territory. Second, Poland will likely find Russia a useful partner for balancing its relations with an ever-stronger Germany. Third, Russia and Poland have no common border, except in Russia's Kaliningrad region, and consequently no outstanding territorial disputes to complicate their relations.

Chapter 9 | *Peter Hardi*

Eastern Europe and Russia

The dissolution of the Soviet Union and the end of the Cold War have changed the interests of Russia and the East European states. Russia wants to play a game of equals in European politics, but has lost almost all of its ability to do so. The political and strategic significance of Eastern Europe has greatly decreased, and without the Bosnian war would be minimal. Eastern Europe is no longer a subject of East-West rivalry, and is not likely to be so, unless Russian politics directly or indirectly threaten the independence and sovereignty of East European countries, prompting Western concerns. Similarly, East Europe no longer has a significant interest in Russia save for the possibility that Russia might again threaten these countries' independence and sovereignty.

However, the foreign policy of East European countries seems to have been based on assumptions that suited the Cold War period. East Europe's desire to join NATO has sparked a tug of war between Russia and NATO over the region. Mostly because of emerging Russian aspirations to restore at least part of its Soviet-era power and influence in international affairs, Eastern Europe might become entangled in an international power game. The membership of the Visegrad countries in NATO has become a bargaining chip in Atlantic-Russian negotiations, which shows that the West gives more credence to Russian aspirations than does Eastern Europe.

The long-term interests of Russia and Eastern Europe differ substantially.[1] All parts of Eastern Europe aspire to come closer to and become

---

1. Within the narrow framework of this essay, unfortunately only passing reference can be made to the important differences among East European countries. It is a diverse region; what may be a valid statement for, say, the Visegrad group, is possibly false for

Peter Hardi is a Professor of Political Science at the Budapest University of Economic Sciences. From 1988–1990 he was the Director of the Hungarian Institute of International Affairs. He founded the Regional Environmental Center for Central and Eastern Europe in 1990. Presently he is a Senior Fellow at the International Institute for Sustainable Development in Canada.

more like Western European countries; in other words, to catch up to mainstream European politics and economics. For most of them, the key structural issue and the number one goal is to become integrated into the European Union.[2] At this stage, any attempt to revitalize relations with Russia seems counterproductive.

Russia's primary goals are to remain a great power and to benefit more from world markets. These goals can best be realized by preventing further degradation of Russia's political and economic significance. Thus, the number one domestic issue for Russian politics might be to secure internal integrity and stability.

These differences explain why Russians and East Europeans have different priorities in their relations. Eastern Europe — especially the former Warsaw Pact countries — is preoccupied with the problems of compatibility with Western structures, and believes that intensive relations with Russia might hinder or delay the integrative process. Russia is preoccupied with problems of the integrity of the nation-state, as well as preserving its international power and maintaining conditions of international influence; Russia believes that having influence over Eastern Europe is an important means to achieve that goal.

This chapter first surveys the factors that will most strongly affect Russian–East European relations, including how these peoples perceive each other, and then considers whether Russia has "legitimate security interests" that could compromise the sovereignty of Eastern European countries. The following two sections analyze the most important aspects of Russian–East European relations from an East European and (much less authentically) a Russian perspective.

Determinants of Russian–East European Relations

OBJECTIVE FACTORS

A number of factors will determine the character of Russian–East European relations. The following listing attempts to order these determinants by importance.

Romania or Bulgaria, while the Baltic states in general deserve a different treatment.

2. From this broader perspective, NATO membership is a secondary issue. Any of these countries might become a NATO member without completing all the economic and social structural changes that are required for entrance into the European Union.

1. Russia's stability. Russia's stability is the central pillar of any relationship with Eastern Europe. Stability means reliability, and a reliable Russia will generate less fear, and will allow the planning of economic and political ties based on mutual interests. Russia's stability depends on the depth and length of its transformation, and on the vehemence of the accompanying political struggle.

2. East European stability. If the democratic transformation process in Eastern Europe is successful and proceeds well, creating a democratic, market-based system, balanced relations with Russia will be possible. However, if Eastern Europe falls into a pattern of regional conflicts and domestic instability in individual states, systematic relations with Russia cannot be established. If a more hegemonic Russia emerges, intervention into East European affairs and the division of East European countries according to their relations to Russia will be a real possibility.

3. Russia's international role. Russia is a nuclear great power. Even ignoring its nuclear capacity, it is a regional power, possessing one of the world's largest standing armies. It is a permanent member of the United Nations Security Council, and it has important positions in numerous international political institutions. (This could change over time if the West seriously desires to dismantle the international system that was created during the Cold War; such changes would decrease the importance of Russia's international role. But many Western politicians and governments seek to maintain Russia's positions and international role.)

Unless Russia is drowned in domestic chaos, it will behave as a great power in international politics, even if its aims are not always clear. In the context of its East European policy, such behavior could mean claiming the right to influence international negotiations on the future status of East European countries, such as negotiations concerning their membership in Western organizations. It cannot be ruled out that Russia will once again come to consider Eastern Europe as its security backyard.

If Russia maintains all the international commitments it inherited from the Soviet Union and further acts as a global power, this will foster suspicion and fear of Russian interference. Accepting a more modest role would encourage East European countries to develop relations with Russia based on mutuality and equal respect of sovereignty.

4. Respect for sovereignty. Russia's handling of all new democracies emerging from the former Soviet Union will significantly affect its relations with Eastern Europe; its Central Asian or Transcaucasian policy will give signals as important to East Europeans as its handling of Ukraine or the Baltic states. Russia must show that it respects the independence

and sovereignty of countries that had been under Soviet dominance. Unfortunately, there are some incentives for Russia's political elites to believe that it is in Russia's security interest to dominate states with a tradition of subservience to Russian or Soviet power, on grounds very similar to those Russia used to justify its consideration of Eastern Europe as a zone of its special interests.[3] On the other hand, by following democratic principles in foreign affairs, Russia could gain not only a partnership with the Western world but a more peaceful future, without internal war or continuous fights against separatist forces.

5. Attraction of Western institutions. Most East European countries are very attracted to Western political and economic institutions such as NATO, the European Union, the European Parliament and the Council of Europe, and the OECD (Organization for Economic Cooperation and Development). Joining these institutions was one motivation for the revolutions in 1989–1990; it has been the main issue on the external political agenda of these countries ever since. It is the yardstick by which East European countries design their foreign policy and shape external relations. These states have made major shifts from their earlier political and economic relations, and not only have economic ties with Russia fallen dramatically; so have economic relations with each other.

The process of joining Western institutions requires that countries establish compatible economic and political institutions: liberal democracy and the rule of law; market mechanisms such as stock, commodity and money exchanges, and a Western-type banking system and communication network are just a few. These changes are already underway; the association agreements with the European Union explicitly require them. As soon as the transformation is irreversible, the interests of these countries will predominantly demand the defense of these achievements, or, more broadly, the defense of the values and institutions of Western civilization. In this sense, the security interests of East Central European countries will be identical with those of the Western countries.

If Russia becomes a democratic country with a market economy, it will have the same interest in joining Western institutions as the states of Eastern Europe. While the similarities in evolving structures would ease Russian–East European relations in the long run, in the short run they might trigger strong competition. Ideally, such competition would increase

---

3. These include a longing for the restoration of Russia's world power status and a hope to overcome economic hardships partly attributed to the loss of that status.

the need for negotiations and concerted efforts in order to find mutually beneficial solutions.

6. Geographic rearrangements. While all ex–Warsaw Pact countries (except East Germany) had joint borders with the Soviet Union, now Russia has virtually no common borders with any of them — only a short border with Poland. More importantly, the countries between Russia and its former communist allies are not necessarily helping Russia to create or maintain closer contacts with East or East Central European countries. Ukraine and Moldova, possibly more than Belarus, are creating new problems: unsolved questions of transit lines, as well as the redistribution of the wealth of the former Soviet Union (including energy sources), outstanding debts, and military power are sources of tension in these relations, limiting the outreach capacity of Russia.

At the same time, the countries in between (again, mainly Ukraine) represent a strategic buffer zone for East Central Europe; they separate it from Russia, holding back Russia's problems and crises, including emigration. By the same token, Ukraine might represent an alternative to relations with Russia, especially if Ukraine stabilizes and recovers economically. Russia's relationship with its neighbors on its western border might have other consequences, especially if relations turn out to be hostile.

7. Ethnic issues. The primary effect of ethnic issues is to influence, if not determine, the relationship of Russia and the former Soviet republics. Their secondary impact is to modify Russian–East Central European relations.

PSYCHOLOGICAL FACTORS: PERCEPTIONS AND MISPERCEPTIONS

While the above-mentioned facts are the decisive factors in shaping Russian–East European relations, an important role is also played by psychological factors. The mixed signals from Russian domestic politics (especially through the emergence of extremists like Vladimir Zhirinovsky) indicate that perceptions affect public feeling — and thus the political elite's ability to make and "sell" decisions — and even influence actual decision making. Perceptions and idiosyncrasies are also shaping longer-term political strategies. Thus, dispassionate consideration of interests and influences is not sufficient; it is also important to consider how East

Europeans think about Russians and how Russians think about East Europeans.[4]

The prevailing feelings of Eastern Europeans toward Russia are fear and suspicion. The fear has different roots and levels of intensity from country to country and sub-region to sub-region, as do specific types of suspicions. Every East and East Central European country has at some time been invaded, occupied, or defeated by Russia or the Soviet Union (or both as in the case of Poland and Hungary). In several cases, Russian or Soviet aggression was linked to the defeat of a freedom fight.

Russia's size also inspires fear and suspicion.[5] It is difficult to ignore the importance of deeply ingrained cultural heritages such as those reflected by idioms, for example, "They are as many as the Russians" or "The Musca [nickname for the Russians] will take you away!" as a reference to the arrival of a danger. The name "Siberia" still reminds East Europeans of the infinite steppes and *taiga* associated with forced labor.

Russians may see East Europeans as unreliable and ungrateful. Russians also remember some East Europeans as enemies in the world wars (especially Hungarians, but in the case of World War II, both Hungarians and Romanians). If any of the polls conducted recently in Russia can be considered reliable, they show that Russians have a low opinion of East Europeans; East Europeans do not rank among the preferred nations, and Baltic peoples in particular rank quite low on the list.[6]

Eastern Europe's leaders cannot help but be influenced by their stereotypes and gut feelings. The process of transition to democracy has not yet changed these stereotypes. It is an open question whether they can be changed at all; and if so, how, and how fast. Analysts also must bear in mind that the collapse of the Soviet Union has helped to revive old arguments that Russia is not really a part of Europe; even liberal Russian intellectuals say that Russia is not *within* Europe but *with* Europe, and that

---

4. As an East European, I might authentically voice many East European perceptions about the Russians, but can refer only to anecdotal encounters with Russians and to several recent polls to explicate some of the Russian perceptions about East Europeans.

5. The first descriptions that come to mind among East Europeans are that Russia is big and that the Russians are many.

6. John P. Robinson, Ted Robert Gurr, Erjan Kurbanov, Stephen McHale and Ivan Slepenkov, "Ethnonationalist and Political Attitudes Among Post-Soviet Youth: The Case of Russia and Ukraine," *PS: Political Science & Politics*, Vol. 26, No. 3 (September 1993), pp. 516–521.

Russia represents orthodoxy, the eastern tradition of Christianity, and a strong dividing line between Western culture and non-Western civilization (including the political framework and the interpretation of individual rights).

NATO and Russia's "Legitimate Security Interests"

It is necessary to challenge any Western or Russian concepts of "legitimate Russian security interests" vis-à-vis Eastern European countries that go beyond the maxim that they should not be attacked, and should not form any hostile grouping with the purpose of blockading Russia or inhibiting its Western contacts. Any extension of that concept seems to be the remnant of "old thinking" and of traditional patterns in foreign policy making. In speaking about legitimate security interests, people usually mean that a country has the right to contain threats against its integrity and sovereignty and, in a somewhat more general sense, to protect its channels of contact with the external world including its access to vital resources. In the current context, however, the most frequently mentioned issue is that Russia has a legitimate interest in preventing East European countries from becoming members of NATO. Should we accept the possibility that Russia might limit the sovereignty of these countries?

In debating whether East European countries should be NATO members, Western policy makers should not frame their arguments in terms of a potential security threat to Russia. This will either come across as a poor excuse to refuse these countries entry, or will serve to revive an East-West (Russia-NATO) controversy, along with the old political dynamic. Implicitly it would mean that NATO might really limit Russia's maneuvering room and prevent it from influencing the region.[7]

The expression "legitimate security interest" was used extensively during the Cold War. The term is an obvious euphemism: when the adversary had strength, including military power to influence or dominate a sphere *unchallenged*, it was acting according to legitimate security interests. In order to clarify what might be a legitimate security interest,

---

7. Even in other regions like the Caucasus or Central Asia, where both border issues and local military conflicts genuinely threaten Russia's security, the term "legitimate security interest" should avoid any reference to a specific sphere of influence or any attempt to hold together these countries with Russia.

let us consider what actual and potential threats are posed by Eastern Europe to Russia:

1. Threats posed by ethnic groups. Minorities outside their own countries have the potential to involve Russia in outside conflicts. Likewise, Russia feels compelled to protect the rights of its citizens in these regions. This threat is limited to a few countries, mostly to the Baltic states and other ex-Soviet republics, specifically Moldova, because of its East-Central European dimension, and its special relationship with Romania.

2. Border disputes. This is a problem of very limited significance, due to Russia's loss of almost all common borders with East-Central European states.

3. The isolation of Russia. Eastern Europe is itself not in a position to isolate Russia either politically or economically. However, Eastern Europe could become an instrument used by Western powers to isolate Russia, at least in European politics, and hinder its Western lines of contact. Even in such a case, Russia's isolation would not be complete: it would still remain open and accessible from all other directions, most importantly from Asia. Russian fears could emerge not because of East European politics (even if those states are aiming to join NATO) but if it detects Western forces hostile to Russia. In any event, it will not be Eastern Europe that is feared by Russia, but the West. That is why the problem is an issue of Russian–Western rather than of Russian–East European relations.[8]

Threats to Russia's security emanating from Eastern Europe should be addressed through the creation of adequate international regimes such as treaties and conventions, and institutions such as the Council of Europe. East European countries have legitimate security interests in curbing Russian activities and involvement in their affairs — interests that are forgotten when discussing Russia's "legitimate security interests," with its corollary that permits certain actions to be taken that might prevent other countries from acting in a sovereign manner. The concept of a "legitimate security interest" might easily be used as a cover-up for interference in the affairs of others.

The relationship of NATO and Eastern Europe will remain a focal issue of Russian–East European relations during the 1990s. East European countries have different motivations for aspiring to NATO membership, and not all of them consider Russia the main threat from which they need

---

8. Of course, Russia could also become isolated as a result of its domestic politics.

the protection of NATO, as Poland does. Some of the Visegrad countries, like the Czech Republic or Hungary, as well as Romania seek protection mostly against possible involvement in ethnic conflicts and local wars. Such a demand introduces a new challenge to NATO in redefining its role in international and especially European politics, a process that has been started by accepting a role in solving the Bosnian crisis.

Unfortunately, the first solution offered by NATO — the Partnership for Peace initiative — simply postpones the solution and extends the period of Russian–East European (better to say Russian-Western) controversy over the issue. Even if a careful reading could calm Russia's fears, the Partnership for Peace is not a substantive solution and lacks any kind of Western commitments to provide a defense umbrella for Eastern Europe in all cases. Eastern European politicians accepted the offer with disappointment, but with realistic pragmatism, understanding the limitations of their influence. On the other hand, the inclusion of Russia did not help dissolve suspicion among Russian policy makers.

East European Interests in Relations with Russia

In order to make any points of analytic value, certain simplifications are inevitable. First, it is important to avoid the debate on national consensus in interpreting interests. Second, it is necessary to presuppose a minimum of stability within the region. The following is a summary of Eastern European interests with regard to relations with Russia:

1. First and foremost, it is the paramount interest of every East European country to avoid domination by Russia, most directly by eliminating any chance of military intervention or occupation. In the making of foreign policy, it matters little how realistic such a threat may be — traditions, perceptions, the legacy of the distant and immediate past, and present tendencies in Russian domestic politics keep this issue on Eastern Europe's political agenda.

It is also an East European interest to circumvent any agreement between Western powers (specifically the United States or NATO) and Russia on defining spheres of interests that might again place Eastern Europe in the Russian sphere of influence. While most politicians no longer consider the former Warsaw Pact countries as part of Russia's domain, many are still willing to speak about "legitimate Russian security interests" in the context of Russia's East European policy.

2. The continuation of democratic rule in Russia is an interest of Eastern Europe. A totalitarian, nationalist Russia would present a clear and imminent threat to Russia's immediate neighbors as well as to the East European countries. Such a Russia could pursue a policy of both recapturing ex-republics and expanding influence to the former satellite countries, and would undoubtedly try to regain superpower status and would challenge Eastern Europe's orientation toward and integration with the West.

If Russia remains on the democratic path, its chance to pursue a different, non-expansionist foreign policy is much greater. The internal rules of the democratic game imply certain regulations for international behavior, including tolerance of other nations and acceptance of other's interests based on reciprocity and mutuality. It also implies a need to participate in international regimes that are open only to democratic states.

3. It is an interest of East European states that Russia not remain a military superpower. Old thinking and old patterns of behavior were supported by a solid foundation of military power, and it is the "old thinkers" who insist upon preserving Russia's superpower status. It is in the interest of the Eastern European states to help find and promote international solutions to neutralize this trend. A likely solution might be the incorporation of Russia into existing all-European and Western structures. Another possible avenue is to rely upon an international regime of arms control and treaties to reduce Russia's nuclear capabilities. Such agreements, however, are viable only if the trend of Russian liberalization and integration with the West prevails.

4. Eastern Europe has an interest in economic relations with Russia should it become a compatible and reliable trading partner and if commerce is based on mutual advantage. After upgrading existing infrastructures (such as transportation lines and storage capacities) and solving problems such as currency conversion and debt issues, Russia could provide badly needed raw materials, including energy, while opening a huge market where East European goods might be quite competitive. Using the obsolete terminology, Eastern Europe has a "legitimate interest" in securing the availability of vital resources in Russia, especially where East European investments have also been made (as in the gas fields).

Such economic relations might well function. In Russia and in Eastern Europe, part of the former communist elites have gone into business. They are reviving their old ties, transforming them into business relations. Though it is difficult to estimate their share of the Russian–East European market, it would be a mistake to underestimate their economic influence. The underworld also capitalizes on weak government. Both groups are interested more in business and liberal governments than in any restoration of the previous system or the creation of a strong totalitarian power.

5. Though present political elites in Eastern Europe are not aware of the extent of the problem, they regard environmental issues as important to their security interests, especially in their relations with Russia (and Ukraine). Concern is greatest over nuclear issues and in some cases water and air pollution. An understanding is emerging that Russia has no right to create environmental risks for Eastern Europe. Russia's environmental problems are clearly global issues and need to be addressed by global means. At the same time, as the ongoing negotiations over the environmental legacy of the Soviet military occupation demonstrate, each East European country is affected.

Unsolved environmental conflicts, and a systematic disregard of the environmental interests of other countries, will make political relations tense and will create an indirect threat to security. Environmental issues *are* of strategic importance when they threaten to degrade vital resources or the wellbeing of a nation.

Russian Interests in Relations with East Europe

Russia's interests in Eastern Europe will depend upon its development. This section considers Russia's interests depending upon three broad outcomes: first, if Russia pursues a democratic, liberal, Western-oriented modernization; second, if it pursues a nationalist-traditionalist, inward-oriented restoration; and third, if it establishes an étatist but not fully authoritarian regime, somewhere between the first two possibilities.

WESTERN-ORIENTED MODERNIZATION

Should Russia integrate into a Western culture–dominated international political system and market economy, its main interest would be to promote its welfare goals and find ways to realize its economic aims. Russia would not need to pursue any major military role in international affairs and could reduce its military power to a level adequate for defense, concentrating mostly on its capacity to deter threats from its neighbors (including China and the Muslim countries to its south), and the spread of local conflicts and disturbances. In this case Russia would no longer pose a nuclear threat to the West. On the basis of this general assumption, Russia's interests in its East European relations could be the following:

1. Economic cooperation. Russia would foster close economic cooperation with Eastern Europe based on mutual advantage. An era of strong economic competition would likely emerge in which mutual interests require international regulation. Agreements similar to EFTA (European Free Trade Association) or NAFTA (North American Free Trade Association) would well serve Russian business interests; such arrangements would ultimately foster Russia's closer links to the European Union and the integrated European market. Monopolistic tendencies, however, might favor Russian interests because of the country's important raw materials. Tradeoffs would be necessary in order to achieve mutually acceptable solutions through international trade regimes. Russia might seek to become a regional center to organize trade relations and create a genuine flow of goods and services in both directions. Attempts in the economic sphere would help to disperse East European fears of Russian aspirations for dominance.

Serious efforts should be devoted to creating a cooperative system of energy transportation and an energy supply network. A regional solution for quick and efficient energy distribution might be extremely beneficial for Russia's economic development, while it would serve the interests of East European economies well, including their need to diversify their energy dependence. This system might include a network for fossil fuel transportation and distribution as well as an electricity transfer system.

2. Renounce intentions of domination. In order to develop economic, political, social and cultural ties with Europe, Russia must give clear signals to Eastern Europe that it abandons all hegemonic aspirations, has no intentions to dominate Eastern Europe, and does not consider Eastern Europe as a specific sphere of Russian interest. Through a series of bilateral treaties Russia should attempt to neutralize any political efforts to isolate it or exclude it from the benefits of the Western-based international regimes. Here the West might play an important and influential role. Democratization and the stabilization of a democratic system in Russia must be supported by the West, but not at the expense of the independence of Eastern Europe.

3. Promoting solutions for ethnic minority issues. The situation and the rights of Russian ethnic minorities living in different East European countries are among the most delicate problems the Russian political leadership must address in developing its East European policy. These issues must be handled with tact and a firm obligation to cooperative

solutions and dialogue. Though Russian minority problems have emerged exclusively in ex-Soviet republics, like the Baltics, the handling of the issue is relevant for overall Russian–East European relations, including countries with no Russian ethnic minorities. If Russia tries to find negotiated guarantees and handles the problem within the context of all-European institutions of human and minority rights, this would signal to East and East Central European countries that Russia is committed to democratic institutions and democratic solutions.

4. Political-military cooperation. If Russia fears isolation from Eastern and Central Europe, and by extension from the rest of Europe, it might try to establish closer cooperation with Eastern Europe beyond economic fields: first in politics, but also in military affairs. This idea might sound far-fetched, but there are good reasons to pursue it. The conversion and modernization of the ex-Soviet military industry might enable Russia to reconsider its role in the international arms trade. After economic modernization, especially with the help of Western (including U.S.) technological assistance, Russia might become a competitive local supplier for East European countries. A revitalization of Russia's military industry seems almost inevitable. If it happens, it is in the best interest of both Eastern Europe and Russia to create friendly and legitimate markets instead of increasing the chances that Russia will act as a player in the obscure international arms market.

There are other areas where Russia can try to promote its political role in East European relations. We already can see a certain Russian willingness to mediate in debates between East European countries. However, this does not seem compatible with East European expectations, and might create more problems than solutions. Despite Russia's best intentions, all East European politicians would regard such an effort as a sign that Russia intends to dominate the region. Russia has inherent advantages over any Western powers in terms of being able to act as a mediator, but in general, Western powers are better accepted in Eastern Europe (with the exception of Serbia) due in part to perceptions about Russia.

5. Environmental initiatives. Though the scarcity of capital resources and the economic crisis do not permit any rapid transition to sound environmental policy in Russia (or anywhere in Eastern Europe), it has a huge interest in promoting regional environmental regimes. Such a policy is justified not only by the devastation of Russia's own environment but by the effects of its pollution problems beyond its borders, and the need for international solutions to many of these issues. Russia could and

should be an important participant in international efforts to introduce patterns of sustainable development into economic and business decision making. Both geographic vicinity and the similar heritage of the communist past make cooperation quite sensible. Any progress along this line presupposes a negotiated solution to the debate on how to compensate East European countries for the environmental damage caused by occupying Soviet garrisons.

INWARD-ORIENTED RESTORATION
While Russia could choose a liberal, democratic system, it is almost equally likely to choose an authoritarian, nationalist system that rejects Western modernization patterns. Following an isolationist and anti-modernization course, Russia would be shut off from mainstream international politics, and would be perceived as a potential adversary of the West.

This development alone would be enough to make Russia a threat in international politics, especially since Russia would likely again emphasize the build-up of military power. A revival of Cold War–type East-West conflict could be expected, with less ideological underpinning than before and with a more blunt appearance of power politics. This would present the danger of a comeback of obsolete, pre–World War II power struggles for international domination and influence, based upon force.

In such a case, Eastern Europe would legitimately fear Russian aspirations for dominance in the region. This could easily create divisions in Eastern Europe, bringing some Slav countries with potentially strong nationalist and pan-Slavic oriented leadership (like Serbia, Slovakia, and eventually Bulgaria) closer to Moscow, and leaving other countries with no other option than to call for Western patrons, further deepening the division in European politics.

AN ÉTATIST REGIME
As a further possibility, the emergence of a political rule in Russia similar to that of present-day China is not excluded. Russia would be an authoritarian state with a controlled and more or less closed society tempered by isolated clusters open for trade with the West in order to promote Russian industrial and commercial interests. Russia might in this case pursue less confrontational relations with Eastern Europe, demonstrating more willingness for cooperation — though less on issues that represent long-term and global interests such as the environment, than on issues of immediate interest such as transportation, trading zones along

bordering territories, etc. At the same time, Russia would still try to maintain its international great power role and expend considerable effort to influence Eastern Europe.

Conclusion

East European–Russian relations will have an unequal importance for Russia and for Eastern Europe in the coming years. If democratization and stabilization do occur in Russia, its relations with Eastern Europe will remain of secondary importance. Both Russia and Eastern Europe are now looking for political and especially economic support from the West; this will require a healthier and more resourceful Russia to be an important, competitive partner for an Eastern Europe capable of changing its economic priorities. Similarly, an economically depressed Eastern Europe cannot offer badly needed resources or purchasing power to Russia, as can the West and the Far East.

With regard to security policy, the countries of Eastern Europe will still focus on protecting themselves *against* Russia, not on allying *with* Russia. The greater the Russian threat is for Eastern Europe and its interests, the worse relations with Russia will be. Russia's security policy will encompass primary issues like nuclear arms, China, and its rapid deployment capability; Eastern Europe will be secondary. Another important area of Russian security policy might be its policies toward the former Soviet republics, which may partially overlap with its East European policy.

The Eastern European countries are too small and uninfluential to represent a key area in Russian foreign policy. Eastern Europe as a unit might be more important, but the region is deeply divided, and no significant regional integration has emerged which could be regarded as a serious party in international affairs.

Only in a worst-case scenario, during a renewal of Western-Russian controversies, would Eastern Europe's importance for Russia be direct: then the West might want and try to create a buffer zone between Russia and itself. The West might have two main reasons to do this. First, it would isolate and limit the spin-offs from political and economic crisis and disarray in Russia, block the flow of refugees, the impact of organized crime, and the spread of ethnic conflicts. Second, after the consolidation of an authoritarian, nationalist regime in Russia, the West would want to contain the potential military threat, to protect itself from the direct exposure to Russia's conventional forces, and to prevent direct Western-Russian confrontation in the heart of Europe. If this scenario evolved before Eastern Europe had been integrated into the Western political and economic system, and into its institutions (like the European Union), it would have significant negative consequences for those countries.

Russian foreign policy lends credence to this scenario, even in the absence of a repressive, authoritarian regime, fitting the étatist scenario for Russian development. When key Russian policy makers identify Eastern Europe as a sphere of vital Russian interests, it is not in order to develop friendly relations,[9] but to enhance the policy goal of preserving a strong international position vis-à-vis the West. Most countries of Eastern Europe, especially the former members of the Warsaw Pact, do not represent any security threat to vital Russian interests. If Russia still considers this area as a vital sphere, it is only a consequence of a geostrategic policy framed within its Western and not East European policy.

---

9. Cf. the statement of Russian foreign minister Andrei Kozyrev, cited by Interfax on February 14, 1994. See *Radio Free Europe/Radio Liberty Daily Report, Russia*, No. 31 (February 15, 1994).

Chapter 10
Russia and Western Europe

Igor F. Maksimichev

The end of ideological conflict in Europe has created a unique opportunity for the formation of a Greater Europe. However, it has also raised many questions concerning the future stability and prosperity of the region: How will the new Europe be defined? Who will participate in its construction? What will be the nature of the relationships among its nations? Will we learn from the past?

The current situation in Europe has been best characterized as a "recurrence of history."[1] The process by which Russia is moving closer to Western Europe is not new. Russia has always strongly believed itself to be a part of the European family of nations, with which it shares similar historical roots, culture, genealogy of language and literature, religious morals, and world view. As Russia enters a new stage in its development, it needs not only business partners, but reliable allies to help it develop on a variety of levels. Russia cannot look to the North, the South, nor even the East to find such a kindred spirit to support its transformation. Furthermore, relations between Russia and Central and East–Central Europe remain strained. Only Western Europe, and in a broader sense the United States, can provide a solid base of support for Russia during its movement toward a new future.

However, the past also reveals deep fears in Western Europe about the Russian threat and the Asian onslaught. Such fears have fueled enormous catastrophes throughout European history, such as the rise of Hitler's National Socialism in Germany from 1933–1939. Once again, an opportunity for peace and stability in Europe may be wasted if Western Europe

---

1. Rummel Reinhart, "Die westeuropaische Sicherheitszusammenarbeit: Richtung und Spielraum" (West European security cooperation: Direction and Scope), in Jakobeit, Cord, Yenal, and Alparlan, *Gesamteuropa: Analysen, Probleme, und Entwicklungsperspektiven* (*Europe: Analysis, Problems, and Perspectives in Development*) (Bonn: 1993), p. 380.

Igor F. Maksimichev is the head of the Political Problems of European Security Section of the Institute of Europe at the Russian Academy of Sciences. From 1956–1992 he served in the Diplomatic Service of the former Soviet Union and Russia.

excludes Russia from the European context due to a resurgence of anti-Russian or anti-Asian sentiment.

Reorganizing European Security

For half a century following the end of World War II, the safety of Europe and the entire world relied on the balance of power between the two greatest military and political unions in modern history — the North Atlantic Treaty Organization (NATO) and the Warsaw Pact. The opposition between these two alliances represented the global confrontation between East and West and operationalized the irreconcilable contradictions between Eastern and Western Europe. However, these organizations also embodied the very system of collective safety in Europe that the continent had tried unsuccessfully to establish between the first and second world wars. For fifty years, increasing interaction between NATO and the Warsaw Pact protected Europe and the world from global catastrophe and gradually forced the confrontational elements of their relationship into the background. Strict Eastern bloc discipline was maintained to prevent internal conflicts from spreading and threatening the peace. Europe was without war throughout the period of bilateral opposition between the forces of capitalism and "real socialism." Indeed, the further we move from this period of opposition, the more reasonable sounds the thesis that the threat of bipolar nuclear confrontation was the strongest guarantee of the peace and safety of the planet. This statement, which should serve as the point of departure for any discussion of Europe's future, is not meant to idealize the past situation, when any mistake in political or military leadership could have led to mutual annihilation, but instead to promote efforts to learn from the past and to reach an equal or greater degree of peace and stability in Europe today.

Western European political leaders believed in 1990–1991 that the most effective way to maintain assurances of peace and stability in Europe during the dissolution of the Cold War structure was to bring together the previously opposing parts of Europe and establish a single organization dedicated to European safety. German unification was viewed as a first step in this direction. Bringing together NATO and the rapidly transforming, newly independent Eastern European countries held great promise as a way to preserve the stabilizing elements of the previous confrontational security system, while negating its destabilizing military and political impulses. Furthermore, the looming conflict in Yugoslavia led all parties to recognize the need to act quickly to consolidate the post–Cold War security system.

However, few could have anticipated the complications that arose from the disintegration of the Soviet Union. The Warsaw Pact dissolved without an attempt to define new rules for peaceful coexistence. The tragic conflict in Yugoslavia failed to motivate the European states to join forces; it also demonstrated the lack of power and credibility of existing security instruments, including the CSCE and NATO. The former has not fulfilled its vision as an organ for peaceful conflict resolution within Europe. Although in form it has become something like a miniature United Nations, the CSCE lacks the authority and power of a true security alliance and the ability to act in crucial situations. The powerlessness of the CSCE as a European confederation was sealed when it included the Asian republics of the former Soviet Union. Furthermore, the fact that NATO was created as an anti-Eastern body greatly challenges its ability to assume the role of a common European security institution.

In addition, early efforts of West European governments to establish a common European security alliance threatened to exclude Russia. This continues to jeopardize the forces of stability in Russia by promoting fears of isolation, creating a nationalist political backlash against Western influence. The American proposal for a "Partnership for Peace," subsequently endorsed by NATO, does not exclude Russian participation, and may present a way out of the present situation, but only if the plan actually results in a change to the structure and mission of NATO, and is not just an intermediate stage for Eastern European nations aspiring to join NATO. The Partnership for Peace plan does promote the possibility of restructured relationships not only between the members and non-members of NATO, but also among the NATO non-members. If the proposal does not exclude Russia and allows real interaction between non-members of the alliance, NATO may yet develop into a security base for the entire European continent, as envisioned in 1990-1991.

More ideas may surface in the process of completing work on the Balladur Plan, which, due to its emphasis on the equality of all participants, represents perhaps the most promising proposal yet. By sidestepping the NATO dilemma of how to deal with states outside the Alliance, this plan could serve as a valuable starting point for a future all-European alliance. Key to this process will be the creation of an organization that is capable of enforcing its rules. Such plans, however, should be considered only intermediary steps toward the creation of all-European security structures and institutions that can guarantee stability on a continental scale.

Three issues illustrate the dramatic importance of stable, constructive relations between Russia and the West. First, the crisis in the former Yugoslavia leads even those removed from politics to recognize the benefits of Russia's independent participation in the search for resolutions to such conflicts. The problems that provided the pretexts to begin both world wars arose within Eastern Europe, indicating the need to delicately control events in that subregion. It is hard to imagine the burden that would fall upon all of Europe if Russia did not have a place in the discussions concerning the conflict in the former Yugoslavia. The threat of destabilization emanating from the Balkans demonstrates better than anything else the need for close interaction between Russia and Western Europe.

Second, Western Europe and Russia both have an interest in preventing the Soviet Union's successor states from becoming nuclear powers. This problem has intensified over time due to poorly reasoned policies and actions of Russian and Western political leaders. In particular, several American politicians, among others, have flirted independently with Ukraine's leadership, severely complicating efforts to ensure that nation's anti-nuclear status. The satisfactory resolution of this potentially explosive problem will require the closest interaction between Russia and the West.

Third, the progressive decomposition of the Soviet military mechanism and its weakened control over its nuclear arsenal may increase illegal access to nuclear weapons. This possibility has been seriously considered in the West. For example, U.S. Director of the Central Intelligence Agency James Woolsey expressed such concern in a report submitted to a U.S. Senate committee on January 25, 1994. According to Woolsey, order in Russia has been undermined to a dangerously low level by poor morale in the army, activities of organized crime, and attempts by countries such as Iran to purchase nuclear materials or technologies.[2] The surest way to prevent the illegal spread of nuclear arms is full and open cooperation between Russia and the West.

---

2. *Segodnya*, February 4, 1994.

Attraction and Repulsion

Since the height of cooperation between East and West at the beginning of the post-confrontational era which led to such achievements as German reunification, the distances — both geographic and geostrategic — between Russia and the West and between Russia and Western Europe have increased, not decreased. This phenomenon is acquiring a long-term character despite the growth of cultural homogeneity in Russia, which greatly reduces the possibility that "psychological incompatibility" will give rise to conflicts in the upcoming process of European integration. What accounts for this expanding gap between Russia and the West?

Throughout history, leaders of the West have repeatedly dismissed the idea of cooperation with Russia once its immediate and apparent usefulness has ended.[3] With the ideological division of Europe after 1917, anti-Soviet sentiment was simply layered upon anti-Russian sentiment. Therefore, it is no wonder that following the dissolution of the Soviet Union, mistrust and enmity toward Russia have again taken the lead.

The West has outwardly accepted, with varying degrees of political rapture, Mikhail Gorbachev's idea of a Common European Home, which would unite under one roof all Europeans and the Asian peoples of the former Soviet Union. However, no practical steps have been taken to build such an edifice. Much of the reproach lies with Gorbachev himself, who was often occupied with building political castles in the air rather than constructing concrete foundations for European unity. However, since achieving German reunification in cooperation with Gorbachev, the West has again looked with only limited interest at the prospect of Russian involvement in European affairs. This has been especially true since the

---

3. Consider for example the Crimean War (1853–1856). Following the defeat of Napoleon II and the destruction, with Russian help, of the centers of revolutionary ferment in Central and Eastern Europe, the West decided that it no longer needed Russia's support. One result of the period of Russian isolation that followed was the first unification of Germany in 1871. Immediately after unification, Germany began military preparations to restructure Europe. An analogous situation appeared after the Allied forces defeated Germany in World War I, again with Russia's help. After consolidating the dependent status of the defeated Germans within the Versailles framework, Britain and France chose to ignore Russia's travails by drawing its line of European interests at Russia's western border. Once again, Russia's isolation, magnified by powerful trends of self-isolation, resulted in the rise of Germany and the dizzying success of the German army during the first stages of the Second World War.

disintegration of the Soviet Union, when Russia entered a period of great internal crisis.[4]

Western Europe's tendency to exclude Russia is compounded by Russia's own tendency toward self-isolation. At the beginning of Russia's movement to a market economy, Russia's political leaders planted illusions of substantial Western assistance that would lead Russia quickly toward prosperity and wellbeing. The Russian logic was simple: Russia's ideological shift and renouncement of aggressive overtures had liberated the West from the need to maintain colossal military expenditures, and if even a small amount of the money saved was made available to support Russia's movement toward a free market economy, the process could be greatly accelerated. However, the reality in both Russia and the West is that defense conversion actually consumes capital. Disarmament costs not less, but often more than armament — a factor not to be underestimated, especially considering that Western nations are experiencing their own economic difficulties.

Therefore, Western economic assistance to Russia and the East, according to such associations as the Organization for Economic Cooperation and Development (OECD), was less than originally promised and continues to decrease. In 1991, OECD member nations contributed approximately $7.8 billion in U.S. dollars to Eastern Europe. In 1992, the amount was $8.1 billion. Correcting for price increases, the sum allotted in 1993 is actually 3 percent less than in 1992. Approximately one-half of the 1992 assistance, $3.9 billion, came from Germany. The European Community contributed $1.2 billion, the United States gave $740 million, and Italy, Austria, and Japan allotted $460 million, $410 million, and $240 million respectively. In addition, total investment by the International Monetary Fund (IMF) decreased about 50 percent. The IMF allocated $2 billion to Russia, almost as much to Poland, $600 million to Ukraine, and $300 million to Belarus. Such support amounts to an insignificant fraction of these countries' gross national products, and, therefore could not play a substantial role in the process of revitalizing their economies.[5]

Meanwhile, in Russia, the decrease in Western aid is compounded by the swift and dramatic reduction in Russia's economic cooperation with the outside world that began during the period of Gorbachev's perestr-

---

4. One of the few Western politicians who consistently considered Russia to be a necessary participant in the European concert was President George Bush.

5. *Segodnya*, February 4, 1994.

oika. The Russian Ministry of Foreign Economic Relations reported in February 1994 that, while Russia's export volume will likely remain at the 1993 level of $43 billion, imports will be reduced again by 27 percent to $27 billion.[6] Finally, the Ministry also reported that in 1993, Russia exported more primitive products. For example, industrial machinery and equipment fell to only 7 percent of export volume (it accounted for 9 percent in 1992). In comparison, metal-cutting machinery alone comprised 10.5 percent of Soviet exports in 1984.[7] This decrease in advanced exports has been compensated for by an increase in the volume of raw materials exported. However, world prices for raw materials have fallen, so a dramatic increase in the amount of raw materials exported is necessary simply to maintain current monetary returns on trade. In addition, imports to Russia fell 30 percent in absolute terms from 1992, with much of the volume now comprised of foodstuffs.[8]

The early expectations of the Russian people following the Soviet collapse are analogous to the hopes of the former East Germans who voted almost unanimously to abolish the German Democratic Republic (GDR) and supported its immediate incorporation into the all-powerful Federal Republic of Germany (FRG). However, even in unified Germany with its powerful economy and abundant resources, the process of reform caused acute social dissatisfaction. Such dissatisfaction is heightened in Russia, where the incompetence of local elites is compounded by decreasing Western assistance and the ineptitude of outside advisers. Therefore, many Russians have developed a grudge against the West. The defensive reaction is, "If the West refuses its assistance, we can manage without the West."

Another factor that fuels disenchantment within Russia is the realization that the new Russia retains practically no friends in the world. The euphoria caused by Russia's declaration of peace toward its former enemies has quickly disappeared. It has become obvious that any attempt by Russia to discard such notions as national interest, geopolitical imperatives, and the balance of power will harm it. Thus, the Russian elite's sympathy for the Serbians in their fight for national survival is

---

6. *Kommersant Daily*, February 4, 1994.

7. *Statistical Bulletin*, Secretariat of the Congress for Economic Assistance, Moscow, 1985, pp. 343, 366.

8. *Kommersant Daily*, November 25, 1993.

motivated by the instinctive desire not to lose the last Russian friend in Europe.

The lack of assistance and friendship from the West forces Russia to return to a policy of harsher, more insistent defense of its national interests in foreign policy, including, to some degree, the use of power and force. However, the world is no longer accustomed to a kind of Russia that strongly defends its positions and interests. As a result, the potential for conflict has grown.

One potential area of conflict centers around the continuing failure of the West to recognize its obvious double standard toward human rights. For example, the CSCE has repeatedly pressed Russia to respect the civil rights of its non-Russian citizens, while failing to recognize that the rights of Russians have been violated by non-Russian majorities in former Soviet territories. This has a profound effect on public opinion in Russia. Approximately 17.4 percent of all Russians, a total of 25.3 million people, live outside the borders of Russia as a result of the dissolution of the Soviet Union. It is unreasonable to demand that Russia be indifferent to their fate. The West's uncaring attitude toward the plight of Russian minorities fans the smoldering sparks of nationalism in Russia. The potential dangers of such action were illustrated by the success of Vladimir Zhirinovsky in the Russian parliamentary elections of December 12, 1993. Russia is not a conquered country, and the Russians will not allow themselves to be treated as a conquered people. In fact, some of the former republics of the Soviet Union received their freedom and independence from Russia against their will, as in Central Asia.

According to a February 1994 joint report by the Russian Academy of Sciences Economic Division and the international fund Reforma, "The scale of economic and social troubles which have fallen upon Russia are a real threat to its national security. The country finds itself at the threshold of losing forever the chance to be reborn as a great power."[9] Is the West ready to accept the possibility that Russia will forever be the sick man of Europe, requiring constant social help, instead of being a source of strength for a Greater Europe? If not, then immediate action is necessary. Such action does not mean simply a careless and limitless increase in financial credits; such credit dissolves in the Russian expanse leaving no identifiable traces, only increasing the financial burden to be carried by future generations of Russians. What is needed is normal

---

9. *Nezavisimaya Gazeta*, February 4, 1994. The report is entitled *Social and Economic Changes in Russia: Contemporary Situation and New Approaches.*

cooperation between East and West, including support for the emerging class of Russian entrepreneurs, promotion of Russian participation in markets where its products are now exemplary and competitive, and the gradual opening of world markets to Russian goods, including cooperative ventures in the Third World. Such initiatives would constitute true and valuable assistance.[10]

The incorporation of Russia's human, natural, and industrial resources into the European fund will not provide the ship of Europe with immediate stability in sailing the turbulent waters of international competition; however, it is crucial to its long-term seaworthiness. The process of full European cooperation must begin as soon as possible. The further degradation of Russia's industrial potential threatens to cause the rates of economic development in Western Europe and Russia to grow irreversibly disparate.

Prospects for Russia's Relations with Western Europe

The West's struggle to develop a Greater Europe could have been lessened by enhanced communication between Russia and Western Europe. Germany, France, Great Britain, and the United States (which despite its location is indivisible from Western Europe on a number of levels) all share with Russia similar strategic interests in maintaining political and economic stability in Europe. However, only the United States maintains the open dialogue with Russia that is critical for sustaining such stability. Communications between Russia and Western Europe consist only of proclamations of mutual sympathy. This must change.

The greatest potential for leadership within Western Europe unquestionably resides in Germany. All of Eastern and Western Europe shares this conviction. Unified Germany is the only country with the experience to promote a Greater Europe: geographically, it is located in the center of the continent, which forces Germany to think on a regional scale. Politically, Germany has historical traditions of coexistence and cooperation with many Eastern European nations. Economically, the citizens of the former GDR are experts in "real socialism" and are gaining unparal-

---

10. In February 1993, Jaques Attaly, former President of the European Reconstruction and Development Bank, proposed the creation of a "continental market" in which all European countries would participate, including Russia and the European republics of the former USSR.

leled experience in the transition from a national economy to a free market economy. Also, Germany is supported by a powerful economic base. Finally, Germany is so closely integrated with Western institutions that historically-based fears of German nationalism and hegemonic ambitions seem completely absurd.

The leaders of Germany recognize their responsibility to encourage the inclusion of all nations of the East in the Common European Home. For example, Germany remains the largest donor to Russia in terms of financial support, humanitarian aid, and commercial trade. This reflects in part the special obligation of the FRG to compensate for the loss to Russia caused by the absorption of the GDR, which previously provided approximately 10 percent of the Soviet Union's imports. Still, Russian-German cooperation is decreasing. First, the scale of trade is declining, with imports into Russia affected first. According to preliminary information from Russia's trade representative, the volume of product exchange between Germany and Russia during the first nine months of 1993 was 14.1 billion marks and is projected to have been between 16-17 billion marks for the year. This compares to 21.5 billion marks in 1992. Russian exports, of which 90 percent are raw materials and energy, comprise approximately two-thirds of current trade. Of its imports, 55 percent are machines and equipment, and 17 percent are produce, alcohol, and tobacco.

The growing divide between Western Europe and Russia raises the question: After a certain period of "thwarted expectations," will Russia look for an alternative to the notion of a Common European Home? A significant part of Russia's territory lies within Asia, and a spacious apartment is reserved for Russia in the common Asian home. It would be wrong for leaders of Western Europe to believe that the participation of Russia in both the European and Asian continental communities is mutually exclusive or that it would cause conflict. There already exists a growing bond between the two spheres, and in the future they will inevitably become part of a single, global security system. For example, in his speech on January 27, 1994, before the Chinese Association of National Diplomacy in Beijing, Russian Minister of Foreign Affairs Andrei Kozyrev pointed to the growing importance to Russia of the Asian-Pacific region, where one-third of its foreign trade is already concentrated. He emphasized that it would have been "absurd for Russia to make sharp divisions between the 'Western' European and 'Eastern' Asian directions of foreign policy."[11] Until now Russia took upon itself the role of a "sovereign representative" of Europe and Asia — a position which is now threatened. The Asian economic "tigers" have already secured strong positions in the Russian economy and will likely be among Russia's powerful competitors in the future competition to secure market power.

Relations between Russia and Western Europe can develop in two possible directions: the optimistic, and the pessimistic. In a very optimistic scenario, Russia quickly overcomes its internal economic and political crises, remains a great power, and is actively included in all European structures on all levels. Several prerequisites for the realization of the optimistic version are already in place. First, Russia has been acknowledged as the main heir and national representative of the former Soviet Union, taking its prestigious place in the United Nations and in the still exclusive company of nuclear states. Furthermore, the political situation within Russia has stabilized and will likely remain stable at least until the 1996 election. Finally, Russia is beginning to interact with the former Soviet territories in the mode of voluntary cooperation between independent nations.

Still, this optimistic scenario is not likely to be realized in the near future, not only due to the forces of instability in Russia, but also because of poorly orchestrated actions of Western (especially Western European) powers toward Russia. The West cannot afford to waste time arguing the merits of building a European Community or the proper role of Russia within that structure. The declaration of a new "Marshall Plan" for nations in the East is unlikely. Therefore, Western Europe must coordinate with other Western powers to support Russia's redevelopment as a major economy in its region during its movement from a national to a market economy.

In a very pessimistic scenario, all movement in Russia toward Western reforms ceases, and the Cold War reemerges. This would require that the current economic crisis become a catastrophe and the political system collapse, resulting in mass emigration from Russia, and a state of civil war. Despite recent nationalist movements, the pessimistic version, too, remains highly unlikely.

More likely for the present is an "intermediary" scenario. It is characterized as "intermediary" because it is moderate compared to the optimistic and pessimistic extremes and because it is temporary. Under

---

11. *Segodnya*, February 4, 1994.

this scenario, there will be a considerable deepening of the crisis inside the country, but without the political and economic extremes of the Gaidar period. People gradually become accustomed to the inevitable worsening of their situation; a half-democratic and half-authoritarian regime without extremes is established; there is continuous deterioration of communication between centers and provinces without the actual collapse of the state; emigration grows without becoming explosive; there is the undeclared inclusion of several parts of the country into the orbit of influence in the various centers of world power; and the destructive potential of nationalism furtively accumulates. For the outside world such a scenario presupposes "a little" isolation, "a little" help, and "a little" interference, without the chance to exercise the determining influence. However, the temporary nature of this intermediary scenario means that it will inevitably move toward either the optimistic or pessimistic extreme. This current hiatus in the rapid deterioration of the situation provides the opportunity to lead Russia's development in the positive direction.

Conclusion

If all parties recognize their long-term strategic interests in European stability and act rationally to promote the current potential for positive developments, the relationships between Russia and the West and between Russia and Western Europe in the next several years will be characterized by the following factors:
- Russia's movement toward self-isolation will not overstep reasonable bounds. Russia will move toward a stable democracy and free market economy, likely following to a limited extent the Chinese model of social transformation. Relations between Russia and Western Europe will not be dramatically weakened.
- The United States will remain Russia's closest partner with regard to questions of European and global security. This condition should not complicate the process of building a Common European Home because the inclusion of Russia in Greater Europe is consistent with America's national interests.
- The political culture in Russia will not be swayed by authoritarian movements and interests, but will continue to evolve toward Western European standards.
- Russia will be able to control, with the support of the West, the forces of instability within its borders and throughout the former Soviet

areas. Furthermore, Russia's efforts to maintain peace will not be misunderstood as a resurgence of imperialism.
- The United States and Western Europe will recognize Russia's limited capacity to act as a leader in foreign affairs during this period of national restructuring, which will likely stretch into the twenty-first century. Therefore, the West will consider Russia's national interests in issues of foreign policy and pursue a line of conduct that promotes Russian participation and establishes a foundation for long-term foreign policy cooperation between Russia and the West.

It would be extremely unfortunate if the fundamental mistake in foreign policy between the two world wars were repeated: the West's erroneous conclusion that it could manage without Russia (that is, the Soviet Union). World War II proved that when there are substantial reciprocal interests, there is also a possibility of cooperation — even between Western democracies and the Stalinist dictatorship. There would be fewer excuses for Western politicians now holding power if they had been unable to interact with the new Russia, which, faithful to its nature, strives to be included among the European nations. Greater Europe, and the security and stability it can provide, can materialize only with the participation of Russia.

The West could find a multitude of reasons why Russia should not be included, especially if Russian participation in building an all-European security system is made contingent upon Western judgements of what in Russia constitutes democracy and what does not, who is reformist and who is not, which decision of the Russian voters is correct and which is not. Now more than ever, firm political will is needed in order to cooperate with a difficult partner, and to insist on the policies that can respond to the long-term interests of all Europeans. This will is lacking in the West now. Everyday concerns push visions of Europe's future to the background. It is unlikely that the situation will change for the better in the near future.

The lack of Russian leadership regarding advancement toward the all-European goal is not evidence that Russia does not want close relations with Western Europe. Russia's readiness to see speedy integration of Russian and Western institutions on all levels — sub-regional, regional, transregional and global — and in all spheres — economic, military-political — resembles the European excitement of the first post war years in Western Europe, when those countries began the movement to create regional unity. Russia is tired of being a "superpower." By the 1980s,

Russia itself had begun to reject the doctrines that had forced it to install wherever possible its inefficient and oppressive order; it passionately desired to live "like everybody else." Russia has not yet recovered from the hardships of the transition period, which have been greater than all expectations. Nationalist and isolationist movements have not yet overpowered the integrational movement. The votes cast in the December 1993 parliamentary elections for Zhirinovsky still only record protest against an overdose of "shock therapy," and support for separatist slogans, chauvinism and antagonism. At the same time, this signal of dissatisfaction should be taken seriously, and East and West Europe should correct the course of their politics, keeping their main goal in sight — the safety of a stable, prosperous, and unified Europe.

Chapter 11
Karl Kaiser

Western Europe and Russia

The Cold War, though global in scope, was above all a confrontation over Europe. Although both sides increasingly realized that any outbreak of war would carry incalculable risks, East and West built up the most formidable, destructive, and costly military machine ever produced in peacetime.

During the early phase of the Cold War, Western Europe was but an object in the growing conflict between the Soviet Union and the United States. By the late 1960s, the terms of the East-West relationship were no longer exclusively defined by the two superpowers; increasingly the Western European states made their own contributions, and developed more intensive relations with Moscow. During the CSCE negotiations in the 1970s, the European Community for the first time acted as a group and spoke with one voice. Nevertheless, differences over how to deal with the Soviet Union in arms control and détente policy became a frequent if not constant issue of intra-Western relations.

With the end of the Cold War, new security problems have arisen in Europe. Most of them are very old problems — unresolved disputes reflecting ancient hatreds — and are being fought with the weaponry piled up during the superpower rivalry. The European peace that was maintained since 1945, at the price of vast repression, has come to an end. Wars are taking place in Southeast Europe and on the territory of the former Soviet Union. The theoretical possibility of a great war between East and West has now been replaced by the reality of multiple smaller conflicts.

The termination of the East-West conflict did not end Europe's security problem, it only changed it. Though the United States will remain a major actor in determining Europe's future, Russia and Western Europe will shape Europe's destiny to a greater degree than during the early postwar

---

Karl Kaiser is a Professor of Political Science at the University of Bonn and is the Otto Wolff Director of the Research Institute of the German Society for Foreign Affairs in Bonn. He was a member of the Council of Environmental Advisors of the Federal Republic of Germany and of the Government Commission for the Reform of the Armed Services.

period. Yet uncertainty reigns: Russia is suffering from internal turmoil and is undecided about its own future; Western Europe is still trying to come to grips with the end of the East-West conflict and is unclear about the future of its unification process.

New Challenges

There is a striking and momentous disparity between Russia, Europe's largest power, and the Western group of states: Western Europe, though plagued by various difficulties, is not in crisis, whereas Russia definitely is. The challenges facing both will affect their relations in the post–Cold War period.

RUSSIA'S FOUR TASKS

The course and outcome of many of the crises besetting Russia are of profound importance to Western Europe; indeed, in many ways Western Europe is likely to suffer more from negative outcomes in Russia than would other regions. Four tasks are of particular importance to Western Europe.

First, Russia must transform an ossified communist state into a democracy. The West Europeans realize what a tremendous stake they have in this evolution, for its outcome will profoundly influence the external policy of Europe's largest power. The success of the Russian reformers would improve the prospects for a cooperative relationship with Russia; consequently, supporting reformers is in Western Europe's interest. For reform-oriented Russian policy makers, the path toward democracy defines a new framework for external relations and ultimately global politics; for example, one goal might be to become a partner of the Group of Seven. Domestic changes in Russia profoundly affect Western Europe's perception of Russia, the redefinition of its security policy, and its willingness to assist Russia.

Russia's second task is to transform its seventy-year-old centrally planned socialist economy into a social market system. Here again Western European countries, Germany in particular, are considerably affected, since they have traditionally been Russia's main external trading partners. (West and East Germany were Russia's most important trading partners.)[1] Russia's transformation to a democracy with a market economy is a central interest of Western Europe; a consolidation of the reforms in Russia is the prerequisite for a realization of the extraordinary potential for mutually advantageous, complementary economic relations.

A third Russian task of concern to Western Europe is the political reorganization of the Russian Federation, reconciling the principle of shared powers and decentralization with the need for strong national government. While reforming the political regime along democratic principles, the central Russian government must preserve its capacity to govern, to mobilize resources, and to ensure the loyalty and support of its population, which encompasses so many cultural and ethnic communities. Some unresolved questions have assumed crisis proportions and could well escalate into violent confrontation. West Europe is concerned that unless these conflicts are resolved peacefully, they could sour Russia's relations with other countries. Moreover, if Russia is bogged down in violent conflicts over the integrity of the Russian Federation or the internal distribution of power, it is unlikely to be a viable partner for contractual arrangements. Consequently, the evolution of Russia according to genuinely federative principles that preserve its ability to act internationally is a central interest for Western Europe.

Finally, a fourth task is to redefine Russia's foreign policy. The dissolution of the Soviet Union has terminated the empire built up by the czars and their communist successors; at the same time hegemonic rule over the Warsaw Pact countries has ended. The most dramatic consequence of this change is the outbreak of civil war and wars between the new states of the former Soviet Union. Conflicts have emerged between Russia and some of the successor states, including the newly independent Baltic states. These conflicts with what Russians call the "near abroad" pose great problems for Russia and touch upon central Russian interests: stability at the southern and western periphery, the presence of nuclear weapons outside Russian territory, the fate of Russian minorities outside

---

1. Interestingly, in pure numerical terms trade relations between Russia and the European Union have roughly maintained their 1989 level, but Russia imports fewer investment-related goods (the main item of Germany's exports which is consequently decreasing), and more consumer products (resulting in increasing exports from other European Union members). The decrease of investment-related imports is indicative of the breakdown of existing patterns in the division of labor; this will likely further aggravate dislocation and unemployment in Russia; and contribute to severe shortages and further impoverishment of the population.

the country, and the potential loss of Russian lives through the deployment of Russian troops in unstable areas.

It remains an essential truth that a peaceful Russian foreign policy is crucial for the stability of the entire continent and a necessary prerequisite for the reorganization of security between Russia and Western Europe, as well as for cooperative relations in general.

CHANGES IN WESTERN EUROPE

Western Europe has also changed profoundly since the early Cold War period. Both democracy and the market economy are well established in Western Europe, though all states are plagued by economic problems and unemployment. There is no war, nor any danger of war. The process of European integration has wrought fundamental changes. First, a new system of interstate relations based on the peaceful resolution of conflict has been securely established. Rooted in many years of intensive political work toward reconciliation and trust-building, the relationships among peoples, elites, and political systems has changed in such a way that war has become inconceivable. Second, European integration has established a new system for managing interaction among highly developed economies.

As the Cold War came to an end, the European Union — with its flourishing democracy, internal stability and remarkable prosperity — became a magnetic pole for all of Europe. Both old and new European democracies are now trying to become members or associates, or at least establish cooperative relations with this community of states.

Only European integration, and the stability of German democracy, could have made the merger of the two German states and the recreation of Western Europe's most powerful country acceptable; integration binds Germany into a system of mutual constraints, transfers of sovereignty, and multilateral commitments. The European Community, therefore, not only provided a solution to the German question, which had been one of Russia's major concerns in modern history, but it has become the focus for the restructuring of relations between Russia and Western Europe.

To be sure, the European Community is not without problems. While the Treaty of Maastricht has transformed it into the European Union and further advanced the process of unification, this process will most likely evolve in unexpected ways, and more slowly than envisioned. Part of the uncertainty is rooted in the common foreign and security policy established by the Maastricht Treaty. Western Europe remains part of the Atlantic structures of NATO but at the same time the treaty aims to strengthen the "European pillar" through the growing convergence of the European Community and the Western European Union military alliance.

As they face the challenge of restructuring their relations, both Russia and Western Europe start from situations very different than in the past. Throughout modern history, West European powers have sought either to keep Russia out or to induce it to take sides in the affairs and conflicts within Europe. Today Russia is out of Western Europe; its final troop withdrawals from Germany in summer 1994 made Russia more distant from the borders of Central Europe than ever before in modern times. The notion of Russia playing a role in the internal disagreements of the European Union, for example between France and Germany, appears ridiculous.

Russia's Security Debate

Russia's foreign and security policy, will, of course, be decided by Russians. Western Europeans may have preferences, but their capacity to influence the course of events within Russia according to these preferences is marginal to nonexistent. Indeed, they may be able to affect Russian policy negatively, if at all, by causing unwanted effects, for example, by reinforcing Moscow's perception of encirclement.

Still, whatever is decided in Russia will no doubt affect the course of West European and Atlantic security policy, which in turn will likely have some influence on events in Russia. There is a widespread conviction among West Europeans that the outcome of Russia's internal transition will profoundly affect their security, and they follow with particular interest the Russian internal debate about the future priorities of its security policy.[2] In fact, these discussions affect Western and West

---

2. See for example Hannes Adomeit, et al., Stand and Perspectiven des deutsch-russischen Verhältnisses (The state of and future perspectives on German-Russian relations), Workshop given at the German-Russian Forum, Bonn: September 1993; Olga Alexandrowa, *Entwicklungen der außenpolitischen Konzeptionen Rußlands (Developments of the foreign policy conceptions of Russia)* (Cologne: Bundesinstitut für ostwissenschaftliche und internationale Studien) Bericht No. 13 (March 1993); Jeff Checkel, "Russian Foreign Policy," *RFE/RL Research Report*, Vol. 1, No. 41 (October 16, 1992), pp. 15–29; John Lough, "Defining Russia's Relations with Neighboring States," *RFE/RL Research Report*, Vol. 2, No. 20 (May 14, 1993); and Heinz Timmermann, "Rußland auf der Suche nach einem neuen aussenpolitischen Profil" ("Russia in search of a new foreign policy profile"), *Osteuropa*, Vol. 42, No. 10 (1992).

European thinking about the future of their policies much more than many Russians realize.

Three elements of Russia's security policy debate are of particular importance to West Europe's debate on its future security relations with Russia. The first element is the declining persuasiveness of arguments for an orientation toward Europe, the Atlantic region, and the West as a whole. During the transition from communism, many individuals and groups agreed that adherence to Western values such as democracy and a market economy was the essential basis for the modernization of Russia, and a prerequisite for its integration into the system of democracies and the world economy. They no longer considered the West an enemy, but rather an ally in Russia's transformation. Foreign Minister Andrei Kozyrev was a forceful proponent of this view, as was President Boris Yeltsin at the beginning of his term. However, these views are under growing attack, increasingly criticized for tying Russia too closely to the West and for being contrary to Russian interests. Indeed, Kozyrev felt compelled to respond to criticisms of the high priority given to relations with the United States and Western Europe by declaring that the "romantic period" of relations with the West had come to an end.

A second element, and the main reason for the decline of pro-Western thinking, is the rise of nationalist and geopolitical-realist thinking. It revives the idea of a greater Russia in combination with notions of autarky, and a specifically Russian or Eurasian "third way," and rejects the concept of Russia's integration into a world dominated by Western values. According to this view, Russia is the natural dominant power in its own zone; the world is basically conflictual; and Russia, surrounded by rivals, must fight to regain lost areas in the West, the South, and the Southeast.

The third element in the Russian security policy debate — and the most important to West Europeans — is the growing importance of the distinction between the "near abroad" and the "distant abroad." This distinction removes the former members of the USSR from the realm of normal foreign relations and relegates them to a special status, and suggests to a number of European observers a restricted concept of independence and sovereignty.

To be sure, there is much understanding for the special importance that Russia attaches to the neighboring successor republics of the former USSR and the Baltic states. Movements for ethnic independence in these areas have an immediate impact on the internal struggle over the future of the Russian Federation. The fate of the Russian minorities in many of these states is a concern, and the migration of Russian refugees is becoming a serious problem. Economic relations within the formerly interdependent socialist economies remain crucial to Russia's future. War is being waged in these regions, often involving Russian troops, and is threatening to spill over into other areas. Moreover, there are major unresolved conflicts between the newly independent states, notably over nuclear weapons and frontier issues. It is natural that Russia focuses most of its immediate attention on these problems.

The security status of Eastern Europe is the most important potential source of conflict between Russia and Western Europe. It is closely linked with Russia's policy in the "near abroad" and is a central issue for Russian–West European relations. The more tense the relations between Russia and West Europe, the more important will be the status of Eastern Europe. Ironically, Western European efforts to integrate these countries into its institutions have so far tended to increase this tension.

Western reactions to Russia's foreign policy debate include proposals to change NATO or the Western European Union, and proposals on the treatment of Central European states by these institutions. West European opinion on the developments in Russia is divided. The majority view, on the whole shared by all West European governments, tends to accept Russian concerns about stability in this area as legitimate, and considers the re-emergence of a neo-imperial Russia (which some experts and politicians constantly warn of) as by no means a foregone conclusion. However, to some West Europeans, the new military doctrine adopted after the October 1993 coup suggests that the military may be used to legitimize a neo-imperial policy; it stresses the defense of Russian minorities abroad as a central task of the armed forces and asserts the necessity of a common defense at the outside borders of the CIS. Others have a more benign view; they point to certain regional instabilities, for example in the Caucasus, that only the Russians (and certainly not the West Europeans) are able and willing to deal with, and cite the legitimacy of the concern about Russian minorities.

A common theme in Russia's foreign policy debate — voiced by liberal and democratic thinkers and neo-communists, orthodox and chauvinistic thinkers — is Russia's natural claim to great power and superpower status.[3] West Europeans do not doubt that Russia is entitled to such a

---

3. This claim was expressed by Andrei Kozyrev in particularly frank terms. See "No Sensible Choice but a True U.S.-Russia Partnership," *International Herald Tribune*, March 19–20, 1994.

status, but are concerned by the potential combination of such goals with an anti-democratic posture or the resurrection of a repressive Russian hegemony over the independent successor republics, not to mention a new type of dominance over the former members of the Warsaw Pact.

The New Nuclear Question

No issue is as important to the future Russian-West European security relationship as the problems deriving from the new nuclear question in the CIS.[4] The first element and possibly the most important is the problem of nuclear proliferation within the CIS. If Belarus, Kazakhstan, and Ukraine do not implement their pledges to become non-nuclear states, a problem of profound importance for the stability of Europe will arise. Given the intensification of conflict between Ukraine and Russia, this problem has already assumed crisis proportions.

The large quantity of warheads and fissile material piled up in the former Soviet Union, as well as the know-how of the nuclear military-industrial complex, could represent a second major threat. The decay of political authority could lead to a loss of control over these weapons; it is possible that some could end up in radical states or in the hands of terrorist groups.

A third dimension consists of the problems involved in dismantling the nuclear arsenal in an environmentally safe manner — a formidable scientific and technical challenge even for a country like the United States. A failure would likely have disastrous consequences far beyond the borders of Russia. The safe functioning of Russia's numerous nuclear power stations is also a concern. The first Chernobyl accident cost thousands of lives and devastated a large region. The destructive impact

---

4. On these questions see Graham Allison, et al. eds., *Cooperative Denuclearization: From Pledges to Deeds*, CSIA Studies in International Security No. 2 (Cambridge, Mass.: Center for Science and International Affairs, Harvard University, 1993); Erwin Häckel and Karl Kaiser, "Kernwaffenbesitz und Kernwaffenabrüstung in Europa: Bestehen Gefahren der nuklearen Proliferation in Europa?" ("Possession of nuclear weapons and nuclear disarmament in Europe: are there dangers of nuclear proliferation in Europe?"), in Joachim Krause, ed., *Kernwaffenverbreitung und internationaler Systemwandel* (*Proliferation of nuclear weapons and change in the international system*) (Baden-Baden: Nomos, 1994), pp. 239–264; Karl-Heinz Kamp, *Probleme nuklearer Abrüstung: Die Vernichtung von Kernwaffen in der GUS* (*Problems of Nuclear Disarmament: The destruction of nuclear weapons in the CIS*) Interne Studien, No. 45 (Sankt Augustin: Forschungsinstitut der Konrad-Adenauer-Stiftung, 1993).

of the accident extended far into Western Europe, further undermined public acceptance of nuclear energy, and caused major financial burdens for Western governments. Another accident would likely have a much greater impact on a critical public and its attitude toward nuclear energy, and could cause destabilizing migration, possibly extending into Central and Western Europe.

Finally, it remains to be seen whether the forceful non-proliferation policy which the Soviet Union once pursued (in relative agreement with the West European powers and the United States) will be continued in the future. Will a Russia weakened by internal crises be able to support the extension and strengthening of the non-proliferation regime when the Nuclear Non-Proliferation Treaty comes up for review in 1995? The chances for prolongation are also jeopardized if Ukraine or Kazakhstan are not clearly heading toward denuclearization.

An Agenda for Russian–Western European Relations

During the Cold War, efforts to bring about a détente between East and West could be pursued by reliably committed governments, largely exclusive of domestic politics. Today, efforts to organize security relations between Russia and Western Europe must address the close interaction of domestic and external affairs. The legitimacy and effectiveness of governments are not guaranteed, and the volatility of domestic politics can suddenly change the course of events. As a consequence, security policy must address a broad spectrum of issues and adapt to a dynamic environment.

NUCLEAR ISSUES

Nuclear questions deserve priority in Russian–West European security policy not only because nuclear events can cause such catastrophic damage, but also because they could precipitously change the course of history. This is a field where West Europeans must make a major contribution, though on most issues American participation is crucial.

First, to prevent the rise of new nuclear states, Western Europe must assist Russia, Ukraine, and Kazakhstan in the process of nuclear disarmament, the dismantling of nuclear weapons, the safe transformation of weapons materials, and the scaling down of the oversized nuclear sector. The United States has started a quite substantial program. France, Britain, Germany, and Italy have followed suit with modest — if not inadequate

— programs that deserve significantly enhanced funding by countries of the European Union.

West European governments and the United States should explore all avenues to induce Russia to follow a cooperative and prudent policy toward the nuclear successor republics, notably Ukraine. The January 1994 trilateral agreement between Russia, Ukraine, and the United States represents a major breakthrough that deserves full support from West European countries. A failure in the denuclearization of Ukraine could have disastrous consequences for the security of Europe and the advancement of global nonproliferation policy. A West European policy that contributes to stability and democracy within Ukraine and to cooperation and the resolution of conflict between Russia and Ukraine deserves top priority in West European policy. The West should extend low-level security guarantees to Ukraine in exchange for it becoming a non-nuclear state.

A second issue on the nuclear security agenda is the shared goal of Russia and Western Europe to assure that nuclear weapons reductions in the former Soviet Union do not result in nuclear proliferation elsewhere. Hence, any Western-supported strengthening of political stability in Russia, Belarus, Kazakhstan, and Ukraine is a contribution to non-proliferation, since it creates better conditions to effectively control materials and know-how. For the same reason the planned international center for technology and science, which would give employment to technicians and scientists in the shrinking nuclear sector, could contribute to non-proliferation once Russia creates, as the West has, the necessary political and legal conditions.

Finally, the issue of reactor safety in Russia is of such concern to West Europeans that a more substantial effort must be made to quickly provide advanced Western safety technology to remove threats to both Russians and West Europeans. So far the willingness of Western governments to provide financial help has been modest. There are still Russian fears about Western intrusion in its internal affairs. A new effort must be made by both sides; the economic and political cost of another nuclear accident would exceed by thousands of times the cost of a sensible program. Such a program would include modernizing or closing down unsafe reactors at Western expense, subsidizing the provision of alternative sources of energy in certain cases, and training personnel.

Nowhere else is the discrepancy between West European interests and deeds as large as in the nuclear field. While the concerns about the consequences of nuclear proliferation or a detonation in Europe are considerable, the real consequences would likely be much worse. Yet the willingness to act and invest resources to preclude such developments is shockingly inadequate.

ECONOMIC REFORM, DEMOCRACY, AND SECURITY

Democracy provides the most important basis for security. Democracies tend to be more prudent in their external behavior and more opposed to adventurism than do non-democratic regimes, and do not go to war with each other (though authoritarian regimes can also have friendly relations with their neighbors). Thus, any Western policy of assistance to Russia that helps economic and democratic reform will contribute to European security. Since the demise of communism in Russia, the states of Western Europe have acted according to this basic conviction; the European Community has given almost three quarters of all the assistance provided by OECD members.

The European Union is now engaged in redefining its relationship with Russia in fundamental ways oriented toward long-term goals. Better access for Russian exports to the EU market, combined with the inclusion of Russia in its aid programs, as well as regular summit meetings between the Russian government and the governments of the European Union would help provide the basis for a long-term, cooperative relationship, and would contribute to Russia's integration into the world economy. However, the establishment of a free trade area, which the Commission of the EU is examining with Russia, does not make much sense, since Russia is likely to remain a mixed economy for some time. Moreover, a total removal of tariffs would expose Russian industry to Western competition; Russia is not prepared for such competition, nor would there be adequate outside help, as was given to East German industry after German unification (and even with that help, competition was highly disruptive).

There is some justified disappointment in Russia that Western and West European governments have not been more forthcoming with their help. Although Western Europe has contributed far beyond its share (as has Germany within Western Europe), the overall performance has remained inadequate. Of the 40 billion dollars of credit offered to Russia by the Tokyo G-7 summit of 1993, less than a tenth was spent by early 1994. While part of the blame must be borne by Russia, with its ineffective political, administrative, and economic system, most of the blame goes to the West Europeans and Western lack of commitment and imagination.

Western policy should move away from macro-economic assistance programs (aside from debt rescheduling measures), and focus instead on targeting aid to Russia in those areas where it will have an immediate social impact. Such aid could include funds for the construction of food processing plants and housing for military officers and their families, joint programs with the Russian government involving Western personnel to fight organized crime, provision of tax breaks and other incentives to Western companies that engage in joint ventures with Russian companies, provision of funds and expertise for improving the efficiency and environmental safety of oil and gas extraction in Russia (thereby increasing the flow of much needed hard currency), and a substantial increase in programs training low and middle managers in Russia.

In addition to such programs, a complementary effort to overcome Russia's isolation from Western Europe is also needed. A very limited amount of cultural and human contact was allowed and developed during the Cold War; such interaction must be deliberately sought by private groups, political parties, and churches, and must also be supported by governments. Such contacts are indispensable to strengthening transnational links among democracies.

ORGANIZING STABILITY AND PEACE

Russia and Western Europe must be aware that each side has political forces that mourn the disappearance of a clear enemy and the order it created. In Russia, some consider NATO to be anti-Russian and any of its moves as neo-encirclement; in Western Europe, some interpret Russian actions in the successor republics and the new military doctrine as unquestionable evidence of a renewal of expansionist Russian hegemony. The two schools reinforce each other.

The first item on the Russian-West European security agenda is reconciling Russia's special interests and responsibilities in its neighboring republics with the autonomy and sovereignty to which these republics are entitled. How can one differentiate between providing order on the one hand, and pursuing Russian interests in disregard of local aspirations and by repressing opinion in these republics on the other? There seems to be a clear geographical differentiation in the minds of West Europeans. They accept a Russian stabilizing role in the Asian and Transcaucasian republics, but their attitudes change with regard to Russia's western neighbors. The three Baltic former republics are considered to be independent states that have regained their sovereignty; no doubt their independence is at the top of the list of policy priorities in Western Europe. If these countries can find a fair regime for the Russian minority and settle the remaining issues of the Soviet military presence, a functioning relationship between them and Moscow has a chance to emerge.

Ukraine is the most complex problem because of its large Russian minority (constituting half of all the Russians living outside Russia), the nuclear issue, the territorial disputes, and economic difficulties. The evolution of these issues will have a profound impact on the Central European democracies, notably Poland, as well as Western Europe. There are no easy answers, but it is in Western Europe's interest to be as generous as possible in contributing to a resolution of conflicts, and in enhancing stability and cooperation in Russian-Ukrainian relations.

Would a deal between Russia and Western Europe, as well as the West as a whole, with regard to Russia's role in the successor republics be conceivable? Discussion has begun within the CSCE framework, and Russia has shown willingness to discuss the terms of a Russian stabilizing role in this region in exchange for outside recognition and support of such a function. Although one attempt failed at the CSCE ministerial meeting in Rome at the end of November 1993, an agreement might be reached on the basis of certain principles that seem acceptable to all participants, such as not changing existing frontiers by force (although such a method seems to have become legitimized in the former Yugoslavia).

Relations between NATO and WEU and the states of Eastern and Central Europe present the second issue in Russian-West European security. It will be the thorniest, since it directly concerns military dimensions and the structure and quality of European security. Moreover, nowhere else do the memories of the past so obstruct constructive designs for the future.

Former Warsaw Pact countries have become increasingly interested in joining NATO, which is itself undergoing significant change.[5] NATO became a symbol of stability and of acceptance into the Western democratic circle. The difficulties of democratic reform in Russia have deepened the concerns of the Central European democracies about stability in their region. The debate in Western countries has become increasingly divided. Some who favor extending NATO membership to former Warsaw Pact

---

5. Indeed, Russia's acceptance of German unification within NATO and the wholehearted support of this outcome by Central European countries suggested a general recognition in the East that a multilateral alliance could be the best guarantee against a re-nationalization of security policy, and would assure a continued U.S. commitment to Europe's security.

nations agree that the decision should be made by these countries and NATO itself, and that Russia should have no veto on this matter. Skeptics argue that any move that would worsen relations with Russia would aggravate the very problem Western policy was trying to prevent; the appearance of neo-containment would only strengthen old thinking in Moscow. Moreover, a NATO extending further east would inevitably lose its former homogeneity, and thus be weakened; this would undermine its essential function of providing stability.

The decision of the January 1994 NATO summit to create the Partnership for Peace was an attempt to deal with this dilemma. The Partnership would cover joint planning and military exercises, and remove barriers to joint peacekeeping, search and rescue missions, and humanitarian missions, as well as other missions both sides agree upon.

Without excluding future membership for East European countries, this decision offers a pragmatic approach to redeveloping relations between NATO and the other European states. Not unlike the NATO strategy formulated in the Harmel Report of 1967, Partnership for Peace combines the preservation of security, now implicitly extended eastward, with the building of trust among military and political elites. In European politics today, the most important dimension of security consists of changing the political environment — creating new links and systems of integration among the states and societies of Europe. Partnership for Peace offers the possibility of developing and deepening a multitude of such links with Eastern Europe.

Another possibility is that membership in WEU could be an alternative to an extension of NATO, since the European Union has become a major force of stability in Europe. While the EU has adopted varied approaches to these countries, it is involved to some degree with all European countries, including Russia. At its November 1993 Council meeting, the WEU decided to examine a closer relationship between Eastern European states and the WEU, but it was clear that this would fall far short of entering a formal alliance commitment. The barriers to Eastern Europe's entering the WEU alliance are not very different from those involved in full NATO membership; the West European partners are not willing to assume the all commitments up to the last military implication.

In the past, the far-reaching commitment of WEU members to mutual defense has been based on the assumption that any security guarantee would be backed by the United States, due to the close interaction and division of labor between WEU and NATO. But the United States does not want to make such a commitment to Eastern Europe. The states of

Western Europe want to reassure the Central European democracies with regard to their security by giving priority to the political and economic environment rather than by resorting to classical alliance commitments at this stage. However, they wanted to open the prospect of full membership in WEU at a later point, and did so by a May 1994 decision of the WEU Council of Ministers to associate the democracies of Central and South East Europe with WEU, notably the Baltic states, Poland, the Czech Republic, Slovakia, Hungary, Romania and Bulgaria.

At this stage, the CSCE can be little more than an instrument to complement the approaches discussed above. It continues to make contributions by developing its role in mediation and in organizing observer missions. Moreover, the establishment of common rules for peacekeeping in Europe, which has begun under the auspices of CSCE, could contribute significantly to solving Western Europe's dilemma about Russia's legitimate role in its neighboring regions.

Conclusion

Western Europe and Russia must redefine their relationship to deal with common problems in Europe and an unstable international environment. Their first priority must be to maintain security — that is, stable relations with each other. In concrete terms, this means that both sides must make a constant effort not to let potential conflicts, such as those in the Balkans or Central Europe, escalate to dangerous levels or cause a new Cold War between Russia and the West. Moreover, Russia and an enlarging European Union must learn to become partners in dealing with threats to their common security, notably the proliferation of weapons of mass destruction and of missile technology.

Their second priority should be to end Russia's isolation from Western Europe. While recognizing that Russia's Eurasian location and status as a world power rule out membership in the European Union, Russia should be connected through a multitude of links with the cooperative institutions of Western Europe and the West: association with the European Union and the Council of Europe leading to membership on the Council once democracy is securely established; partial participation in the G-7, ultimately leading to full membership as Russia becomes a market economy, and regular and intensive cooperation under Partnership for Peace in NATO.

Nothing is as important to Western Europe's security as Russia's successful transformation into a modern and market-oriented democracy.

Consequently, support of that process is profoundly in Western Europe's interest and must be a priority of the European Union's policy.

So far, however, there is a shocking disparity between Western Europe's rhetoric and deeds. Public opinion and policy makers in Western Europe are all too easily overwhelmed by the obvious difficulties of a Russia in turmoil, stymied by the radical noises emanating from certain Russian politicians. The result is a paralysis of Western policy. Even substantial programs assisting Russia — for example, in denuclearization, reactor safety, and building up democratic institutions and a market economy — would only cost a small fraction of what a nuclear weapon in the wrong hands, a reactor accident, or the adventurous expansionism of a non-democratic chauvinistic government in Moscow would entail for Western Europe and the West.

As Western Europe contemplates its future it must do everything it can to avoid threats to its security arising from developments in Russia. But more is at stake than avoiding negative outcomes from Russia's inevitably long and arduous evolution. After the end of the Cold War a new system of international politics is emerging. Although its ultimate shape cannot be foreseen, some structural trends are already visible today, such as the rise of Japan and China to global power. Japan appears to have drawn its own conclusions and is quietly making a long-term investment in China to ensure a cooperative and beneficial relationship with Asia's largest country and market in the future.

In Europe two trends are visible today: the consolidation of the European Union as 1) Western Europe's encompassing framework for organizing its economy; and 2) as a significant actor in political and security affairs. Moreover, Russia's resources are such that its economy will eventually pick up strength and then be able to support its claim to world power status.

For West Europeans the time has come to look at Russia in long-term geostrategic terms (similar to Japan's approach to China), and make a substantial and enduring investment in the future of Russia. Though a realistic assessment of Russia's developments must take into account and prepare for set backs, even catastrophic ones, Western Europe has no choice but to work toward a lasting cooperative relationship between the two European giants: the European Union and Russia, Europe's largest country, which also extends to Asia. These are the most crucial elements, along with a functioning American-European partnership, of the stable international system to emerge at the beginning of the next century.

Chapter 12

Russia and the States of Central Asia and the Transcaucasus

Vitaly V. Naumkin

Moscow and the leaders of the Central Asian and Transcaucasian states realize full well that the Central Asian and Transcaucasian region (CATR), except, perhaps, for Georgia with its outlet to the Black Sea, depends for its contacts with the outside world almost entirely upon countries adjacent to them and upon communication lines and trade routes that run across their territories. In addition, since the Central Asian region, especially, is of only secondary importance to the leading world powers, it is vulnerable to Russian moves in all important spheres.

Russia has several long-term security interests in the CATR. First, Russia has a vital interest in preventing armed interstate and inter-ethnic conflicts in the CATR states, as well as the engagement of other powers that could compete with Russia's hegemony in the region. Thus, it is important for Russia to maintain sufficient influence in the affairs of these regions to ensure the effective protection of its interests. This means that it is in Russia's interest to maintain economic and political links with the CATR states and to check the involvement of these states in military-political blocs hostile to Russia. In addition, Moscow seeks guarantees that no anti-Russian action is launched from the territory of CATR states, that ethnic chauvinism and Islamic extremism do not spread from the region into Russia, that the environmental safety of the CATR is guaranteed, and that drug trafficking, terrorism, and arms smuggling into and out of the region do not spread to Russia.

Second, Russia has a vital interest in ensuring that there is no discrimination against the Russian community in the CATR states. In fact, according to the new Military Doctrine of the Russian Federation adopted on November 2, 1993, "the suppression of the rights, freedoms, and

---

Vitaly V. Naumkin is the Deputy Director of the Institute of Oriental Studies at the Russian Academy of Sciences. He is a member of the Council for Foreign Policy at the Ministry of Foreign Affairs of the Russian Federation, and is head of the Russian Center for Strategic and International Research.

legitimate interests of the citizens of the Russian Federation abroad" constitutes a threat to Russian security.

In general, the limited possibilities for Russia to spread its influence beyond its borders compels Moscow to concentrate on its "near abroad," where the Russian government is seeking to construct a friendly environment. If the above-mentioned threats become acute, Russia would be plunged into a whirlpool of endless local armed conflict and would be flooded with refugees from the CATR. Russia's protracted embroilment in conflicts in this region would impede normal communications with neighboring states, break down existing economic ties, and sow mistrust toward its leadership both inside and outside the country, strengthening the political forces that favor empire.

While it is difficult to imagine Russia being targeted for aggression by any Asian state south of its borders, an offensive could only be successful if there were an agreement or alliance among the CATR states. Therefore, it is in Russia's interest to minimize the potential for such a strategic arrangement to crystallize, both through formal treaties with the CATR states and also through significant economic and political engagement in the region.

This chapter examines Russia's interests in the southern regions of the former USSR, the threats to its national security, and what moves Moscow would be well advised to make to alleviate or contain those threats.

Differences Between the Two Regions

Some Russian experts argue that there are fundamental differences between the security situation in Central Asia and that in the Transcaucasus.[1] Russia does, in fact, have a differentiated approach to security issues with regard to the two groups of states. Since Transcaucasia is generally of greater concern to Russian foreign and security policy, it is considered in more detail. Features specific to this region are:
- Of the three Transcaucasian republics, Georgia and Azerbaijan were outside the CIS until fall 1993.
- All three republics are involved in armed conflicts involving bloody warfare.

---

1. Alexei Arbatov, "An empire or a great power?" *Novoye Vremya*, No. 50 (December 1992).

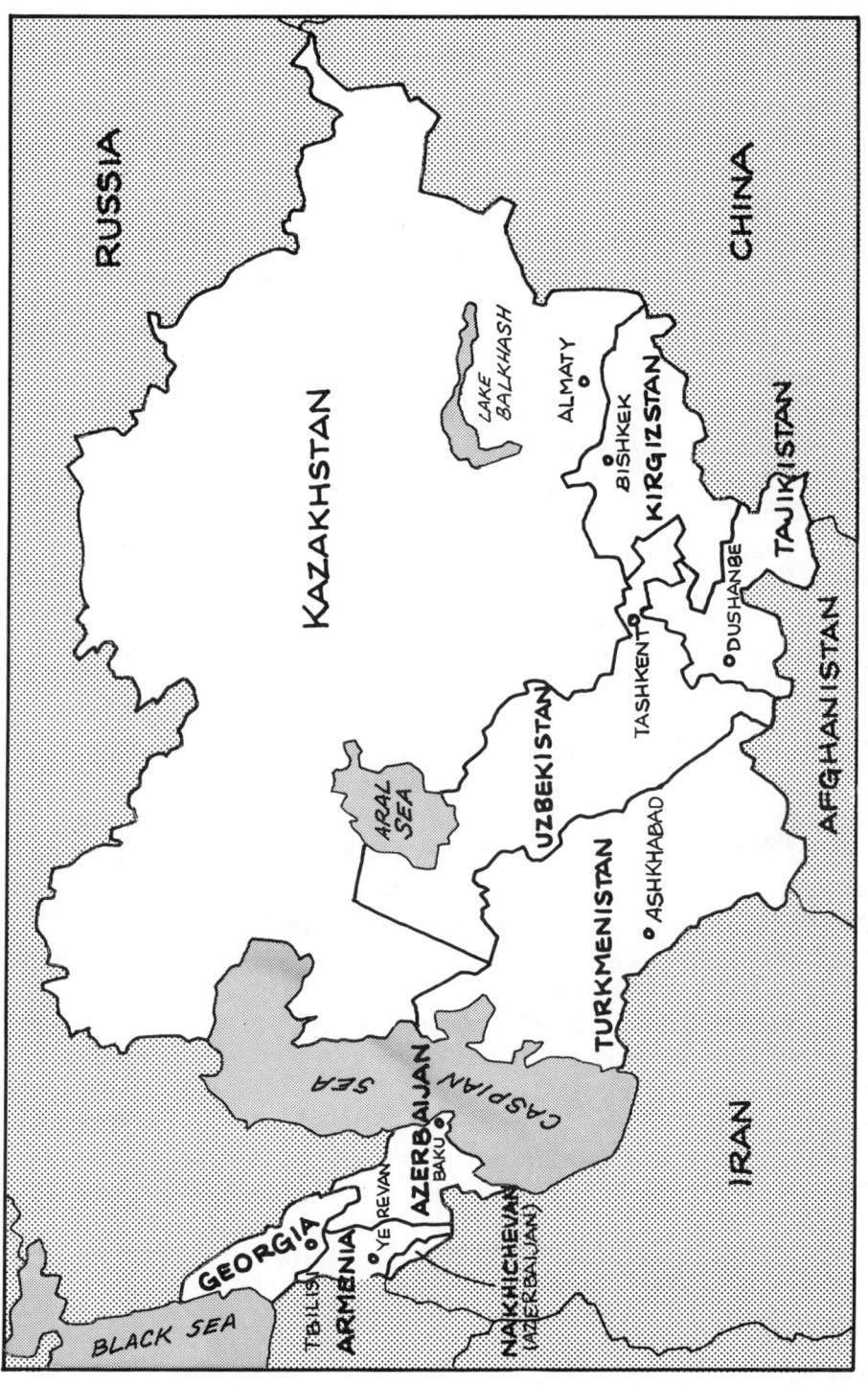
Transcaucasia and Central Asia

- The Transcaucasian republics border the Northern Caucasus, a primary pocket of instability in Russia.
- Georgia's outlet to the Black Sea gives the Transcaucasian republics an economic and geostrategic advantage over the Central Asian states, which depend entirely upon overland routes for transport and communications.
- Azerbaijan has special bonds linking it with its southern neighbors (Azerbaijan and Iran are both Shiite Muslim countries; Azerbaijan and Turkey are both Turkic countries). However, Armenia and Turkey are involved in border disputes, and two-thirds of ethnic Azerbaijanis live in Iran; this creates a potentially explosive situation.
- Armenia and Georgia are Christian, while most of the residents of Central Asia are Muslim.
- In the Transcaucasian states there are no Russian communities as large as the ones in Central Asia. For example, the Russian community of Kazakhstan accounts for 38 percent of the state's population. In Kirgizstan the figure is 22 percent, in Turkmenistan, 10 percent, and in Uzbekistan, 8 percent. In Azerbaijan Russians comprise only 6 percent of the population, in Georgia, 6 percent, and in Armenia they account for a mere 2 percent.[2]

Transcaucasia represents a potentially more explosive threat to Russian interests than Central Asia, and is therefore a greater priority in a geopolitical and geostrategic sense. Conflicts in Transcaucasia threaten the interests of Russia; they often contribute to arms and drug smuggling, as well as acts of terrorism, and in general add to the export of instability. At the end of 1993 there were approximately 2 million refugees residing in the Russian Federation, including a sizable number from the CATR states. The need to accommodate increasing numbers of refugees has become a heavy burden on the Russian state budget.

However, the presence of a large Russian population in Central Asia, especially in Kazakhstan, the length of the Russian-Kazakh border, and the enormous oil and gas resources of Kazakhstan and Turkmenistan, confirm the long-term importance of that region to Russia.

---

2. "Russians Abroad: Pawns or Knights?" *The Economist*, July 10, 1993.

Economic Interests

Immediately following the collapse of the USSR, Russian opinion was divided about how Russia should conduct its relations with the newly independent Central Asian states. Many wanted to see Russia as part of the Western world. They felt that if Russia intended to return to Europe and to Western civilization, then Russia should distance itself from Central Asia and reduce its obligations to those states to a minimum. The Eurasianists, who insist that Russia has a special status on the Eurasian landmass that cannot be contained in the "European idea," are convinced that it is vitally important for Russia to preserve its ties with Central Asia and the Caucasus.

The unpreparedness of Central Asian regimes to carry out reforms on the Russian model constitutes one of the main obstacles to economic reintegration with Russia. In fact, according to experts at the International Research Center of the Moscow International Relations Institute, "The non-uniform development rate of the CIS member-states will lead to the fragmentation of the Commonwealth, while the consolidation of its nucleus may lead to the transformation of the CIS from a Eurasian commonwealth into a Russian-dominated association with Kazakhstan and Central Asia."[3] The differing rates of development in the Central Asian and Transcaucasian states and Russia have become an important factor in policy debates.

Russia's leadership decided against closer economic ties with the Central Asian states because of the incompatibility of the economic policies of those states with that of Russia, in particular the greater role played by the state in their economies. It was also the case that certain Russian politicians believed that a close economic alliance with Central Asia would entail the inevitable regression of the economic reform process in Russia. Neither Kazakhstan nor Uzbekistan has proved willing to accept Russia's terms for entrance into the ruble zone, and both countries have opted to introduce their own national currencies. Tajikistan, economically the weakest of all the Central Asian states and the most dependent upon Russian aid, became the only state in the region to continue to use Russian currency.

---

3. "Sodruzhestvo nezavisimykh gosudarstv: protsessy i perspektivy" ("Commonwealth of Independent States: processes and prospects"), *Report of the International Research Center of the Moscow International Relations Institute* (Moscow, September, 1992), p. 10.

Russia's economic relations with the Transcaucasian states proceed from somewhat different premises. First, Georgia and Azerbaijan are, on the whole, bent on distancing themselves from Russia. Second, the establishment of closer economic ties between Russia and Transcaucasia has been hindered by the extreme political and strategic instability in that region. Of the three republics, Armenia alone is seeking closer integration with Russia and wanted to stay inside the ruble zone. But as a result of Russia's failure to reconstitute the ruble zone and to provide sufficient economic guarantees, in November 1993 Yerevan too declared that it intended to create its own currency. By the end of 1993, Georgia found itself in such deep crisis that its only option was to request aid from Russia; in February 1994, it signed a treaty of friendship and cooperation with Moscow.

Russia's national interests demand that the long-established economic links with the CATR states be preserved. Apart from being of immediate benefit to both sides, economic cooperation between Russia and the CATR helps preserve stability in the region, prevent any of its parts from falling under the influence of other external powers, and enable Russia to use the communication links located in the region to gain access to the countries south of Central Asia and the Caucasus.

Independence has presented all the CATR states with formidable challenges, including the termination of economic subsidies from Moscow, the switch to selling raw materials and food supplies on a commercial basis at world market prices, and the exodus of skilled Russian laborers and specialists. These difficulties are further exacerbated by persistently high rates of population growth, and economic pressures stemming from the need for the CATR states either to introduce their own currencies or to join the ruble zone on terms acceptable to Russia.

Preserving the remaining economic links with Russia while establishing new diversified foreign ties and gradually gaining a firm foothold in the world market would represent the ideal path of development for the CATR states today. The restructuring and reorientation of their economies is indispensable and inevitable, but this will require the ability to draw substantial resources from outside this framework. A solution to the problems facing the CATR calls for a well thought-out economic growth strategy — something that has yet to be worked out. For the present the states of Central Asia and Transcaucasia continue to survive economically by selling mostly raw materials to industrialized countries for hard currency, while producing very little on their own.[4]

Economic links with Russia would also strengthen the position of the reformists in the CATR states, at least as long as pro-market reformers remain in power in Russia. Over the long run, attempts to establish alliances with extremist authoritarian regimes would likely be counterproductive. In Leonid Fridman's opinion, there is no ruling out the prospect that some of the new independent Soviet successor states will for a time become something akin to a "sedimentation tank" of backward politico-religious structures and ideas. This would be the luxury of those states that can survive economically on the marketing of fuels and other valuable resources.[5]

If any of the CATR countries becomes a major producer of fuels, this could go some way toward stabilizing the situation in the region. However, it could also stir up antagonism between various political forces and invite the involvement of external forces interested in drawing those countries into their own zones of influence. This, in turn, would threaten Russian interests. No CATR state has yet become, or is likely to become in the near future, a major producer of fuels. However, Kazakhstan has large oil deposits, and the largest deposit, located in Tengiz, is slated to be developed with the cooperation of the Chevron Company and the Uzbek government.

The creation of a network of pipelines for the export of oil and gas from Central Asia could affect the security equation in the region. It makes a great deal of difference to Russia, and to many other states, where Turkmenian gas will go, and along which routes. There are plans to pipe oil and gas southward to the Persian Gulf and to Black Sea ports, and to Europe via Russia and Ukraine. The inclusion of the territories of Russia and Ukraine into the pipeline system would contribute toward integration. In contrast, laying the pipeline outside the CIS boundaries would substantially undermine the oil extracting countries' long-term economic and geostrategic ties with Russia and other existing and potential partners in the CIS.

The strategic importance of oil and gas in the CATR will depend on the rate at which the oil and gas industry is developed in Russia and its

---

4. *Nezavisimaya Gazeta*, October 30, 1993.

5. Cit. in Apostolou, "The Problems of Creating Economies in Central Asia," paper presented at "The Gulf and the Central Asian Republics" symposium, Exeter, July 12–14, 1993.

performance in the foreign market. If Russia becomes a major oil and gas exporter, it may, in cooperation with the CATR, compete with the oil extracting countries of the Persian Gulf. If Russia and the states of the CATR can guarantee secure delivery by ending armed conflicts in the region, they may succeed in luring oil and gas customers from the Gulf states.

Political Interests

The effectiveness of Russia's policy instruments has declined throughout the CATR. The region is badly in need of funds for economic development and is looking elsewhere for new, more reliable partners. In their attempts to assert themselves in the international community and to secure the support they need, the CATR states have pinned their hopes on their new Eastern partners, particularly Turkey and Iran. The countries of Central Asia and Transcaucasia are currently conducting bilateral trade with those and other states. In addition, a number of Central Asian republics and Azerbaijan have gained representation in regional economic organizations such as the Economic Cooperation Organization (ECO).

The attitudes of the individual states of Central Asia and Transcaucasia toward participation in regional economic and security arrangements are influenced by a number of factors:

- The CATR states have embarked upon the road of sovereign political and economic development and will shape their policies to avoid dependence on any external force.
- None of the CATR states has yet worked out a general framework for development or fully elaborated its foreign policy orientation.
- All of the CATR states have so far remained closely tied to Russia, and always take the "Russian factor" into consideration in their policy decisions.
- The Central Asian states and Armenia are members of the CIS, which imposes certain obligations upon them. Their positions vary from actively pro-integrationist (Kazakhstan) to isolationist (Turkmenistan).
- All of the CATR states and Russia are signatories to the Collective Security Treaty; each has bilateral security arrangements with Russia.
- The promotion of cooperative relations with their southern neighbors — above all Turkey and Iran — is among the top priorities of the CATR states, especially the Muslim ones.

- Stability in the CATR is threatened by border and territorial disputes, inter-ethnic and social conflicts, and the power struggle among the local elites. Transcaucasia is going through a period of critical instability. In Central Asia, stability has been maintained so far through a policy of unhurried and smooth reforms, "restrained" democratic freedoms, and the effective preservation of authoritarian rule.
- The CATR countries vary considerably in their levels of development, the availability of natural and mineral resources on their territories, demographic patterns, and geostrategic importance to Russia.

Since the collapse of the Soviet Union, the Transcaucasian states have sought above all to consolidate their newly acquired independence. Integration within the framework of the CIS became an increasingly remote possibility in Central Asia. On January 4, 1993, Kazakhstan, Uzbekistan, Turkmenistan, Kirgizstan, and Tajikistan established an interstate community, the Central Asian Regional Union. Its primary purpose is to deal with economic problems, but the possibility of cooperation on military and security issues was not excluded.

In Russia, attitudes toward Iran, Turkey and other new partners of the CATR countries in south-central Asia and the Middle East differ, but in general fall between the extremes of realism and alarmism. Alarmist politicians think that Russia is facing today a large-scale expansion into the zone of its economic and geopolitical interests by countries that aim at ethno-cultural (Turkey) and ideological (Iran and Afghanistan) expansion. They warn that the spread of Turkic chauvinism has the potential to lead to the radicalization of nationalist sentiments in Russia's Turkic enclaves, and to violations of the rights of Russian and other ethnic communities.

Alarmists also fear that the likely spread of Islamic extremism in the CATR is a serious potential threat to Russia's interests because it will lead to the ousting of Russian-speakers from many localities and cause the emigration of non-Muslims to Russia, as well as Muslims unwilling to live under Islamist regimes. They also feel that "political Islam" is a threat to the Muslim regions of Russia, where it has the potential to become an alternative to secular democratic rule. A range of political views can be found in the alarmist camp. On the whole, alarmists argue for the containment of the activities of Iran, Turkey, Afghanistan and other states attempting to become actively involved in the affairs of the region, accompanied by efforts to maintain Russia's influence in the CATR.

The realists feel that a partial loss of Russia's influence in the CATR is a *fait accompli*. It is virtually inevitable, they argue, that Russia will lose a part of its economic and security leverage in the CATR to the new economic and political partners being cultivated by those states. Realists reason that this will not endanger Russia's long-term interests unless military-political unions are formed in the CATR, or forces having aggressive intentions with respect to Russia come to power. Certain segments of Russia's policy elite are, however, apprehensive about any attempts to form integrative blocs or alliances in Central Asia without direct Russian involvement. The economic and military dependence of the Central Asian states upon Russia, and the fact that no external forces are willing to tackle the region's complicated problems make it highly unlikely that the Central Asian states will seek to realign themselves completely. In general, realism predominates in Russia's current policy toward the CATR, punctuated by occasional alarmist sentiments.

For example, in July 1993 Russia's leading centrist opposition party criticized the attempts by the ECO's founder states to weaken Russia's influence in the Central Asian region. They also warned that the threat of expanding this bloc to the southern borders of Russia was "not just economic." To dramatize the point, Russia's Vice-Premier Alexander Shokhin called on the Republics of Central Asia to choose between the ECO and economic alliance with Russia, Ukraine and Belarus. Yet Moscow is currently neither willing nor able to effectively counter the ever more active cooperation between Turkey and Iran and the CATR countries, above all in the economic and cultural spheres. The spread of this cooperation to areas directly connected to the maintenance of Russia's national security has obviously put Moscow on the alert. Russia has so far opted for a policy of limited containment.

Military Cooperation

Since Russia signed the Collective Security Treaty in Tashkent on May 15, 1992,[6] no practical efforts have been made toward military integration among the signatories, while the treaty's failure to put an end to the Armenian-Azerbaijani conflict has revealed its ephemeral character. It has been argued that although widely advertised in the CIS as a "collective

---

6. The document was ratified in the Russian parliament in August 1993.

security structure," the Tashkent accord can guarantee defense against challenges from outside but has no mechanisms to provide security within the CIS itself.[7] In fact, even when Tajikistan was attacked from the territory of Afghanistan, initially only Russia and Kazakhstan remained faithful to their commitment to fortify the Tajik-Afghan border.

Most of the Central Asian states still trust Russia as a mediator,[8] and readily rely upon its aid both economically and militarily. In Transcaucasia, however, at least until the fall of 1993 the conflicting parties preferred to appeal to the UN, NATO, the CSCE and the West instead of Moscow. By its behavior in the Tajik conflict Russia has demonstrated that it is not indifferent to the fate of the Central Asian states, and that it is prepared to intervene for the purpose of restoring stability, law and order — but only in cooperation with the states of the region.

The Central Asian and Transcaucasian states, with the exception of Georgia, are fully aware of the need to promote military cooperation with Russia.[9] These states could face threats to their security from China, Iran, Turkey, and Afghanistan, and from militant nationalist and Islamist groups. Other threats include domestic conflicts on ethnic, political, regional, and religious grounds, and disputes over borders and the control of resources and lines of communication within the region. The CATR states face severe problems obtaining weapons for and training their national armies. Finally, the limited military potential of the states in this region creates problems in the reorganization of an effective system for regional deterrence.

Even if military cooperation with Russia goes smoothly, guaranteeing the long-term security of the CATR countries will be no easy matter. As a result of the disintegration of the Soviet Army, the CATR states have found themselves in possession of a military heritage out of proportion to

---

7. M. Shashenkov, "Security Issues of the Ex-Soviet Central Asian Republics," *Defence Studies*, No. 14, London, 1992, p. 49.

8. During the February 1994 visit to Uzbekistan of E. Rakhmanov, Chairman of the Supreme Soviet of Tajikistan, Uzbek President I. Karimov stated that the presence of Russian peacekeeping forces in Tajikistan is a guarantee of stability in the region. Television Broadcast, Moscow, February 22, 1994.

9. In Georgia, Eduard Shevardnadze was forced to call on Russia for help after multiple setbacks in the Abkhazian armed conflict and the start of another military offensive by the supporters of ex-president Zviad Gamsakhurdia in the autumn of 1993. In this way Georgia changed its attitude toward military cooperation with Russia.

their actual needs. Turkmenistan, for example, has more weapons and combat equipment than Uzbekistan, which is far larger.

Unlike in Central Asia, the Transcaucasian states brought strong pressure to bear on Russia in military matters. They demanded the withdrawal of Russian troops, tried to bring military units remaining on their territory under their national jurisdiction, and seized weapons and other military hardware. In addition, these governments accused the Russian military of giving support to this or that side in various conflicts in the region. None of the Transcaucasian states have succeeded in creating a battleworthy national army in the brief time since they gained independence; not surprisingly, groups involved in armed conflicts recruited mercenaries from among Russian, Ukrainian and other servicemen.

Kazakhstan: A Special Status?

Kazakhstan is more important to Russia than the other CATR states for a number of reasons. Kazakhstan and Russia share a border of approximately 6,000 kilometers. Kazakhstan is Russia's gate to Central Asia. Kazakhstan has the second-largest Russian community in the CIS (after Ukraine), about 6.5 million who live in a largely compact area in the north. Kazakhstan is rich in mineral resources, including oil, and is also one of the CIS's leading grain producers. Kazakhstan has nuclear weapons on its soil. The present Kazakh leadership is, despite serious differences in political views, still considering options for the development of closer ties with Russia.

Kazakhstan has tried to use the nuclear weapons deployed on its territory as a political trump card in its bid for concessions from the international community. The possibility of external threats from China and, under certain circumstances, from Russia, and the desire to carry more weight with the world community constitute concrete incentives for Kazakhstan to hold onto its weapons.

In 1993, Kazakh politicians discussed the advisability of keeping nuclear weapons on the territory of Kazakhstan but under the control of Russia. This would not only deter external threats to Kazakhstan, but would also deter Moscow from supporting Russian separatism in Kazakhstan. Russia is still insistent about bringing all these weapons to Russia, preventing nuclear proliferation, and ensuring strict adherence to all international agreements relevant to this issue.

A second issue that has strained Kazakhstan's relations with Russia is the Baikonur space launch complex, which Kazakhstan claimed as its own, although it does not have the means to maintain it. Presidents Yeltsin and Nazarbayev met in Moscow on August 6, 1993, to settle all the issues involved in Russian-Kazakh relations, and decided that Baikonur remained "undivided." Still, the issue remained unresolved. Tensions grew after the parliamentary elections in Russia in December 1993 in which the communists and the chauvinistic Liberal Democratic Party of Vladimir Zhirinovsky won a considerable number of seats in the Federal Assembly; Almaty's fears about the possible revival of Russian imperialist policies have served to reaffirm its demand to secure joint control over Baikonur in order to prevent it from being used as a Russian military base.[10] However, in the end, a compromise was reached and Russia was granted a twenty-year lease on the facility for $115 million annually.[11]

During the autumn of 1993 the strain in relations between Russia and Kazakhstan was further increased after Almaty rejected the conditions under which Moscow agreed to provide the state with new rubles, and Kazakhstan moved to introduce its own currency. Kazakhstan's refusal to grant dual citizenship to its residents remains another factor negatively affecting relations between the Kazakh authorities and the Russian community. Graham Fuller is of the opinion that the Republic of Kazakhstan represents the most extreme case of potential confrontation between local nationalists and Russian national interests.[12]

---

10. *Nezavisimaya Gazeta*, February 12, 1994.

11. If it chooses, Russia can extend the lease for an additional ten years. Rather than pay Kazakhstan, Russia will deduct the amount of the lease from Kazakhstan's debt to Russia. Russians employed at Baikonur will be subject to Russian law. Bess Brown, "Agreement on Baikonur Signed," *RFE/RL Daily Report*, March 29, 1994, p. 1.

12. Graham Fuller, "Central Asia: The New Geopolitics," National Defense Research Institute, Santa Monica, 1992, p. 41. This view corresponds to that of A. Migranyan, member of the Presidential Council of the Russian Federation, who considers the potential for Kazakhstan to fall apart on ethnic grounds inevitable if it succeeds in separating itself from Russia using guarded borders, customs checks, and other means of underlining the division between them. *Nezavisimaya Gazeta*, February 12, 1994.

Domestic Conflicts

Armed inter-state and inter-ethnic conflicts are among the most serious threats to Russian interests in Central Asia and Transcaucasia, for many reasons:
- By violating the status quo, inter-state and inter-ethnic armed conflicts set a precedent for resolving outstanding issues by forcible methods.
- By weakening the CATR countries' already shaky economies, inter-state and inter-ethnic conflicts will hinder economic development in the CIS as a whole.
- Conflicts may draw Russia and its troops that are stationed in the region into hostilities.[13]
- Armed conflicts may compel Russia to make new military commitments.
- Conflicts may provoke intervention by external forces, introducing the possibility that their influence in the conflict zones may increase beyond Russia's control.
- Armed conflicts place the welfare and security of local Russian communities in jeopardy and lead to massive emigration of ethnic Russians to Russia.
- Armed conflicts may spread to the territory of Russia.
- Inter-state and inter-ethnic conflicts place obstacles in the way of political reforms in the states of the region and foster authoritarian and even totalitarian tendencies.
- Armed conflicts fuel fanatical anti-Russian movements, such as radical nationalism and Islamic extremism.

Despite these arguments, some feel that Russia reaps benefits from some of these conflicts. For example, some argue that the Russian government has deliberately encouraged the continuation of the conflict between Azerbaijan and neighboring Armenia over the disputed territory of Nagorno Karabakh so that it can emerge as the arbiter of peace and

---

13. According to reliable estimates, as of July 1993 there were 189,000 servicemen of various national armies, 97,000 Russian servicemen, and 34,000 troops under joint Russian-Turkmenian command in Central Asia. In Transcaucasia, there were 55,000 national army troops and 15,000 Russian servicemen.

consolidate its control over the region.[14] If this was Russia's strategy, it has not been successful.

As a rule, each side in any conflict in Central Asia or the Caucasus accuses Russia of supporting its enemy. Grounds for such charges are furnished by cases of Russian servicemen having been hired as mercenaries, unauthorized arms sales (which Russian authorities find difficult to combat), and the question as to whether Russian army units have taken part in the Georgian-Abkhazian hostilities on the Abkhazian side.

Although exaggerated by Western analysts, the spread of Islamic extremism does threaten Russian interests. Over the short term, Islamists stand no chance of becoming a major political force — let alone coming to power — in the Central Asian states, in Azerbaijan, or in the Muslim regions of Russia, due to the spread of secularism during the years of Soviet rule. However, with the growth of Islam's cultural influence and the aggravation of the economic and social crises in those states and subregions, Islamists may become a powerful force in Central Asia and Transcaucasia. The concept of a theocratic state, in whatever form, is antidemocratic by definition and will be rejected by autonomous republics and regions of the Russian Federation. Nevertheless, the process of democratization will likely contribute to the activeness of Islamist-oriented parties on the political scene of Central Asia, Transcaucasia and Russia. Radical anti-Russian nationalistic extremism may become a much more serious threat to Russia's interests.

As it begins to take an increasingly larger part in settling conflicts on the territory of the CATR, Russia prefers that its actions be legitimized by the appropriate international, regional or bilateral agreements. However, according to the new Russian military doctrine, the armed forces of the Russian Federation have the task of carrying out peacekeeping operations. These operations can take place both within the CIS and outside its borders in accordance with the decisions of the UN Security Council or other collective security bodies, or in keeping with stated international obligations. The doctrine stipulates the conditions and possible forms of Russia's participation in peacekeeping missions sanctioned by the UN,[15]

---

14. D. Sneider, "Big-Power Rivalry in the Caucasus," *The Christian Science Monitor*, July 22, 1993.

15. In September 1993, Russian Minister of Foreign Affairs Andrei Kozyrev in his speech to the U.N. General Assembly for the first time raised the question of giving the Russian armed forces in CIS states the status of international peacekeeping forces. He repeated this request in November 1993 when the foreign ministries of the CSCE states met in Rome.

and assumes that the main threat to peace and stability derives from local wars and armed conflicts.[16] Since a significant share of the world's armed conflicts are taking place within the borders of the former USSR, Russia considers the containment of these conflicts a fundamental security priority.

In addition, Russian officials argue that challenges to Russia's national security may threaten international security as well. If conflicts spread to other Central Asian republics, the immediate result will be the further destabilization of the region; but there is hope that such developments can be prevented. The instruments available to Russian policy makers to influence outcomes in the CATR will largely depend upon the level of stability in Russia itself.

Conclusion

The states of the CATR will feel the need to maintain close ties with Russia for a long time to come, and Russia is likely to play an important peacekeeping role in the region for the foreseeable future. The domestic changes of Russia preclude the re-establishment of a Soviet-style political order in the region; while certain sectors of the Russian political establishment exhibit isolationist leanings as well as messianic and patronizing attitudes, these sectors will not hinder the course of long-term reintegration. The option of maintaining a common military, political, and economic space that includes the Central Asian and Transcaucasian states is based upon political pragmatism and a clear view of Russia's vital national interests.

According to Andrei Kozyrev's address to Russia's ambassadors to the CIS countries and the Baltic states in January 1994, the territory encompassed by the CIS member states constitutes a zone of vital interest for Russia.[17] Russian participation in military peacekeeping actions inside this region seems highly likely, if not inevitable, although many of the existing conflicts will be difficult to manage indeed. Russia's efforts to legitimize its involvement in conflicts in the CATR and other regions by giving its troops the status of international peacekeeping forces is dictated not by

---

16. *Krasnaya Zvezda*, No. 254 (November 4, 1993).
17. *Nezavisimaya Gazeta*, January 20, 1994.

neo-imperialist ambitions, but by its desire to act in accordance with international law and in close collaboration with its Western partners.

However, Russia cannot solve all of the domestic problems of the Central Asian and Transcaucasian states single-handedly. Moscow realizes the necessity of broadening economic ties between these states and other external powers, while reserving for itself the responsibility to provide stability for the region in the form of a military and security shield. At least for the time being, this vision seems, for the most part, to be shared by the leaders of the Central Asian and Transcaucasian states.

Chapter 13

Tonya L. Putnam

The States of Central Asia and the Transcaucasus and Russia

Russia and the former Soviet republics define their national security interests in a multipolar environment that lacks the stability provided by an unambiguous political center of gravity. The vital interests of the newly created independent states of Central Asia and Transcaucasia are not always compatible with the vital national interests of the more advantaged Russia. The central policy dilemma for each state is to minimize the number and level of threats to its political, economic, and security interests, and to achieve the most favorable outcome vis-à-vis the others.[1]

This chapter identifies and examines the long-term geostrategic, political, and economic interests of Russia and the states of Central Asia and the Transcaucasia in their relations with one another, and probes the likely significance of these relations for the West. Finally, an attempt is made to identify and analyze the factors that are likely to affect the willingness of the United States and Western Europe to intervene directly or indirectly in Russia's relations with the states of Central Asia and Transcaucasia.

Russia's Interests in Central Asia and the Caucasus

Russian policy makers identify Russia's vital interests with regard to Central Asia and the Caucasus as the following: to create conditions in which the political and territorial integrity of the Russian Federation and the inviolability of its borders are secure; to retain access to and use of

---

1. The states of Central Asia are Uzbekistan, Turkmenistan, Tajikistan, Kirgizstan, and Kazakhstan. The states of Transcaucasia are Armenia, Azerbaijan, and Georgia.

Tonya L. Putnam is at the Kennedy School of Government at Harvard University. She holds an MA from Harvard University, where she studied Russia, Eastern Europe, and Central Asia.

The author is indebted to Donald Carlisle for his contributions to an early draft of this paper.

military installations, ports and strategic defense facilities located on the territory of these states;[2] to guarantee future access to Central Asian and Transcaucasian oil, gas, and mineral resources; to ensure the maintenance and expansion of beneficial economic ties; and to achieve these ends without endangering the internal consolidation of the Russian state.[3] The greatest threats to these interests stem from the pervasive national conflicts in Central Asia and the Caucasus with their potential to damage Russia's internal political stability and economic prosperity, and to complicate its external relations.[4] The following factors are most important.

1. Nuclear weapons in Kazakhstan. If Kazakhstan were to succeed in acquiring control over the nuclear weapons on its soil, this would have a significant impact on the balance of power, reducing Russia's relative strength in the region and beyond.

2. The need to protect the rights of Russian citizens who reside in the former Soviet republics.[5] This exigency provides Moscow with an ideal pretext for intervention in the affairs of Central Asian and Transcaucasian states, especially in regions torn by armed conflict.

3. Refugees. The ongoing conflicts in Nagorno Karabakh, Georgia, and Tajikistan have already displaced tens of thousands of people, many of them ethnic Russians. Since Russia is already suffering severe shortages of housing and social services, these refugees strain Russia's capacity to provide for the most needy among its own population; this could heighten

---

2. Russian officials argue that the voluntary withdrawal of forces and influence from the Central Asian and Transcaucasian states would entail the surrender of large amounts of military hardware, including radar facilities essential to Russia's early warning systems for nuclear attack. (Interview with Yurii Nazarkin, January 29, 1994, Moscow.)

3. The shift in Russian foreign policy away from its openly Western orientation has prompted more pragmatic assessments of certain aspects of Russia's national security interests, and has led to a more assertive Russian stance in the international arena, especially with regard to the so-called "special threats" to Russia and its national interests emanating from its southern rim, including the Central Asian and Caucasian states.

4. In particular, developments in Russia's relations with these regions may either heighten or assuage the level of nervousness about Russian imperial intentions in the Western republics of the former Soviet Union, especially Ukraine, and thus influence those relations.

5. Ten million Russians live in the five Central Asian states, where they are an important part of the skilled workforce. Anthony Hyman, "Moving Out of Moscow's Orbit: The Outlook for Central Asia," *International Affairs*, Vol. 69, No. 2 (1993), p. 304.

social tensions inside Russia, and lead to the spread of ultra-nationalist sentiments.[6]

4. The involvement of external powers in the former Soviet security space. Instability in these regions could invite the engagement of outside powers potentially hostile to Russia and Russian interests, as could intensive economic and security contacts conducted by the Central Asian and Transcaucasian states with outside powers without the regulation of Moscow.

5. The disruption of markets and resource supply lines. Russian foreign trade has been restricted by existing economic and trade regimes, as well as by its own technological shortcomings, even as a supplier of raw materials. This has led Russia to maintain its economic and military ties with former Soviet republics to ensure markets for its exports.

6. Fear of the spread of religious extremism. Russia's ruling circles, and the public, view the spread of Islamic extremism to the territory of the Russian Federation from the states of Central Asia and the Caucasus as a particularly destabilizing threat. This partially explains why Russia is concerned about the increasing intensity of the Central Asian and Caucasian states' relations with other Muslim countries, especially Iran and Afghanistan, where Islamic extremism has played a significant role in politics.

7. Historical memory and public opinion. Many Russians, including significant numbers in the Russian armed forces, consider these former Soviet republics a legitimate realm of Russian hegemony.

The threats posed by the instability in the Central Asian and Caucasian area suggest that Russia's policy toward this region will be assertive and will encroach upon the economic, political, and military sovereignty of these states. Such encroachment will sometimes be difficult to detect; none of these countries has an effective army, and instead they openly depend almost exclusively on Russia for protection from outside threats.[7] In other cases, coercion is easy to discern — for example Russian demands to be given a full half of Kazakhstan's oil revenue along with the right to restrict Western development of those and other resources.

---

6. See "Russia's Refugees," *RFE/RL Research Report* Vol. 2, No. 37 (September 17, 1993) pp. 46–53.

7. As pointed out in a recent article by Mohiaddin Mesbahi, "the demand for Russian activism is not confined to Moscow, but [is] coming from Central Asia itself." Mohiaddin Mesbahi, "Russian Foreign Policy and Security in Central Asia and the Caucasus," *Central Asia Survey*, Vol. 12, No. 2 (1993), p. 192.

Russia's interests in Central Asia and Transcaucasia vary in type and intensity from state to state. In Central Asia, Kazakhstan, with its nuclear weapons inheritance, vast stores of oil and gas, and high proportion of ethnic Russians among its population (around 40 percent), is the central focus of Russian attention. Recent Western interest in gaining oil concessions in Kazakhstan has intensified Russia's resolve to maintain a strong economic foothold there. Second in importance is Uzbekistan, the most populous and ethnically diverse state in the region, which provides Russia with gold, petroleum, and cotton. Tajikistan appears to be important to Russia as a buffer from Afghanistan and in containing Tajikistan's own political and religious extremism. Moscow is currently taking a benign posture toward Turkmenistan's choice to isolate itself from the region politically and economically; this could quickly change if Russia concludes that relations between Turkmenistan and outside countries threaten its access to Turkmenistan's vast stores of natural gas.[8] Kirgizstan, with its peaceful pattern of political development and its almost complete economic and military dependence upon Russia, has so far not created any problems.

In the Caucasus, Azerbaijan, which returned to Russia's political and security orbit in 1993, is struggling against Russia to maintain control over its substantial Caspian Sea oil reserves. Russia's interest in Georgia is to avoid the export of Georgian conflicts into Russia and to guarantee access to military and port facilities on the Black Sea — an interest that will only increase if relations with the Baltic region take an extended turn for the worse,[9] and if Russian access to facilities in the Baltics is limited. Armenia is likely to continue to defer to Moscow because of its economic and security isolation within its own region.

---

8. Fiona Hill and Pamela Jewett, "Back in the USSR: Russia's Intervention in the Internal Affairs of the Former Soviet Republics and the Implications for United States Policy Toward Russia," Strengthening Democratic Institutions Project, Kennedy School of Government, Harvard University, January 1994, pp. 30–31.

9. Hill and Jewett, "Back in the USSR," p. 33. The authors argue that Russia purposely contributed to the destabilization of the Georgian-Abkhazian situation, both to cripple Georgian resistance to compliance with Moscow, and to convince the West that Russian intervention in the affairs of the former Soviet republics is needed.

The Situation in the Central Asian and Transcaucasian States

Russia's involvement in the countries of the Caucasus and Central Asia will vary; the countries differ from each other in many ways, as do their degrees of dependence on Russia. Anti-Russian feeling is stronger in the Caucasus than in Central Asia, and an abundance of historical animosities find their expression in territorial and ethnic-based conflicts. Turkmenistan, Uzbekistan, and Tajikistan are likely to have authoritarian political regimes for some time. In addition, the social and ethnic reverberations of the conflict in Tajikistan have yet to subside, and it is possible that unrest could spread from the Turkic regions of China.

In the Caucasus further fragmentation is likely. The conflicts raging in Transcaucasia will probably not be resolved without the involvement of Russia. The Georgian civil war has spawned conflicts between the region's ethnic minorities that will drag on, as will spin-off conflicts in the northern Caucasus. The impact of five years of bloody warfare between Armenia and Azerbaijan will also be felt in the region for some time.

In the Soviet era, Central Asia and Transcaucasia were closely tied to Russia through a complex web of political, social, and economic ties. The Central Asian republics served as reservoirs of raw materials for the USSR. During the Gorbachev period, the Soviet Central Asian republics were not animated by the drive for full independence. In the Transcaucasus, Georgia was particularly quick to follow the Baltic example, and Armenia and Azerbaijan seized their independence after the signal had been given by Moscow. Once they achieved independence, the states of Central Asia and Transcaucasia initially attempted to extract themselves from Soviet-era economic ties and obligations, and to find new partners abroad.[10] For a time, the countries hoped that Turkey, the United States, international lending institutions, or some other source would provide short-term solutions to long-term problems through foreign aid and investment. The crush of local and regional crises has forced the leaders of these countries to turn once again to Moscow for support of their

---

10. In 1992, the Central Asian states and Azerbaijan joined the Economic Cooperation Organization trading bloc, which theoretically covers an area of 7.2 million kilometers and a market of some 300 million people in countries of Asia and the Middle East. "Central Asia and Economic Integration," *RFE/RL Research Report* Vol. 2, No. 14 (April 2, 1993), p. 41.

economies and armies.[11] Moscow will not allow these countries to become economically dependent upon ties with Iran and Turkey while relying on Russia for security.

For economic and political reasons, the Central Asian states have not been able to create a common front.[12] Some Central Asian regimes fear that such a coalition would reduce their ability to act independently. In addition, these states must compete with each other for scarce economic and investment resources from abroad. The recent rapprochement between these Asian states and Russia in their joint response to both the civil war in Tajikistan and the need to defend the border with Afghanistan can be explained by Russia's pre-eminence in the making of CIS security policy, and the recognition by Central Asia's political elites that the Tajik conflict poses a threat to their own vital interests.

For a time following the Soviet collapse, Russia contracted its influence in Central Asia, but efforts to contain the Tajik catastrophe have ended Russia's political retreat from the region. Russia has reappeared as a guarantor of the new states' territorial integrity and perhaps also of their internal stability on the pretext of providing security for local Russians. This has led Turkey and Iran to once again recognize Russia's dominance in Central Asia and the Caucasus. Russia has opted to support, at least temporarily, authoritarian rulers such as Saparmurad Niyazov in Turkmenistan and Islam Karimov in Uzbekistan; they view the preservation of stability as their top priority, and are willing to cooperate with Russia in order to achieve this end.

Russia's Options

Whether Moscow views the states of its "near abroad" as real or potential enemies, vassals, or neighbors will be determined to a large degree by the political disposition of future regimes in these states, the larger security framework in which these states interact, and whether the terms of these relations are established unilaterally by Russia or through some form of

---

11. None of these states is economically or technically able to equip its own national army without the support of Russia. See Mesbahi, "Russian Foreign Policy and Security in Central Asia and the Caucasus," p. 206.

12. Domestic politics in the Central Asian states are characterized by a tension between political structures and patterns inherited from the Soviet era, and ethnic and religious pressures that undermine these structures.

concord. Obviously Moscow would prefer to have the voluntary compliance of the Central Asian and Transcaucasian states in the protection of its interests, but this will be more difficult to achieve if these states become economically and politically more self-reliant. Russia has three main options for responding to threats to its national security emanating from Central Asia and Transcaucasia.

First, Russia could attempt to seal the southern borders of the Russian Federation and maintain a neutral stance in all conflicts in the former republics. Russia is most likely to choose this option if it suffers a severe economic downturn or internal fragmentation, or if a nationalist-isolationist regime comes to power. While this option would allow Russia to focus on its domestic difficulties, it would invite the Central Asian and Transcaucasian states to become economically and politically tied to, or even dependent upon Iran, Afghanistan, Turkey, or China. This might be the most costly option for Russia over the long term.

Another extreme solution is for Russia to openly and urgently resume military and political control over the destabilized regions, force a settlement in conflicts, and direct the external relations of the Central Asian and Caucasian states. Even if a neo-imperialist faction were to assume power, Russia would likely be unable to carry out such a policy effectively due to the depleted state of its ground forces and its lack of available resources. The most probable option then is for Russia to intervene selectively in conflicts in Central Asia and the Caucasus, either unilaterally or under the auspices of the CIS.[13] Since late 1992, this has been the policy of the Russian government. Although most reasonable for Russia in terms of costs and commitments, it may ultimately prove to be creeping imperialism.

Globally-oriented security organizations are unlikely to provide adequate means for managing instability on Russia's borders. The United

---

13. Some argue that Russia's maneuvering in Nagorno Karabakh and in the civil war in Georgia was calculated to weaken the political forces in Georgia and Azerbaijan that refused to join the CIS or to acquiesce in promoting Moscow's interests in the region following the Soviet collapse. The tactic appears to have paid off in Georgia; in November 1993, the newly appointed Georgian president, Eduard Shevardnadze, agreed to bring Georgia into the CIS in exchange for assistance in halting well-armed separatists from Abkhazia and the northern Caucasus. Similarly, leadership changes in Baku and the overwhelming success of Armenian military offensives throughout the summer and fall of 1993 also forced Azerbaijan back into the CIS fold. As a result of these changes the boundaries of the CIS have expanded and are now identical with those of the former USSR in Central Asia and the Caucasus.

Nations will likely continue to be unwilling to embark upon an effective peacekeeping operation in Central Asia and the Caucasus. The CSCE has attempted to maintain an active role in mediating solutions to these conflicts, but cannot enforce its resolutions. By refraining from exerting pressure through bilateral relationships, the West is, in effect, tacitly recognizing that Russian interests extend beyond the borders of the Russian Federation, while at the same time resisting an actual definition of a "Russian sphere of interest" in the post-Soviet security space.

If Russia opts for a more heavy-handed approach to securing its interests in Central Asia and the Caucasus, this will create moral and policy dilemmas for Western governments. Central Asia and the Caucasus are geographically far removed from the Western industrialized world, and in this century have been at most a minor concern for Western Europe and the United States. However, this is changing.

The Role of the Region's Resources

Of the factors that are increasing the West's interest in Central Asia and the Caucasus, critical is the region's immense energy resources, particularly oil.[14] In Kazakhstan alone there may be as many as 35 billion recoverable barrels of oil.[15] In the Tengiz oil field located on the northern shore of the Caspian Sea, Kazakhstan possesses what is estimated to be one of the world's ten biggest fields; another of the top ten is located in Azerbaijan. Turkmenistan is heir to one of the world's largest stores of natural gas, estimated at some 350 trillion cubic feet.[16]

For Russia, this raises several objectives: guaranteeing Russian access to the resources, receiving adequate compensation for the development of

---

14. Other concerns are the proliferation of Soviet weapons and weapons technology, especially nuclear technology; the spread of nationalist and religious extremism; and the growth of the narcotics industry in these regions and the trafficking of drugs to Western markets. Central Asia has long been a producer of opium poppies, hashish, and other narcotic plants. The dire economic situation in these states has resulted in a surge in the drug trade, introducing the possibility that the region could become a new world supply center for illegal substances. *RFE/RL Research Report*, Vol. 3, No. 1 (January 1994), p. 60.

15. "The Rush to Alma-Ata," *Newsweek*, February 7, 1994. Experts estimate that the region around the Caspian Sea holds the world's third largest deposits of oil. *Washington Post*, March 18, 1994, p. A24.

16. *Washington Post*, March 18, 1994, p. A24.

these resources during the Soviet era, and achieving the construction of transport pipelines through Russian territory. Although it possesses the world's second largest oil deposit (in Siberia), Russian oil and petroleum production has dropped during the past several years as part of the overall contraction of the economy;[17] if the trend continues, Russia could cease to be a net exporter of oil by the end of the decade,[18] making developed reserves in Central Asia and the Caucasus vital to its long-term economic security. The majority of the deposits currently at issue were explored and partially developed before 1992 using Russian capital and expertise; the Russian government maintains that it has a proprietary interest in these sites. The level of Russian control over these deposits is likely to be roughly inversely proportional to the level of access Western companies and consortiums receive, making this a case in which Western interests could be significantly and negatively affected by Russia's influence in the Central Asian and Transcaucasian states.[19] The Russian government has demonstrated a preference for blocking large-scale Western development of energy resources on the territory of the former Soviet Union by trying to make it difficult for Western oil and mineral extraction companies to do business.

The future routes of resource pipelines may also affect the West's access to oil. The resources extracted from reserves in Central Asia and the Caucasus will find their way to Western markets by a northern route through Russia leading to the Black Sea; south through Iran leading to the Persian Gulf; or southwest to Turkey, through Kurdish territory, and on to the Eastern Mediterranean. Each possibility has different geopolitical ramifications, and it is not at all clear that the West should prefer that the fossil fuels flow through Russia.

---

17. "Russia Oil Output Said to Fall in '94," Clarinet Communications, Reuters wire, March 23, 1994.

18. Interview with Sergei Karaganov, January 29, 1994, Moscow, Russia.

19. *Washington Post*, March 18, 1994, p. A24.

Recommendations for Western Policy

For the West, maintaining stable, cooperative relations with Russia is far more important than forging close ties with the Central Asian and Transcaucasian states.[20] In general, any Western policy toward these states that destabilizes relations with Russia is not in the Western interest: Central Asia and the Caucasus will inexorably be dominated by Russia, and the West will be able to do very little about it. In their policies toward the states of Central Asia and the Transcaucasus, Western governments should therefore focus on the few interests associated with these states. The West has a vital interest in the denuclearization of Kazakhstan. Azerbaijan, Turkmenistan and Uzbekistan represent an important interest for the West because of their natural resources, while Georgia, Armenia, Tajikistan, and Kirgizstan are unimportant.

If the West focuses on denuclearization and energy resources, it is less likely to collide with Russia over other issues emanating from this area. In particular, the industrialized democracies should be wary of making rhetorical statements about Russia's conduct in these regions that they are not prepared to back with political and economic actions.

---

20. One possible exception is Turkey.

Chapter 14
Russia and China

Vladimir S. Miasnikov

In the post–Cold War international security setting, Russia will, as it has for centuries, look to the East as well as to the West to safeguard its vital national security interests. International security in the "new world order," unlike in the old bi-polar arrangement, will be structured primarily by regional sub-systems of power. Russia has a vital stake not only in securing an advantageous position in North Atlantic political, economic, and strategic alignments, but also in those taking shape in the Asia-Pacific region. China will emerge in the not too distant future as the undisputed leader in the security affairs of East Asia; Russian-Chinese relations will be critically important to the future of Russia's security, as well as its overall status in the Asia-Pacific region.

The ability of China to affect Russia's interests in the Asia-Pacific region will increase. With its military and nuclear capabilities, Russia will maintain the potential to influence the balance of power in the Asia-Pacific region, as well as the area's long-term regional stability and security. It is virtually impossible to imagine a secure Asia-Pacific region where relations between Russia and China are hostile, or even largely antagonistic.

In the Asia-Pacific region, conflicts and coalitions with their roots in the Cold War political and security system are gradually being displaced by other issues brought on by new conditions in the international environment. In many countries of the Asia-Pacific region a re-examination of Cold War era values is still ongoing. Many, especially the smaller states, still feel insecure; their insecurity is exacerbated by the continuing militarization of the region.[1] In 1991, the states of East Asia, including China, Taiwan, Japan, both Koreas, Indonesia, Malaysia, and Singapore

---

1. See Gary Klintworth, "Asia-Pacific: More Security, Less Uncertainty, New Opportunities," *Pacific Review* Vol. 5, No. 3 (1992).

Vladimir S. Miasnikov is Deputy Director of the Institute of the Far East, and a Corresponding Member of the Russian Academy of Sciences.

purchased 35 percent of all the weapons produced that year for the world market.

The redefinition of national interests in both Russia and China is a complex process. This chapter explores Russia's enduring national security interests with regard to China, and compares them to Chinese national security interests concerning Russia. Where appropriate, points of potential conflict and opportunities for cooperation in Russian-Chinese relations are highlighted. Finally, some analytical conclusions are offered as to how these interests are likely to impact the future development of Russian-Chinese relations.

Interests and Approaches

In essence, Russia's vital national interests during its protracted period of economic and political reform may be summarized as: self-preservation, self-enhancement, cooperation, and pragmatism. For Russia, self-preservation entails the consolidation of the means of national endurance during a long and hard period. It means preserving and ameliorating the material basis of the nation's existence, including its territorial integrity, raw material and energy sources, and ecological and environmental wellbeing, as well as its general demographic composition and cultural wealth. In addition, national self-preservation demands the creation of an effective economic system suited to Russia's history, culture, and resources. Self-enhancement includes the goals of self-preservation, and also encompasses the endeavor to take a fitting place in the commonwealth of nations. Cooperation with members of the international community in all spheres is a necessary element in the self-preservation and self-enhancement of any nation. Finally, pragmatism requires that Russia's leaders operate according to realistic estimates of the country's national interests and that they ensure that Russia's national priorities are commensurate with its actual means.

China generalizes its approach to securing its vital national interests with the formula "peace and development." According to this prescription, peace entails the establishment of international conditions for the modernization of the country along the path of reform, and the rejection of force as a means to solve international disputes. Development involves achievements in production designed to bring China to a reasonable level of prosperity, the preservation of China's territorial integrity, and solving the country's environmental and demographic problems.

In purely geostrategic terms, Russia and China share a strong interest in preserving stability in the regions along their common border — settling outstanding disputes over territory, preventing the spread of separatism and territorial revanchism in the form of pan-nationalist and religious extremism, and protecting the region from outside threats. The need to deal with these common issues could either create opportunities for cooperation, or provide the basis for antagonism.

It is a vital interest of Russia to establish itself as a preeminent power on the Pacific rim, both for its own value, and as a strategic alternative to exclusive reliance upon integration into Western economic and security structures. In the medium and long term, this strategic goal will require that Russia participate actively in the political affairs of the Asia-Pacific region. The opportunities to do so will increase the more Russia is able to contribute to the regional economy, both as a supplier and a consumer. Russia's available instruments to realize this goal in the short and medium term will be primarily military and political, although economic levers will also play an increasingly important role.

Military-Strategic Interests

BILATERAL ISSUES

From a security point of view the most critical issue in Russian-Chinese relations over the previous decade has been the question of military domination in East Asia. From the mid-1950s China struggled to expel Soviet influence from the Asia-Pacific region — a goal it largely achieved by 1989. For its part, the Soviet Union expended enormous resources to fortify its borders and create an eastern branch of its armed forces capable of handling any unforeseen moves on the part of China. The construction of the Baikal-Amur railroad as well as military bases in Mongolia, Vietnam, and North Korea; the strengthening of India's military potential; and the attempt to bring Afghanistan into the Soviet security fold by force were all elements of the Soviet struggle to counter Chinese hegemony in East Asia. China was the winner; Soviet prestige in the region was practically liquidated in exchange for a reluctant normalization of relations with China.

Russia starts from a weak position with regard to the settlement of border and territorial issues with the People's Republic of China. The potential for resolving these issues in a timely manner is viewed by many experts as problematic.² Disputes over territory and threats to territorial integrity reach to the heart of a state's strategic interests. This is particularly true in Russia, which is struggling to come to terms with a marked loss of strength and status in its own region and internationally.

However, progress has been made on the resolution of several outstanding territorial disputes between Russia and China. By December 1992, there remained only two stretches of territory upon which agreement had not yet been reached, and in the western sector diplomatic solutions were devised to deal with 80 percent of the outstanding problems. In addition to the setting of boundaries, these agreements contained measures to build mutual confidence in the region, including cuts in armed forces deployed on or near the Russian-Chinese border.

Despite these diplomatic advances, border violations have become more frequent over the past few years. Common violations, such as unlawful fishing and grazing of cattle, are very widespread. In an attempt to limit the negative economic and socio-political effects of such activities, both sides are instituting more rigid crossing procedures.³

Firmly rooted in the mass consciousness of the Chinese people are ideas of Russia's historical territorial debt to China. Mao Zedong skillfully played this card in the 1960s and 1970s; there are no guarantees that China's leaders will not again raise this specter. Therefore, it is in Russia's long-term interest to resolve as many of its outstanding territorial conflicts with China as possible if this can be achieved with a minimum compromise of Russia's position vis-à-vis China in the short term. Recent attempts to diffuse tension among troops stationed on both sides of the border and to promote cooperation in the solution of their common dilemmas are a step in the right direction.

REGIONAL ISSUES

Central to the relationship between Russia and China at the regional level are issues of military security and the proliferation of weapons. It could be argued that the sale of weapons to third parties by both China and Russia may soon become a far greater threat to the national security of both states than their disagreements over borders. Although China is somewhat renowned for its liberal policy in the sale of weapons on the

---

2. See, for example, George Ginsbergs, "The End of Sino-Russian Territorial Disputes?" *The Journal of East Asian Affairs*, Vol. 7, No. 1 (Winter/Spring 1993), pp. 261–320.

3. *Isvestiya*, July, 1993.

international market, it has no interest in promoting the severe weakening or collapse of Russia, and will therefore not become a steady supplier to any state which threatens the stability of Russia. Russia officially maintains a tight policy on the proliferation of weapons and weapons technology, but the weakening of the command structure of the Russian armed forces has introduced the possibility of uncontrolled proliferation of Russian military hardware and technology. Overall, however, the sale of weapons to third countries is unlikely to significantly detract from the quality of relations between Russia and China over the long term.

One immediate effect of the collapse of the Soviet Union was the creation of several independent states on the borders of Russia and China. Both Russia and China consider it a vital interest to preserve stability in the region of former Soviet Central Asia for a number of reasons, and Russian and Chinese interests are highly compatible and relatively uncomplicated by other issues in this sphere. China is home to 56 non-Chinese ethnic groups (about 90 million people), many of whom live in China's western-most provinces; a significant part of the population there is Muslim. Instability and armed conflict in Central Asia, with its roots in tribal and nationalist disputes, has the potential to spread and to threaten the stability and integrity of the Chinese state. China's national security is also threatened by the spread of both Turkic separatism and Islamic extremism as political forces. Prolonged conflict within Central Asia could disrupt the spread of Chinese economic activity in the region, and possibly complicate the political and strategic situation by tempting outside powers to get involved. Furthermore, the spread of Islamic extremism could increase political tensions inside China by fueling the fire of separatist forces in the western provinces. The promotion and protection of Central Asian stability and security, therefore, constitutes a policy realm in which long-term Russian and Chinese cooperation is likely.

An equally serious threat to China's national security is the spread of pan-Mongolism, which has as its goal the recreation of Greater Mongolia. This movement threatens Chinese and Russian interests on three fronts. First, the reunification of Outer Mongolia, an independent state, with Inner Mongolia, a part of China, would threaten directly the territorial integrity of China, and seriously destabilize the region as a whole. Second, the Russian Federation is home to a handful of minority nations of Mongol descent. Pan-Mongolism envisions the incorporation of these nations into Greater Mongolia, and thus threatens Russian territorial integrity and its national security interests. Finally, the Mongols share strong cultural ties, including national religion, with Tibet. The possibility that these two nations will forge political solidarity in their struggle for independence from Beijing cannot be discounted by Chinese strategists.

Beijing has a clear interest in forging and strengthening economic ties with the states of Central Asia. Unlike Russia, however, China has no interest in promoting the overt political or economic integration of any of the Central Asian states under its administrative umbrella in the short or medium term. Such a scenario would go against China's millennia-old tradition of gradualist state-building, and would detract from far more economically and politically lucrative Chinese activities in the coastal regions of East Asia. Therefore, China is unlikely to object to any future Russian activities in the Central Asian region that have the effect of promoting political stability and economic normalization.

Due to the unstable situation in many of the former Soviet republics, Russia, and to a lesser extent China, will be unable to define a new system of geopolitical interests for some time. This makes it imperative for the interests of both Russia and China that the territorial provisions of the Yalta accords for the Far East continue to be observed until an agreement of the Helsinki type is established for Asia.

INTERNATIONAL ISSUES

Many Russian policy makers have concluded that Russia must find alternatives to strategic alignment with the West. Russia will continue to seek new ways to consolidate political relations with its eastern neighbors, particularly China. Russia and China have largely similar long-term interests with regard to the future of the international security structure. Both hope to carve out a position of influence largely independent of predominant Western security arrangements.

China is joining the new system of international relations as a country possessing a reasonably advanced market-based economy. Russia, by comparison, faces a largely uphill battle to consolidate a new position in the international community. Few Russians yet realize the enormity of the Chinese challenge to Russia's long-term political and economic interests. Attempts have already been made, both by China and by the United States, to exclude Russia from the discussion of Asia-Pacific issues vital to it national security.[4] Like Russia, the United States is both an Atlantic

---

4. For example, Winston Lord's formulation of the ten main goals of U.S. policy toward the Asia-Pacific region gave even less attention to Russia than to North Korea. ("The Ten Primary Goals of American Policy in the Asia-Pacific Region," presented to the U.S.

power and a Pacific power, and is likewise struggling to balance its interests. China would prefer that the United States deal primarily with Beijing with regard to economic and strategic planning in the Pacific Rim, and envisions that the Russian-American dialogue will be replaced by the Chinese-American dialogue in U.S. national security. In such an arrangement, U.S. relations with China would largely determine the United States' political, economic, and military engagement in the region as a whole over the long term.

The growth of Chinese power and influence in the Asia-Pacific region will affect relations among all powers in this area. The emergence of China as an economic colossus will decrease the security of Taiwan, Singapore, and South Korea, and detract from their world market leverage. It will also give China a freer hand to dictate the terms of its relations with lesser powers in the region, including Thailand, Vietnam, and Malaysia. It is unclear how China intends to use the leverage; the result will likely be an increase in political tensions between many of these states and China, and the undermining of long-term prospects for the stability of the region.[5]

Should tensions among Asia-Pacific powers increase, small states may seek alternatives to alignment with China; their options are to create a strategic confederation, or to seek bilateral alignment with Japan or Russia. A confederation of small states is the least feasible option; it would be complicated, costly, and possibly ineffective due to a lack of policy instruments. Japan may be an ill-favored option for strategic partnership for many states, both for historical reasons, and due to Japan's dependence upon the United States for its own national defense.

Strategic alignment with Russia may present an attractive alternative to alignment with China for many small states in the Asia-Pacific region. In at least a military sense, Russia remains the strongest power in the Asia-Pacific area, and the second strongest in the world. Russia, unlike China, will for the foreseeable future balance its Western interests with those in the Asia-Pacific region, providing states that prefer not to maintain close relations with China with a channel by which to access the West. Russia, for its part, will likewise seek ties in the Asia-Pacific region

---

Congress in 1993.) Second, it was primarily at the behest of China that Russia was not included among the nations represented at the Asia-Pacific Summit in 1993. Finally, only occasionally is Russia invited to participate in the meetings of Pacific Rim leaders.

5. For a fuller explanation of this argument see Denny Roy, "Consequences of China's Economic Growth for Asia-Pacific Security," *Security Dialogue*, Vol. 24, No. 2 (June 1993).

to solidify its position as a legitimate power there, and to balance its own dependence upon maintaining good relations with China.

Political Interests

BILATERAL RELATIONS

Both Russia and China have vital political interests in the future development of a regional security structure. Chinese leaders have formulated a number of specific proposals to strengthen security in the Asia-Pacific region, proceeding from the declared general principles of China's foreign policy;[6] Russia has generally proven receptive to overtures for political cooperation with China. As a result of the December 1992 visit of Russian President Boris Yeltsin to Beijing, twenty-four mostly future-oriented intergovernmental and interdepartmental agreements on various aspects of Russian-Chinese cooperation were signed, helping to lay the foundation for cooperation in a number of spheres of vital importance to both countries.[7]

In the past, political disagreements between the Soviet Union and China were often cast as differences in the interpretation and implementation of socialist theory; in reality, disputes between them more often than not reflected conflicts over territory, nuclear proliferation, strategic alignment, and other issues. Russia's intention to build a market system has in effect removed the ideological layer of contention between Russia and China.

---

6. These principles include sovereignty; commitment to the principles of peaceful coexistence and renunciation of hegemony and the use of force; a refusal to create military bases and deploy armed forces outside its state borders; and support for disarmament and arms control; the destruction of nuclear weapons, chemical weapons, and weapons deployed in outer space; no first use of nuclear weapons; and the prevention of nuclear proliferation.

7. Among the most important of these agreements were the "Joint Declaration on the Principles of Bilateral Relations Between Russia and China," the "Memorandum on Mutual Understanding Between the Government of the Russian Federation and the Government of the People's Republic of China on the Issue of Reciprocal Cuts in the Armed Forces and on Confidence-Building Measures in the Military Sphere in the Border Regions," the "Protocol Between the Government of the Russian Federation and the Government of the People's Republic of China on Trade and Economic Cooperation in 1993," the "Intergovernmental Agreement on the Construction in the People's Republic of China of a Nuclear Power Plant," and agreements on scientific cooperation. *Diplomaticheskii Vestnik*, Foreign Ministry of the Russian Federation, No. 1–2 (1993), p. 11.

For the past several years, China has been slowly changing its political interpretation of socialist theory to accommodate its new economic policy; China has found that its social system is obstructing the development and protection of its vital national interests, particularly in the international sphere. Ideological residues from the Cold War era have made it disadvantageous for China to define itself to the outside world as a communist power. While China may retain many aspects of its socialist system, its trend is toward more explicit acknowledgement that the interests of the Chinese state are the driving force behind policy. This will ultimately contribute to a more open and frank political dialogue between Russia and China on the issues that divide the two countries, and the interests that unite them.

REGIONAL AND INTERNATIONAL RELATIONS
Although in the political sphere, there currently exists a foundation for stable cooperative relations between Russia and China based upon principles of respect for sovereignty and policy independence, it is not a foregone conclusion that such a climate of political cooperation between Russia and China will persist over the long term. A drastic worsening of domestic political conditions in Russia could result in threats to China's national security for reasons outlined above.

In contrast to Western governments, which tend to assume a strong correlation between Russia's democratic development and the potential to build some form of strategic partnership, the Chinese government takes a much more pragmatic approach to relations with Russia. Both in theory and in practice, China is neutral toward Russia's internal political struggle. Of course, this policy rests on the assumption that internal affairs in Russia will not deteriorate enough to endanger the future integrity of the Russian state. Such a development would pose a definite threat to Russia's neighbors, and possibly to states farther afield if control over nuclear weapons were to become an issue.

The disintegration of the Russian Federation would go against the long-term interests of China on at least two important counts. First, if the Russian state collapsed, the minority nationalities in Russia's central and eastern regions would gain sovereignty. This could trigger a separatist chain reaction in China and threaten the integrity of the current borders of the Chinese state.

Second, as China's relations with the United States develop and intensify over the coming decades, it will be to China's advantage to have a third party that it can usher into the political dialogue from time to time to check the power of U.S. interests in the Asia-Pacific area. Russia and China, as large continental powers with abundant resources, are likely to have roughly similar interests with regard to economic and strategic development in the Asia-Pacific region; therefore, the Chinese government will place a far higher premium upon stability and continuity in Russia's conduct of its international affairs over the long term than upon the fate of any particular individual or political camp within Russia. For this reason, China may prove to be a valuable partner for the United States if events in Russia do not develop as the West hopes.

The Chinese approach to diplomatic relations is colored by the fact that for an extended period it was the victim of the colonial policies of European powers. To many Chinese, Russia is a predominantly European countries. Thus the Russian-Chinese border is not merely a border between two states, but the point where civilizations come into contact. For this reason, while relations between Russia and Asian-Pacific states obey international laws of interstate discourse, they bear an imprint of ethno-cultural influences. This may prove to be a stumbling block in Russia's pursuit of an economic and political role in the region.

Many experts in Russian-Chinese relations, including Li Jingjie, predict a rosy future for Russian-Chinese political cooperation based upon their similarity of interests in the economic and strategic sphere. Such a prognosis, however, assumes that the division of political, economic, and strategic power between Russia and China will maintain a rough consistency over the long term. If China fulfills current expectations for its long-term economic growth, this could threaten Russia's prospects for becoming a Pacific Rim power and would directly affect Russian-Chinese relations.

Economic Interests

For hundreds of years, China has been Russia's chief economic and trading partner in the Far East; it will likely become more important to Russia's external economic activities for the foreseeable future. As Russia seeks to consolidate a new political system and complete its transformation to a market-based economy, it must seek outside partners for trade, investment, and the acquisition of new technologies. Real economic recovery will be impossible for Russia to attain without securing dependable trading partners and markets for Russian exports. China offers both to Russia.

The West will likely continue for some time to be Russia's most direct source for the transfer of technology. But Western markets are proving difficult or impossible for Russian producers to penetrate, even with goods and materials for which Russia meets or exceeds world market quality standards. Without a minimum level of trade, Western investment in Russia is not likely to approach the level needed to start Russia back on the path to economic growth. China, therefore, presents itself as a potentially strong economic partner for Russia in trade and other forms of economic intercourse, both immediately and over the long term.

Russia and China share a border of 4,375 kilometers. In recent years it has exploded into a zone of cross-border micro-economic activity. In March 1992 Russia and China signed an Agreement on Trade and Economic Ties, extending to one another Most Favored Nation status, and suspended a number of specific customs duties and taxes on commerce. Free trade zones have begun to crop up in the provinces and autonomous regions bordering on Russia, Mongolia, and the former Soviet republics. The establishment of a "northern belt of openness" along China's border with Russia may also strengthen China's economic interest in Russia.

However, the economic activity along the Russian-Chinese border is not purely beneficial, especially for Russia. The increasing transparency of this border causes concern not only among border guards, but also among local and national authorities. In recent years, nearly one million Chinese have settled on Russian territory without permission from Russian authorities. Another million or so Chinese traders and entrepreneurs live in China, but rely upon economic activities in Russia for their sustenance.[8] Some feel that this threatens Russia's rather sparsely populated Far East.

Economic intercourse between Russia and China could contribute to the strengthening of cooperative ties between the two, but only if there is a measure of economic parity and commercial reciprocity, which is beyond the capacity of Russia to deliver, at least over the short term.[9] If

---

8. A feature called "The Chinese Are Coming? They're Here" in *Komsomolskaya Pravda*, June 15, 1993, reprinted from the November 26, 1992 issue of *Japan Times*, describes the dramatic situation in cities in Siberia and Russia's Far East: "Chinese have become local hawkers — every day they cross the [Russian-Chinese] border which is only fifty kilometers from Khabarovsk by the thousands, laden with huge bags which bulge with jackets, running suits, and T-shirts. Far from all the Russians welcome their unruly street-vending, which is causing a rise in anti-Chinese sentiments."

9. By the end of the 1990s the ratio of the Russian to the Chinese GNP will have changed from 2:1 in Russia's favor in the early 1990s to 0.75:1 in favor of China.

Russia experiences a severe economic crisis with hyper-inflation and the complete breakdown of productive activity, it would become dependent upon economic ties with China; this would likely have a disruptive effect upon their long-term political relations.

It is highly probable that sharp economic competition will develop between Russia and China.[10] Their economic and trade relations may become strained in the future by competition for markets in the Asia-Pacific region and beyond. China is actively striving to develop its means of production in many lines of machinery and equipment traditionally exported by Russia. It will not be difficult for China to overtake Russia economically, as both states have about the same rate of technological development. In the next decade, the sharpest economic competition between Russia and China is likely to occur in machine building, especially in the production of medium-level technical equipment, and in military technology.

Russia is not yet a serious competitor to China in attracting foreign investment due to the considerably higher risks involved in putting money into the Russian economy. As the economic and political situation in Russia stabilizes, competition between Russia and China in this sphere will undoubtedly grow. Competition will also emerge in the market for the transport of goods. A new railway has been proposed to connect the east coast of China with Western Europe. This route would run from Xinjiang through Kazakhstan and Turkmenistan, bypassing Russia, and would divert a significant proportion of the freight currently transported across Russian territory.

Conclusions and Policy Recommendations

Relations between Russia and China will become an increasingly important component of Russia's national security in the coming decade and, by extension, will affect the structure and character of the emerging international security system. Intensive development of Russia's economic and strategic ties in the Asia-Pacific region constitutes the most direct path

---

10. Although both Russia and China possess enormous labor forces, which must find niches in the world market, this is unlikely to cause any friction between them. China's labor force is largely comprised of unskilled and poorly skilled workers, while the Russian labor force is, by comparison, highly skilled and highly specialized.

now available to Russia to secure its long-term position as an economic and strategic great power.

The Beijing Declaration of 1992 formulated the fundamental principles for the conduct of relations between Russia and China. The document emphasizes the friendly and cooperative basis of relations between the two states, and formalizes the Russian and Chinese commitment to observe international standards and norms in their relations with one another. The Beijing Declaration also states the need to respect the right of each nation to choose its own path of development, thus explicitly rejecting the role of ideology and domestic affairs as determinant factors in relations between Russia and China. The document represents the political and diplomatic intent of both sides to pursue good-neighborly relations and to strengthen Russian-Chinese economic ties.

The ratification of the agreement on border issues was an important step toward securing stable and productive Russian-Chinese relations over the long term. However, if the threats to Russia's national security stemming from the increase in cross-border social and economic activities are not handled properly, they could erode the basis of this cooperation.

There is a solid foundation for Russian-Chinese cooperation in managing the threats to their respective national security interests at both the bilateral and regional levels. Both Russia and China have a strong interest in the other's economic and political reforms. The pace and character of Russian and Chinese development, however, appear to be quite different; depending upon how economic, political, and military relations between them are structured, this could result in a new rivalry between Russia and China in which China will likely be more advantaged, especially in the economic sphere. Never before has China developed so much more quickly than Russia.

Russia must carefully balance its future relations with China with bilateral and multilateral ties with other states in the Asia-Pacific region. Russia must avoid over-dependence upon Chinese commerce and markets, and take measures to enforce a rough balance in Russian-Chinese international trade. The United States constitutes an enormously important variable in Russia's national security equation. Russia should use the Russian-American dialogue to increase American awareness of Russia's interests in the Asia-Pacific region.

In order to secure for itself the role of a great power on the Pacific Rim, Russia must establish a place in the ongoing regional discussion of political and security issues; this requires that Russia divert some of its attention away from Europe. In China the potential for Russia to reemerge as a great power is taken seriously, as illustrated by a statement by Deng Xiaoping: "Don't think of Russia as a dead tiger. It is a great state that will again demonstrate its might. It is necessary to be attentive in the conduct of relations with Russia: It is never simple diplomacy — it is never a simple country."

Chapter 15 — Li Jingjie

China and Russia

Since the end of the Cold War, Chinese-Russian relations have undergone a fundamental transformation. Both Russia and China are undergoing historic economic and political transitions, and in internal and external environments that differ markedly from those of the past. One cannot simply apply pre–Cold War and Cold War–era conceptions of international relations between the two communist powers to predict future relations between Russia and China. Rather, the challenge is to isolate enduring factors and accurately grasp the linkages between them, and, through identifying patterns and regularities, to apply them to prospects for the future development of those relations.

The end of the Cold War has brought about a decline in the importance of purely military factors in determining relative strategic advantage, and has sharply elevated the significance of economic ones. Because the possibility of the outbreak of a new world war or wars between great powers is minuscule, competition among nations has shifted from the military to the economic sphere. More and more, the strength of a nation is calculated in terms of its market shares and scientific and technological prowess, rather than by the power of its military arsenals.

For Russia and China — two large countries sharing a lengthy border — reliable long-term guarantees for mutual security will be determined not by the size of the military forces deployed on each side of that border, but by the level and intensity of Sino-Russian economic ties over the long term. Their economic relations will greatly affect the future of their broader political relations.

Over the past two years, relations between China and Russia have, on the whole, been developing smoothly, and remarkable progress has been achieved in virtually all aspects of their relations. During this period old antagonisms have subsided and the foundation has been laid for mutual cooperation and the development of productive future ties.

Li Jingjie is the Deputy Director of the Institute of East European, Russian, and Central Asian Studies at the Chinese Academy of Social Sciences. He also serves as a professor at the Academy.

This chapter analyzes the current status of Sino-Russian relations and provides some predictions with regard to the prospects for development of these relations into the beginning of the next century, rooted in a basic understanding of the history of Russia's diplomatic and strategic interaction with China.

Recent Landmarks in Sino-Russian Relations

At the end of 1991, when the Soviet Union was in the last stages of its disintegration, a delegation from the Chinese government visited Moscow. During that visit, a number of agreements were reached between China and Russia. First, China agreed to recognize Russia as the exclusive heir to Soviet power, and, hence, as a permanent member of the United Nations (UN) Security Council.

Second, the two sides acknowledged the Five Principles of Peaceful Coexistence as the basis for Sino-Russian bilateral relations.[1] In addition, the two countries reaffirmed their commitment to the fundamental principles laid out in two joint communiqués, one signed during Mikhail Gorbachev's 1989 visit to China, and the other signed during the visit to the USSR by General Secretary of the Central Committee of the Chinese Communist Party Jiang Zemin.

Third, it was agreed that treaties and diplomatic documents signed in the past between China and the USSR would remain valid. Finally, the countries agreed to continue two sets of negotiations, those on the mutual reduction of military forces in Sino-Soviet border areas and strengthening mutual security measures in the military field, and those concerned with Sino-Soviet border disputes. Both sides have expressed an interest in facilitating the ratification of the agreement already reached concerning the eastern section of the Chinese-Russian border, and continuing discussions on sections still in contention.

On January 31, 1992, Prime Minister Li Peng of China and President Boris Yeltsin held talks in New York, and reached a consensus concerning the development of good-neighborly and cooperative bilateral relations. In summary, the Chinese-Russian relationship was not hampered by the

---

1. These are the five principles for handling state-to-state relations advocated in the 1950s by China, India, and other countries. They are mutual respect for sovereignty and territorial integrity; mutual non-aggression; mutual non-interference in their respective internal affairs; mutual benefit; and peaceful coexistence.

collapse of the Soviet Union; on the contrary, it continues to march forward on the basis of positive trends initiated in previous years.

Russia and China have also made progress in developing mutually beneficial economic and trade relations. In March 1992, Russia and China signed a trade agreement in which each side guaranteed that it would confer "most favored nation" status upon the other. In August 1992, the first session of the Sino-Russian Inter-governmental Economic, Trade, Scientific, and Technological Cooperation Committee was held in Moscow. A series of concrete agreements was reached on expanding the scope of bilateral economic and trade cooperation, on perfecting the forms and measures of cooperation, and on promoting trade among different localities in the border regions, including an agreement that established economic and technological zones of cooperation.

Specific spheres of economic cooperation between China and Russia have expanded to include agriculture, energy, transportation, and peaceful utilization of nuclear energy and outer space, as well as retail trade and the conversion of defense industries for civilian production. By the end of 1992, the two countries had signed more than 200 agreements on establishing joint ventures. More than 2,000 Russian firms and companies have entered the Chinese market, and many Russian technicians have been attracted to Chinese enterprises to work. In Russia's Far East and Siberia alone, there are over 30,000 Chinese workers. In 1992 and 1993, the total volume of Russia's foreign trade decreased by 23 percent and 12 percent respectively, but its trade with China increased 69 percent and 52 percent over the same period, making China Russia's second most important trading partner.[2]

Significant progress has been made in promoting local and border-region trade between the two countries. Since the establishment of diplomatic relations between China and Russia, China has further opened its border areas, and the two governments have decided to allow cross-border commercial trade in twenty-one border cities. In addition to developing a cooperative bilateral relationship, both countries are actively promoting multi-lateral cooperation in Northeast Asia. A prime example

---

2. In 1991, the total volume of Sino-Soviet trade was $3.7 billion; in 1992, $5 billion; and in 1993, $7.6 billion.

is the enthusiastic participation of both China and Russia in the joint development of the Tuman River Delta.[3]

China and Russia have also had frequent interaction in the sphere of military security. Since 1992, they have encouraged reciprocal visits by top military leaders, dramatically increasing contact between the top ranks of the various branches of the armed services. A series of agreements has been reached between China and Russia to develop friendly ties between their military establishments, and to facilitate technological cooperation in the military sphere. One concrete result has been Russia's decision to allow the export of arms and advanced military equipment and technology to China. In 1992, Russia withdrew all of its armed forces stationed in Mongolia, and the two countries' frontier force commanders held talks for the first time in forty years.

Negotiations on arms reductions and mutual security measures have continued, and agreements were reached that resulted in the withdrawal of forces on both sides to 100 kilometers from the Chinese-Russian border, and the establishment of zones of limited military activity within 200 kilometers of the border. It is expected that a Chinese-Russian agreement on the disarmament of border areas and mutual security will be reached soon; this will be the first genuine disarmament agreement among nations in the Asia-Pacific region.

The successful ratification of agreements between Russia and China with regard to the eastern section of their common border led to an expanded effort in this sphere. In February 1992, talks aimed at resolving outstanding territorial disputes were resumed. A joint delegation with representatives from Russia, Kazakhstan, Kirgizstan, and Tajikistan met with Chinese officials, and the first steps in solving disputes in the western zone were taken. The second round of talks was held in July 1992; again, progress was made.

President Boris Yeltsin's 1992 visit to Beijing resulted in the issuance of the "Joint Declaration on the Basis of Bilateral Relations between the People's Republic of China and the Russian Federation,"[4] as well as twenty-four other documents concerning future Russian-Chinese

---

3. The Tuman River Delta cuts across China, Russia, and North Korea. This ten-year, $30 billion project includes plans for a free trade zone and a special investment zone of 1,000 square kilometers, as well as the construction of a world-class port. South Korea and Mongolia are also becoming actively involved in the Tuman project, and Japan is participating as an observer.

4. *People's Daily*, December 19, 1992, p. 1.

cooperation. Thus, a solid legal and diplomatic foundation was laid, opening up new prospects for the development of Chinese-Russian relations.

PRINCIPLES OF SINO-RUSSIAN RELATIONS

Judging from recent developments between China and Russia, these relations are characterized by greater openness and respect. First, since the normalization of Chinese-Soviet relations, leaders of both countries have been very careful to prevent ideological differences from affecting bilateral relations. For example, the Joint Declaration explicitly stipulates that "the right of peoples of various countries to choose their path of domestic development should be respected" and that "ideological differences between social systems must not hinder the normal progress of state relations."[5] The smooth advance of Chinese-Russian relations is precisely the result of the implementation of this principle.

As is well known, ideology was an important factor in Sino-Soviet relations. The Soviet-Chinese alliance in the 1950s was, to a great extent, the result of shared ideology. Similarly, the confrontation between the two countries from the 1960s until the 1980s was primarily due to ideological differences that arose between them. The determination of both China and Russia to separate ideological differences from state-to-state relations has created the opportunity to establish and develop a healthy relationship based upon liberal-democratic principles.

Second, both Sino-Soviet and Sino-Russian relations have emphasized the Five Principles of Peaceful Co-existence. A further point has been added to the basis of Sino-Russian relations: "No side will participate in any military or political alliance directed against the other; neither side will conclude any treaties or agreements with a third party which threaten the sovereignty or security interests of the other; and neither side will allow the use of its territory by a third party for activities detrimental to the sovereignty or security interests of the other."[6]

This idea is central to the concepts of mutual non-aggression and neutrality. After the breakdown of bilateral relations, the Soviet Union increased its deployment of forces along the Sino-Soviet border, and also supported Mongolia, India, and Vietnam against China, creating a hostile ring of encirclement around it. For its part, China did its utmost to join

---

5. Ibid.
6. Ibid.

with the United States, Japan, and even NATO in forming an anti-Soviet united front. The Sino-Soviet summit of 1989 put an end to this abnormal relationship.

Third, among the various factors that constitute Sino-Russian relations, geopolitics and geostrategy are giving way in importance to "geo-economics." Economic relations will be the most important element for guaranteeing the stability of friendly bilateral relations between Russia and China. If the basic principles guiding political relations between the two countries can be summarized as "good-neighborliness and goodwill," then the guiding principle for the Chinese-Russian bilateral economic relationship is epitomized by "equality and mutual benefit." The development of Chinese-Russian economic relations based upon equality and mutual benefit will facilitate the blending of their most important national interests, and thus will be a key factor in strengthening their cooperative relations.

Fourth, in the past, interaction between China and the USSR was confined to the government level. Since the establishment of diplomatic relations between China and Russia, direct contacts have greatly increased. With the opening of the borders between China and Russia, thousands of citizens from both countries have ventured to the other side to work, study, travel, engage in business activities, and conduct scientific and cultural exchanges. In 1992, over 80 percent of the volume of trade between Russia and China was in the form of deals negotiated directly between firms and enterprises. Such firm-to-firm and person-to-person contact, if it continues, will have far-reaching implications for the development of Sino-Russian bilateral relations.

Although various negative phenomena may emerge in this process, over the long term the participation of the masses in international contact will improve mutual understanding and enhance the friendship among peoples. Such interaction can also help states and societies to more accurately and deeply identify and explore their own national interests. Cross-national contacts among individuals have the potential to create pressures from below for governments to create and maintain bilateral relations, and will give non-government actors an increased voice in the foreign-policy process. This may help states to avoid mistakes caused by the inherently myopic style of policy making in which a small handful of people make all the decisions.

Fifth, both sides have succeeded in abiding by the principle of mutual respect and equality in the handling of their bilateral relations. In summing up the reasons for the deterioration of the Sino-Soviet relationship, Deng Xiaoping stated, "The essential issue was inequality. The Chinese people were made to feel humiliation."[7] China has not taken advantage of Russia's crisis to impose outside pressures; Russia, unlike some Western countries, has refrained from attempting to interfere in the internal affairs of China.

The new Sino-Russian relationship has been forged at a time of great change, both in the international system, and in Russia and China. It is imperative that relations between Russia and China continue to adapt to the new situation; new methods, new approaches, and new mechanisms in all fields of cooperation must be constantly sought after by both countries to ensure that necessary agreements are reached, and that bilateral relations continue to develop effectively. In this sense, relations between China and Russia are still in an experimental stage, with both sides exploring different paths of development.

Russian and Chinese Interests

In general, the development of Sino-Russian relations has been healthy and beneficial for both nations. A Sino-Russian relationship based upon goodwill and good-neighborliness will constitute a positive factor for the achievement of long-term peace and security in the Asia-Pacific region, and throughout the emerging international security system.

While the political leaders of both countries have avoided many of the pitfalls that plagued China's relations with the Soviet Union, and have ensured that this relationship will continue to advance, the causal drive behind Sino-Russian relations is, and will continue to be, the protection of the national interests of each. Both Russia and China have a vested interest in securing cooperative bilateral relations with the other over the long term. This section examines the enduring interests that underlie Sino-Russian relations.

RUSSIA'S INTERESTS

During his stay in Beijing, Yeltsin told the Chinese leaders that "developing Russian-Chinese relations has priority in Russia's foreign policy," and that "a powerful and unified China is in keeping with Russia's interests."[8]

---

7. *Selected Essays of Deng Xiaoping* (Chinese edition), Vol. 3, p. 295.
8. *People's Daily*, December 19, 1992, p. 4.

Judging from other speeches by Russian leaders and Russian foreign policy documents, the "priority" assigned to China in Russia's foreign policy will manifest itself in the following interests:

First, Russia will try to form a "good-neighborly zone" around itself, as described in "The Conception of Foreign Policies of the Russian Federation."[9] At present, the stability of Russia's western and southern border areas is threatened by the complex territorial and national problems existing between Russia and the newly independent post-Soviet states, and the armed conflicts in Eastern Europe, Transcaucasia, and Central Asia. In contrast, Russia's 4,375-kilometer border with China has remained secure and stable. The chronic instability of Russia's other border areas has heightened the necessity for Russia to maintain good relations with China. Confrontation with China would endanger many of Russia's most pressing vital interests, including the need to create favorable international conditions for Russia's domestic reforms, and, above all, to ensure a peaceful and stable periphery.

Second, Russia wishes to develop mutually beneficial and complementary economic cooperation with China. One of Russia's main objectives in its attempt to develop a market economy and pursue a policy of openness abroad is to ensure the incorporation of Russia into the world market and international economic cooperation regimes. Russia enjoys especially favorable conditions for the development of trade and economic cooperation with China. First, the countries are near each other, and both have extensive transport facilities. Second, in many ways the two economies are highly complementary. For example, China is fairly advanced in the production of agricultural goods, products from light industry, and household electrical appliances, which are precisely what Russia lacks. Russia has an advantage in aerospace technology, nuclear energy utilization, heavy industry and machine-building, agricultural machine-building, and other similar areas for which there is a demand in the Chinese market. Russia also has an advantage in natural resources, while China has the advantage in labor power to develop those resources.

Although Russia has emphasized the forging of economic ties with Western industrial nations, for the forseeable future it will be very difficult for Russian-made machinery and equipment to penetrate the Western market on a large scale; to a great extent, Russia can serve only as a supplier of raw materials to the West. China will very likely become the

---

9. "Russia's Foreign Policy," *Rossiyskiye Vesti*, No. 103 (1992).

most important market for Russian exports of machinery and equipment, due to the similar level of technological development in native industry, and the rapid rate of growth and development of its central and western regions.

The eastward shift of Russia's western border resulted in the loss of direct Russian access to many of the USSR's most important centers of industrial production; it has therefore become a vital imperative of the Russian state to direct the focus of economic growth and development eastward in order to utilize the enormous potential of regions formerly largely outside of the Soviet industrial pale.

Of course, the economic development of its eastern regions will also strengthen Russia's political and strategic position in the Asia-Pacific region. However, Russia cannot rely on itself alone if it intends to establish a more formidable presence in Asia; it must enlist the participation and cooperation of other countries, above all those of the Asia-Pacific region, including China. In order to begin attracting foreign capital into Siberia and the Far East, Russia has initiated or intends to initiate the establishment of free trade zones in Sakhalin, Nakhodka, Vladivostok, Kharbovsk, Blagoveschensk, Krasnoyarsk, the Altai Krai, Yakutiya, and other areas along the Chinese border. At present, Chinese and Russian experts are studying concrete proposals for the establishment of three zones of regional economic cooperation.[10]

Third, Russia has an interest in conducting a balanced diplomacy, both regionally and globally. Russia's ruling elites are gradually formulating a clearer, more consensual understanding of the demands of post–Cold War international relations and the new imperatives for international security. Russia is in the process of redefining its role and status in the emerging international security system. From a Russian perspective, the defining characteristic of this new system appears to be the vacuum left by the collapse of the bipolar security structure, and the opportunities this has created for the development of regional centers of power.[11]

Although the Russian Federation is less imposing than was the Soviet Union, it still possesses a great deal of potential to influence world politics, and to affect the formation of new international security structures

---

10. These include a zone between Russia's Far East and China's northeastern provinces, a zone between Russia's eastern Siberia and China's eastern provinces, and a zone between Russia's western Siberia and China's northwestern provinces.

11. "Russia's Foreign Policy Perceptions," *Rossiyskiye Vesti*, No. 103 (December 3, 1993).

and regimes. In short, Russia remains a great power.[12] Increasing numbers of Russian policy analysts advocate abandoning the Eurocentric mentality and a Western-oriented foreign policy. Instead, they advocate a more balanced account of Russia's interests, both east and west. In January 1993, President Yeltsin identified the foci of Russia's eastern policy as China and India.[13]

Since the end of the Cold War, the United Nations has begun to play a larger role in attempting to solve regional conflicts and other issues of global importance. As permanent members of the UN Security Council, the cooperation of Russia and China within the UN and the coordination of their positions could enhance Russia's potential to secure an important role among world powers, and to influence the future of international affairs.

Central Asia and the Asia-Pacific region will be spheres of long-term vital interest for both Russia and China. At present, Russia is participating in the affairs of the Asia-Pacific region more actively than did the Soviet Union, because Russia urgently needs to attract the participation of Asia-Pacific countries in the development of Siberia and the Far East, and because Moscow is beginning to realize that the Asia-Pacific countries will emerge as the leaders of the global economy in the not-too-distant future. Some Russian analysts have gone so far as to predict that "the shortest journey to the twenty-first century is through the Asia-Pacific region."[14]

Russia will seek to play a great power role in the Asia-Pacific region. It will attempt to become a balancing influence in relations between the region's three actors: China, Japan, and the United States. Historically, both czarist Russia and the USSR viewed some measure of control over China as key to furthering Russia's hegemonic aspirations in the Asia-Pacific region. Moscow's current leaders surely know that only by maintaining good relations with China can the new Russia secure a smooth path to a bright future in the Asia-Pacific region.

Many factors suggest that Russia will have difficulty making its mark as a great power in the Asia-Pacific region, at least over the short term.

---

12. See V. Chernov (Deputy Director of the Strategic Security Bureau under the Russian State Security Commission), "Yeltsin Has Approved the Perception of Russia's Foreign Policies," *Nezavisimaya Gazeta*, April 29, 1993.

13. "Russian President B. Yeltsin Gives an Interview in New Delhi," ITAR TASS Agency, January 29, 1993.

14. M.L. Titarenko and B.T. Kulik, "Russia's Foreign Policy: The Far Eastern Dimension," *Far Eastern Problems*, No. 1 (1993).

For a long time to come, it will not be possible for Russia to become a center of power, economically or politically; it is still too preoccupied with problems inherited from the Cold War era and from the aftermath of the collapse of the Soviet Union. Russia is ill-equipped to positively affect many of the political realities of the Asia-Pacific region, including the enormous U.S. military presence in the area and the ramifications of the U.S.-Japan Security Treaty. At most, Russia may be able to resolve the Northern Territory issue with Japan, but even this appears unlikely in the short run. In addition, there is no substitute for time and experience accumulated through extended bilateral relations in building partnerships and trust in the region. Among the countries of the Asia-Pacific region, Russia has comparatively few outstanding problems and contradictions of interest with China. In these circumstances, to maintain and augment good relations with China will serve Russia's vital national interests, and will directly strengthen its economic and political position on the Pacific rim.

Russian leaders worry that the stirring of ethnic, nationalistic, and confessional tensions in Central Asia will spark new confrontations and conflicts that might threaten Russia's southern border. Faced with such a situation, China, with its own Turkic provinces and borders with the newly independent states, could become an invaluable partner for the maintenance of stability in Central Asia.

CHINA'S INTERESTS

China's policy toward Russia centers first and foremost around serving its own national interests. Modern Chinese history has shown that China's national security has been closely intertwined with that of Russia, and later with that of the USSR. In May 1989, when President Mikhail Gorbachev visited Beijing, Deng Xiaoping remarked that historically, two countries — Russia and Japan — have threatened China, and that Russia has greatly benefitted from its proximity to China. Over the course of history, Russia has seized some 1.5 million square kilometers of territory from China.[15] During Stalin's reign, the Soviet Union attempted to bring China's Northeast and Xinjiang provinces into its sphere of influence. In the 1960s and 1970s, confronted with the Soviet military threat, China had no choice but to throw a large amount of its resources into a military buildup. One strategy was to shift many of China's industrial enterprises

---

15. *Selected Essays of Deng Xiaoping* (Chinese edition), Vol. 3, pp. 292–293.

away from its borders and into the mountainous interior. As a result, China's economic growth suffered tremendously.

The situation has now changed. Since embarking on the road to reform, China has adopted the tactic of liberalizing its domestic economy, as well as creating favorable international conditions for economic reconstruction. This goal is complemented by the chief objectives of Chinese foreign policy; during the past few years, China has regarded the development of good relations with the states on its periphery and the assurance of a stable regional environment to be central points of its policy. With the breakup of the Soviet Union, the most immediate threat to China's national security disappeared. Due to the dramatic improvement of relations with post-Soviet Russia and other neighboring countries in recent years, China now enjoys perhaps its most stable and promising security environment in almost a century and a half. This has provided a historic opportunity for China to deepen its domestic reforms, to become more open to the outside world, and to quicken the pace of economic reconstruction.

The new Russia is China's biggest and strongest neighbor. Russia's nuclear weapons capacities are only the most obvious source of its strategic significance, and will ensure Russia's status as a formidable military power well into the next century. Establishing and maintaining friendly relations with Russia is important to China's long-term national security interests, both for its foreign policy goals, and for the vital task of domestic economic development.

Another vital national interest of China that will be served by cooperative relations with Russia is the development of foreign trade and economic cooperation. The level of mutual benefit and complementarity in Sino-Russian economic and trade relations has been dealt with earlier; what bears mentioning here is Russia's position in China's strategy of opening itself up to the outside world. Russia's parallel attempts to form a market-based economy and pursue a policy of openness will allow great maneuverability for China's foreign economic policy, and will help strengthen incentives for China to continue upon its own path of economic openness. The operative strategy is to spur economic development by giving free reign to the economic consequences of opening regions to outside relations, including coastal, river, and border areas, as well as the capital cities of land-locked provinces. The greater transparency of the Sino-Russian border areas is an important aspect of China's new strategy. It is only natural that China will attach great importance to developing trade and economic relations with Russia.

In international affairs, China also needs to develop a broad cooperative relationship with Russia. China maintains that the world is experiencing a historic period of political and strategic change; various forces are in the process of disintegration and realignment, and the international system is headed toward multipolarity. For the modern world, peace and development are the two primary imperatives. As the world's largest developing country and a permanent member of the UN Security Council, China will seek to positively influence the conduct of international affairs; to do so, it must try to forge strong cooperative relations with all the countries of the world, especially world powers, including Russia. China welcomes Russia's entry into the Asia-Pacific region as a stabilizing factor. Due to differing export structures and means for absorbing international capital, economically there will be no direct competition between Russia and China, at least in the short and medium term.

At present, it is difficult to predict what kind of policy Russia will pursue and what kind of role it will play in the Asia-Pacific region; however, three points are clear. First, like China, Russia does not want to see a breakdown in the balance of forces in the Asia-Pacific region at present. Second, Russia and China share a common interest in maintaining the stability and non-nuclear status of the Korean Peninsula. Third, neither Russia nor China wishes to see Japan follow a militaristic path.

The two countries also share many interests in the Central Asian region. China hopes to develop friendly and mutually beneficial relations with the newly independent Central Asian states. Since a great number of Muslim national minorities live in compact communities in China's western regions, like Russia, China has a strong interest in minimizing the emergence of aggressive nationalist and religious forces in the Central Asian region. Threats to the security and stability of the independent states of Central Asia could endanger the security and stability of China's western provinces. Hence, China and Russia share identical interests in securing the long-term stability of this region. China hopes that Russia will respect the integrity, sovereignty and independence of the Central Asian states, and that it will choose to maintain peace and stability in this region.

Several conclusions can be drawn from the above analysis. First, China is trying to create "a peaceful and stable environment on its periphery," while Russia wants to establish around itself a "good-neighbor zone." In this respect, the two countries have the same strategy for achieving long-term security within their immediate regions. Second, both China and Russia are pursuing a policy of openness, and each perceives the other as an important partner in the new economic and political conditions. Third, in the sphere of international security, the national security and stability of both China and Russia are closely tied to their relations with each other. Working together, China and Russia can both exert an enormous influence on the evolution of the emerging multipolar international security structure, and ensure peace and stability in their own regions. In sum, the long-term interests of China and Russia in the international security sphere are largely complementary, and can be pursued without generating conflict. Indeed, the pursuit of these national interests provides ample opportunity for strategic collusion.

Prospects for Long-Term Relations

The policy path being followed by the governments of both China and Russia is in conformity with the short-term needs of both countries, as well as with their long-term needs and interests. This is because the long-term interests of both Russia and China are derived in part from similar goals and strategies of domestic reform and development.

The leadership of China has decided that, barring a large-scale external invasion, it will devote the bulk of its considerable resources to the development of its economy. China hopes to have constructed a mature, modern market system within thirty to fifty years, supported by a complementary political superstructure. Russia too is in the midst of a radical process of transformation, but it will be impossible for it to build a genuine market economy and modern democratic political system within a short period. To narrow the development gap between itself and the Western industrialized countries, and to eventually reach a comparable level of development, Russia must invest a great deal in its domestic development over a long period. Thus, for the foreseeable future, China and Russia will have strong incentives to create an international environment favorable to domestic reform and economic development. This will include opening their states and economies further to outside activities and investments, both to each other, and to other potential partners in Asia and beyond.

In a multipolar world, as in the past, China will not enter into an exclusive alliance with any power or group of powers. China will pursue an independent foreign policy and will not relinquish its initiative to pursue cooperative relations with any country, Russia included, based upon the Five Principles of Peaceful Coexistence. If Russia places emphasis on both the West and the East, this will augment its role as a world power and will help it to exert a broad influence on international security developments. For Russia to serve as a junior partner of Western countries or to enter into an alliance with the West against other countries, however, would run counter to its interests.

It is not in China's interest to attempt to directly influence the outcome of Russia's domestic political struggle. Such an attempt could only hurt Sino-Russian relations in both the short and the long term. The leaders of China maintain that it neither can nor needs to influence the development of Russia's domestic situation. The painful deterioration of Sino-Soviet relations in the 1950s through the 1970s adequately demonstrated to leaders on both sides that attempts to interfere in the internal affairs of the other will have dangerous consequences for bilateral relations. For this reason, China has declared many times that it will respect the Russian people's choice of government, and has emphasized that regardless of the changes that take place in Russia, and regardless of who comes to power, China will seek friendly and cooperative relations with Russia. So far, this policy has withstood the test of time. As for Russia, it is encouraging that the entire spectrum of Russia's political forces have declared their intention to support a stable and cooperative relationship with China.

Thus, the foundation for friendly and good-neighborly relations between China and Russia over the long term is deep. A cooperative relationship built according to the Five Principles of Peaceful Coexistence is the optimal model for the future of Sino-Russian relations; such a relationship would be conducive to the peace and security of the Asia-Pacific region and the world as a whole. In contrast, an exclusive alliance between China and Russia would serve the long-term interests of neither; it would provoke other nations into developing a hostile stance toward them, and would run counter to the interests of stability and security in the Asia-Pacific region and globally.

A famous Chinese proverb states, "Consider the worst possible outcome, while working to achieve the best." As applied to the question of Sino-Russian relations, it is necessary to anticipate sources of conflict and antagonism that might cloud the prospects of a bright future in Russia's relations with China. At present, few doubt the irreversibility of the general direction of reforms in Russia, but no one can guarantee that there will not be twists and turns along the path of political and economic reform. The domestic situation in Russia is highly complex and riddled with uncertainties, and changes in Russia's domestic political situation could affect the course of Russia's foreign policy, including its policies toward China. Several factors could lead to tensions in Russian-Chinese relations over the long term. First, there is currently a great deal of talk about the danger of the resurgence of Russian imperialism. If Russia does pursue an imperialist foreign policy, its main targets will be the former Soviet republics. Next on the list would be Eastern Europe. If Russia were to continue its drive for expansion, the next most likely targets would be Mongolia and the border regions of China. If Russia began to redispatch troops into Mongolia or redeploy heavily armed forces near the Chinese border, for example, China's leaders would perceive these actions as a direct threat to Chinese national security, and would respond in defense.

Second, there are still boundary disputes between Russia and China. The two sides have agreed that "the two parties will accept as a basis for further negotiation all treaties concerning the current Sino-Russian border, and in accordance with the established principles of international law and in the spirit of equal consultation and mutual understanding and mutual accommodation, continue to hold talks over the border areas which have not been agreed upon between the People's Republic of China and the Russian Federation." Nevertheless, it is possible that Russia's leaders could opt not to abide by the boundary agreements already reached between China and Russia. If Russia perceives China's interest in resolving the border issues as an opportunity to press for territorial claims against Russia, then it may consider China a potential enemy. If Russia intensifies its efforts to expand its influence in China's periphery, instigating countries like India and Vietnam (both of which have border disputes with China) into taking actions against China, then China is bound to strike back.

Third, on the issue of Taiwan, the former Soviet and the current Russian governments have declared that they support the position of the Chinese government. But frictions would be generated if in the future Russia forgets all moral and diplomatic principles in pursuit of short-term investments and profits and does not abide by existing agreements on this issue, or uses the issue of Taiwan as a means to exert pressure upon China for any purpose. If it were to change its traditional stance on the status of Taiwan, Russia would place further obstacles in the path of Chinese reunification and would damage goodwill between itself and China.

Fourth, Russia has time and again declared that it wants to establish a strategic partnership with the United States and other Western countries, but has not clearly defined what constitutes a strategic partnership. If Russia concludes agreements with the United States on nuclear disarmament or security arrangements in the Asia-Pacific region that run counter to China's interests in order to curry favor with America, or in exchange for Western economic aid, the relationship of trust and cooperation between Russia and China would be damaged. Their relationship will also suffer if Russia joins the United States and other Western countries in criticizing China's handling of its internal affairs.

Finally, Russia still maintains a powerful military presence in the Asia-Pacific region. While this presence is a legacy of Soviet power, rather than a result of post-Soviet Russian actions, how Russia deals with this force is a question of common concern for all of the Asia-Pacific nations, including China. Russia has reportedly reached an agreement with Vietnam to maintain a military presence in Cam Ranh Bay equal to that of the former Soviet Union. This decision contradicts Russia's repeated declarations that it would not maintain military forces abroad. What is the purpose of Russia's maintaining forces here? If, as some foreign media suggest, Russia's purpose in maintaining forces in Cam Ranh Bay is to "contain China," then this will serve to stir some doubt in the minds of China's leaders as to the sincerity of Russia's policy of cooperation and goodwill toward China.

It would be possible to list other factors that might negatively affect the future development of Sino-Russian relations; however, the above list is itself speculative. One thing is certain: for both Russia and China, Sino-Russian relations are qualitatively different than the relations that each maintains with other outside powers. China and Russia are two great powers with nuclear capabilities and a shared border thousands of kilometers long. The history of Sino-Soviet relations has shown that once bilateral political relations between Moscow and Beijing begin to deteriorate, tension along the border regions will immediately follow; that is, political conflict between Russia and China has the potential to escalate quickly into a military confrontation. This constitutes a serious danger for the security of China and Russia, and for peace in the Asia-Pacific region and the world as a whole. Therefore, it is the common task of the Russian and Chinese peoples and their governments to handle their disputes cautiously, and to treasure the friendly relations between these two countries.

At present, Russia is concerned that because of China's rapid economic development and the prolonged economic crisis in Russia, by the end of the century there may be a "rich China" and a "poor Russia." If this happens, Russia fears, China might contend for the upper hand in regional and global affairs. This concern is groundless. Even if current trends were to continue for a decade, China would not find itself among the world's rich countries, nor would Russia find itself in the ranks of the poor majority. Russia has more or less completed its industrialization, whereas China is still undergoing the transition from an agrarian to an industrial society. China would be very fortunate if it were to catch up to Russia in only ten years.

Over the long term, China will become richer, and will acquire the incentives and means to modernize its military forces. However, even then China will not constitute a threat to Russia and its neighboring states. First, over the short and medium term, and even into the long term, China will not become strong enough to pose a serious challenge to the force levels already held by Russia. For example, China developed its nuclear weapons capabilities solely to break the U.S. and Soviet nuclear monopoly, and for self-defense. Compared with the United States and Russia, China's nuclear might is negligible both in terms of the quality and quantity of its weapons and weapons systems.

Second, in the course of the next twenty to thirty years China will be occupied with domestic tasks, and will not choose to instigate a new arms race. For every government in China, the number-one priority has been to feed and provide for the 1.2 billion citizens living in China, and to improve their standard of living. In addition, in the years to come the Chinese government will emphasize national reunification; this will include not only resuming sovereignty over Hong Kong and Macao, but even more importantly, unification with Taiwan. In order to achieve its domestic goals, China will avoid becoming a threat to other countries or initiating conflicts with other states.

Rather, through its policies of reform and openness, China will be increasingly incorporated into emerging international economic and security structures. An economically successful China will serve as a force of stability in the international security environment, and will avoid being perceived as a strategic threat by its neighboring countries.

Chapter 16

Russia and Japan

Konstantin Sarkisov

Russia and Japan both have key roles to play in international relations, but their bilateral relationship is one tight knot of problems, and an obvious misfit in the post–Cold War international environment. This relationship is in many ways politically and historically anachronistic and contains many elements reminiscent of the Cold War and World War II. It was in this era that the most painful issue of Russian-Japanese relations — the controversy over the Kurile Islands — had its origin. Russian-Japanese relations are characterized by a cool hostility and a general lack of mutual trust. In addition, there are cultural and psychological barriers to understanding, and few reliable lines of political and diplomatic communication. These factors doom relations between these two countries to chronic stagnation and a high degree of susceptibility to issues and circumstances outside the substantive core of Russian-Japanese bilateral discourse.

It is becoming increasingly clear that Russia and Japan are unable to resolve their differences through their own efforts alone — they need constructive backing from the international community. The international community is concerned about the direction in which Russian-Japanese relations develop because of their impact upon global security, particularly in the Asia-Pacific Region. One would be hard put to visualize a stable and enduring security system in this region without the normalization of relations between Russia and Japan.

In the absence of dramatic changes in the international environment and Russia's domestic situation, Russia's foreign policy, influenced as it is by the logic of the transition period, will be geared toward two principal tasks: the democratization of political structures, and the establishment of a free market economy. The coupling of democratic values and the defense of human rights with an increasing awareness of Russia's new national interests will invariably create tensions and

---

Konstantin Sarkisov heads the Center for Japanese Studies at the Institute of Oriental Studies at the Russian Academy of Sciences, and is Deputy Director of the Institute.

and contradictions will not be easily resolved and may lead to instances of Russian great power posturing. The dramatic outcome of the December 1993 general elections in Russia introduced even greater instability into Russia's foreign policy debate by calling into question its basic principles and orientation.

The dispute with Japan over the status of the Kurile Islands has become hostage to a political struggle between various parties and groups in Russia. President Boris Yeltsin's varied course on this issue has reflected his struggles with the political opposition. Neither Russia nor Japan is prepared to make any dramatic moves in the immediate future, largely due to the increasingly critical internal situation in Russia and uncertainties about future political developments in Japan. The situation, therefore, remains a stalemate. No major shifts in bilateral relations are to be expected in the short term, making it all the more important to examine the factors that may alter this situation over the long term.

This chapter first discusses Russian and Japanese national interests, including prospects for cooperation and likely points of policy discord. Second, the impact of developments in the external policy environment on Russian-Japanese relations is examined. Finally, several possible scenarios for the future of Russian-Japanese relations are elaborated.

Factors Likely to Influence Russian Policy Toward Japan

Of the numerous factors that will influence Russian policy toward Japan, the most important is the volatility or stability of Russia's domestic political situation. Only if democratic and market reforms succeed can Yeltsin afford to pursue more active attempts to achieve a breakthrough in relations with Japan. Still, any viable solution to the territorial question will come in the form of a peace treaty that must be ratified by the Russian Parliament. The current Parliament would not favor any solution to the Russian-Japanese territorial conflict; it would block any movements in this direction, and might even take steps to decrease the likelihood of an eventual solution to this dispute. Thus, for at least the term of the 1994–1996 Parliament, no substantive moves toward improving the Russian-Japanese bilateral relationship can be predicted. Even if democratic groups prevail in the next Parliament, it would be very difficult to work through the territorial question without the ability to impose intense pressure on Russian lawmakers. That requires strong leadership and cohesive government policy, neither of which have shown themselves to

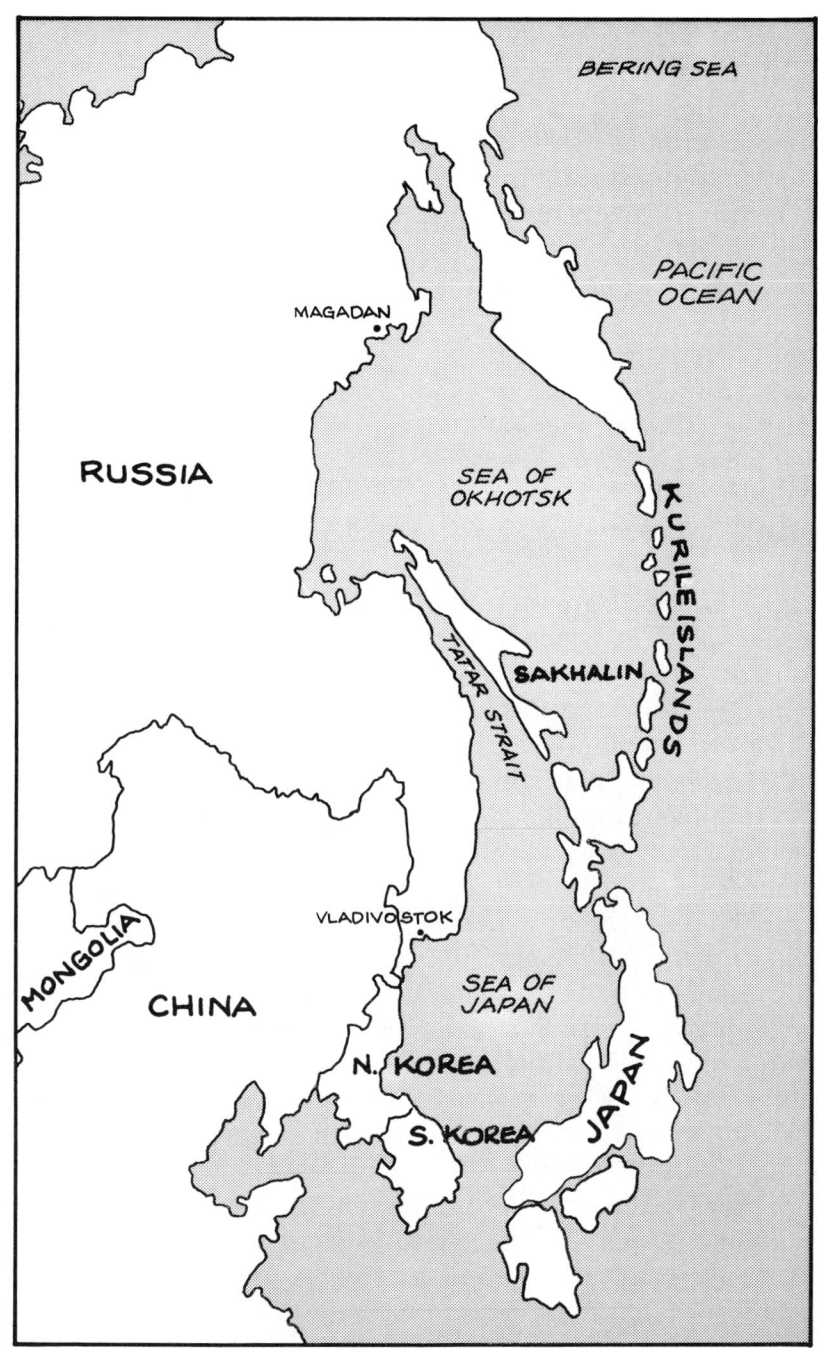

The Russian Far East and Japan

be pervasive elements in post-Soviet Russia.

If an authoritarian regime is established, it might be easier to go through with unpopular measures such as agreeing to territorial concessions in order to secure improved relations with Japan. But such a course would impose an immense political cost upon any Russian leader. If the Yeltsin government collapses before the 1996 elections, for whatever reasons, the situation will be so complicated and fluid that the possibility of territorial compromise with Japan will not even be on the agenda.

FOREIGN INVESTMENT

Russia's prospects for economic recovery in the short and medium term rest largely upon its mineral and natural wealth. Many of the economic assets that were accumulated over the Soviet period in the industrial and production sphere are either outmoded or otherwise unusable; oil, coal, rare-earth metals, timber, gold, and diamonds comprise Russia's most important — if not its sole — economic reserve. The economic future of Russia will depend greatly upon the effective exploitation of its natural resources, many of which are located in Siberia and the Far East. In the initial period of its economic revival, Russia will have to export growing amounts of energy and raw materials.

However, it will take a great deal of money to develop the resources of these regions. Enormous capital investments and active efforts are needed to convert munitions plants, which are pervasive in industrial and technological enclaves like Novosibirsk and Krasnoyarsk. In addition, much money will be needed to ensure the social protection of servicemen who will be discharged in line with cuts to the armed forces stationed in this over-militarized region. To achieve its goals, Russia must become an active presence in the Asia-Pacific community of states, apply for membership in regional economic organizations, and attract foreign capital. All of this is possible only if Russia pursues an active Asian policy; this would make it imperative or at least extremely desirable that Russia fully normalize its relations with Japan, which plays the key economic and a leading political role in the Asia-Pacific region.

The Yeltsin government is attempting to initiate cooperation with China, South Korea, and the ASEAN (Association of South East Asian Nations) countries, and to find acceptable forms of economic relations with Taiwan. But it will become ever more obvious to Russia with the passage of time that these countries cannot compensate for the lack of normal relations with Japan.[1]

THE MILITARY-STRATEGIC FACTOR

The growing importance of the Asia-Pacific region for the economic resurrection of Russia will have a long-term impact on its security interests. Moscow will be increasingly interested in maintaining a stable environment in this region, as well as in forming an effective system of regional security based upon cooperative relations with all of the countries of the region, particularly Japan. Russia has inherited the enormous and largely obsolete military potential of the Soviet Union. Primarily for financial reasons, Russia must make substantial reductions in its armed forces and armaments. At the same time, Russia must retain a sufficient defense potential. In order to ease the burden of its military spending, Russia will attempt to achieve stability and gain security guarantees through political means, including cooperation with leading regional powers and efforts to create a regional security system. It will seek to link inevitable cuts in its military presence in the region to similar steps by the United States, with Japan and China likely also to participate. A necessary condition for this will be not only the forging of some sort of partnership with the United States, but also more intensive relations with Japan.

Obviously, Russia and Japan should fully normalize their relations on the basis of a peace treaty that includes a solution to the territorial dispute. Over the long term, Russia's engagement in the economic affairs of the Asia-Pacific region will create an increasing interest in a close economic relationship with Japan. The territorial question will become a more annoying matter for both sides, prompting an eventual compromise. If Russia and Japan were to acknowledge the drastic changes that have occurred in the political and geostrategic underpinnings of their relationship, the resolution of the territorial dispute would become merely a technical problem, rather than a political and national-psychological problem.

THE GEOPOLITICAL FACTOR

Russia's foreign policy is still oriented toward the West, but this is likely to change. As they are developed more intensively, the resources currently

---

1. The normalization of Russian-Japanese relations will not automatically entail an inflow of Japanese capital to Russia; the creation of various types of economic and transportation infrastructure, as well as the consolidation of a reliable legal system, will also be required.

lying dormant in Siberia and the Far East will shift Russia's strategic concerns from Europe to Asia; this will have a significant impact on its foreign policy.[2] It is more to Russia's advantage for Tokyo to be its political ally, rather than an adversary, particularly over the long term. Russia's relations with the United States may run into difficulties as imperial tendencies in Russia's foreign policy become more pronounced. The United States will not depend for its security upon good relations with Russia, because it has always had much more varied interests. China's development is still too unpredictable to be able to foresee that country's likely role.

In addition, the intensity of Russian-Japanese relations is important to the prospects of forming workable relations between states in the Asia-Pacific region. For Russia to maintain good relations with the United States and China while failing to have a good relationship with Japan will foster in Tokyo a sense of isolation, or even a feeling that a collusion is being mounting against it. This, in turn, could lead to greater tensions between Tokyo and Washington, which would be a disaster.

Thus, Russia clearly has no interest in promoting divisions between Japan and the United States or in prompting a crisis in the United States-Japan Mutual Security System. The disappearance of this system would potentially entail an extremely dangerous turn in the overall balance of power in the region. The emergence of a vacuum of power might provoke the growth of Japanese nationalism and give a shot in the arm to those who demand that Japan employ its immense industrial and financial might to become a nuclear weapons state.

HISTORICAL AND PSYCHOLOGICAL FACTORS
The territorial question is the subject of acute political infighting in Russia, and is exacerbated by the ignorance of the larger part of the Russian population about its history and legal aspects. President Yeltsin's incumbency will be a period of intense political struggles and he is, therefore, unlikely to be the Russian leader who will eventually solve the painful territorial problem in relations with Japan. Over time the territorial issue will only give Russia more pain, aggravated as it is by the emergence of new territorial disputes arising from the dissolution of the Soviet

---

2. Culturally, Russia will continue to gravitate toward Europe for a long while, which can be explained as a reaction to the seventy years of Bolshevik efforts to bar it from all European influences. The Russian dream of becoming a developed European state will diminish little, if at all.

Union. In this context, the Kuriles cease to be just a problem of the postwar settlement and come to epitomize the challenges to Russia's integrity from all sides.

Both Russia and Japan should develop a strategy that takes into account all aspects of the dispute, including psychological factors. The solution will most likely be found in a compromise that will not injure the national pride of either party, but will rather convince the Russians that far from losing, they will only profit from solving the territorial issue.

The history of Russian-Japanese relations is marked more by periods of wars, conflicts and hostility than by peaceful and fruitful coexistence. However, a deeply entrenched hostility toward old enemies is largely absent in Russia nowadays. (A striking case in point is the attitude toward Germans and Germany prevailing in present-day Russia.) The Russian and Japanese peoples have traditionally viewed each other with respect. To this day, the Russian cultural tradition contributes immensely to the positive image of Russia in Japan.[3]

The gap in understanding between Russia and Japan is a product of their past negative relations and the lack of real contacts between the two countries and the two peoples. Every generation of Soviet and Russian leaders spoke of the importance of good relations with Japan, but none understood Japan. Old national wounds cannot be healed at once. The intensification of contacts and economic and geopolitical interdependence will move both countries closer to this end.

Japan's Foreign Relations

Japanese foreign policy has reached a limit in its development and is ripe for a serious revision of its course and strategy. Based upon the Yoshida Doctrine formulated in the 1950s, Japanese foreign policy was geared toward a rapid postwar economic recovery. Japan, therefore, opted for a close alliance with the United States. The disintegration of the bipolar system that followed the collapse of the Soviet Union has exploded the entire system of Cold War values. Economic relations have moved to the forefront as the principal focus. Increasingly loud voices in the United States assert that Japan is now the number-one enemy of U.S. national interests. The Japanese policy of non-interference in regional conflicts and

---

3. In the early years of this century Russian culture was one of the principal sources from which the Japanese drew their knowledge of European civilization.

non-involvement in military operations against aggressive regimes and international terrorism has also come under sharp criticism. Tokyo is accused of economic snobbery and unwillingness to contribute anything more than money for peace and stability. Western pressure on Japan has led to a grave crisis in the conceptual underpinnings of Japanese foreign policy.

However, because of the internal diasarray of the Japanese political party system, it is possible to predict that in the short and medium term, there will be no dramatic shifts in the character of Japanese foreign policy, including the nature of its political power structures. The conservative presence is in no danger of disappearing, making it highly unlikely that Tokyo will renounce the Yoshida Doctrine. More likely, Japan will continue to rely upon its partnership with the United States to guarantee its military security.

Still, there are a number of signs that Tokyo is beginning to give serious thought to finding a long-term alternative to the Security Treaty with the United States. Japan is seeking to start a positive dialogue with Russia and China on issues of security, military transparency, and all factors that can build trust. Japan has shown interest in proposals to form regional structures similar in nature and functions to those in Europe, particularly the CSCE. Over the long term, the main concern of the Japanese will be the willingness and ability of the United States to continue to provide a strategic "umbrella" over Japan. The deteriorating situation around North Korea, combined with evidence that the Kim Il Sung regime has or will soon have a nuclear device and the means to deliver it, are unnerving to Tokyo. There should not be any doubt that in the worst case, Japan will become a nuclear power — with all the repercussions that would carry for stability in the Asia-Pacific region.

In its relations with Russia, Japan is facing a dilemma. It could freeze relations with Russia in their present state and conduct a "two-level" policy — one within the G-7 framework in which Japan will be urged to give aid to Russia, and the other within the framework of Russian-Japanese bilateral relations. This would entail maintaining a tough stand on the territorial issue and making economic aid conditional upon concrete progress on that issue. A second option is to use the principle of a "balanced expansion" of bilateral relations coined by former Foreign Minister Sosuke Uno, in which relations would develop gradually, without any dramatic leaps and bounds and with a minimum of policy linkage to the territorial issue. It is possible that Japan might pursue both options simultaneously. A number of factors will influence Japan's policy toward Russia.

THE ECONOMIC FACTOR

Russia and Japan operate at different levels of economic activity in the Asia-Pacific region. Japan is the economic epicenter of the region. Russia's economic involvement is marginal, and the development of its Siberian and Far Eastern districts will require much time and enormous investment. It is not vitally important for Japan today to have access to Russian resources; it is not even particularly enthusiastic about gaining access to Siberian energy and oil stocks. Japan is unwilling to initiate cooperation with Russia because of Russia's lack of economic and political stability, and its unpreparedness to absorb large-scale investments in its energy-producing industries.

The Japanese are not afraid that they may be "late for the train" in terms of becoming economically engaged in Russia; they are convinced they will always be able to make up for lost time. Japan will be content to wait out the period when the least profitable groundwork is occurring in Russia, and to later take advantage of the work done by others. When the time is ripe, the Japanese will likely flood the Russian market, primarily in the Far East region and Siberia. One can see even now a growing slant in Japanese policy toward these regions, which consists of increasing humanitarian aid and establishing direct ties with local authorities. However, the United States and China will remain the countries of highest priority to Japanese foreign and economic policy.

STRATEGIC AND GEOPOLITICAL FACTORS

The force of mutual attraction between Russia and Japan in the geopolitical sphere is much stronger than in the economic sphere. Both countries have a stake in securing stability in the Asia-Pacific region and both want a more durable international security system to be created there. Russia especially needs such a system; to single-handedly ensure the security of its vast territory and extensive borders would be an enormous economic burden, especially in the transition period. For Japan, the Soviet military threat dominated strategic thinking throughout the postwar years, but today, the territorial dispute and the conditions of interaction with Russia in the context of Asia-Pacific regional intercourse loom larger.

The returns to be gleaned from the normalization of relations with Russia are growing for Japan as a new, post–Cold War security configuration takes shape. It is not to Japan's advantage to have a politically lethargic relationship with Russia now that its own partnership with the United States is under serious threat, and while its partnership with the People's Republic of China and the emergence of a Japan-dominated Asian market remain highly problematic issues.

Even if Russia does not become an ally of Japan, Russia will provide a natural counterbalance to the growing influence of China in the Asia-Pacific region. China is becoming an increasingly dynamic economic force in the region, and the modernization of the Chinese armed forces being promoted by the current regime is also a source of worry to the Japanese. There is a lingering Russian influence in the conflict between North and South Korea as well.

Japan wants to maintain some leverage with the Russian government over Russian arms exports to Asian countries, where the arms are likely to constitute a destabilizing factor that directly affects Japanese interests. The dumping of Russian nuclear waste in the Sea of Japan has become a hot issue for Tokyo. The resolution of these and other small but pressing problems requires closer Japanese interaction with Moscow, and Japanese economic cooperation with Russia can serve as a source of leverage.

Japan will have to rely upon the instruments of multilateral diplomacy to be in a position to neutralize potential threats as they emerge. One such threat is perceived to be an excessive U.S.-Russian rapprochement. The threat of finding itself strategically isolated may compel Japanese diplomacy toward compromises with Russia, including over the territorial dispute. But there is a limit that Japanese diplomatic flexibility will not exceed: Russian diplomats should not stress the Russian rapprochement with the United States in order to browbeat Japan and force it to accept a territorial settlement on Russian terms. Such a strategy could even force Japan to look for geostrategic allies in the Asia-Pacific region, including some form of strategic partnership with China. Japan might also attempt to organize its own economic bloc in the Asia-Pacific region.

Russia may well back the Japanese ambition to become a permanent member of the UN Security Council. This may, of course, upset the balance of forces in the territorial issue, but on the whole the consequences of this step will not be bad for Russia.

External Factors in Russian-Japanese Relations

During the Cold War, no state or bloc of states wanted Russia and Japan to resolve their territorial dispute; it helped ensure that these two countries would remain politically distant. After the collapse of the Soviet Union, the situation changed but not completely, since old geopolitical considerations still prevail in the strategy and policies of many countries.[4] However, as economic momentum in the Asia-Pacific region begins to lead all other regional processes, there will be growing pressure from both great and small powers in the region to forge good or at least normal Russian-Japanese relations.

The United States can play a key role in the settlement of the territorial dispute between Russia and Japan.[5] First, it can act as an honest broker by encouraging the search for a compromise, and can act as a guarantor of the means to implement it. For example, Russia will need to feel more, not less, secure by resolving the territorial dispute with Japan, and it is to this end that the United States ought to direct its efforts. Ideally, the territorial settlement and the signing of a peace treaty between Russia and Japan should be accompanied by the conclusion of a number of tripartite agreements on disarmament, security guarantees, and new regional mutual security structures.

The United States should shed additional light on the history of the issue by opening to the public more of its wartime archives, which contain all of the details of the Roosevelt-Stalin agreement on the Kuriles, as well as its postwar archives, which record how U.S. diplomacy stamped out all timid attempts by Japan to reach a compromise with Russia. Access to these materials could help both nations to better understand the history of the conflict and to lay the psychological groundwork for an eventual solution.

---

4. The nature of the Russian-American confrontation over the option of a NATO bombardment of Serbian positions around Sarajevo in the conflict in former Yugoslavia proves that remnants of the Cold War era are still around. It also suggests that Russia in transition cannot be a real and coherent strategic partner of the West.

5. The United States appears not to be fully aware of its own responsibility for the emergence of the territorial problem in relations between Russia and Japan. President Franklin D. Roosevelt endorsed the transfer of the Kuriles to Russia in exchange for Russia's involvement in the war against Japan. This saved American lives, cut off a part of Japanese territory, and drove a permanent political wedge between the Soviet Union and Japan.

China's indirect impact on the Russian-Japanese territorial issue could be immense. Beijing has no positive stake in an excessive Russian-Japanese rapprochement that would strengthen both Russia and Japan and could divert Japanese capital and investments away from China. However, China would benefit from a Russian-Japanese rapprochement in other ways, due to its interests in a number of regional development projects and economic cooperation schemes, most notably the Tuman River project; such initiatives are likely to move forward much more quickly if Moscow and Tokyo find a more cooperative basis for their relations. As long as its interests remain divided, China will probably not assume an active stance on the issue of the Russian-Japanese territorial dispute.

South Korea has always reacted more vigorously to all shifts in Russian-Japanese relations. As a state with only modest potential for political influence, South Korea exploits as far as possible the differences between the great powers in the region, and keeping Japanese power confined to the economic sphere is of primary importance for Seoul. While Seoul will support Russian-Japanese rapprochement in word, it will indirectly resist it in practice. However, Seoul wields little power on this issue.

Scenarios for Russian-Japanese Relations

The first scenario for the development of Russian-Japanese relations entails gradual evolution and slow progress toward a settlement of the territorial dispute sometime in the twenty-first century. Acknowledging the existence of deterring factors and insufficient incentives for large-scale cooperation in general, both Russia and Japan would agree to move slowly with an eye to a distant future. Talks on the territorial issue would begin at a stalemate, with four outcomes possible.

The first possible outcome is a political compromise on the territories, that is, a concession by one of the sides; the second outcome would be a search for some intermediate solution, including the possibility of dual possession of the islands; the third is to put the issue before the International Court of Justice in the Hague; and the fourth is to preserve the status quo, that is, to put off the matter indefinitely. The first outcome is unlikely, because politically and psychologically the issue is extraordinarily sensitive and the Russian political leadership is too weak and divided to overcome this barrier. The fourth possible outcome cannot be regarded as a positive solution, although it may be the most probable.

If a solution is achieved, the third outcome — trying the case before the International Court of Justice — may be the most likely means; most Russian experts are confident that Russia would win the case. Applying to the International Court of Justice has its merits and demerits. One chief advantage is that a court ruling would be accepted with a measure of grace, because it would be based on legal regulations rather than a political deal. But the loss of the case by one of the sides will form a poor basis for friendly relations in the future. To avoid a deterioration in Russian-Japanese bilateral relations, the best policy may be pragmatic incrementalism. The conceptual basis for such a policy may be the idea of "balanced expansion" generated some years ago by the Japanese Ministry of Foreign Affairs.

In the second scenario, a positive solution to the territorial dispute is found within a shorter period of time. For this to be feasible, Yeltsin must consolidate the situation in Russia in short order, gain a victory over his opposition, and strengthen his political hand. In this case, Yeltsin may attempt a territorial solution within, say, a period of three to five years; there will be talks, a choice among several political compromises, and agreement upon some interim formulas, likely to be followed by an application to the International Court of Justice.

This scenario introduces the prospect of some intermediary and palliative solutions which might suit the Japanese side more than the circumstances of the first scenario. In this scenario it is possible to envisage agreement on a special status for the islands, their greater demilitarization, or their declaration as a zone of special interests for both countries. A plan could be adopted that would minimize the potential for political and psychological damage to Russia and also enable the Japanese to save face. In other words, a quick solution to the territorial issue involving the transfer of all four islands to Japan is impossible even if events in Russia develop in accordance with the best-case scenario.

In the third scenario there will be a sharp worsening in the domestic political situation in Russia. The current government will fall and President Yeltsin will be sent into retirement, there will be a complete destabilization of the balance of political forces, and a new regime will attempt to deal with Russia's internal problems by authoritarian methods. In this case, progress in Russian-Japanese relations will not occur until long into the future. Yeltsin will be accused of intending to sell off the Kurile islands to the Japanese; he is already dodging such reproaches from the right chauvinist and centrist opposition. Paradoxical though it may seem, the consummation of such a pessimistic scenario would hardly do great damage to bilateral relations between Russia and Japan. Instead, it would take the edge off the territorial issue, and force both sides to seek some interim terms of coexistence.

Of course, these scenarios do not cover the entire spectrum of possibilities, but they show that a quick and mutually acceptable solution to the chief problem in Russian-Japanese relations — the territorial dispute — is unlikely to be achieved soon, and in any case not before the end of the century. But Russia and Japan must not allow their relations to deteriorate on account of this dispute. With the end of the Cold War, both Japan and Russia should reexamine their interests regarding each other. If in some measure this can be accomplished in the less charged realms of economic, political, and environmental cooperation, it is possible that new opportunities will appear for the settlement of the territorial issue.

Chapter 17 | *Tsuyoshi Hasegawa*

Japan and Russia

The end of the Cold War and the collapse of the Soviet Union have not significantly altered the basic nature of Russo-Japanese relations. While Russia's relations with other major powers have gone through fundamental readjustments to the new reality, Russo-Japanese relations continue to be in a state of stalemate. The abnormality of this situation becomes immediately apparent when we recall that Russia and Japan have not concluded a peace treaty half a century after the end of World War II.

This situation appears more extraordinary if one takes into account the fundamental changes that both Russia and Japan have undergone in recent years. After the end of communism and the collapse of the Soviet Union, Russia embarked on a tortuous path toward democracy and a market economy. Japan's political system, dominated by the conservative Liberal Democratic Party for almost the entire postwar period, ceased to operate in the summer of 1993, setting into motion a process of political realignment. While both Russia and Japan go through fundamental restructuring, they are simultaneously redefining their national interests, their own identity, and their role in the new international environment. Foreign policy and domestic policy are now intertwined more closely in both countries than in previous years. Despite these changes, Russia and Japan find themselves unable to overcome the legacies they inherited from the Cold War and World War II.

This chapter assesses the significance of the current stage of Russo-Japanese relations against the background of the factors that have impeded rapprochement between Russia and Japan, and speculates on how their relations might evolve.

Tsuyoshi Hasegawa is currently a Professor of History at the University of California at Santa Barbara. He received his BA from Tokyo University, and his MA and Ph.D. from the University of Washington.

The Northern Territories Problem

On August 9, 1945, the Soviet government declared war against Japan, thus violating the Neutrality Treaty that existed between the Soviet Union and Japan, and began military operations against the Japanese forces in Manchuria. In the last stage of the war, between August 28 and September 5, Soviet forces seized the southern Kurile Islands.[1] Altogether, these islands comprise 4,894 square kilometers off Hokkaido, and had been recognized by Russia as Japanese territory until this time. In 1947, the Supreme Soviet of the USSR created an independent Sakhalin oblast, which included the Kurile Islands, and amended the Soviet Constitution to include the Kurile Islands as a part of the Russian Soviet Federated Socialist Republic. In 1947 and 1948, approximately 17,000 Japanese were evacuated from the islands to Hokkaido.[2] The islands are now populated by 43,000 citizens of the Russian Federation, comprising only 4 percent of the total population of Sakhalin oblast. Of these, 85 percent are Russians, while Ukrainians, Belarussians, Tartars, and Caucasians account for 10 percent. Fishing and the military are the economic backbone of the islands, with 21 percent of the population engaged in the fishing industry and one-third of the islands' population serving in the military.[3]

These small islands, which the Japanese call the Northern Territories,[4] constitute the great stumbling block that has prevented either country from making a great leap toward rapprochement. The most puzzling aspect of this dispute is its intractability. The Northern Territories cannot be considered an issue that threatens Japan's national existence. As some Japanese describe it, the Northern Territories dispute is like a fish bone stuck in the throat, an irritant rather than a deadly struggle.

---

1. For the most recent Soviet work on Soviet occupation of the Northern Islands in 1945, see Boris Slavinsky, *The Soviet Occupation of the Kuril Islands, August-September 1945: A Documentary Research* (Cambridge, Mass.: Strengthening Democratic Institutions Project, John F. Kennedy School of Government, Harvard University, 1993).

2. John J. Stephan, *The Kuril Islands: Russo-Japanese Frontier in the Pacific* (Oxford: Clarendon Press, 1974), pp. 166–170.

3. For the contemporary situation on the islands, see Oleg Bondarenko, "Paper on the Contemporary Situation in the Kurile Islands," in Graham Allison, Hiroshi Kimura, and Konstantin Sarkisov, eds., *Beyond Cold War to Trilateral Cooperation in the Asia-Pacific Region: Scenarios for New Relationships between Japan, Russia, and the United States*, Appendices F–N.

4. In this chapter I use the term "Northern Territories" for these islands, without attaching any value judgement on the issue of their sovereignty.

Far more difficult issues have been resolved when the benefits that could be derived from their resolution far outweighed the cost of not resolving them. For instance, the United States and the former Soviet Union were able to conclude major arms control agreements, and before the revolutions in 1989, few would have predicted that German reunification would be achieved before the Soviet return of the Northern Territories. This section examines why the Northern Territories problem has proven intractable.

SOVIET PERCEPTIONS OF THE NORTHERN TERRITORIES QUESTION
From the Soviet or Russian point of view, the acquisition of the Northern Territories during the last weeks of the Pacific War was justified; it made the Soviet Union finally safe from the Japanese militarism that had constantly threatened the country throughout the twentieth century.[5] Moreover, the occupation of the Kuriles was not a unilateral action by the Soviet Union, but was based on a prior agreement by its wartime allies, the United States and Britain. Japan has no legal claim to the islands, the Russians argue, since Japan renounced its claim to them in the San Francisco Peace Treaty of 1951. From 1960, when Japan renewed the U.S.-Japan security treaty, until the Gorbachev period, the Soviet government officially took the position that no territorial question existed between the Soviet Union and Japan.[6]

Concealed behind this intransigence are four factors. The first is national prestige; the territories acquired during World War II have served as a reminder that the Soviet Union was a victor in the war, not merely in Europe but also in Asia. Second, the farther the Russian economy lagged behind Japan's, the more tenaciously the Soviet leadership attempted to cling to the Northern Territories. This psychological need to reassert Russia's victory over Japan has, if anything, been more intense since the collapse of the Soviet Union.

Third, for the Soviet leadership, adherence to the World War II settlements was the foundation on which Soviet domestic and international stability rested. The Soviets had good reason to believe that any

---

5. See Jonathan Haslam, "Patterns of Soviet-Japanese Relations Since World War II," in Tsuyoshi Hasegawa, Jonathan Haslam, and Andrew Kuchins, eds., *Russia and Japan: An Unresolved Dilemma between Distant Neighbors* (Berkeley: International Area Studies Publications, 1993), pp. 3–48.

6. In the second half of the 1970s, the Soviet government temporarily softened its position in order to block Sino-Japanese rapprochement.

territorial concessions would start a floodgate of irredentist demands from other countries.[7] This paranoia persists; in fact, the fear of irredentism, combined with the wounded sense of national pride, constitute the most powerful psychological factor explaining the upsurge of a Russian national-patriotic movement against any territorial concessions to Japan on the Northern Territories.

The Northern Territories are also strategically valuable to Russia. One important component of Soviet strategy for a nuclear war was to turn the Sea of Okhotsk into an impregnable bastion from which Delta-class SSBNs could attack the United States. The possession of the Northern Territories became a linchpin in this strategy.[8]

Since the end of the Cold War, the loss of the large buffer zones that existed in Eastern Europe, the independence of the "near abroad" republics in the West and the South, and the marked reduction of the conventional forces have led to the increasing strategic weight of Russian nuclear deterrent. The Russian military thus still considers the Sea of Okhotsk an area vital to Russian security, making the possession of the Northern Territories an essential defense requirement.

JAPAN'S PERCEPTIONS

The possession of the Northern Territories is also a matter of utmost national pride for Japan. The Soviet occupation of the Northern Territories has been a constant reminder that Japan has not eradicated the humiliation suffered by the defeat of World War II.

Here, too, the psychological dimension needs to be emphasized. The Pacific War and the period preceding it provoke among the Japanese depressing memories that offer no consolation; but the Soviet attack on Japan in violation of the Neutrality Treaty gave the Japanese a sense that they, too, were victims from the outside. The Northern Territories are a symbol of this sense of victimization.[9]

---

7. Kimura Hiroshi, *Hoppô ryôdo: kiseki to henkan eno jyosô* (*The Northern Territories: it would be a miracle if they were returned*) (Tokyo: Jijitsûshinsha, 1989), pp. 16–19.

8. See Tsuyoshi Hasegawa, *Gorbachev's Asian Initiative and Asian Security: Final Report to the National Council for Soviet and East European Research*, pp. 6-7; and Michael McGwire, *Military Objectives in Soviet Foreign Policy* (Washington, D.C.: Brookings Institution, 1987), pp. 174–175.

9. Gilbert Rozman, *Japan's Response to the Gorbachev Era, 1985–1991: A Rising Superpower Views a Declining One* (Princeton: Princeton University Press, 1992), pp. 12–13.

The Japanese government has also effectively exploited the Northern Territories issue for its geopolitical purposes. During the Cold War, the Japanese government made the immediate return of the four islands a precondition for rapprochement with the Soviet Union. This was a peculiar position on at least two accounts. First, if Japan's ultimate goal was to regain possession of the islands, its approach made this goal most difficult to achieve; it was tantamount to an ultimatum that no Soviet leadership could seriously entertain. Second, this policy led to a bizarre situation, in which Japan's entire policy toward the Soviet Union was reduced to the Northern Territories question; as long as the territorial dispute had no prospect of being resolved, there was no need for Japan to craft a comprehensive Soviet policy.

These peculiarities tell us more about one of the Japanese government's goals, if not the sole goal, for the Northern Territories issue — to prevent rapprochement with the Soviet Union and to build a national consensus for its close alliance with the United States. The Northern Territories issue provided a convenient excuse for Japan to keep its relations with the Soviet Union adversarial.

The drastic changes in international relations during the perestroika and post-perestroika periods have eliminated one of the most important goals of Japan's policy toward the Northern Territories. No longer is there any overarching reason for Japan to avoid rapprochement with Russia. On the contrary, Japan has been under considerable pressure from its allies to hasten the process of reconciliation with Russia. The Northern Territories dispute, which once anchored Japan firmly in the Western camp, has become a source of friction. Nevertheless, the sense of national prestige, historical memory, and psychological antipathy toward Russia that the Japanese government once effectively exploited to justify its policy toward the Northern Territories has come to haunt the Japanese government as it seeks to change its policy. This explains many of the contradictions in Japan's policy toward Russia in the post–Cold War period.

LACK OF INCENTIVES

In addition to the symbolic importance of the Kurile Islands to both Russia and Japan, there is a marked lack of incentives to break the current Russo-Japanese stalemate. First, although Russo-Japanese relations are often characterized as "bad," both countries have displayed a remarkable ability to manage their relations in a generally hostile environment.

Russo-Japanese relations are not "bad" in the sense that they are on the verge of a serious breakdown. Nor does this poor state of relations imply any imminent risk to the political, diplomatic, and economic ties between the two countries. On the contrary, within certain limits bilateral relations have markedly improved, not deteriorated, since Gorbachev's accession to power.

Second, while resource-rich but technologically poor Russia and resource-poor but technologically advanced Japan seem to be naturally compatible economic partners, Russia's domestic troubles make it an unattractive business partner for Japan. Economic motivation no longer drives Japan's policy toward Russia, as it did in the early 1970s, when the Japanese business community was eager to seek Soviet energy resources. Currently, the business community exerts no pressure on the government to change its Russia policy. Moreover, Japan is well aware that its financial and economic resources are not unlimited, particularly since it is experiencing an unprecedented recession; thus, it must give financial aid selectively. An overwhelming consensus in Japan is that in purely economic terms Japan's investment in and financial assistance to Russia do not make sense. Accordingly, Russia is rightly skeptical that the return of the islands would result in a sudden infusion of Japanese capital, economic and technological aid, and an increase in trade.

Third, in Russia's new political context, characterized by the resurgence of nationalism, the territorial dispute with Japan has become a subject for domestic politics. Early public opinion polls (which became possible only under glasnost) indicated that an overwhelming majority of Soviet citizens, especially those who lived on the disputed islands, were opposed to giving up any territory to Japan. The more the Japanese government propagated its view on the Northern Territories, the more deeply the Northern Territories issue penetrated into the consciousness of ordinary Russian citizens, and the more widespread and vociferous the opposition to Japan's demand became. Ordinary Russian citizens who had never heard of the Southern Kuriles and may not know where they are located are now convinced that the islands must be protected at any cost.

Prospects to resolve the territorial question have varied with the political winds. For example, in September 1992 domestic pressures forced President Boris Yeltsin to cancel a trip to Tokyo only three days before his scheduled departure. The momentum for improvement in bilateral relations that had been built up step by step was suddenly disrupted.

Despite Yeltsin's stridently anti-Japanese pronouncements, which were patently intended to gain domestic popularity at the expense of Japan, the Japanese government wisely attempted to diffuse the crisis, and patiently waited for an opportune moment to repair the damage. Throughout the critical period of uncertainty, the Japanese government continued to pledge support for Russia's reform process, despite the cancellation of Yeltsin's second promised trip in May 1993. It was impossible, however, to expect that Yeltsin could come up with any major proposal that would satisfy both the Japanese government and his domestic opponents, as long as he was waging a deadly political struggle, with his opponents firmly entrenched in the parliament.

One week after Yeltsin crushed his opponents in October 1993, he flew to Tokyo to hold a summit meeting with Japanese Prime Minister Hosokawa. No breakthrough took place, but Yeltsin's visit succeeded in repairing the damage inflicted by the cancellation of his previously planned visit, thus bringing bilateral relations back on the right track. The joint Tokyo Declaration stated that the Russian Federation, as the Soviet Union's successor state, should abide by all treaty obligations made by the Soviet Union.

This momentum for improvement turned out to be ephemeral. The December 1993 election in Russia pushed Vladimir Zhirinovsky's Liberal Democratic Party into the newly created parliament as one of the dominant parliamentary parties. The result of the election immediately led to the conservative swing of the Yeltsin government's economic and foreign policies. For all practical purposes, the possibility of Russia's coming up with a more flexible policy than that taken by Yeltsin at the October 1993 summit has vanished.

Fourth, Japanese domestic politics have also constrained Russo-Japanese relations. Japan's policy toward Russia is distinguished from any other part of Japan's foreign policy by the small number of players involved in the decision-making process; there is still a marked absence of influential advocacy groups that challenge the government. This is related to the low priority given to Russia in Japan's foreign policy. Russia is not necessary for Japan's immediate economic needs. As long as the U.S.-Japanese security alliance is intact, Japan does not have to worry about being threatened by Russia's problems, and can delegate the major tasks of solving security conflicts to the United States. The low priority accorded to Russia is also anchored in a deep-seated Japanese popular dislike of Russia that is largely expressed in the form of indifference.

Russo-Japanese relations have suffered a streak of bad luck. The powerful Japanese politicians who could have taken decisive action on the territorial issue fell victim to a series of political scandals. Every time Russo-Japanese relations showed signs of improvement, the Japanese cabinet collapsed. The political instability in Japan is likely to continue for some time. Weak governments will have little time or energy to devote to a fundamental reorientation of Japan's foreign policy; therefore, there is little likelihood that Japan will take the initiative to break the deadlock on the territorial issue.

Finally, in the prevailing Japanese perception, Russia does not fill any of Japan's economic needs, while Japan is absolutely essential for Russia's. The only advantage that the Japanese can think of gaining from improved relations with Russia is on the territorial issue. Thus, the Japanese tend to reduce Russo-Japanese relations to a simple quid pro quo: economic aid (Russia's gain) for the return of the Northern Territories (Japan's gain). This formula affronts the Russian sense of pride. Even if there were no political opposition, it would be impossible for any Russian political leaders to accept this formula without abandoning the status of a great power. Russia is prepared to do without Japan's economic aid for this reason, particularly when Russia is not ready to make effective use of massive economic aid.

Long-Term Interests of Russia and Japan

The analysis above suggests that rapprochement between Japan and Russia is an impossible task, at least in the foreseeable future. In order to assess the implications of this stalemate, we must examine where the national interests of Russia and Japan converge and diverge in the long term.

RUSSIA'S ECONOMIC REFORM

First, Russia's and Japan's national interests converge in their common desire to see Russia's economic transition successfully completed; Japan could play a major part in this. Not only does Japan have sufficient financial, economic, and technological resources to make a substantial difference in this process; it is also indispensable to the economic development of the Russian Far East.

A revitalized market-oriented Russian economy would in the long run also serve Japan's interest. It would create a huge market for Japan's trade and investment, while the resource-rich Russian Far East, buttressed by a well-developed infrastructure, would complement Japan well. The economic progress of the Russian Far East will also strengthen the integration of traditionally hostile neighbors along the Sea of Japan, leading to economic interaction and contributing to stability in the region.

The outcome of Japan's refusal to actively participate in Western aid policy would be to earn the enmity of the Russians. Japan would lose its chance to penetrate a reinvigorated Russian market. Japan's non-cooperation would also alienate its Western allies.

Is Japan's economic aid indispensable for Russia's economic reform? Despite the importance of foreign aid, it would not directly determine the outcome of Russia's economic success; it merely serves as a facilitator. Without Japan's aid, however, Western aid would not be as substantial, and its effectiveness, even as a facilitator, would diminish. In this case, Russia would be forced to adjust its economic reform strategy in such a way as to reduce its dependency on foreign economic aid. The economic reform process would become more tortuous, and its outcome more uncertain. However, while Japan's refusal to extend aid to Russia may not substantially alter the outcome of Russia's economic reform as a whole, it would inevitably affect the Russian Far East's ability to recover from the present crisis.

The failure of Russia's economic transition would run counter to Japan's interests, most importantly because it would contribute to Russia's social unrest, political instability, the possible resurgence of authoritarianism, or even disintegration. The domestic consequences of failed economic reform would inevitably spill over into foreign-security policy, posing a serious threat to global stability, and especially to the stability of the Asia-Pacific region.

In addition, the failure of economic reform would have immediate implications for the conversion of the Russian defense industry. It would lead Russian leaders to the conclusion that the only way for the ailing defense industry to survive is to sell arms abroad; this process has already begun under Yeltsin. However, arms sales would not solve the fundamental problems that face the defense industry. As a result, managers, engineers, and workers employed in the defense industry would become disgruntled, and thus potential supporters of an authoritarian regime. Some of them would be lured by foreign governments opposed to Western interests.[10]

---

10. This process has already been taking place. See James Clay Moltz, "The Russian Economic Crisis: Implications for Asian-Pacific Policy and Security," Institute on Global Conflict and Cooperation, San Diego., CA, May 14–15, 1993, pp. 3–4.

GEOPOLITICAL INTERESTS

Russia's and Japan's interests are diametrically opposed on the territorial question. As an emerging nation, territorial integrity and the protection of Russians living beyond its borders constitute a high priority for Russia's foreign policy. Japan has also identified the territorial settlement as the most important goal for its policy toward Russia. The Northern Territories dispute is basically a zero-sum game, and cannot be resolved unless other factors become more dominant in the relationship.

This does not necessarily mean that a compromise solution would be impossible. In fact, it is widely believed both in Russia and Japan that the only solution acceptable for both would be the so-called "two plus alpha" formula, in which Russia would return to Japan the two smaller islands after the conclusion of a peace treaty, as was agreed in 1956. In addition, Russia and Japan would agree on the demilitarization of the entire four islands, joint economic development, and travel on the islands without visas. Russia and Japan would continue to negotiate on the status of the other islands.[11]

The territorial question is also a part of the broader geopolitical differences between the two countries. While Japan no longer identifies Russia as its number one threat, it does continue to view the Russian military presence as a threat to Japan. The Russian military also continues to approach the security problem in Northeast Asia through the perspective of superpower conflict between Russia and the combined forces of the United States and Japan.

Nevertheless, geopolitical interests between Russia and Japan are conflictual only when they are viewed from the old stereotypical security thinking. When one breaks out of this mould, however, geopolitical interests between Russia and Japan in Northeast Asia have the potential for convergence rather than divergence. First, it is clear to both sides that neither harbors secret intentions to attack the other by force, and that both have common interests in maintaining stability in the region. Second, during the Cold War, direct security dialogue between the Soviet Union and Japan was impossible, since their conflict was an integral part of the larger strategic relations between the Soviet Union and the United States. The time is ripe for the United States, Japan, and Russia together to begin

---

11. For the "two plus alpha" formula, see Tsuyoshi Hasegawa, "Soviet-Japanese Relations in the 1990s," in Mike Mochizuki et al, eds., *Japan and the United States: Troubled Partners in a Changing World* (Washington, D.C.: Brassey's, 1991), pp. 75–78.

discussions as to what security system they should strive to create in Northeast Asia.

DEMOCRACY OR AUTHORITARIANISM

It is possible to agree that the question of whether Russia should be under democracy or authoritarianism does not necessarily have any direct bearing on Japan's national interests. Some even argue that an authoritarian regime willing to make territorial concessions to Japan might be preferable to a democratic regime that refuses to give the islands back. This is a short-sighted argument; democracy, even with its attendant contentiousness that may temporarily contribute to political instability, is by far the best system to ultimately contribute to economic reform and to constructive foreign policy. Economic reform and foreign policy not backed by national consensus will remain fragile at best.

There is no question that an authoritarian regime in Russia that takes a clearly anti-Western attitude would be a threat to the Western world. It is also possible to see the emergence of an authoritarian regime that favors market-oriented economic reform and pursues an independent foreign policy that does not necessarily threaten the vital interests of the Western world, although it may domestically suppress democracy. Still, compared to a democratic regime, an authoritarian regime is more likely to be wedded to nationalist sentiments, and would be unencumbered by any institutional restrictions; it would be more likely to pursue a foreign and security policy that would increase the possibility of friction with the Western world, especially if the military increases its voice.

It is not clear whether an authoritarian regime or a democratic regime is more likely to make territorial concessions to Japan, but it would be a mistake for Japan to place the return of the territories above the objective of supporting Russia's reforms for democracy and a market economy. It follows that Japan's national interests will be best served by pursuing a policy that fosters the democratic elements in Russia; Japan's active participation in Western aid to Russia will strengthen democratic forces.

UNITED RUSSIA OR DIVIDED RUSSIA

Some in Japan might argue that a weak, divided Russia will be more advantageous to Japan. All its energies would be devoted to the handling of internal problems and the fragmented and weakened military would not pose a serious threat to the security of Japan. The desperate need of such a divided Russia for international recognition or for economic assistance might induce Russia to grant concessions to Japan's demands on the territorial settlement. However, a disintegrating and chaotic Russia would be rife with uncertainties, danger of violence, civil war, masses of refugees, and authoritarian resurgence.

Japan's interests would not be served by a divided Russia, even if Japan might regain the territories; Japan's global interest depends on stability. To bargain for the repossession of the Northern Territories at the expense of international stability will lead to isolation from its major allies. Moreover, to have a politically unstable Russian Far East, detached from Moscow, will create a destabilizing security environment in Northeast Asia, particularly since an economically bankrupt Russian Far East could only maintain its regional coherence with the help of the military. Such a Far Eastern unit would more likely look to China for support than to Japan, and would also be more likely to resist any territorial concessions that Moscow might accept. Thus, Russia's and Japan's interests converge again in their common desire to prevent the disintegration of Russia.

THE NORTHERN TERRITORIES ISLANDERS

The Northern Territories debate has neglected the plight of those who live on the islands. The islanders have expressed their irritation at the political leaders of both countries who, in their perception, exploit the dispute for political purposes, attempting to determine their fate without consulting them. Their standard of living has declined precipitously, and the islanders have resorted to a method of harvesting fish that can be characterized only as criminal destruction of sea fauna and flora. At the same time, the ecological degradation of the islands is proceeding at a frightening pace.

Both the Russian government in Moscow and the Sakhalin regional government have largely ignored the catastrophic situation that faces the islanders. A concerted effort on the part of both Russian and Japanese governments to alleviate the economic and environmental plight of the islands will be in the national interests of both.

Long-Term Prospects

Japan's policy toward Russia has inherent contradictions between its short-term and long-term objectives. On the one hand, Japan continues to make the Northern Territories issue the centerpiece of its policy toward Russia. On the other hand, Japan has clearly elevated economic assistance to Russia to become another central focus of its Russia policy on the assumption that Japan's interests are closely tied to Russia's successful transition to a market economy and democracy.

This inevitably raises the question of the relationship between the two goals of Japan's policy toward Russia. To balance the two goals, the Japanese government has in the past adopted two operational principles: the principle of inseparability of politics and economics, which ties Japan's economic aid directly to the resolution of the Northern Territories question; and the principle of "balanced expansion," adopted in 1989, which means that both countries can expand the realm of cooperation even before the settlement of the territorial dispute. Clearly, these two operational principles are mutually exclusive, and Japanese policy has the tendency to swing like a pendulum between these contradictory aims.

Despite the Japanese government's explicit endorsement of Russia's reform process, there is a widespread perception in Japan that its aid to Russia is dictated not by Japan's interest in Russia's reform process, but rather by pressure from the G-7 nations, particularly the United States. If we take a long-term perspective, however, it becomes clear that from the political, security, and economic perspectives Japan's active participation in assistance to Russia's transition to democracy and a market economy will best serve Japan's interests, although this may not immediately lead to the resolution of the territorial dispute.

Still, it is unlikely that either Russia or Japan will break the stalemate in the context of bilateral relations. However, a drastic change in the power configuration in Northeast Asia might eventually jolt Russo-Japanese relations out of stalemate. Three factors are likely to affect the future of Russo-Japanese relations: the future of U.S.-Japanese relations, the future of China, and the nuclear issue.

THE FUTURE OF U.S.-JAPANESE RELATIONS

The United States and Russia are no longer enemies. Although their interests may not coincide, they are not directly in collision, either. This has created a new situation where Russia can now play a "balance of power" game. In addition, the economic realm, rather than the military-strategic factor, has become the primary area of competition among nations. Thus, it is inevitable that the economic conflict between the United States and Japan has become a central focus for both countries. There is a psychological shift in the American public: America's major enemy is now seen to be Japan, not Russia. Although the United States has not moved decisively to form a coalition with Russia against Japan, the trend in this direction is clearly discernible.

The deepening economic friction between the United States and Japan is bound to change the nature of their military alliance. There will be an increasing voice in the United States that demands the scaling down, if not the complete withdrawal, of the U.S. commitment in Asia. In any case, the continued U.S. military presence in Asia, which is perceived as serving to protect Japan's economic interests, is no longer tenable. Thus, both in economic and security areas U.S.-Japanese relations could be seriously damaged. If this happens, Russia would reap the greatest benefit.

Given the degree of interdependence of the economic relations between the United States and Japan, however, it is unlikely that both nations will allow their relations to deteriorate to the point of breaking the alliance. The United States will welcome Japanese moves to assert its global leadership, including opening its market to reduce trade deficits and shouldering responsibility for international peacekeeping. In this context, the United States would be open to more active participation by Japan in Western aid to Russia and the resolution of the territorial dispute through mutual compromise. It is important, however, for the U.S. government to make sure that the United States is not a balanced, neutral arbiter, but rather a partial partner committed to support Japan's policy, and to convey to the Russians that they cannot expect to take advantage of the differences between the United States and Japan. Nor should the United States suggest, openly or behind the scenes, specific ways to resolve the territorial dispute; outside pressure will more likely move Japan toward intransigence and the "go-it-alone" strategy.

THE CHINA FACTOR AND THE NEW POWER BALANCE

The second important factor to consider is China. The Chinese approach to Russo-Japanese relations has been dictated by its geopolitical interests and the balance of power approach. China would prefer continued stalemate between Russia and Japan. The tensions between China and Japan would undoubtedly be exacerbated if Russia and Japan achieved rapprochement. Japan's military capability, which has been aimed at the Soviet Union in the past, would create anxiety for China. The continuing stalemate also means that China will not have to compete with Russia for Japan's economic aid.[12] Meanwhile, China would take advantage of

---

12. See Tsuyoshi Hasegawa, "Conclusion: Russo-Japanese Relations in the New Environment — Implications of Continuing Stalemate," in Tsuyoshi Hasegawa, Jonathan Haslam, and Andrew Kuchins, eds. *Russia and Japan: An Unresolved Dilemma between Distant Neighbors* (Berkeley: University of California, International and Area Studies Publications,

Russia's plight to modernize its military capability by purchasing Russia's military hardware. Clearly, Russia and Japan would stand to lose in this arrangement. By continuing the stalemate, Russia and Japan might be contributing to the creation of a regional power that might threaten the security balance of the region. The emergence of an economically and militarily powerful China as a major Asian power will pose a serious dilemma for Russia and Japan. This may place the territorial dispute in a fundamentally different context.

OMNIDIRECTIONAL STRATEGY
Instead of playing a balance of power game, Russia could choose an omnidirectional strategy, aimed at forging good relations with all major powers. Russia may seek good relations both with China and Japan, while pursuing membership in the "G-8." An obstacle to this policy will be Japan, which will continue to insist on the resolution of the territorial dispute as the price for Russia's membership. Japan's objections to Russia's omnidirectional strategy, however, will have the consequence of pushing Russia into seeking a balance of power strategy. For Japan to avoid diplomatic isolation and not be forced into adopting such a strategy, the wisest course is to achieve rapprochement with Russia by reaching a modus vivendi on the territorial dispute.

JAPAN'S NUCLEARIZATION
Finally, the nuclear issue may drastically change the dynamics of Russo-Japanese relations. As long as Russia maintains a nuclear deterrent, Japan will have to find ways to protect itself from a Russian nuclear attack. If the U.S.-Japanese alliance is unravelled, it might trigger Japan's decision to go nuclear. Japan's nuclear decision may also be prompted by North Korea's possession of nuclear weapons. This will have an incalculable consequence on the dynamics of Northeast Asian security. It is imperative, therefore, that the United States, Japan, and Russia begin security dialogues to map out long-term cooperation so that they can reduce the possibility of nuclear proliferation in Northeast Asia.

1993), p. 443.

Conclusion

Neither Japan nor Russia have the incentives to break the stalemate over the territorial dispute; both countries would be hard put to sell a solution to their publics. And continued stalemate jeopardizes the possibility of forging a new stable international order.

Chapter 18

Russia and the United States

Andrei Kortunov

The accession of Bill Clinton's new Democratic administration in the United States was interpreted by most outside observers, Russians included, as an important event — perhaps even a turning point in international politics. Clinton's team was the first U.S. administration to gain power after the Soviet collapse. For forty years, the Cold War had exerted a deeply deforming influence on America's foreign and military policies, as well as on its domestic politics, economy, and even the American psyche. It would not be an exaggeration to state that since the end of the 1940s, the United States had been in the process of creating a national security state in which the central priority was confrontation with the outside enemy: the Soviet Union and global communism. The end of the Cold War has stripped many political and economic institutions of their justification.

A number of challenges demanded urgent attention. First, in foreign policy and in the sphere of national security, Clinton encountered threats that were more economic, technological, and social than military. With the Soviet Union gone, the problems of American economic competitiveness, leadership in key technologies, free trade and protectionism, illegal immigration to the United States and international drug traffic have become much more visible.

Second, the Clinton administration needed to reevaluate the whole system of American defense alliances. With the disappearance of a common enemy, America's allies all over the world started to emancipate themselves from old complexities that assumed obedience or even certain forms of political services or payments to the United States in exchange for protection from the communist threat. Likewise, in the absence of a mortal enemy looming on the horizon, the American public ceased to consider the loyalty of U.S. allies so necessary that it could overlook the financial burdens of defending others' interests.

Andrei Kortunov heads the Department of Foreign Policy at Moscow's Institute of USA and Canada Studies. His present research focuses on the emergence of security systems and the development of foreign policies in the states of the former Soviet Union.

Third, the Democrats faced the uneasy task of forging new relations with the countries of the ex-Soviet bloc, especially Russia.

These foreign policy tasks were even more complicated because they overlapped with the necessity to overcome the deforming legacy of the Cold War in the United States' domestic affairs: extreme militarization of the economy and public life, an inflated bureaucratic apparatus, infringement on America's democratic traditions during decades of confrontation, and struggle against the real or mythical intrigues of an external enemy.

In addition, Clinton represents a generational change. Particularly during the final stage of his campaign, Clinton gathered relatively young Democrats from the "lost generation" of the 1970s who entered politics on the wave of the post-Watergate success of their party. They are united by the experiences of their youth — participation in the protests against the war in Vietnam, liberal universities, and for some even the search for "alternative lifestyles" in the late 1960s and early 1970s. They entered politics with a complex mix of personal ambition, enthusiasm, a loss of belief in the American Dream, and disillusionment in liberal ideas. Psychologically, they seemed to be better prepared to seek new paradigms in foreign and defense policies than their Republican predecessors.

The Clinton administration has shown thus far that great expectations about future Russian-American relations were at least premature. True, as one could have predicted, Clinton demonstrated readiness to make very significant cuts in the military budget and to reduce the U.S. military presence in Europe and the Far East. Such moves reflected both the changed perceptions of the American public and the mood in the U.S. Congress. In arms control, the administration has emphasized "non-traditional" aspects (such as preventing the proliferation of nuclear weapons and other means of mass destruction, limiting international arms trade, broadening confidence-building measures, etc.). Yet for a number of reasons, Bill Clinton's approach did not lead to any boom in U.S.-Russian military cooperation.

First, further progress in arms control was blocked. The Republicans had left a pile of already signed treaties and agreements waiting for ratification or implementation (START I and START II, CFE, etc.) But numerous political, technical and financial constraints may limit Russia's ability to comply with these agreements, at least within the initially agreed time. Second, severe cuts in the U.S. defense budget limited opportunities for joint military-related ventures and projects, such as Russian-American space programs. Third, the end of the Cold War did not stop the competition between Moscow and Washington in the global arms market;

on the contrary, with domestic markets shrinking, the competition became more fierce and neither side was ready to make major concessions.

Nor were any breakthroughs reached in the field of economic relations. In trying to promote economic ties with the United States, the Russian government seemed to forget that American and Western governments only make grants in extraordinary cases, and these must be returned with interest. The only way to build a natural relationship is to create a favorable investment climate for American private businesses in Russia.

The United States' attitudes toward Russian politics have also disappointed many. At least until the December 1993 elections in Russia, the Clinton administration acted on the assumption that there was no viable alternative to President Boris Yeltsin — that his defeat would mean Russia's return to communism, totalitarianism and maybe even a turn toward fascism. To the Russian political opposition, the unconditional support of Boris Yeltsin during the October 1993 events in Moscow signified the U.S. blessing of the new Russian authoritarianism and raised suspicions of American hypocrisy. Likewise, the unwillingness of the White House to see many evident shortcomings of Yegor Gaidar's economic policies led to frustration and disappointment within the benign opposition looking for a more balanced and comprehensive economic reform program.

In short, the new administration has shown clear limits in its ability and desire to expand Russian-American cooperation. At the same time, it demonstrated that there are ample grounds for a quarrel: Russia's desire to revise the articles of the Paris Treaty on conventional arms in Europe, the reluctance of the Clinton administration to increase significantly its economic aid to Moscow, differences over the Bosnian problem, and possible conflicts of interest on the world arms markets, to name a few.

Amid the numerous problems and disagreements are two areas of particular importance in defining the future of Russian-American relations: 1) the need to avoid strategic disengagement between the two countries; and 2) Russia's posture in the so-called "near abroad."

Avoiding a Strategic Disengagement

Russia inherited the vast infrastructure of U.S.-Soviet nuclear arms control negotiations, along with its respective obligations, rights, and responsibilities. It also obtained traditional Soviet nuclear doctrines, basic concepts of nuclear stability, strategic parity, unacceptable damage, etc. However, what Russia has not inherited is no less important. First, it rejected the political foundation of U.S.-Soviet nuclear interaction that guided nuclear arms control negotiations between the two superpowers. Indeed, President Yeltsin has stated on several occasions that Russia considers the United States to be its ally rather than a competitor or adversary.

Second, Russia did not preserve the Soviet-style decision-making process on nuclear issues characterized by centralism and secrecy. The major decisions in the USSR, even during Gorbachev's years, had usually been made at the very top, boldly and promptly, without extensive consultations with legislative power, without major media interference, and with no public discussion. The Russian leadership obviously lost this advantage through its exposure to democratic, but quite frequently cumbersome, procedures of budgeting and ratification.

Finally, the Soviet Union was an extremely stable environment for the production and deployment of nuclear weapons. In contrast, Russia, from the very beginning of its independent existence, faced numerous regional instabilities, ethnic conflicts and communication failures, not to mention rigid economic constraints and at least potential nuclear challenges from some other former Soviet republics.

Given these differences between the Soviet Union and Russia, the future of Russian-American nuclear arms control largely depends on the ability of both sides to find a proper balance between continuity and change. To what extent should the experience of more than twenty years of Soviet-American nuclear arms control be preserved, revised, or discarded? How can the old principles, mechanisms and institutions of arms control be adjusted to a radically different political environment?

IMPLEMENTATION OF START II

Highlighting the difficulty of making such a transition are the conservative critics of President Yeltsin, who argue that the implementation of START II would break the principle of parity established during the two decades' history of U.S.-Soviet strategic arms control negotiations. Worse, they argue, is the ban on the MIRVed ICBMs (Multiple Independently-targeted Re-entry Vehicles, Intercontinental Ballistic Missiles), which have always been the core of the Soviet nuclear arsenal. The problem cannot be discarded as artificial. The MIRVed ICBMs account for more than 60 percent of the former Soviet nuclear arsenal; to eliminate them completely means to reconsider the very foundations of the traditional nuclear posture, moving away from ICBMs to SLBMs (Submarine-Launched Ballistic Missiles) and strategic bombers.

But the interpretation of START II as Russian "unilateral disarmament" or "capitulation" does not hold water; the reductions are balanced, not unilateral. While Russia will have to cut more ICBMs and SLBMs than the United States, the United States will reduce its number of aircraft much more drastically than will Russia. The United States will also reduce its number of warheads more than Russia will. For the first time, the United States has agreed to radical cuts of its sea-based strategic arms component. Finally, the United States has agreed to cut some of its most modern and most destabilizing systems — above all, the MIRVed MX (Peacekeeper) ICBMs, considered by the Russian military as a key first-strike weapon.

These U.S. concessions do not mean that START II will have absolutely symmetrical effects on the Russian and American strategic forces. The United States will be able to preserve most of its current composition of the strategic triad and will be relatively less affected by the Treaty. Yet do Russians really need parity in order to preserve stability? Even in the worst-case scenario, if Russian-American relations were to dramatically deteriorate, Russia could still inflict "unacceptable damage" on the United States in its second strike. In fact, the second strike capabilities of Russia increase with START II.

A second concern of Russian conservatives is that Yeltsin has made a decisive step on the road toward "Americanization" of the Russian nuclear potential, turning it into a carbon copy of U.S. strategic forces. By reducing dramatically the ground leg of the strategic triad, Russia is doing what the Soviet Union resisted for four decades: it is following the U.S. lead in shifting to sea-based and air-based systems. Thus, the United States has imposed its own strategic structure on Russia and from now on will direct the evolution of the Russian strategy, putting the latter in an unequal and in some respects dependent position. First, the United States has a dense network of military bases scattered around the periphery of the former USSR; second, American submarines have much better access to the high seas than Russian ones; and finally, submarine-based missiles are seven to ten times more expensive than ground-based missiles (ICBMs). In addition, the United States is more advanced in anti-submarine warfare (making Russian submarines less survivable), and has superior strategic bombers. This criticism of the START process seems more to the point. Indeed, Russia was too receptive to American proposals, especially at the initial stages of negotiations.

A third concern is that the implementation of START II — requiring the elimination of thousands of missiles, hundreds of launchers and aircraft and dozens of submarines — will be an expensive undertaking. According to preliminary estimates, the cost for Russia alone will run as high as 40 billion rubles (in constant 1992 rubles) over the next ten years.

This can hardly be considered a convincing argument against the Treaty. As leading Russian arms control expert Alexei Arbatov put it, "The implementation of only START I, which has met no opposition in Russia, would cost us not much less — about 30 billion rubles. In addition to large savings on strategic modernization programs, Russia will receive substantial compensation for expenses related to START II implementation. Without cuts, the cost of maintenance for the already deployed forces only within ten years would amount to no less than 200 billion rubles."[1] Moreover, proponents of START II emphasize that, thanks to the Treaty, Russia might expect substantial savings after the year 2000.

Still, Russia's implementation of START is linked to a future agreement on assistance programs promoting the implementation. If such an agreement is reached the financial burden on Russia will be considerably eased. The critics of START II will undoubtedly point out that the record of American assistance programs does not look very promising. Currently, the Department of Defense budget includes an $800 million allocation (the Nunn-Lugar account) for the dismantling of weapons of mass destruction on the territory of the former USSR. But the money remains largely unspent due to differing views on mechanisms and procedures.

NUCLEAR NON-PROLIFERATION
Beyond the START I and START II Treaties, the future of Russian-American strategic relations is difficult to predict; there are too many variables. Domestic Russian politics could dramatically affect these relations, and the overall global strategic situation could fluctuate considerably. Under different conditions the same military systems might appear stabilizing or destabilizing, the same programs can look affordable or not affordable, the same strategies can turn out to be manifestations of prudence and realism or displays of irresponsibility and recklessness.

However, in the sphere of nuclear concerns, the United States and Russia will pay the most attention to the problem of non-proliferation. Cooperation between Moscow and Washington on this problem has a long

---

1. Alexei G. Arbatov, "Dogovor dorozhe deneg" ("A treaty is worth more than money)," *Novoye Vremya*, No. 2–3 (1993), p. 24.

history. In a sense, it has been one of the major successes in superpower strategic relations. As early as the 1960s, at the height of the Cold War, the Soviet Union and the United States acknowledged that they had to limit the number of states with access to nuclear weapons, and that this goal was not only in the interests of international security at large, but also in the national interests of both superpowers. The modern non-proliferation regime is to a large extent the result of bilateral Soviet-American efforts. Their persistent pressure was a key factor in bringing 140 countries to join the Nuclear Non-Proliferation Treaty (NPT) by 1990. Every year, despite very uneven political relations, the United States and the USSR held consultations aimed at coordinating their policies in this field of international relations. In 1989 the Soviet Union and the United States launched a collaborative project on preventing nuclear terrorism.

But by the beginning of the 1990s it became evident that Soviet and American efforts were not adequate. In fact, during the Cold War there was a slow but steady inflow of new members to the "nuclear club" (usually through the back door). Nowadays, it is even difficult to give an exact answer to the question, "How many nuclear states are there?"

It is not even clear if the NPT will be preserved after 1995 or if it will be "revised" in a way that will flash a green light on the road to rapid and irreversible nuclear proliferation. The potential dangers to international security posed by proliferation — especially in unstable Third World countries — might well exceed those of the bilateral Soviet-American nuclear confrontation during the Cold War.

Thus, incentives for both the United States and Russia to concentrate primarily on their bilateral nuclear equation will be reduced. The age of nuclear rivalry between the superpowers has come to its end, but the age of nuclear proliferation is just beginning.

Two factors seem especially important for the future of Russian-American strategic cooperation in the field of non-proliferation. First, much will depend on whether nuclear weapons continue to play a major political role after the Cold War — whether a nation's nuclear weapons will confer upon it a special status in the system of international relations. The collapse of rigid bipolar structures could increase the relative military and political weight of a nation's nuclear arsenals and, accordingly, the overall international importance of the nuclear factor. In addition, the current shift in the economic power balance in favor of non-nuclear states (Germany, Japan, newly industrialized nations in Asia, etc.) should stimulate members of the nuclear club to rely on their unique asset to preserve their former political positions.

If the end of the Cold War means greater nuclear multipolarity, accelerated modernization of nuclear arsenals will probably become essential both for the United States and Russia. The members of the nuclear club will see the new generation of missiles and strategic defense as insurance against the devaluation of their strategic potentials.

A second important question is whether nuclear weapons can be used in the context of possible "North-South" conflicts. Is it feasible to apply nuclear weapons to deter regional conflicts, that is, to threaten new Saddam Husseins in Asia, Africa and Latin America? If Northern countries do not distance themselves from conflicts in the chronically unstable South, nuclear weapons will inevitably become an important factor in North-South relations. For Russia this prospect might be especially significant, since it borders some of the most explosive regions of the Third World.

To find a basis for policy the United States and Russia must admit that it is no longer possible to preserve the exclusive character of the "nuclear club." In order to prevent the "nuclear club" from growing it is necessary to disband it or at least to move in this direction. (The nuclear test ban as well as a formal ban on production of enriched uranium and plutonium might be important first steps.)

Of course, one can claim that to stop or to slow down the nuclear programs of the threshold states it is necessary first of all to upgrade the existing international non-proliferation regime by creating additional disincentives for these states. But, paradoxically, to stop the majority of threshold states from working to attain nuclear status, they should be treated as de facto nuclear powers. For example, threshold countries might pledge to abstain from nuclear testing, but only under the Comprehensive Test Ban Treaty; they might stop producing fissile materials for military purposes, but only under a formal moratorium on such production, as adopted by the United States and Russia.

But it seems that the only radical alternative to the nuclear renaissance after the Cold War is to gradually internationalize nuclear weapons (an updated edition of the old "Baruch plan"). The feasibility of this option depends to a large extent on the United States, the only remaining military superpower.[2] The collapse of the Soviet superpower and postwar

---

2. The internationalization of nuclear weapons could not develop under the aegis of the United Nations; the members of the nuclear club are too sensitive to any steps that can be interpreted as interference in their defense planning. Deepening of bilateral and multilateral interaction of nuclear states appears to be more promising.

international security system will lead to increasing anarchy in world politics. There is no central authority in modern global politics other than a set of rudimentary international institutions with no practical power to enforce law and order.

At the same time, military power — nuclear power, in particular — remains an important and legitimate factor in world politics, and will continue to play a significant role in different regions of the globe. Neither the arms race nor conflicts among nations have ended with the Cold War. Facing a highly unstable and sometimes dangerous world, the United States must define its new security policy.

The United States could adopt a "nationalistic" approach that aims to ensure immediate American security interests, even at the expense of international stability. This does not necessarily imply a return to isolationism; the United States might still have an active foreign policy, but would follow principles of unilateralism, might withdraw militarily from Western Europe, might aim to preserve its exclusive spheres of influence in the Third World, etc. It might also try to use the multipolar balance in Eurasia in order to play one power center against another, in the classical Nixon-Kissinger mode.

The main outcome of this option would be further disintegration of the global security system, extreme fragility of the multilateral strategic balance, and the decline of the American international position. Some of the traditional regional contradictions would reemerge from the ruins of the bipolar Cold War system. Arms control would have somewhat limited importance for all the participants in the international system.

How would these policies affect Russian-American relations? The loss of its superpower status and American egotism in Geneva might combine to make Russia much less interested in a bilateral arms control process with the United States. Instead, it could choose "nuclear isolationism," complete independence in the strategic sphere ("asymmetrical response") and rejection of American strategic culture (including unacceptable damage criteria, the concept of strategic stability, etc.). This could leave the United States as the only nuclear superpower, with no partner to negotiate arms control agreements.

This option for the post–Cold War nuclear Russian posture seems feasible because profound political and strategic changes in recent years have gradually undermined the notion of parity as the basis for strategic stability. Both Russian and U.S. strategic arsenals are militarily redundant. Russia could take substantial unilateral actions to lower the level of its forces and change its defense structure.

In contrast, the United States could adopt a "globalistic" approach, in which it does not separate its own security interests from global security interests. Rather than working toward another version of the classical multipolar system in Eurasia, the principal American goal will be a kind of international security structure of "Greater Europe" that will be able to repulse numerous destabilizing impulses from the chronically unstable South.

TOWARD A NEW WORLD SECURITY ORDER

Of course, American security policy will not be a clear-cut choice between the first and second options. Rather, it will fluctuate between them, depending on the political situation in the country and international developments. But if it is closer to the second option, which seems both more feasible and preferable, post–Cold War nuclear arms control might become a key factor in the creation of the new world security order. Four policy changes are key.

First, nuclear arms control cannot remain a bilateral Russian-American venture. In a few years, the effectiveness of arms control will directly depend on the ability of the United States and the Russian Federation to engage other nuclear powers in this process. The United States should play a more important role than the Russian Federation, by bringing its allies to the negotiation table. The political and technical difficulties of this approach cannot be underestimated. Indeed, multilateral nuclear arms control talks certainly cannot be conducted according to the old model: first, the traditional principles of parity, equal capabilities, and mutual concessions must give way to new, incomparably more complex principles and criteria; moreover, geopolitical, geostrategic, and other factors must be taken into account even more than in the talks hitherto conducted.

It would be tempting to suggest that in the future, strategic arms control talks between nuclear powers (at least, nuclear powers of the northern tier) will resemble current NATO discussions on sharing the defense burden. Yet such a model seems too optimistic for the foreseeable future. Nuclear arms will remain an important symbol of political status for relatively weaker countries (France, Russia, Great Britain). Besides, the security concerns of nuclear powers will be different even if they find complete accommodation among themselves. For example, Russia might find an "extended deterrence" strategy indispensable to counter a potentially overwhelming conventional threat from the South or East.

It would probably be easier to achieve some progress in multilateral nuclear arms control if its goals can be specified as strictly arms control, rather than disarmament goals.[3] Multilateral arms control should not be directed primarily at reductions or even rigid limitations of the existing forces, but rather at coordination of their modernization as well as confidence-building measures. Smaller nuclear powers can be engaged into the bilateral Russian-American strategic interaction gradually and flexibly. As a first step one can imagine, for example, multilateral risk reduction centers instead of existing bilateral and multilateral launch notification agreements. Each nuclear power will be able to choose its own level of participation in the arms control process based on its national analysis of related costs and benefits.

Second, it is clear that the time for comprehensive arms control deals is over. Many experts favor the "bite after bite" model, in which negotiators try to reach a number of agreements in a specific order; these agreements both resolve specific problems, and advance the whole front of the talks. Such an approach will not necessarily facilitate negotiations; in the 1970s and 1980s the United States and the USSR persistently tried to reach comprehensive agreements not just because of their political significance, but also because the larger the package of agreements, the easier it was to find a compromise by trading concessions in one sphere for concessions in another. Given the existing asymmetries in the structure of the Russian and American forces, to say nothing of French and British forces, it seems very difficult to find an acceptable solution that would cover only one area. The answer might be to keep packages but make them just as large as is needed to exchange concessions and reach a compromise.

Another danger of the "bite after bite" approach is that it can rationalize, not retard, the arms race by closing off militarily ineffective channels. Negotiators will be inclined to solve easy questions without trying to address the principal problems. There will be many loopholes devaluating agreements that have already been achieved. Even in the START I and START II agreements one can see such loopholes, though these were initially designed as comprehensive treaties.

Third, the sides should try to adjust to a new balance between negotiated agreements and unilateral actions. If the current political

---

3. The aims of modest, limited arms control cannot be just stability and a controlled nuclear arms race. Leaders of nuclear powers cannot afford such a pragmatic approach: they negotiate arms control not just among themselves but also with their powerful domestic anti-nuclear constituencies. There are no reasons to believe that these constituencies will soon disappear in the United States, Europe, or the Russian Federation.

developments in Russian-American relations continue, one can expect that unilateral restraints in strategic forces will outpace and even revise an accelerated arms control process. In order to avoid Russian-American strategic decoupling, it becomes extremely important to make these unilateral steps parallel and, when possible, coordinated.

This does not imply that negotiated agreements are of no significance. When meaningful, they turn into a political and psychological impediment, in particular for the side that leads in the arms race, hindering it from building up its advantages in the most favorable areas. They also promote a stronger opposition to the arms race and have a definite positive effect on the general international situation. Indeed, the prospect of attaining further accords checks the arms race in certain areas, influences developments in defense-related efforts, and intensifies political strife around them. Dialogue on arms limitations adds to each country's knowledge of the other's capabilities and intentions, and creates greater confidence. The arms control process simply cannot catch up with political changes, and should not be used as a building block on the way to unilateral steps.

Coordinated unilateral actions will save both sides the difficulties of the ratification process. In the record of Soviet-American relations, some unilateral steps that had no legal power were still politically binding and played an important role in curbing the arms race (SALT-II is just one example).

Such "soft" arms control might be more attractive to the smaller nuclear powers. None of them seem ready to participate in any classic arms control negotiations, even with observer status. Non-legal coordinated actions will in no way compromise their nuclear independence, but would create additional reliability and predictability in the overall nuclear balance.

Fourth, the format of negotiations should be changed to provide expert advice at the outset, and a chance to resolve problems at every step. Four stages may be necessary.

At the first stage, a permanent forum of military, political and technical experts from all the participating sides would exchange information on strategic systems and technologies in the process of development. They would discuss the possible impact of specific programs on strategic stability and the arms control process. The function of this forum is to coordinate the future strategic posture of both sides. Participants would discuss programs that exist only in blueprint, and would find it easier to avoid current political considerations than the participants in the START process. The forum would present its recommendations on the most dangerous trends in nuclear technologies and possible ways to block these trends to the governments of the nuclear powers.

In the second stage, the governments would either make unilateral decisions and inform the partners about them, or start consultations in order to reach an accord on issues at the highest level or at the level of foreign ministers.

In the third stage, negotiators would translate the accord into the language of legally formulated agreements in a very short period. Afterwards, the talks would close (unless negotiators received directives on any new problems). If the problem discussed is not very important the agreement could be signed by high officials and could then take the form of executive agreement not subject to ratification.

If the accord touched upon really vital issues, a fourth stage would be needed: a second summit would be held and the document would be signed by the political leaders and then go to the national legislatures for ratification.

Russia, the United States and the Near Abroad

It is clear that Moscow's policy toward the near abroad is becoming tougher. The protection of the rights of Russian minorities by diplomatic and other means is becoming an official strategy. Russian armed forces are being drawn into military operations in other republics, while officials from the Yeltsin administration call for a "Monrovsky Doctrine."

The impression is that politicians in the Kremlin and the Foreign Ministry count on not only understanding but active support from the White House. They put forward these reasons: Russia is guided by not only its own reasons but the interests of the whole civilized world in maintaining peace and stability in Eurasia; and Russia has turned into an important Western outpost to hold back the waves of religious fundamentalism, nationalism and political extremism generated in the Caucasus, Central Asia and other regions of the former Soviet Union. In other words, Russia is a "front-line state," the gatekeeper for the West, like Germany was throughout the Cold War. This is why, Russian officials say, the West should approve Moscow's actions and assist them with everything possible, including financial and military aid.

Of course, leaders in Kiev, Kishinev and Almaty see Russia's policy in a different light. Calls for a "Monrovsky Doctrine" are viewed as a clear manifestation of imperial thinking. In most cases these leaders refuse even to acknowledge the existence of a problem with the Russian minority, and the prospects of Russia again becoming Eurasia's policeman are perceived as a way to restore the Soviet Union. In the former Soviet republics, critics of the United States are becoming more vocal in accusing Washington of being exclusively pro-Moscow and applying double standards that could threaten the interests and even the survival of the newly independent states.

In the United States, the administration is often criticized for concentrating its efforts on helping Russia, which is detrimental to U.S. policy toward other countries in the region, especially such major and potentially significant players as Ukraine and Kazakhstan. The pro-Moscow position of official Washington is underscored by its support for Russia's demands for nuclear disarmament of Ukraine, Kazakhstan, and Belarus, and for Russia's permanent seat on the UN Security council; it has also recognized Russia as the "sole and lawful inheritor" of the Soviet Union.

Concerns that the United States is too pro-Russia reflect a deep mistrust of Moscow. These concerns are supported by two concepts. First, many believe that a power balance is the only stable system of international relations. If Russia is the most powerful country in the region, then the United States should promote the formation of a coalition of all other nations to offset Russia's might and provide guarantees against the resurrection of Russian imperialism. This concept was best elaborated by former Secretary of State Henry Kissinger in a number of his speeches and articles.

Second, some argue that the U.S. influence on Russia's development will always be marginal because Russia continues to be the leading power in the region. Russia is simply too big to be influenced from the outside; it will develop according to its internal dynamics. Efforts to influence smaller nations like Belarus, the Baltic states and even Ukraine may be more productive; here even relatively small investments of American money and effort promise significant political return, and will provide indirect influence over Russia. This concept is elaborated by the former national security adviser Zbigniew Brzezinski.

The Clinton administration so far does not listen to advice from Kissinger and Brzezinski. Off the record, State Department officials often talk in favor of a Russian sphere of influence in Eurasia. But the toughening Russian policy toward the former republics will force the White House to distance itself from the Kremlin's political and military claims at least at the level of rhetoric. It is impossible to exclude more serious conflicts between Moscow and Washington if Russian neo-imperialist inclinations in the near abroad become too provocative.

OPTIONS FOR U.S. POLICY

Is it at all possible to prevent a Russian-American clash over the near abroad? One solution might be the "finlandization" of the former Soviet republics: the pledge of the West not to engage these countries in implicitly anti-Russian alliances in exchange for a Russian commitment to abstain from interference in the domestic affairs of its neighbors.

Such a solution would considerably lessen the chances for a conflict of interests between Russia and the United States over Eurasian affairs and would stabilize the situation in the region. Such an understanding — even a tacit one — would pre-empt possible manifestations of radical imperialism from the Russian side, rendering irrelevant the Russian "Monrovsky Doctrine" in the near abroad. One additional Russian responsibility based on adequate Western assistance could be the role of an economic balancing state in Eurasia (primarily to prevent trade and financial imbalances within the CIS). Finally, Russia could take care of the regional infrastructure: the financing and maintaining of transportation and energy systems, development of information channels and communications, etc.

However, even a tacit Russian-American understanding on "finlandization" of the near abroad appears very unlikely. First, neither conservative Republicans nor liberal Democrats in Washington would support it; the notion of "finlandization" has acquired a derogatory meaning within the American political elite.[4] Second, such a solution would mean a new division of Europe, this time along the Western border of the former USSR. It would block attempts to promote the common European political and defense space, setting different rules for the Central European countries and those of Eastern Europe.[5] Furthermore, the near abroad

---

4. A most explicit rejection of the American endorsement of any Russian influence in the near abroad can be found, for example, in publications of the conservative Washington-based Heritage Foundation.

5. It should be noted that new security arrangements on the European part of the former Soviet Union will make sense only if they form an open, not closed, system. It means that the Baltic states, in order to balance the Russian military might, have no choice but to try to work on some kind of Nordic subregional security system with the Scandinavian countries; Ukraine will do its best to have a special partnership with Poland or Germany, etc. Russia, in its turn, is likely to try to reach over its immediate neighbors to get special deals with Central and West European countries as well as with European transnational institutions. On the other hand, Central European nations that have broken almost all

states, feeling betrayed by the West and considering Russia to be the prime threat to their security, might try to circumvent "finlandization" by forging an anti-Russian alliance of their own, without Western participation. Finally, the current political instability in Russia itself and its mixed foreign policy prospects endanger the validity of any long-term strategic compromises with Moscow; such compromises could be unilaterally rejected or revised by a new Russian leadership.

The other option the United States has in the Russian near abroad is to follow an activist policy, acting as an "honest broker" between the former Soviet republics, depriving Moscow of any chance to display its imperial instincts. This activist position, including the use of economic and political sticks and carrots, mediation and peacekeeping, undoubtedly would be cheered in the capitals of the smaller successor states to the USSR. But the option of an active American involvement in Eurasia to keep Russia in check seems even less probable than the "finlandization" option.

But the fundamental impediment to an effective U.S. foreign policy in the near abroad is the United States' new-found security: to what extent can a democratic state pursue an active and consistent foreign policy without permanent outside pressure? Can it mobilize adequate social and political support for sizable programs abroad when mortal dangers to the national security seem remote, and the possible benefits to the national wellbeing also seem rather distant?

The Clinton administration has confirmed once again that democracies, if not hit by a crisis, tend to be egotistic, shortsighted and clumsy — no matter how wise, energetic and idealistic their leaders might be. Foreign policy is probably the first victim of newly acquired security. A democracy is usually not ready to allocate considerable resources to foreign aid, because it will always find many domestic problems demanding urgent decisions. A democracy is not inclined to involve itself in armed conflicts abroad, because voters do not want to watch on television how their compatriots die, even for a noble cause. A democracy is suspicious of international organizations, considering them a threat to national sovereignty and independence. Finally, a democracy is extremely reluctant

---

political and military ties with former Soviet republics but have been granted a place only in the "waiting room" of Western security structures will sooner or later engage themselves in security cooperation with some of their Eastern neighbors. (These countries have agreed to more or less symbolic participation in such bodies as the North Atlantic Cooperation Council, the North Atlantic Assembly, Partnership for Peace, etc.)

to make radical concessions and introduce major changes to its initial positions, since each concession and each change immediately becomes a matter for domestic politics and partisan clashes.

Only a very painful shock (such as Pearl Harbor) or a mortal threat to the mere existence of the democratic society (the Cold War) can push a democracy toward an active foreign policy. Moreover, an active and firm foreign policy almost inevitably cripples the democratic process, and deforms it with elements of authoritarianism.[6] While the American public can be shocked by the slaughter of civilians in Tajikistan, war crimes in Abkhazia and Nagorno Karabakh or political terrorism in Crimea, and experts and officials can speculate about various real or potential threats to American security coming from the vast Eurasian land mass, these challenges cannot mobilize power in the same way in America as the overwhelming and hypnotizing threat of Soviet communism.

If meaningful American leadership or even an active U.S. policy toward the Russian near abroad does not look very likely, the idea of a "collective Western leadership and responsibility" cherished by Clinton, is even less likely. Neither West Europe nor Japan is eager to share with the United States the burden of building the "new world order" — especially in dangerous and unpredictable places like the Russian near abroad. The former Soviet republics might need resolute and firm Western leadership more than ever before, but the West is less than ever prepared to provide this leadership.

The least politically and financially costly U.S. strategy is not to attempt to settle local conflicts, but rather to work toward their insulation — the prevention of escalation through limitations of arms transfers to sides in a given conflict, imposition of embargoes and the building of stable regional balances. Some level of violence in the Caucasus, Central Asia, and even Moldova (as well as in remote areas of sub-Saharan Africa, South Africa or Central America) might appear politically acceptable to the United States and the West in general, even if this violence lasts for decades; the real question will be whether such conflicts have a noticeable impact on the stability of the global international system, or affect vital interests of key players in world politics.

Thus, the territory of the former Soviet Union will not be the top priority for the United States. In the case of a more aggressive Russian policy toward its near abroad, one could expect plenty of critical rhetoric

---

6. Political biographies of Winston Churchill, Charles deGaulle, and Franklin D. Roosevelt provide vivid examples.

coming out of the White House, but not much in the way of action or alternative strategies. The only really sensitive issue is the Baltic states; here a Russian imperialist policy might confront a tough American response. Otherwise, one could expect that even a gradual reabsorption of Ukraine by Russia in some form would be met with indifference, if not understanding, by the United States, provided this reabsorption does not produce much violence or regional instability. Both sides will, nevertheless, exchange ritual accusations and reproaches: Washington accusing Moscow of aggression and imperialism, Moscow accusing Washington of hypocrisy and reluctance to participate in building stability in Eurasia. The subsequent deterioration of Russian-American relations will be practically inevitable but not fatal.

Chapter 19

The United States and Russia

Philip D. Zelikow

During the Cold War, Washington needed to pay close attention to Russia's military power and security policy. Now, after the Cold War, Russian security policy still commands the attention of U.S. officials. The breakup of the Soviet Union and the decline of its military establishment have created an entirely new situation. But a vast, abstract threat has been replaced by dangers which, though smaller in scale, are far more acute.

After Russian-U.S. rapprochement swelled into a genuine entente between Moscow and Washington during 1990 and 1991, the Bush administration and then the Clinton administration were hopeful that they might press further to turn the relationship into a true "strategic partnership" or quasi-alliance. These hopes are now fading. The task ahead is more limited. It will be hard enough just to preserve the entente which prevailed at the beginning of the 1990s amid the turmoil in the former Soviet Union and growing Russian restiveness with a geopolitical relationship Russia now thinks of as a one-way street.

During its first year the Clinton administration deliberately and consistently portrayed the United States' choices in Russia as a straightforward decision between "reform" and "reaction." The rhetoric was extraordinarily simple, in what was probably a conscious imitation of Dean Acheson's decision to be "clearer than truth" in the 1947 enunciation of the Truman Doctrine. The forces of reform were portrayed as democracy, synonymous with peace and national contentment; reaction was equated with authoritarianism, which equals imperialism, which equals the prospect of a new Cold War.

As with the Truman Doctrine, the simplified rhetoric has been used to persuade the U.S. Congress and public to support large aid programs. In a similar way, this simplistic rhetoric infected the public's image of the

---

Philip D. Zelikow is Assistant Professor of Public Policy at Harvard University. Formerly a career diplomat with the United States Department of State, he served as Director for European Security Affairs on the staff of the National Security Council from 1989 to 1991.

problems being faced in Russia and did not adequately prepare either Congress or the public for murkier realities; Russian policy reversals have led the public and Congress to question the basis for U.S. assistance to Russia. Many Russians, in turn, became convinced that U.S. proclamations of alignment with "democracy" were hypocritical, since Washington backed President Boris Yeltsin even after he adopted undemocratic measures to preserve his hold on power during fall 1993.

If Washington makes clear that its policies are guided by the consistent lodestar of furthering clearly articulated U.S. interests, whatever the Russian government may be, this position can be explained and defended to the Congress and the public. Meanwhile the United States remains free to support whichever Russian leaders seem likely to help achieve these security goals. Such a position may be more candid; it will certainly be more durable.

The United States' Interests in Russia

Before the Second World War Russia did not have an important role in the history or interests of the United States. Usually friendly, sometimes hostile, U.S. relations with Russia were above all distant.[1] The United States is not bound to Russia, Ukraine or other republics on the territory of the former Soviet Union by deep or intrinsic ties of history, culture, demography, or commerce. Its interest in Russia during and after World War II arose from Russia's involvement in or threat to areas where the United States did have such deep and intrinsic interests. In other words, the United States' national interests in the Soviet Union during the past half century are an outgrowth of concerns about Soviet security policy.

This condition has not changed. The real and latent military capabilities, threat of conflict, and possible imbalances of power emanating from the former Soviet Union remain the primary reasons for U.S. interest in the region. Statements from the Clinton administration to the contrary, there is nothing especially compelling about Russia's value to the United

---

1. See John Lewis Gaddis, *Russia, the Soviet Union, and the United States: An Interpretive History* (New York: Wiley, 1978); Thomas A. Bailey, *America Faces Russia: Russian-American Relations from Early Times to Our Day* (Ithaca: Cornell University Press, 1950); and George F. Kennan, *Soviet-American Relations, 1917–1920*, 2 vols. (Princeton: Princeton University Press, 1956–1958).

States either as a market for goods or as a source of commodities (except for oil).[2]

Even if U.S. economic policies were so successful that trade with Russia and other Eurasian republics grew 20 percent per year, it would still be a number of years before such interactions became important to the U.S. economy. In 1991 the United States exported more to Malaysia than to Russia and all of the other republics of the former Soviet Union put together.

So traditional security concerns about conflict and military power are still the principal motives for strong U.S. interest in the fate of Russia and the Eurasian republics. These have both a negative and a positive dimension. Russia should still command the United States' respect either as a potential foe or friend.

U.S.-Russian Entente: A Global Perspective

The United States' perspective on Russia is conditioned by its perspective on the world. In its international policies, the United States finds itself positioned atop a hierarchy of political, economic, and military power.[3] This has two important consequences. First, the United States is a status quo power. Any significant disruption of the current hierarchy is more likely than not to have a negative effect on the United States' position. Second, the United States can best exert a positive influence over the direction of world events if it is at the center of a coalition, or "concert," of other great powers. These powers are Great Britain, France, Germany, Japan, and — perhaps — Russia. This concert, when it acts together, readily dominates the leading international institutions of the post–Cold War era, from the G-7 and World Bank to NATO or the United Nations.

All of the great powers, except for the United States, present mixed or lopsided pictures of political, economic, and military capacity. None are close to supplanting the United States as a global leader, but they can

---

2. For example, see President William Clinton, address to the American Society of Newspaper Editors, in *Dispatch*, April 5, 1993, p. 192; and Strobe Talbott, statement before the Subcommittee on Foreign Operations of the House Appropriations Committee, April 19, 1993, in *Dispatch*, April 26, 1993, p. 284.

3. Philip Zelikow, "The New Concert of Europe," *Survival*, Vol. 34, No. 2 (Summer 1992), pp. 12–30.

provide crucial support or crucial resistance to any major U.S. policy initiative.

The position of Russia in relation to this group is the great question of the 1990s. (The position of China may be the great question of the next decade.) In theory Russia could, after its defeat in the Cold War, quickly take the seat being held for it at the table of the great powers as France did so soon after the defeat of Napoleon. But historic distrust of Russia, as well as Russia's own turmoil and ambitions, raise doubts about Russia's ability to become an integral member of a coalition made up of states committed to democratic values. Politically, the West is increasingly inclined to preach to the Russians. Economically, the Russians are concluding that their industries can thrive if they guard them from the world trading system rather than plunge into it. Both trends would push Russia and the West further apart in the 1990s.

The United States should no longer embark on a vain attempt to seek an alliance or partnership with Russia of the kind the United States has with other members of the great democratic coalition. Yet rivalry and confrontation are not the only alternatives; rather, U.S. leaders should strive to sustain an entente, a cordial understanding, which concedes that a general alignment of policies and interests is unlikely but stresses the value of cooperation on issues of importance to both countries.

In this phase of entente, agreements on some major areas of tension are in place and maintained, and both sides further recognize some common interests for positive cooperation. Yet the understanding between the two countries is limited only to certain issues and the improvement of relations, stopping short of an "alliance" or wholesale "conciliation" that methodically removes all principal causes of disagreement between the parties. While the Clinton administration has reaffirmed its wish to seek a security "partnership," it has not succeeded in describing the basis for significantly broader cooperation. Entente therefore remains, and should remain, the best description for U.S.-Russian relations in the current period.[4]

A slide into rivalry and confrontation with Russia would be dangerous. The coalition of free nations simply is not strong enough to be able to discard the good possibility of Russian cooperation. The West European states are struggling to recapture a sense of global political vision that atrophied during the Cold War. Their military establishments are in

---

4. For a sharp expression to the contrary, see Robert Blackwill, "Forget the Grand Bargain," *Washington Post*, October 12, 1993, p. A19.

decline; none could independently mount significant combined arms operations against even a moderately armed state. The European Union's machinery reflects and even amplifies these weaknesses. Nor can Japan erase any of these deficits.

The great challenges to the current world order are likely to arise within the Eurasian landmass or the rim of the Mediterranean. Russia is the only great power situated in Eurasia that *might* be counted on for cooperation with the United States. Russia has great potential to affect events for good or ill in the Balkans, Turkey, Iraq, Iran, South Asia, or China. Russia's nuclear weapons arsenal and arms-making potential are second only to those of the United States.

If some cooperation with Russia, an entente, is in the United States' interest, the task is to identify a short list of vital issues on which cooperation is required. Then Washington should reflect upon its objectives for this understanding and consider whether or how its policies make such an understanding appealing to Russia as well as being defensible to the U.S. public and its representatives.

Reducing and Securing Russia's Nuclear Weapons

No area of U.S.-Russian cooperation is more important than the fate of the enormous nuclear arsenal that belonged to the Soviet Union. The United States will strive, as in the past, to deter and defend against a nuclear attack emanating directly or indirectly from the former Soviet Union. Since the Russian government is far from threatening such an attack, the immediate goal is to make sure the Russian government can exert control over the Soviet nuclear legacy. That means preventing the dispersal of nuclear weapons or the means of making nuclear weapons outside of firm, secure Russian central control.

This objective has two parts. The first is to prevent overt nuclear proliferation by keeping Ukraine, Kazakhstan, and Belarus from becoming nuclear weapons states. The second is to prevent unauthorized loss of Russian central control over nuclear weapons or the means of making them within the Russian Federation itself.

THE UKRAINE ISSUE
Ukraine, Kazakhstan, and Belarus have all pledged repeatedly that they will be non-nuclear states, that they will ratify the Lisbon protocol to the START I treaty which provides for elimination of strategic offensive arms

on their territory, and that they will accede to the NPT (Nuclear Non-Proliferation Treaty) as non-nuclear weapon states "in the shortest possible time." Those pledges were offered in May 1992 and renewed repeatedly thereafter. Belarus has kept its word, and with less alacrity so has Kazakhstan. Ukraine has not.

In December 1991, just after the dissolution of the Soviet Union, Ukraine allowed the removal — in about six months — of all tactical nuclear weapons on its territory (over 2,000 weapons) back to Russia. Russia agreed, in April 1992, to dismantle these weapons and allow Ukraine to monitor their dismantlement. This process is reportedly working and the majority of these weapons have been dismantled as agreed.

What remains are 176 SS-19 and SS-24 ICBMs (Intercontinental Ballistic Missiles) in Ukraine, based at two different locations, armed with about 1,240 nuclear warheads. Also in Ukraine are about 600 nuclear-armed air-launched cruise missiles, stored for the use of long-range strategic bombers. If Ukraine acquired effective control over these weapons it would be the third most powerful nuclear weapon state in the world.

In 1991 and 1992, pending the return of all nuclear weapons to Russia, operational responsibility for nuclear forces in Ukraine, Kazakhstan, and Belarus was placed in the CIS Joint Armed Forces High Command. In succeeding years Ukraine has distanced itself from CIS security structures and asserted "administrative control" over supply and manning of the nuclear bases,[5] and in June 1993 Prime Minister Leonid Kuchma told Parliament that Ukraine might ratify START I but would keep the 46 modern SS-24 ICBMs.

In the late summer of 1993 the Clinton administration embarked on a new effort to negotiate a trilateral understanding between Russia, Ukraine, and the United States. In January 1994 Presidents Boris Yeltsin, Leonid Kravchuk, and Bill Clinton signed a Trilateral Statement (not a treaty) and an annex which renewed Ukraine's non-nuclear obligations, set some interim deadlines for specific actions, listed the reciprocal assurances Russia and the United States would offer (repackaging security assurances already codified in the UN Charter, NPT and CSCE Helsinki Final Act), and outlined arrangements for additional compensation to Ukraine in the

---

5. See Philip D. Zelikow, Appendix 1-E to "Ownership and Control of Nuclear Weapons," in Graham Allison, Ashton Carter, Steven Miller and Philip Zelikow, eds., *Cooperative Denuclearization: From Pledges to Deeds*, CSIA Studies in International Security No. 2 (Cambridge, MA: Center for Science and International Affairs, 1993), pp. 72–78.

form of low-enriched uranium fuel assemblies for civil nuclear power plants.

The great danger is that any agreement with the Ukrainian government is written on the wind. Kravchuk, desperate for Russian economic support, had agreed with Yeltsin at a September 1993 meeting at the Crimean resort of Massandra to proceed with the transfer of all the remaining nuclear weapons.[6] But the status of the SS-24 ICBMs or the nuclear-armed cruise missiles had never been nailed down, and by the end of September that deal had fallen apart, along with the Ukrainian government. Kravchuk began ruling by emergency decree. Shortly after the January 1994 Trilateral Statement, Kravchuk announced that he would step down as president after elections for that office were held later in the year. Ukraine, besieged by hyperinflation and plummeting economic output, is also contending with separatist threats from the Crimea and unrest in its more Russified eastern half. Ukraine's ability to carry forward any major policy initiative may be overwhelmed by its economic and political crisis.

As the issue drags on, Ukraine has tightened control over the nuclear weapons on its territory. Ukraine undoubtedly has the capability to develop and manufacture its own interlocks to replace the existing ones and assume positive control over the ICBMs. Yet Ukraine could still only "re-aim" the missiles in a process that would be visible to the United States and Russia and would take at least several weeks. Ukraine's ability to utilize the nuclear-armed ALCMs in their current form is also uncertain.[7]

More likely would be a Ukrainian decision to cannibalize the nuclear weapons in order to build new, much cruder weapons with lower yields. Again, though, this process would take time and could not be concealed.

The process of Ukrainian removal of nuclear weapons is itself delicate and potentially unstable. Once taken from their ICBMs or usual storage sites, the weapons are expected to be placed in a Ukrainian "halfway house" awaiting final transport to Russia. While en route to and in the "halfway house" the weapons are separated from the arrangements as well as the custodial system designed for their security and safety. Both

---

6. Celestine Bohlen, "Ukraine Agrees to Allow Russians to Buy Fleet and Destroy Arsenal," *New York Times*, September 4, 1993, p. 1.

7. Positive Ukrainian control over nuclear weapons would be a costly proposition. Other small nuclear powers have found that the infrastructure needed to support long-term deployment of nuclear weapons can cost billions of dollars.

the United States and Russia have a strong interest in seeing that the removal and dismantlement process, once set in motion, moves swiftly.

All of this discussion presumes that Washington should press Ukraine to give up the nuclear weapons on its soil. Since some prominent commentators have questioned whether the United States is right to oppose Ukrainian nuclear ambitions,[8] it is worth citing six reasons why — from a U.S. perspective — the current position should be vigorously maintained:

First, Ukrainian conflict with Russia is not inevitable, but Russia cannot be expected to acquiesce passively in the creation of yet another nuclear power targeting hundreds of weapons against it. Danger of Russo-Ukrainian conflict would increase dramatically, and some experts have underestimated the potential effectiveness of the (destabilizing) strategic options Russia could develop to meet the new threat.

Second, the United States has no reason to be complacent that a Ukraine armed with nuclear weapons would serve U.S. interests as a foil to the presumed danger of future Russian expansion. A Ukraine so armed which instead formed a strategic alliance with Iran, China and other revisionist states could pose significant new dangers to U.S. interests. Nor should it be casually assumed that Ukraine will evolve into a stable, democratic state; it is currently moving in the opposite direction.

Third, Ukrainian security will be undermined by an attempt to gain positive control over nuclear weapons. Ukraine would become a target for the strategic arsenals of both Russia and the United States. It will be less likely to find Western political support in the event of a conflict. And Ukraine's conventional military position is not hopeless if CFE (Conventional Forces in Europe treaty) allocations and constraints remain in force. An extraordinarily generous CFE entitlement enables Ukraine to have the second-largest army in Europe. This fact has "generally gone unnoticed in the West, perhaps due to the fact that some hard-line nationalists in the Ukrainian parliament have chosen not to highlight their conventional strength because it undercuts arguments on the need to keep nuclear

---

8. See John Mearsheimer, "The Case for a Ukrainian Nuclear Deterrent," *Foreign Affairs*, Vol. 72, No. 3 (Summer 1993), pp. 50–66; Barry Posen, "The Security Dilemma and Ethnic Conflict," *Survival*, Vol. 35, No. 1 (Spring 1993), pp. 27, 42, 44–45; and comments of Richard Haass in Strategic Planning International, *Counter-Proliferation: Deterring Emerging Nuclear Actors*, Compendium of Proceedings of the Strategic Options Assessments Conference, Offutt AFB, July 7–8, 1993, pp. 4–5.

weapons for their own defense."⁹ But Ukrainian nuclear ambitions, unchecked, could offer Russia an excuse to break out of the CFE treaty's constraints.

Fourth, the scenario for a Russian-Ukrainian conflict is not likely to be the simple, deterrable threat of Russian conventional invasion. It is far more likely to arise from the internal disintegration of Ukraine itself, as Kiev struggles to hold its more Russified eastern half and the Crimea. The Russian approach is much more likely to rely on covert or underground aid to friendly factions in the neighboring countries — subversion, not invasion.

Fifth, if Ukraine becomes a nuclear weapons state, prospects for implementation of START I and START II become bleak. These treaties are not purely Cold War anachronisms since they will help radically reduce the Russian nuclear weapons stockpile, thereby helping to address the new danger of unauthorized diversion of weapons within Russia (discussed further below).[10]

Sixth and finally, Ukrainian violation of its NPT pledge will damage the general credibility of the worldwide NPT regime, already under siege in both the Middle East and Northeast Asia.[11]

RUSSIAN NUCLEAR WEAPONS SECURITY

Unfortunately, even the quite serious nuclear problem in Ukraine is only part of the problem of nuclear weapons dispersal in the former Soviet Union. There are only about 1,200 nuclear weapons in Ukraine; there are at least 20,000 more in the Russian Federation.

The United States does not know exactly how many nuclear weapons there are in Russia; it is possible that the Russian government does not know either. Atomic Energy Minister Viktor Mikhailov, who might know, has indicated that the Soviet nuclear stockpile peaked in 1986 at about 45,000 weapons and had declined about 20 percent (to about 36,000) by mid-1992. U.S. experts estimate that there are between 20,000 and 35,000

---

9. Lee Feinstein, "CFE: Off the Endangered List?" *Arms Control Today*, Vol. 23, No. 8 (October 1993), pp. 3, 4.

10. The United States is rapidly and unilaterally implementing START I and START II reductions in its force and budget plans for its strategic forces. Russian failure to proceed with implementation of either of these treaties could create the worrisome prospect of a superpower nuclear balance at the end of the 1990s radically tilted toward Russia.

11. See Steven E. Miller, "The Case Against a Ukrainian Nuclear Deterrent," *Foreign Affairs*, Vol. 72, No. 3 (Summer 1993), pp. 67–80.

weapons held now in Russia, the majority of which are not even assigned to operational forces.[12]

Although the Russians have many more nuclear weapons than the United States, Washington's concern should not revolve around calculations of the strategic military balance. The much more urgent issue is the safety and security of this vast arsenal, related stockpiles of fissile material, and other human and material assets used in building nuclear bombs. One-tenth of 1 percent of the Russian nuclear arsenal could devastate dozens of large cities and kill millions. Yet Russia today is a country where the government cannot confidently assert effective control over anything.

Russian nuclear forces are scattered at more than 200 locations throughout the Federation. At a fraction of these sites, operational security is very reliable, with weapons lodged in modern missile systems using advanced designs. At others, isolated detachments guard aging stockpiles of obsolete bombs or missiles.

The Russian nuclear custodial system was designed for a very different environment than the one which now exists. It depends on social assumptions about hierarchies and authority that can no longer be taken for granted. As in much of Russian society, lines of authority, unit cohesion, and predictable routines in the military are breaking down. Manning levels are low due to a liberal draft deferment policy and massive unchallenged draft evasion. In many units officers actually outnumber the enlisted men, so that career commissioned professionals do sentry duty and perform menial tasks. They also engage in widespread corruption and crime, with even senior officers — generals — being linked to the very powerful organized criminal groups that dominate significant parts of Russian economic life.

The consequences are easy to imagine. Practically every Russian weapon system that can easily be moved is already available for sale on the black market, from tanks to jet aircraft.[13] No item would bring a higher price on the black market than nuclear weapons or the means to make them. Nuclear materials that should be under lock and key, such as low-enriched uranium and radioisotopes, have already appeared on the black market and have led to arrests of smugglers in Europe.

---

12. See Robert Norris and William Arkin, "Nuclear Notebook," *Bulletin of the Atomic Scientists* (July/August 1993), p. 57.

13. See "The Threat that Was," *The Economist* (August 28, 1993), pp. 17–19.

Although none of the many reports of actual nuclear weapons smuggling have yet been substantiated, there are undoubtedly nuclear custodial units where relatively junior officers might have near-autonomous control over dozens of nuclear weapons. The danger of unauthorized diversion is obvious, and neither the United States nor Russia could even be sure of knowing that such a diversion of weapons or fissile material had occurred.

The danger of theft or unauthorized diversion is compounded by the threat of political fragmentation within the Russian Federation itself. In the event of the breakup of Russia or of civil conflict, fissile materials and nuclear weapons could readily fall into the hands of local governments or warring groups.

There are four major ways the U.S. government should tackle the problem of nuclear weapons security in Russia.[14] First, the United States should work to see the Russian nuclear stockpile reduced as rapidly as possible. Smaller numbers are more manageable; they can be concentrated in fewer, safer installations. Since most stockpiled Russian weapons are not operational even now, the START I and START II treaties are neither necessary nor sufficient for achieving these stockpile reductions. But START II, in particular, can help because its implementation would reduce Russia's operational requirements for strategic weapons to about 3,000 deployed warheads.

More significant was the Bush administration initiative to buy highly-enriched uranium (HEU) from dismantled weapons for cash (billions of dollars). The Clinton administration has concluded an agreement with Russia which would set the price for HEU and help Washington ensure that the HEU is really coming from dismantled weapons.

Second, the United States should aid improvements in the safety and security of the nuclear weapons dismantlement and custodial system. Thanks to a congressional initiative in 1991, led by Senators Sam Nunn and Richard Lugar, a considerable sum of money has been made available for "safety, security, and dismantlement" (SSD) assistance. Problems both in Washington and Moscow have delayed the effective delivery of SSD aid, but these obstacles are slowly being overcome.[15]

Third, the United States could devise ideas for "strategic disengagement" of U.S. and Russian strategic forces. Though the missile detargeting

---

14. See also Allison, Carter, Miller, and Zelikow, eds., *Cooperative Denuclearization*.

15. On SSD assistance, see "U.S. Security Assistance to the Former Soviet Union," *Arms Control Today* (June 1993), p. 36; and Dunbar Lockwood, "Dribbling Aid to Russia," *Bulletin of the Atomic Scientists* (July/August 1993), p. 39.

initiative announced by Clinton and Yeltsin in January 1994 was not especially significant, other possibilities being considered in Washington include lowering the alert status of active forces and even separating warheads from delivery systems. Even if proposals along these lines prove viable and win Russian support, they will only affect the minority of weapons which are operationally deployed. New problems could arise if weapons in storage sites prove more vulnerable to diversion than weapons sitting in a massive silo inside ICBM reentry vehicles.

Fourth, the United States is working to increase Russia's ability to dismantle much larger numbers of weapons. Russian officials say they can dismantle a maximum of about 2,000 weapons per year. Maintaining even this rate will be difficult, though, because Moscow is running out of space in which to store the tons of plutonium and HEU produced by the dismantlement process.

Current Russian ideas for ultimate plutonium disposal assume burning it as fuel in a new generation of plutonium-fueled power reactors. Such reactors do not yet exist in Russia and would be *very* expensive to build.[16] Such reactors would also, of course, add to the growing quantity of "civil plutonium" being produced worldwide. Many U.S. scientists insist that such "civil plutonium" presents a serious proliferation danger and can be used in making low-yield weapons. Russian nuclear officials, like some in Western Europe and Japan, tend to dismiss these fears.

The United States is still searching for its own best answer to the "ultimate disposal" problem.[17] Energetic U.S. efforts will be vital in putting these ideas on the Russian agenda for action.

Arms for Revisionist States?

As mentioned above, the greatest threat to U.S. interests will arise from those states that hope to overthrow the hierarchy of political, economic, military and even cultural influence headed by the United States. The danger these "revisionist" states may pose is directly proportionate to their access to levers of world power. Since only a few states can produce

---

16. See Lydia Popova, "Russia's Nuclear Elite on Rampage," *Bulletin of the Atomic Scientists* (April 1993), p. 14.

17. See Committee on International Security and Arms Control, National Academy of Sciences, *Management and Disposition of Excess Weapons Plutonium* (Washington, D.C.: National Academy Press, 1994).

the sinews of modern military power, the United States must care deeply how these strong potential "arsenals of anti-democracy" are aligned.

This does not mean alignment in the old sense — into capitalist or communist camps — but, more generically, whether these arsenals are harnessed to the forces of revision, supplying valuable military commodities to revisionist states preparing to confront or challenge the United States. China, for example, cannot seem to resist temptations to support such states.

The stance of Russia and Ukraine will plainly be critical to the fate of revisionist challenges. States like Iran do not need to match the United States' military might; they need only start by building up enough sophisticated forces to offset the portion of U.S. power regularly available in the region, raising the stakes for U.S. involvement in a crisis and threatening U.S. freedom of action.

Russia and Ukraine are among the few states able to sell the sophisticated military technology that can even aspire to the levels of quality of U.S. military technology. Both states know this, and are anxious to sell more arms. Konstantin Sorokin has pointed out that:

> Today in Russia, any criticism of arms sales practices on moral or other grounds is rare. Moscow has come up with a "new look" arms sales strategy ostensibly designed to invigorate exports and make them more profitable and somehow less destabilizing. This strategy has a broad and influential constituency as well as full governmental backing...[18]

In 1991 Russia signed a deal to sell three Kilo-class diesel attack submarines to Iran and appears to be renewing substantial military cooperation with China. Ukraine has already begun turning to Iran as a source of oil to replace Russia; arms sales have been reported as a likely medium of exchange. The lure of the Iranian, Chinese, and even, if possible, Iraqi markets will be powerful as Russia's traditional arms markets in Eastern Europe dry up or, as in India, turn to other sources.

Russian-U.S. disputes over the new arms export policy were crystallized in 1993 by the Russian sale of cryogenic rocket engines to India. Elements of the sale were prohibited under the international Missile Technology Control Regime (MTCR). Russia is not a formal member of the

---

18. Konstantin Sorokin, "Russia's 'New Look' Arms Sales Strategy," *Arms Control Today*, Vol. 23, No. 8 (October 1993), p. 7.

MTCR but had pledged to respect its guidelines. Months of high-level negotiations finally produced an agreement that turned a blind eye to some transactions which had already taken place while forbidding new ones. In return for Russia's forbearance, the United States and Russia concluded a new agreement for cooperation in future manned space exploration.

The cryogenic engines themselves were less important than what the dispute revealed about the governance of Russia:[19] the obvious lack of connection between the international pledges of Russia's political leaders and the international behavior of Russia's state enterprises. The intentions and promises of Russia's leaders appeared to be correlated only loosely, if at all, with the activities of Russia's companies. A disturbingly similar pattern seems to be emerging in continuing Russian discussion of a possible sale of nuclear reactors to Iran.

Increasingly, U.S. officials are finding that as the political crisis of Russian central authority continues, traditional channels for handling international problems through Russia's foreign ministry seem inadequate, or even irrelevant. While some deals can be struck more or less directly with the entities wielding power over the issue in question, the long-term trend can only worry the United States. The Russian government openly approves of expanded arms sales, and the climate for authorized and "partly authorized" arms exports seems permissive.

Global Problem Solving

The transition in U.S.-Russian relations during the Bush administration, from the rapprochement it inherited to a strategic understanding on vital issues, yielded enormous security benefits for the United States in its global policies — from its stance toward German unification to marshaling the unprecedented and successful coalition for the confrontation and war against Iraq in 1990–1991, to co-sponsorship of the renewed Middle East peace process and beyond. The Clinton administration pledged it would follow suit. Yet the record of U.S.-Russian joint global problem solving has become cloudier since the end of the Soviet Union.

Russia has done little to interfere with U.S. policy initiatives through the United Nations in regions where Russia took little interest, such as

---

19. The engines had military value to India, but the cryogenic rocket design arguably has severe drawbacks for military use. Such engines are not used in modern ballistic missiles.

Somalia or Haiti. Little cooperation has been needed on Middle Eastern issues. But Russia has already begun to balk at cooperating on smaller matters, disassociating Moscow from the U.S. punitive strike against Iraq in January 1993, refusing to pay Russia's share of the peacekeeping assessment for UN forces in Cyprus, and resisting a movement toward harsher UN sanctions against Libya.

The major global problem in 1992–1994 of concern to both countries was the Bosnian crisis. Russia's policy in the Balkans was usually passive, but invariably aimed at muting or thwarting pressure for collective military action against Serbia. Moscow's first important diplomatic initiative came in May 1993. Russia intervened to propose that the Bosnian Muslims be safeguarded by UN-protected "safe havens." Russia energetically pursued this initiative, and despite initial resistance — even scorn in some quarters — Moscow actually won the support of President Clinton and Secretary of State Warren Christopher.

It is hard to determine which U.S. interests were served by the "safe havens" proposal, a policy whose fate soon outran the most pessimistic predictions made for it, since the Bosnians became both less safe and less strong. At the time the initiative also undermined what little coherence remained in U.S. Bosnian policy. The initiative was a success, however, from the Russian perspective. It dissipated the ripening threat of anti-Serb military action. The initiative must have vindicated the aspirations that nationalist Russian officials privately harbored for it. The subsequent movement toward partition has been encouraged by Moscow.

Similar Russian interests can explain Moscow's February 1994 intervention in the Bosnian dispute, with the insertion of a small number (400) of peacekeeping troops into a Serbian enclave, as Russia claimed it had persuaded the Serbs to comply with NATO's demand to stop the bombardment of Sarajevo. Beyond that immediate humanitarian objective, the ultimate fate of both the United States' and Russia's renewed involvement in Bosnia remains unclear. Both countries appear willing to see a peace settlement that would partition the country and ratify most Serbian territorial gains.

These depressing Russian ventures into global problem solving should not keep the United States from continuing to explore possibilities for an understanding on more important issues. Three examples stand out: potential civil conflict in or disintegration of Ukraine; the United States' "dual containment" policy toward both Iran and Iraq; and the U.S. interest in developing stable lines of supply to the oil reserves being discovered in the Caspian Sea region.

The United States will also wish to seek Russian understanding for any unstable developments in its relationship with China or on the Korean peninsula. In this light, it is noteworthy and somewhat worrisome that current prospects for warmer Russo-Chinese political, economic, and military cooperation appear to be excellent.

Threats to the U.S.-Russian Entente

The U.S.-Russian entente is widely perceived in Russia to have benefited only the United States. The major undercurrents of emerging opinion are pressing for a more "balanced" policy[20] (which includes closer ties to China). The centrists are struggling to ward off a rising backlash of anti–United States sentiment.[21]

Developments in at least three areas could threaten the still young entente between Washington and Moscow: the size and disposition of Russia's armed forces; U.S. policy toward the republics of the former Soviet Union; and the future of Russian reform.

RUSSIA'S ARMED FORCES

The political-military aims of Russia's armed forces are unclear. Stabilizing Russia's southern frontiers is certainly one objective. The military's view of the Western countries is ambivalent and suspicious. Debate is continuing within the ranks of the Russian high command over how to prioritize the relative threats posed from the West, East, or South — or those from within.

The United States' concerns about Russia's military intentions have been muted for a time by the troubled condition of Russia's forces. Government spending on the military has sharply declined. Most major conventional weapons procurement has been suspended. The system of conscription has collapsed and military manpower has fallen to less than half the number fielded in 1990, apparently below the 1.5 million figure. It will also take years to remedy the dislocations produced by the

---

20. See, e.g., S. Neil MacFarlane, "Russia, the West and European Security," *Survival*, Vol. 35, No. 3 (Autumn 1993), pp. 4, 12, 17–18.

21. See Alexei G. Arbatov, "Russia's Foreign Policy Alternatives," *International Security*, Vol. 18, No. 2 (Fall 1993), pp. 5–43. See also Teresa Pelton Johnson and Steven Miller, eds., *Russian Security after the Cold War: Seven Views from Moscow*, CSIA Studies in International Security No. 3 (Washington, D.C.: Brassey's, 1994).

withdrawal of forces from Germany, Eastern Europe, and the former Soviet republics.

One obvious result is an increased Russian reliance on nuclear deterrence, as Russia currently lacks the ability to mount a large-scale conventional military campaign. Moscow has therefore renounced its nominal military doctrine of no first use.

But Russia's military remains powerful and largely autonomous. Both its power and autonomy have been strengthened by the political turmoil in late 1993, and sooner or later its conventional military strength will be revived. Even in its weakened state the military retains an evident capacity to tip the balance in local conflicts on its borders.

The United States must hope that, once it is complete, the rejuvenation of Russia's military will reveal armed forces designed for a posture of global cooperation with the United States and the West, not for confrontation. Washington must endeavor to convince Russia's leaders that such a posture adequately defends Russia's real interests.

U.S. POLICY TOWARD FORMER SOVIET REPUBLICS

Fears have grown in the West that Russia is adopting a "Monrovsky doctrine," declaring the republics of the former Soviet Union to be a Russian sphere of influence.[22]

U.S. strategy toward Ukraine and other new states starts from the assumption that the creation and continued independence of all these states commands U.S. support. This view is an outgrowth of U.S. sympathy for forces of self-determination and national autonomy in the declining years of the Soviet Union. But some have argued that the United States should use its influence to confront and contain Russia in republics of the former Soviet Union, the near abroad, or Central Asia. Each of these regions present distinct problems, however, and requires a differentiated response.

---

22. Analogies to the United States' Monroe Doctrine are misplaced. U.S. President James Monroe declared a doctrine of *non*-intervention, and the doctrine was applied in this spirit for most of its history. Russia could argue that it is exerting power to thwart the intervention of other powers in nations along its frontier, or that anarchy or chaos could, as in Lebanon, tempt other states or violent nonstate groups to take advantage of these conditions. If, on the other hand, Russia is simply determined to prop up certain factions in an effort to resist legitimate internal pressures within these countries for social and political change, these efforts have all the vices of the occasional and misguided U.S. efforts to accomplish this same feat.

In considering the danger of instability in Ukraine, the United States should reflect carefully upon the nature of its interests in the fate of this country. The nuclear question is paramount, but open warfare between Russia and Ukraine would be dangerous even without the possible nuclear dimension. But the United States cannot pledge credibly that it will defend Ukraine militarily against attack from Russia, and Washington will have difficulty finding the basis for any active policy in the event of civil disorder within Ukraine itself.

In other former republics, Russian policy has become more and more activist in extending Moscow's influence, for example in the conflict between Armenia and Azerbaijan, and in Georgia.[23] The U.S. government has preferred to turn a blind eye to the extent of Russian intervention in the Caucasus and Transcaucasus, although for reasons of personal attachment and domestic politics Washington remains strongly interested in the personal welfare of Shevardnadze and in the survival, within borders to be determined, of the Armenian republic. This nuanced approach would be harder to sustain if Russian activism took a more violent turn or extended to countries like the Baltic republics or Ukraine.

In searching for broad themes to determine U.S. policy two considerations should stand out. First, U.S. security interests in the region: except for Baltic independence, U.S. stakes in the fate of other republics are limited. The United States lacks strong intrinsic interests in Moldova, Georgia, or Tajikistan. Indeed, a continued posture of disinterested detachment may be the only basis for aid in defusing potential conflicts.

The second guiding principle should be the preservation of global respect for critical norms of international behavior. One of these is the promotion of peaceful settlement of international disputes. Yet "self-determination" may not be such a norm, if taken in the collective sense asserted by ethnic groups or nations. (A narrower interpretation of "self-determination" could define it as allowing all *individuals* the opportunity for some form of effective participation in their government's political process.)

Nor does the norm of Western-style democratization invariably promote civil peace. Several examples suggest that the process of democratization actually inflames or institutionalizes ethnic tensions in severely divided societies until conditions or political procedures better

---

23. For a vivid portrait of covert Russian military activity in the near abroad, see Thomas Goltz, "Letter from Eurasia: The Hidden Russian Hand," *Foreign Policy*, No. 92 (Fall 1993), pp. 92–116.

reward the formation of multi-ethnic governing coalitions and encourage needed devolution of federal control.

THE FUTURE OF "REFORM"

The U.S. government appears to assume that its security interests are synonymous with a choice between the forces of reform and reaction in Russia. Ambassador Strobe Talbott has described the new U.S. approach as a "strategic alliance with reform" in Russia.

Yet Washington cannot be sure that "reform" will win, or that the reformers, in winning, would be able to maintain all the features of democratic governance that the U.S. government now says are vital. It also appears increasingly probable that Russia will need to take extraordinary measures to restore basic conditions of public order in Russia. For example in Marshal Yevgenii Shaposhnikov's July 1993 elaboration of Moscow's new security concept, it was striking how often he mentioned crime as a "threat" to be addressed by Russia's armed forces.[24]

Whether "reform" wins or not, the United States will want a relationship with Russia that furthers U.S. security objectives. The real U.S. alliance should be with any group of leaders in Russia who will guide their state in this direction.

Democrats are more reliable allies than authoritarians: democrats in Russia do tend to be more congenial partners for U.S. leaders and help sustain harmony between U.S. global policies and the popular and congressional backing for those policies; democratic institutions are also more conducive over the long term to both domestic and international stability; and market reform will make Russia stronger in time. Yet the United States got on quite amicably with czarist Russia during the first century of U.S. history because the two countries shared common strategic interests.[25] While Yeltsin was plainly preferable in the fall of 1993 to Alexander Rutskoi and Ruslan Khasbulatov, the political situation in Russia is just too diverse to fall into neat polar caricatures; understanding the political battle as one against "ex-communists" may soon be of very

---

24. Interview by Interfax with Marshal Yevgenii Shaposhnikov, July 29, 1993, in *FBIS-SOV* 93-145-A, July 30, 1993, p. 5; see also Stephen Handelman, "The Russian 'Mafiya,'" *Foreign Affairs*, Vol. 73, No. 2 (March–April 1994), pp. 83–96.

25. See Benjamin P. Thomas, *Russo-American Relations 1815-1867* (Baltimore: Johns Hopkins University Press, 1930); and John Lewis Gaddis, *The Long Peace: Inquiries into the History of the Cold War* (New York: Oxford University Press, 1987), pp. 4–6.

little use. The United States government should therefore take care about how it draws political portraits of its idealized Russia.

Democrats and advocates of greater freedom are not necessarily opposed to expansionist foreign policies. The same Jacksonian democrats who wanted to open up U.S. politics and society during the 1820s and 1930s, helping build the modern United States, were also among the principal authors of the U.S. doctrine of "manifest destiny" to expand the West. Idealistic French socialists who hoped to make Algerians into Frenchmen were leading supporters of France's war to keep Algeria during the 1950s.

Worst of all, some Russians have come to believe that the use of labels like "democratic" or "pro-reform" represents pure hypocrisy. They can see that Washington supports Yeltsin whether or not he behaves like a democrat. Therefore they infer, with good reason, that other considerations shape U.S. policy. Washington should also recognize that even if Russian economic reform succeeds, such success is no guarantee of political stability. Social forces unleashed by economic transformation can place insupportable demands upon governmental institutions and fiscal structures. Quite possibly the revolutionary flood in Russia has not crested; it is still rising.

Conclusion

The recognition of strong anti-democratic and imperial tendencies in Russia's political direction has led some observers to assume that the United States must prepare again to contain Russian expansion. Or, as Zbigniew Brzezinski more delicately put it, "the central goal of a realistic and long-term grand strategy should be *the consolidation of geopolitical pluralism within the former Soviet Union.*" The cutting edge for Brzezinski would be American "political assurances for Ukraine's independence and territorial integrity."[26] (The goal is to prevent the restoration of a Russian empire, though Brzezinski does not provide or refer to an analysis to buttress his assumption that history would repeat itself in producing a Russian hegemonic danger to other countries in Europe.)

This essay makes a different argument. Rather than confront Russia in a region where the United States has few vital interests and no capacity

---

26. Zbigniew Brzezinski, "The Premature Partnership," *Foreign Affairs*, Vol. 73, No. 2 (March-April 1994), pp. 67, 79, 80.

to back up its pledges short of the hollow but damaging blow of severing U.S. political and economic ties to Russia, Washington should seek to enhance its leverage and apply it where it will do America the most good. The United States needs understandings with Russia to defuse or avert threats to its vital interests both from Russia and from areas neighboring Russia. None of its interests would be served as well by a confrontational stance. If even these understandings prove elusive, the option of abandoning cooperation still remains. But it is not yet time to give up on the U.S.-Russian entente.

From this perspective, U.S. economic assistance has two goals that are more important than the quest to reform Russia's economy. The first is to remain so deeply engaged in Russia's future that U.S. views carry disproportionate weight in Moscow. The second is to promote the establishment or consolidation of democratic political institutions within Russia. The United States could look, though on a far smaller scale, to the Marshall Plan for illustrations of how aid can be used to build and promote certain institutions in the recipient countries, rather than just adding new donor bureaucracies.

In trying to sustain a U.S.-Russian entente the United States enjoys a great asset: for historical, cultural, and social reasons, many Russians are actually predisposed to pay special attention to U.S. opinion. Despite the Cold War, the relationship is not colored by the powerful emotional undercurrents that tug at Russian attitudes toward virtually all its neighbors. Therefore, in the period of turmoil ahead, Washington's real alliance should be with "the United States' friends" rather than with the internal cause of "reform." This is *not* an argument against support of democracy and the free market.

But in the final analysis, the United States cannot dictate the outcome of Russia's internal debates; Russians will choose the government and society they wish to live in. The United States will want to attempt to find a basis for an enduring, positive relationship with Russia regardless of the choice which the Russians make for their future.

The prospects for an American-Russian entente along the lines described in this essay are only fair. Washington must find the self-discipline to select the small number of objectives from the relationship with Russia that it considers truly vital. The Russians must be invited to do the same. Then both sides must try to forge an understanding that shelters these core areas of agreement from the storms that will buffet the relationship. Each side must deliver on its core commitments, accepting that achieving core interests may entail the sacrifice of more peripheral ones. This effort would be difficult, but not impossible. Such hard choices would include, for example, a decision that Russian arms sales to America's foes are more dangerous than Russian disagreements with America over Bosnia. They could include, even more importantly, recalling that America's support for Ukraine's nationhood and territorial integrity have, from the day Washington recognized the new state, been conditioned on Ukraine abandoning the nuclear weapons option.

Chapter 20

Robert D. Blackwill and Sergei A. Karaganov

Afterword

With the disintegration of the Soviet Union, some strategists argued that the West should commit significant economic resources and political capital to promote democracy and market institutions in Russia, always contingent upon tangible evidence that Russian reforms were progressing, and closely cooperate with the Russian government to address the instability and violence of the post–Cold War international environment. The theory was that the West, and indeed the world, had an enormous stake in the outcome of the Soviet and then the Russian reform process, and that the industrial democracies should commit their energies, creativity, and resources in a momentous endeavor analogous to the Marshall Plan in the late 1940s. It is impossible to judge whether such a joint effort between the West and Russia would have had the desired effect, because, unfortunately, neither side made the full-scale attempt necessary to test the theory.

The West did not provide sufficient economic assistance to secure its part of this grand bargain. Although the Group of Seven trumpeted huge figures for assistance to Russia at many summits, the actual new resources reaching Russia have been modest. Most of the money in these summit aid packages consisted of export credits, which are loans largely designed for market penetration by individual G-7 nations; debt relief; and potential IMF loans with conditions that were virtually impossible for Russia to meet. Furthermore, the West continues to be very slow in opening its markets to Russian goods.

During this crucial period, the West performed better politically than it did economically, especially at times of Russian political crisis. In August 1991 and early October 1993, Western rhetorical statements were hardly decisive in the eventual results, but they were apt and important. However, there were long periods between these extraordinary events when Russia all but disappeared from the West's policy screen and was replaced by the Maastricht Treaty, the European economic downturn, the U.S. presidential election, Bosnia, Somalia, Haiti, and so forth.

This insufficient and sporadic Western political and economic engagement in the future of Russia was most broadly speaking a consequence of the withdrawal of Western nations into insular psychologies and internal problems. From Bill Clinton's preoccupation with America's domestic ills to Germany's fixation on the challenges following unification, to the difficulties of the Major government in Britain, to France's post–Cold War confusions, to Italy's endemic political crisis, to Japan's self-absorption, Russia had the bad luck to launch its historic reform at a time when the West was more inward looking than in the past sixty years.

Russia must also bear an important share of the blame. It is difficult to exaggerate the governmental chaos that has existed in Russia since 1991. The task of reforming Russia is gargantuan in character, and is necessarily compromised by the absence of a democratic political culture and the enormous burden of seventy years of communism. These daunting internal Russian factors certainly gave faint hearts and myopic policy makers in the West plenty of excuses to hold back.

Historians are unlikely to be kind to Western and Russian leaders who failed to take sufficient advantage of the extraordinary opportunity that presented itself in the period immediately following the Soviet collapse. In this book, we have addressed the melancholy consequences of that failure.

Center for Science and International Affairs

William C. Clark, Director
John F. Kennedy School of Government, Harvard University
79 JFK Street, Cambridge MA 02138
(617) 495-1400

The Center for Science and International Affairs (CSIA) was established in 1973 to advance understanding and resolution of international security problems through a program of research, training, teaching, and outreach. Founded by Paul Doty, a biochemist long involved in arms control, national security, and science policy, CSIA became in 1978 the first permanent research center of Harvard's John F. Kennedy School of Government.

The Center places special but not exclusive emphasis on the role of science and technology in the analysis and design of public policies to address international problems. CSIA's research addresses four interrelated areas: international security affairs, science and technology policy, environment and natural resources, and public policy issues in the Pacific Basin. Current research includes new international security conceptions after the Cold War; nuclear arms control; nonproliferation; U.S. policies toward the former Soviet Union; science and technology policy; information infrastructure; economic competitiveness; technology transfer; global environmental risk management; land use policy; environmental economics; climate change strategies and policies; and interactions among major policy initiatives in Asia and the Americas with the aim of improving decision-making processes in the Pacific region.

Each year the Center hosts a multinational group of approximately twenty-five scholars from the social, behavioral, and natural sciences. More than fifty Harvard faculty members and forty adjunct research fellows from the greater Boston area also participate in CSIA activities.

CSIA sponsors seminars and conferences, many open to the public; maintains a substantial specialized library; and publishes a monograph series and discussion papers. The Center's International Security Program, directed by Steven E. Miller, publishes the CSIA Studies in International Security and sponsors and edits the quarterly journal *International Security*.

The Center is supported by an endowment established with funds from the Ford Foundation and Harvard University, by foundation grants, by individual gifts, and by occasional government contracts.

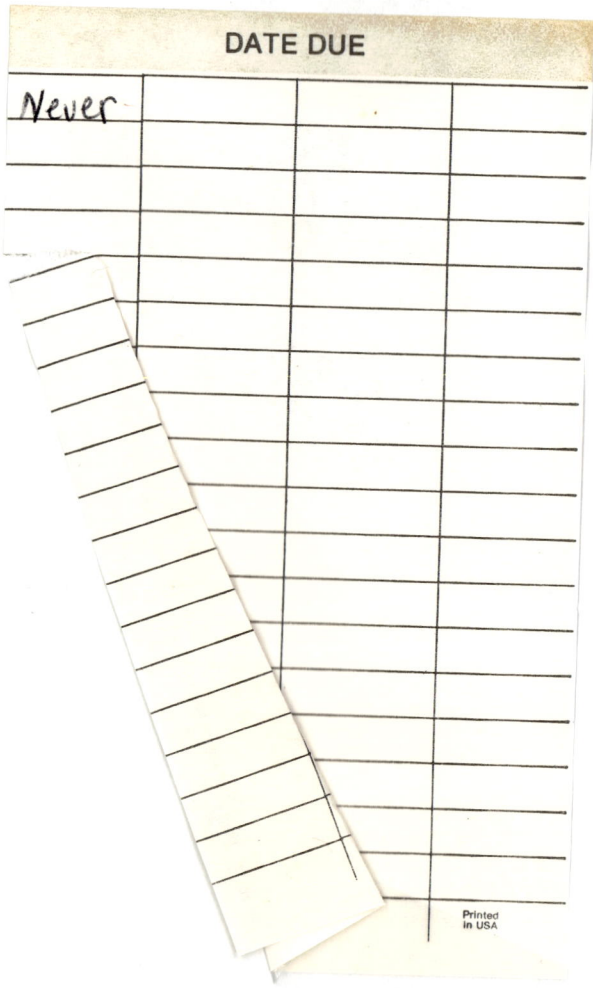